The Asiatic Mode of Production

Explorations in Social Structures

General Editors: Patricia Crone and John A. Hall

State and Society in Soviet Thought
Ernest Gellner

Creating Capitalism: The State and Small Business since 1945
Linda Weiss

The Asiatic Mode of Production
Brendan O'Leary
By the same author
Theories of the State: The Politics of Liberal Democracy
(*with Patrick Dunleavy*)

The Asiatic Mode of Production

Oriental Despotism, Historical Materialism and Indian History

Brendan O'Leary
with a foreword by Ernest Gellner

Basil Blackwell

Copyright © Brendan O'Leary 1989

First published 1989

Basil Blackwell Ltd
108 Cowley Road, Oxford, OX4 1JF, UK

Basil Blackwell Inc.
3 Cambridge Center
Cambridge, Massachusetts 02142, USA

British Library Cataloguing in Publication Data
O'Leary, Brendan
The Asiatic mode of production: oriental
despotism, historical materialism and
Indian history. − (Explorations in social structures)
1. Asiatic production. Theories of Marxists,
to 1988
I. Title II. Series
338'.001
ISBN 0-631-16766-8

Library of Congress Cataloging in Publication Data
O'Leary, Brendan.
The Asiatic mode of production : Oriental despotism, historical materialism, and Indian history : by Brendan O'Leary : with a foreword by Ernest Gellner.
p. cm. − (Explorations in social structures)
Based on thesis (Ph. D.) − University of London, 1988.
Bibliography: p.
Includes index.
ISBN 0-631-16766-8
1. Asiatic mode of production − India. 2. Historical materialism.
I. Title. II. Series.
HB97.5.O455 1989
338.6 − dc19

Typeset in 10 on 12 pt Ehrhardt
by Setrite Typesetters Ltd.
Printed in Great Britain by
Camelot Press, Southampton

Contents

Foreword

The first thing I wish to do in writing the preface to this powerful, incisive and definitive study is to disagree with the author's opening remark in his own Introduction. The Asiatic Mode of Production is far more than merely a bastard child of historical materialism. The name itself may indeed have such an origin. But the idea behind it has preceded Marxism and will, I suspect, survive it. The 'Asiatic Mode of Production' is the projection into the Marxist scheme of thought and terminology of one or two of the deepest fears and preoccupations of political thought.

The first of these is the problem of power. Man is indeed a social and political animal, but, unlike the social insects, he is not so constructed as to form, spontaneously and automatically, a well-ordered and viable community. On the contrary, he is a genetically under-programmed animal. He is capable of internalizing a wide variety of quite distinct cultural values and constraints, and of modifying them. His comportment is not channelled in a unique direction. This alone makes possible the wide range of cultures encountered in history. It is also this alone which renders possible sustained and cumulative improvement; in other words, progress. But it carries with it the inescapable consequence that the preservation of minimal social order is precarious and problematic. Some additional, non-genetic element is required for our collective perpetuation.

If order is neither self-generating nor self-preserving, how then does it arise, and how is it maintained? Certainly not, as some optimistic liberals have hoped or even maintained, by rational calculation or spontaneous benevolence. The information available to any given individual does not unambiguously and persuasively convey to him the advisability of being a good citizen. It does nothing of the kind. The power of human reason either to convince or to motivate us in that desirable direction is sadly limited. Other factors must operate if we are to comport ourselves in a way which will enable our society to survive.

What then? If neither nature nor reason can turn us into tolerable citizens and neighbours who will co-operate sufficiently to make society viable, then order can only be sustained by socially recognized force; or, in other words, by political authority. As the available logical justifications of conformity are woefully inadequate, authority must be either arbitrary or based on superstition, or both. Good reasons not being given, authority must be sustained either by bad reasons or by none at all. Authority will then need to be not merely arbitary, but also absolute. It is always best to eliminate rivals, including potential ones, before they eliminate you, and to establish a monopoly of effective force. This internal logic is reinforced by an external logic: societies not endowed with a firm, cohesion-enforcing centre are at a grave disadvantage in comparison with societies which are so endowed. In due course, they are liable to find themselves eliminated.

This powerful abstract argument is reinforced by historical evidence. The great majority of complex societies rich enough to sustain a complex social organization at all are characterized by authoritarian political regimes. Those which are free of them are but a minority, and constitute a kind of exceptional social condition. The normal political state of mankind is absolutism. The prevailing outcome of the interaction between culturally developed human nature and the surrounding environment is centralized and uncontrolled power. It is the absence and not the presence of absolutism which calls for special explanation.

Marxism is an optimistic philosophy, a variant of the Enlightenment and nineteenth-century theory of Progress, a promise of guaranteed collective salvation on earth made to all mankind. It maintains that a social order free of violence, domination, oppression, exploitation and institutionalized superstition is not merely possible, but is somehow the normal and normative condition of humanity. The ultimate emergence of such an order is, for Marxism, the manifest destiny of mankind.

In order to maintain such a view, the pessimistic theory which insists on the pervasiveness of arbitrary and falsehood-sustained domination must somehow or other be refuted. Marxism claims to do this by a well-known argument. Violence and political domination are not, it insists, inherent attributes of human society. They may indeed be pervasive in *recorded* history, but the reason for this is special rather than general. Recorded history is the story of class struggle; but classes and the conflict they engender are not inherent in human society as such. All possible levels of the development of human productive forces — with the exception of the last and, strangely but significantly, the first — do indeed produce differential relations to the means of production, and thereby produce social classes. But it is this resulting class structure, and not human society as such, which alone requires and produces political reinforcement.

Social order as such does not need coercive reinforcement. Thus Marxist eschatology contains a marked anarchistic element. It is only class-endowed social systems which cannot manage without force. This is the Marxist theory of the state, in a nutshell. Its optimistic implications are tremendous and obvious. Oppression, domination, superstition can all be eliminated from human life; in a sense, effortlessly. They will evaporate of their own accord once exploitation and class stratification have gone.

The thinkers of the Enlightenment felt a profound despair when they contemplated the powerful hold of superstition, false belief and deference over the minds and hearts of men, and in particular of "the people". The effective diffusion of their own enlightenment seemed dreadfully difficult. If Marxism is right, they need not have felt quite so daunted by the task which lay ahead. Domination and institutionalized falsehood will disappear of their own accord once their social base, i.e. class structure and the differential access to the means of production which is of its essence, have been destroyed – or rather, when they have destroyed themselves through their own inner contradictions.

This is not the place to discuss whether this view has much merit, and whether there ever was a time when it was reasonable to endorse it. What is relevant is that even within that untidy mass of materials and ideas which constitutes Marxist scripture – as opposed to the elegant coherence of its central guiding ideas – there is *already* a blatant, dramatic contradiction of the optimistic vision of the collective Salvation of Humanity. Its name is the Asiatic Mode of Production.

The picture contained in this notion is one of a social order in which domination, oppression and ideological befuddlement prevail and are stable and secure – and have not simply been brought into being by a pre-existent and ultimately unstable system of class exploitation. The social classes which constitute the crucial dramatis personae of the Asiatic Mode of Production, the hydraulic bureaucrats, soldiers and hieratic specialists, do not and cannot exist prior to the system. They only come into being with it. They create it, they are not its creation. So domination, in one important and recurring case, enters history not as the handmaiden of economic exploitation, but independently and as a prime mover. Worse still, it is functional. Repellent though the social order in question may be, without the centralized irrigation system and its authoritarian personnel it would not survive at all. Its members would starve. Better Red than dead; and better under a Hydraulic Despotism than famished. So, if the Asiatic Mode of Production is indeed to be found in the historic world, the entire optimistic Marxist vision goes by the board.

The theory of the Asiatic Mode of Production is a kind of dreadful mirror-image of the hopeful Marxist eschatology. It strikes terror where Marxism offers hope. Marxism teaches that the abolition of non-social property will lead to a harmonious social order in which the fulfilment of human potentialities will at long last be possible; where centralized coercion will be redundant, and will, in the famous phrase, wither away. The model of the Asiatic Mode of Production presents the opposite argument, to the effect that the absence of special, socially localized rights over resources leads not to freedom and harmony but, on the contrary, to despotism. This not only contradicts the central idea of Marxism, without which it loses boths its coherence and its appeal; it also provides an all-too-plausible explanation of why, when Marxism was implemented for the first time in Russia, it led, for over three decades, not to the liberation of man but to an appalling nightmare; a *kashmar*, as the Russians say. It also provides a powerful parable, as well as an explanation, for the mechanics of that nightmare. No wonder that, at the time, the idea and its name were rapidly excised from canonical Marxism.

There is another way of putting all this. Within Marxism, there always was a tension, not to say a contradiction, between the functionalist and the reductionist-epiphenomenal views of the state. Both were conspicuously present, but questionaly compatible with each other. The idea that the state serves the needs of the social base clearly attributes an important and presumably indispensable function to it. The doctrine that the superstructure merely *reflects* the base and follows its transformations, possibly with an occasional delay, would seem to contradict the first point. The shadow is redundant: look to the base; that is where the action is. Don't waste your time on the mere reflection. In the theory of the Asiatic Mode of Production, the functionalist element in Marxism takes over completely, and displaces the reductionist element altogether. But in so doing, it also totally and fatally undercuts all justification for the Marxist promise of general salvation, the expectation that oppression can and will be eliminated from human society by the overcoming of property and class differentiation and exploitation. If this is so, then no institutional political devices will be needed thereafter to prevent their reappearance. It is this preposterous optimism which led to the conviction that no checks are required on the privileged institution which is charged by history with setting up classless society on earth: the Party. The baselessness of this expectation is highlighted by the theory of the Asiatic Mode of Production, and by its reapplication, whether as parable or as sociology, to the society engendered by the Soviet path to rapid and forced industrialization. If the Asiatic Mode of Production ever existed, there was no reason to expect the disappearance of coercion: no wonder that the attempt to set up a classless, coercion-less order only led to a new version of the Asiatic Mode.

The question concerning the extent to which Marx and Engels actually perceived the problem inherent in having one theory for the West and another for the East must be left to the specialists of Marxology. My own guess is that at least one element in the answer must be that Marx and Engels, in common with most of the thinkers of the nineteenth century,

were profoundly Euro-centric. On such a view, the philosophically significant sections of mankind, so to speak, lived or had lived roughly between
the Eastern Mediterranean and the North Atlantic. What happens elsewhere
was not to be taken very seriously. It is perhaps for this reason that the
contradiction between their central vision and the ideas contained in the
notton of the Asiatic Mode of Production did not trouble them as much as
it should have done. On this view, formally speaking the philosophy of
history may apply to all mankind; but really it only concerns us Europeans.
All men are human but we are more so, and the others enter World
History only by courtesy of incorporation in our story. What happens to
Asiatics and what they do to each other does not matter too much, certainly
not as much as would a contradiction found in the European mainstream.
If a form of social organization is found in Asia which is forever stagnant,
in which violence is a prime mover and is functional; and if, as Marx
actually said, the only real social revolution in India was the work of the
English, all that need not upset us too much. East is East and West is
West, and the twain do meet only when *we* take *them* in tow; through
capitalism, we have already done so.

This highlights the second reason why the idea of the Asiatic Mode of
Production is so profoundly disturbing. Is the human race, and human
history, One or Many? There is a long tradition, going back to the Greeks,
of the European sense of uniqueness. Machiavelli's observations about the
distinctive characteristics of the Asian state, whether ancient Persian or
contemporary Ottoman or Mamluk, reintroduced this theme into political
thought. Is there one social law for the West, and another for the East?
The recent fashion of Orientalism-bashing has attempted, not very convincingly, to destroy all the ideas of this tradition in one fell swoop. Some
social scientists, eager to atone for colonialism by a facile and uncritical
cultural relativism, have eagerly joined the chorus. Alleged 'Orientalists'
are blamed equally if they say that the East resembles the West and if they
say that it does not. They are blamed not for what they say but for what
they are. This indiscriminate abuse, though often entertaining, does not
advance the serious purpose of comparative study of human societies and
of their potential for freedom and oppression.

When the first self-proclaimed Marxist society became effectively centralized, politically and ideologically, under Stalin, the idea of the Asiatic
Mode of Production was firmly and promptly excised from it. It was all a
little too close to the bone. Russians are a bit touchy about their Asiatic
connection, about *Aziatchina*. 'We are a savage, Asiatic country,' I heard a
Russian say, openly and bitterly, on Soviet TV in January 1989.

It was also natural that critics of the Soviet Union should have seized
upon the idea and used it as a parable for the social system engendered by
forced industrialization. Not for nothing was the Dnieper Dam for so long

a symbol of Soviet technical achievement, the emblem of the new hydro-electric despotism. The parable is frightening for us all. In the long run, an increasingly complex and interdependent technology may produce a social system closer to the Asiatic Mode of Production than to the pluralism and individualism which gave birth to the industrial mode of production.

These are, in stark and simplified outline, the issues which give the entire debate its powerful and disturbing appeal. Dr O'Leary's book provides a superb and authoritative guide both to the logic and the history of the discussion, and it must, as such, be very warmly welcomed.

Ernest Gellner
Moscow

Acknowledgements

This book is based on the PhD thesis which I submitted to the University of London in 1988. As with all books and doctorates it is indebted to many individuals. Most thanks are due to my wife, Lorelei Watson, and my supervisor, Tom Nossiter, for intellectual criticism, advice, editorial assistance, friendship, love and reminding me that it was time it was finished. Tom's abilities to extract effort and inspiration from his PhD students make him a splendid supervisor. I am also generally indebted to the institution of the London School of Economics and Political Science. Many members of the LSE Government Department staff commented with wisdom, severity and wit upon the drafts to which I subjected them. In particular I owe many thanks to Alan Beattie, Patrick Dunleavy, George Jones, Robert Orr and George Schöpflin. Fellow friends, students and researchers, notably Nick Ellison, Paul Heywood, Chris Bertram and Ali Willmore, were equally influential in creating an environment in which I could discuss my exotic interest in the Asiatic mode of production. In 1982−3 Ruth Hobson and Chris Mitchell were helpful in translating obscure French authors. The staff of the British Library of Political and Economic Science continually enabled me to track down material from remote places, for which I am very grateful. Other London libraries − the British Museum, the School of Oriental and African Studies and the Institute of Commonwealth Studies − also facilitated my endeavours. Scholars at many institutions were kind enough to reply to my correspondence and thereby speed my learning − especially L.B. Alayev, Institute of Oriental, Studies, Moscow; Hans Blomkvist, Department of Government, Uppsala; Stephen Dunn, Highgate Road Social Science Research Station at Berkeley, California; David Edgerton, Manchester University; R.S. Sharma, Delhi University; Kate Currie, Lancaster University; and Diptendra Banerjee of Burdwan University. Just as importantly a postgraduate bursary from the Department of Education and Science of Northern Ireland (1981−3) helped keep the wolf from the door and the student in the library. This book could not have been written without the teaching in philosophy, politics and economics which I received as an undergraduate from Larry Siedentop, Paul Collier and Andrew Glyn, or without the teaching of Liam Agnew, who first made me enthusiastic about ancient history at Garron Tower. Thanks are also due to Apple Macintosh computers for coming into existence − even if their UK prices are the only proof that there is something in the theory of monopoly capitalism − and particularly to my father for subsidizing my enthusiasm for information technology. (For those with an interest in these matters I word-processed the thesis with *Write Now* (1.1) and the script for the book with *Microsoft Word* (3.01) on a Macintosh Plus.) I am also grateful to my examiners, Ernest Gellner and Nicos Mouzelis, and to the editors of this series, Patricia Crone and John Hall, for their critical scrutiny of what follows. I must also express my gratitude to Fiona Sewell for her expert copy-editing, to Seán Magee and Sue Vice of Basil Blackwell, and to Anthony Smith for helping me track down the Orientalist painting which forms the cover of this book.

While all these individuals and institutions can be blamed for improving this book, one person is accountable for the final contents.

Brendan O'Leary
Department of Government
London School of Economics and Political Science

The author and publishers are grateful to Macmillan Press Ltd, for permission to adapt a diagram from *Marx and the Third World* by U. Melotti (fig. 4.5, p. 174 in this book).

To Lorelei

Introduction

The last thing you know when composing a book is what to put first.

Pascal, *Pensées*

The concept of an Asiatic mode of production (AMP) is the bastard child of historical materialism. Its lineage and legitimacy, for good reasons, have always been issues amongst Marxists, and partly account for its relative neglect in most elaborations of Marxism, whether written by Marxists or non-Marxists.[1] The lack of attention paid to the AMP by Marxist intellectuals is unsurprising. In comparison to other modes of production, or such topics as alienation, ideology, state, class, party or the labour theory of value, the AMP is an apparently esoteric subject. It is suitable for modern doctoral theses, perhaps, but not obviously germane to understanding, let alone changing, the world. Yet many Marxists and non-Marxists have thought otherwise, and some Marxists are said to have gone to their graves for thinking thus.[2]

---

1 In the most famous recent defence of historical materialism the AMP is mentioned just once, in a footnote in a brief discussion of pre-capitalist epochs (see G.A. Cohen, 1979: 197–201). The most famous recent large-scale critical assault upon Marxism and historical materialism also barely considers the AMP (Kolakowski, 1981: 349–50).

2 One author states that in Stalin's Russia a number of supporters of the AMP 'were sent to their ancestors for instruction' (Draper, 1977: 630). However, he names no names. Stephen Dunn, by contrast, informs us that 'The most that recent Soviet and East European writers will say, in reviewing the history of Soviet Oriental studies and historical research generally, is that from the early 1930s onwards, free discussion was inhibited by political factors' (Dunn, 1982: 35). But he does attribute to the Soviet historian L.P. Danilova the belief that 'N. Kokin', a Sinologist and supporter of the AMP, had to be 'retrained' after discussion of the AMP terminated in the 1930s (Dunn, 1982: 134). He is presumably referring to M.D. Kokin (1906–39). The latter's lifespan was certainly short, but there is no firm evidence that his early death was caused by his 'Asiatic' beliefs. For further discussion of Soviet debates on the AMP in the 1920s and 1930s see Sawer (1977a and 1979). Wittfogel (1981), contrary to popular misconception, did not state that Soviet intellectuals were incarcerated, or killed, for using the AMP after Stalin had expunged it from orthodox Marxism.

The neglect of the AMP, by comparison with the attention paid to other Marxist concepts, has been rectified in the last three decades. The quality and quantity of books and articles produced in defence, elaboration and application of the concept have improved *pari passu* with the calibre of the indictments of its parentage, coherence and explanatory utility. Apart from the thesis that there are more academics in search of exotica there are three obvious explanations for the disinterring of the AMP. First, as a by-product of de-Stalinization, a certain intellectual vitality was restored to Marxist discussions, and the AMP, a taboo subject since the 1930s, was revived and partially rehabilitated amongst Marxist-Leninist intellectuals in European Communist parties.[3] Second, the AMP has played its part in the post-war boom in intellectual investment in Marxology, which includes both Western Marxism and the study of Communist thought and practice in the departments of First World universities. Finally, both the 'successes' and 'failures' of Marxist-inspired revolutionary movements in Asia, and more generally outside the metropolitan heartlands of capitalism, have led both Marxists and non-Marxists to explore Marx and Engels's writings on Asian societies for analytical, strategic and polemical purposes.

An empirical indicator of the academic intellectual boom on the AMP has been provided by one authority who in 1975 counted 'more than one hundred publications on the AMP' produced in twenty countries between 1963 and 1968 (Baron, 1975: 138). The bibliographies in texts produced on the AMP in the 1970s and 1980s provide ample testimony to the acceleration of academic work in this terrain (Bailey and Llobera, 1974–5 and 1981; Melotti, 1977; and Sawer, 1977a). The most scholarly, and scholastic, author of work on the AMP has a weird metaphor to describe the swelling of academic activity around this concept. He contends that 'The literature on this Asiatic mode of production has grown from a rock to a cape to a peninsula' (Krader, 1975: xi).

One purpose of this book is to provide an accessible, up-to-date and critical survey of the literature on the AMP. However, this book is not simply a critical survey in the history of ideas. First, it is not exhaustive. Only the literature available in English and French has been examined. Second, it is not the principal purpose of this book to stand as a complete history of ideas on the AMP. The book has four objectives which cross several disciplinary and sub-disciplinary boundaries within the social sciences. Its primary purpose is to construct, reconstruct and criticize models

---

3 A fair idea of the status of the AMP before de-Stalinization was given by a Hungarian economist: 'the term "Asiatic mode of production" has disappeared from Soviet Marxist literature. It is mentioned neither in textbooks on political economy, nor in textbooks on Marxism-Leninism. Throughout the 51 volumes of the Great Soviet Encyclopaedia there is no mention of an "Asiatic mode of production". All attempts to find out why so important a tenet of Marxist theory has been omitted will be in vain. It is simply passed in silence, condemned and forgotten' (Varga, 1968: 330).

of the AMP with greater clarity than is too often the case in works of Marxology. Part of the book is therefore devoted to the standard methodological protocol of political thought and political philosophy: to conceptual clarification. But such activity for its own sake would be simply indulgent. The task of clarification eases the second objective of this book: to enquire whether any version of the AMP is compatible with any plausible version of historical materialism. The book attempts to demonstrate a dilemma: historical materialism is damned with the AMP and it is damned without it. The third objective of this book is to explore the application of the AMP through scrutinizing the secondary historical literature on India, the country to which the concept was first applied. No pretence can be made to the possession of the professional skills and languages of a historian of India. Rather, my work in this respect depends upon, and is therefore vulnerable to, the primary researches of others. Finally, the utility of both reconstructed and unreconstructed versions of the AMP is explored. Are the enterprises of historical and theoretical explanation, comparative historical sociology, comparative analysis of economic systems, political anthropology and political science aided in any substantive way by the AMP?

In short, it is hoped that this book does some of the work necessary to repair the defects in Krader's analysis of the AMP (Krader, 1975). His massive text, elaborated in other publications (Krader, 1972 and 1976), was rightly criticized on three major grounds (Omvedt, 1977). First, he did not try to explore the logical consistency of the internal elements of the AMP. Second, he did not seriously enquire about the empirical validity of the concept. Finally, he did not try to develop or revise the concept. These omissions are remedied in this book.

Chapter 1, 'The Most Controversial Mode of Production', introduces the AMP and some preliminary definitions of Marxist concepts. But the principal rationale of the chapter is to explain why the AMP has been and remains deeply controversial. The chapter is restricted to the heated ideological controversies generated by discussions of the AMP, and provides an elementary 'sociology of knowledge' of the concept by analysing who finds the concept ideologically useful and why.[4] Chapters 2 and 3 give the necessary background to the explicitly theoretical and analytical chapters 4 and 5. Chapter 2, 'The Antecedents of the Asiatic Mode of Production' surveys the 'history of ideas' *oeuvre* on the origins of the AMP. It also summarizes some of the secondary literature on the accounts given of India by sixteenth-and seventeenth-century European travellers. The history of

4 Jon Elster, amongst others, has cautioned that the sociology of knowledge has produced social science monstrosities worthy of display in any chamber of scientific horrors (Elster, 1986c: 184). Chapter 1 merely establishes the context in which discussions of the AMP have taken place, and does not assume that the interests of theorists *explain* their attitudes towards the AMP. − a *non sequitur* which Elster rightly suggests is often found in the sociology of knowledge.

ideas literature on the AMP is shown to illustrate *post hoc ergo propter hoc* argumentation; that is, it is has been too easily assumed that the AMP is simply a renaming of the idea of oriental despotism. The concept of oriental despotism referred to different phenomena from the AMP, and the idea of oriental society has better claims to be regarded as the authentic ancestor of the AMP. Chapter 3, 'Marx and Engels on the Asiatic Mode of Production and India', provides a systematic exegesis, interpretation and survey of interpretations of the pertinent texts of Marx and Engels on India and the AMP. The thorough presentation of the limited 'textual treasure' both on India and on the AMP puts paid to several myths in Marxological exegesis – propagated by both Marxists and anti-Marxists – and also establishes the context for theoretical and empirical evaluation of the debate about the concept, to which the remaining chapters are devoted.

Chapter 4, 'The Theory, Dilemmas and Contradictions of the Asiatic Mode of Production', builds on chapter 3 in three ways. First, three possible versions of historical materialism are presented. Then the problems, dilemmas and contradictions posed by the AMP for all of these versions of historical materialism are analysed. Improvements which iron out inconsistencies and spell out possible polished reconstructions are considered, suggested, and generally rejected.[5] The conclusion is that no possible AMP, original or reconstructed, is compatible with historical materialism. This conclusion is not original, but it is arrived at in a novel way, and is given force by analysing three rigorous conceptions of historical materialism (which I call the productivist, the structuralist and the neo-Hegelian). These arguments are elaborated in chapter 5, 'The Asiatic Mode of Production and Varieties of Historical Materialism'. Through the demonstration of the problems posed by the AMP for different versions of historical materialism, the argument is made compelling. The crux of these conclusions is that historical materialism and the AMP must be jettisoned as primitive social scientific hypotheses and concepts. The argument is buttressed by showing how Marxists who work without the AMP come to grief in their attempts to be consistent historical materialists.

The remaining two substantive chapters provide evidence which supports these conclusions. Chapter 6, 'Wittfogel and Oriental Despotism' is a theoretical and empirical assault upon one possible reconstuction of the AMP, namely Wittfogel's theory of oriental despotism. Wittfogel's historical

---

5 It has been suggested that 'It may be that attempts at theoretical closure in this field are premature and that the result of ongoing empirical work will be the theoretical production of, not one, but several Asiatic modes of production' (Roxborough, 1977: 410). This thesis partly respects this suggestion. However, the production of several Asiatic modes of production has been the result of attempts to improve the theory of historical materialism more than 'ongoing empirical work', and the results, as will be shown, are not flattering to any version of Marxist theory.

scholarship has been progressively discredited in the course of the thirty years since the publication of *Oriental Despotism*, but since the latter still retains the status of a widely cited 'great book'[6] this chapter can be regarded by the reader as a critical obituary of an influential text.[7]

Chapter 7 concentrates upon 'The Asiatic Mode of Production and Indian History'. The selectivity and poor scholarship evident in Marx's reading of Indian history is highlighted. Then the difficulties in applying any reconstructed model of the AMP to the major formations of Indian history are demonstrated by drawing upon the works of historians of India, both Marxist and non-Marxist. The historiography of Indian scholars, both Marxist and non-Marxist, also leaves little doubt about the weakness of Wittfogel's contentions about Indian history.[8] The chapter concludes with three appendices. The first sketches a 'rational choice' model of pre-industrial imperial government, which captures some of the essential properties of the AMP and Indian society, and which political scientists may find of interest. The phenomena to which the AMP draws attention can be fruitfully explored without the burdens of historical materialism. Its status as an appendix indicates its provisional and preliminary character. The second appendix examines the Soviet Marxist Indian historiography available in English translation, to consider whether or not the AMP intrudes upon their work. It also shows the extent − very little − to which Indian Marxists have used the concept, and I discuss whether this fact has been of any practical consequence. Indonesia arguably corresponded better with the model of the AMP than India ever did, and it has been contended that the failure of Indonesian Communists to use the AMP in their strategic estimation of Indonesian social evolution contributed to their successive political defeats (Tichelman, 1980). Similar reasoning suggests that the (flawed) theory of the AMP might also have helped Indian Marxists avoid making disastrous strategic errors − as judged by their own criteria of revolutionary endeavour. The final appendix surveys the debate over the existence of feudalism in Indian history and its implications for the question of the AMP.

Chapter 8, 'Conclusion', summarizes the discussion. It also answers the question with which the AMP, like a ghost, haunts Marxist social and

6 What constitutes a 'great book' is an interesting question. My colleague Kenneth Minogue insists that *Oriental Despotism* is a great book − if only for the reason that people still write and talk about it thirty years later. Since this standard would make *The Book of Revelations*, *Mein Kampf* and *The History of the Communist Party of the Soviet Union* into great books, I cannot agree.

7 There were striking agreements over the defects in Wittfogel's work in the critical obituaries in the English press which followed his death at the age of 91 − see Gellner (1988), Hirst (1988) and O'Leary (1988).

8 Wittfogel's famous charge that Marx committed a 'sin against science' in his writings on the AMP is found wanting both in evidence and proportion in chapter 3.

political theory: does the AMP explain the European origins of capitalism? My answer is negative. However, despite the ideological abuse of the AMP, its numerous conceptual deficiencies, and its explanatory imperfections, I argue that Marxism's bastard child still stimulates important questioning and speculation.

1

The Most Controversial Mode of Production

La question du mode de production asiatique a longtemps pu passer pour le 'grand serpent de mer' des études marxistes.
Chesneaux, 'Le mode de production asiatique: une nouvelle étape de la discussion'[1]

This chapter introduces the Asiatic mode of production by providing a very brief outline of its chequered history. Some essential Marxist concepts, namely mode of production, basis and superstructure, are then defined to make clear the way they are used in this book. This task enables us to advance a definition of the AMP. Explaining why the AMP has been the most controversial of the modes of production named by Marx is then possible. The conclusion summarizes the contexts in which the AMP has been discussed.

INTRODUCTION: AN OUTLINE HISTORY

The concept of the Asiatic mode of production was introduced to the world by Marx in his famous Preface to *A Contribution to the Critique of Political Economy*, published in 1859. Although the Preface contained Marx's major statement of his theory of history, the concept of the AMP, by that name, was never referred to again by Marx in any of his published writings. (When he did refer to it again he used different words.) Scattered references in miscellaneous parts of Marx's works indicated that he believed, in common with most of his European contemporaries, that Asiatic societies had differed from those of the Occident in their economic, political and ideological structures, but these arguments did not form a major part of his

---

1 'For a long time the Asiatic mode of production has been the Loch Ness Monster of Marxist studies' is a colloquial translation.

theoretical work. Moreover, Marx entered into no public debate or extended discussion of the AMP, under that name or any other. His closest collaborator and friend Friedrich Engels never referred to the AMP at all. Engels had talked of oriental despotism and oriental society in his book *Anti-Dühring* (1878) but made no reference to the AMP in *The Origin of the Family, Private Property and the State* (1884). The latter text became the classical Marxist statement on pre-capitalist societies for the scholars, politicians and cadres of the Second and Third Internationals and consequently served even further to obscure the place of the AMP in historical materialism. The key point is that the concept of the AMP was completely uncontroversial in the lifetimes of both Marx and Engels. Even to describe it as uncontroversial is an exaggeration – it was just not a central part of Marxist doctrine, as understood by either the founding fathers or their followers.

In the Marxism of the Second International the AMP was equally uncontroversial, except in Czarist Russia.[2] There the concept surfaced in 1906 amidst discussions of the Social Democrats about the correct understanding of the agrarian structure of Russia, and the appropriate revolutionary strategy to be adopted on the agrarian front by the emergent Marxist movement. The AMP was raised as a salutary warning about following one strategy. The spectre of an 'Asiatic' restoration, the possibility that a premature revolution and land-nationalization programme might restore to modern Russia features associated with the AMP, was raised by Plekhanov. Lenin rebutted and effectively refuted Plekhanov's analogy. This brief irruption of the AMP into Marxist debate was wholly exceptional in the Second International, and the concept was restored to its previous neglect until the Russian Revolution of 1917.

The success of the Bolshevik Revolution led to the first extended discussions of the AMP in the 1920s. There were three reasons for its resurrection from obscurity. First, the very fact that a society was ruled by Marxists for the first time created space for the expansion of Marxology, and state support for the application of Marxist ideas across the spectrum of the historical, the social and even the natural sciences. Interest in the applications of the AMP developed rapidly in the 1920s amongst Soviet Indologists, Sinologists and Orientalists.[3] These discussions culminated in conferences held by Orientalists and party members in Leningrad and Moscow in 1929 and 1931–2. Second, the AMP was considered potentially relevant to discussions of Marxist revolutionary strategy in the East, given the widespread belief that the Oriental regimes conquered by imperialist powers had neither been fully brought under capitalist hegemony nor

2 See the discussion in appendix 2 to chapter 3.

3 The Marx–Engels–Lenin Institute in Moscow became the chief centre of Marxology and the possessor of the complete works and manuscripts of both Marx and Engels, and thus

developed like the feudal societies of Western Europe. The AMP even figured in the policy documents of the Comintern as a way of describing certain features of the social orders of colonial societies. Third, the AMP – as Plekhanov's prophecy of an 'Asiatic restoration' had already suggested – could be used by Marxists to explain backward features of Russian development, both before and after the Bolshevik Revolution. This feature made the concept especially attractive to dissidents.

These three reasons for the resurrection of the AMP in Russia in the 1920s serve just as well to explain why the concept was censored in the 1930s, apparently as a direct result of interventions by Stalin. In his party catechism *Dialectical and Historical Materialism*, published in 1938, Stalin briskly asserted that: 'Five main types of production are known to history: primitive communal, slave, feudal, capitalist and Socialist' (Stalin, 1973: 323). From then on the five-stage model of history was decreed correct Marxism. The AMP had entered into doctrinal limbo. The stabilization of the USSR was felt to require a rigid codification of Marxism, and the excision of the AMP formed one significant part of a wider vulgarization and simplification of Marxist doxology under Stalin's aegis. The AMP created genuine problems for historical materialism but it also had problematic ideological connotations. Moreover, it allowed far too much Marxist legitimacy to opponents of Stalin's policies in the East and the USSR. These discomforting possibilities led to its disappearance from the accepted doctrine of the CPSU and the parties of the Comintern. This conceptual purge lasted throughout Stalin's life, and was followed, almost unanimously, by all the parties of the Comintern.

In the Soviet academy, debate over the AMP had been most extended amongst antiquarians and archaeologists over the issue of the class-characteristics of the ancient Orient. Academician Struve and his followers had 'won' the debate in the early 1930s with their argument that the ancient civilizations of the Near East had been 'slave-holding' societies. The publication in 1939 of the 'Formen' passages from Marx's hitherto unpublished manuscript, the *Grundrisse*, did not disturb this new 'consensus'. Struve in fact published an article in the Soviet journal of ancient history which asserted that the *Grundrisse* proved that Marx had never believed in a distinctive AMP. Drawing upon an isolated and decontextualized aside in the *Grundrisse*, Struve claimed that Marx regarded Asiatic societies as specimens of 'universal slavery' (Struve, 1940).[4]

facilitated textual scholarship.
    Russian discussions of the AMP are well covered in Dunn (1982) and Sawer (1977 and 1979).
    4 See Dunn (1982: 42–62). Struve's article is also said to have been published in *Vestnik drevnei istorii*, No. 1 – see Shafarevich (1980: 304).

Discussion of the AMP revived amongst Marxists in the 1950s, after Stalin's death, and has gone on unabated ever since. Since de-Stalinization commenced in 1956 theorists in Marxist regimes, intellectuals attached to Communist Parties and independent members of the Western Marxist intelligentsia have found discussions of the AMP stimulating — whether as a heresy to be uprooted or as an instrument for the reform of Marxism. Since a DDR historian and a Hungarian Sinologist revived discussion of the banished idea in 1957—8 (Tökei, 1958; Welskopf, 1957) it has become acceptable to discuss the AMP in Marxist regimes. Debate over its merits was especially animated amongst Soviet antiquarians, anthropologists and archaeologists in the 1960s and 1970s, although it died down again in the early 1980s.

At the same time the more empirically and historically oriented of Western Marxists, notably those associated with the Centre d'Études Recherches Marxistes in Paris, rejoiced in the opportunity provided by the de-Stalinization of Marxism in the East. The way was opened for them to conduct research without the handicaps imposed by Stalin's model of history or the iron grip of their local party bosses. Marxists engaged in revolutionary praxis in Asia were also sometimes receptive to the AMP since it rid them of the dubious requirement to describe as feudal all pre-capitalist 'survivals' in their societies. This widespread enthusiasm for the AMP led to a proliferation of research, articles, books and propaganda on the AMP written by Marxists in most of the world's major languages, notably English, Chinese, Russian, Spanish, German, French and Italian (see *inter alia* Bailey and Llobera, 1974—5; CÉRM, 1969; Krader, 1975; Melotti, 1977; Sawer 1977; and Sofri, 1969).

However, the revival of discussion of the AMP amongst Marxists was partly occasioned by Karl Wittfogel's publications on oriental despotism, which were produced in a steady stream in the 1950s and 1960s. The strongly anti-Communist use to which the concept was put by the ex-Communist Sinologist provoked predictable outrage amongst Soviet loyalists but it also created interest in the AMP amongst Western scholars not noted for an interest in matters Marxist. Although Wittfogel's interventions high-lighted the potential cold war usages of the AMP, they also suggested its non-ideological potential for theoretical and empirical work in comparative political analysis and political anthropology. Writers in comparative politics used Wittfogel's premises to explain the problems of political modernization in Third World countries, and anthropologists employed them to contest the theory of unilineal evolution, then conventional wisdom in that discipline. Consequently since the 1950s there have been forces at work in both Marxist and anti-Marxist regimes which have considerably extended interest in the AMP.

These forces were given a further twist in the 1960s. A brief spurt of growth occurred in the numbers of the non-Communist Marxist intelligentsia in Western universities. This development took place at the same time as hitherto unavailable or inaccessible texts of Marx and Engels, notably the *Grundrisse*, and the writings of both the early and the late Marx, were published in the major Western European languages. The growth of an international network of Marxist sympathizers and scholars ensured that the renaissance of interest in the AMP remained intact long after the debates and polemics initiated by Wittfogel subsided. However, to appreciate why interest has remained sustained in this concept, and why it is controversial, we must first outline some essential Marxist concepts and the defining traits of the AMP.

MODE OF PRODUCTION, BASIS AND SUPERSTRUCTURE

There are three key Marxist concepts indispensable for appreciating the meaning(s) of the AMP: mode of production, basis and superstructure. Consider them in order.

Mode of Production   The modes of defining modes of production merit a serious study in themselves but it is not essential to explore this scholastic history. Broad familiarity is all that is required to understand adequately the controversial status of the AMP in the canons of historical materialism.[5] The concept of a mode of production was generated by Marx in his critique of classical political economy. The notion of modes of production had its primary antecedents in Marx's encounter with the 'modes of subsistence' made famous in the eighteenth century by the thinkers of the Scottish enlightenment and the French Physiocratic writer Turgot. But the genesis of the concept of mode of production must also be understood against the background of Marx's readings of Hegel and Saint-Simon. These authors had a profound impact on Marx and Engels. In different ways, they elaborated philosophies of progress, suggesting that societies passed through various stages of evolution in mankind's journey to perfection and enlightenment.[6] The genesis of the concept of a mode of production explains why it refers both to an economic system (just as the classical economists referred to a mode of subsistence) and to the location of that system in a progressive series of evolutionary stages (similar to those propagated by Hegel and Saint-Simon).

The concept 'mode of production' is ambiguously and profligately used in the writings of both Marx and Engels. However, one authority has

5 The key concepts of historical materialism are discussed in chapters 4 and 5.
6 On the antecedents of historical materialism see *inter alia* Aron, 1968: 140–50; G.A. Cohen, 1979: 1–27; Hook, 1933; Meek 1967 and 1971; and Therborn, 1976: 317–413.

helpfully provided a threefold classification of Marx's principal usages of the term, which he dubs the material, social and mixed modes (G. A. Cohen, 1979: 79).

1   The *material* mode of production refers to the manner or the mode in which persons work with productive forces. Productive forces encompass means of production and labour power. Means of production include instruments of production (or what contemporary economists call physical capital and production premises), raw materials, and spaces. Labour power refers to the capacity of human beings to work.

2   The *social* mode of production refers to the social properties of production processes. The social mode of production can be defined in three ways: by the goals of the production process, by the form of the producer's surplus labour, and by the mode of exploitation. These ways of defining a social mode of production have the same connotation for most Marxists, because the three definitions are usually held to be met once the social relations of production are specified. Social relations of production are relations of effective power over persons' labour power and means of production; that is, over productive forces.

3   The *mixed* mode of production refers to a combination of the material and social mode of production. Marx never precisely defined the mixed mode, nor the conceptual and/or causal relations between the material and social modes, but frequently employs the term in a way which includes both material and social dimensions.

A mode of production, unless specified otherwise, here means a set of productive forces and social relations of production.[7]

In the Preface to *A Contribution to the Critique of Political Economy*, Marx declared that 'In broad outlines Asiatic, ancient, feudal and modern bourgeois modes of production can be designated as progressive epochs in the economic formation of society' (Marx, 1970: 21). This critical sentence introduced, publicly, the AMP. It is listed first in a list of 'progressive epochs', and distinguished from the others by its geographical prefix. Full appreciation of why the first-mentioned in Marx's list is so controversial requires clarification of the rest of the argument in the Preface. For the moment discussion of the definitional problems involved in concepts like material, social, productive forces, relations of production, and progressive epochs, can be postponed in order to focus upon a famous pair of concepts also delineated tantalizingly briefly in the Preface but not elaborated in

7 The conceptual rendering of mode of production in structuralist French Marxism (as in Althusser and Balibar, 1970, or in such post-Althusserian works as Hindess and Hirst, 1975) is discussed below − see pp. 215−22.

detail elsewhere in Marx's writings: basis and superstructure. Arguments about basis and superstructure are fundamental to both the theoretical and ideological difficulties created by the AMP. The misleading architectural and spatial metaphors of basis and superstructure create key difficulties for historical materialist hypotheses. Their clarification is indispensable to any rigorous definition of those hypotheses.

Basis   There are two principal ways in which basis (or infrastructure) has been defined by scholars of Marxism. First, it has been identified with relations of production. Second, it has been identified with the mode of production.

1   *The relations of production basis*. The most reasonable reading of the Preface to *A Contribution to the Critique of Political Economy* suggests a definition of basis which makes it synonymous with relations of production. The relevant passage in the Preface provides strong textual support for this synonymity: 'The sum total of these relations of production constitutes the economic structure, the real basis, on which rises a legal and political superstructure, and to which correspond definite forms of social consciousness' (Marx, 1970: 20). A simple equation is implied: 'economic structure' = 'basis' = 'relations of production' (G.A. Cohen, 1979: 29). This reading of Marx is, unanswerably, literally exact.

2   *The mode of production infrastructure*. The major alternative Marxist 'reading' is to define basis, or infrastructure, as we shall call it for clarity, as a combination of productive forces and relations of production. Such is the creative 'reading' of Maurice Godelier:

By infrastructure ... we refer to a complex combination of:
1. the ecological and geographical conditions within which and from which society extracts its material means of existence;
2. the productive forces, i.e. the material and intellectual means which man invents and employs in different labour processes in order to act upon nature and to extract therefrom his means of existence, and transform nature into 'socialised' nature;
3. relations of production, i.e. all social relations whatsoever, which serve a threefold function: first, to determine social access to and control of resources and the means of production; secondly, to redistribute the social labour force among the different labour processes, and to organise these processes; and thirdly to determine the social distribution of the product of labour (Godelier, 1980: 6; see also Godelier, 1978a: 84−6).

This reading of infrastructure, as with much structuralist French Marxism, has no explicit textual warrant from Marx and Engels. However, we are not especially concerned to define 'what Marx really said' (*except* on the AMP!) and as the Godelier reading is common amongst Marxists and non-Marxists we shall accept for the sake of argument that Godelier's infrastructure is

Marxist, whilst remaining certain that Cohen's basis is that of Karl Marx.[8]

The central difficulty is that, however the basis is defined, problems arise in distinguishing it from the superstructure, problems which recur in discussions of the AMP. The logical possibilities are threefold:[9]

first, basis (or infrastructure) is identical with the superstructure − in which case the potential explanatory utility of the distinction disappears;

second, basis (or infrastructure) is completely distinct from the super-structure; and,

third, basis (or infrastructure) is imprecisely distinct from the super-structure; that is, some things or relations might be both basic (or infra-structural) and superstructural, and/or it might be undecidable whether a certain thing or relation is the one or the other.

All three positions have been upheld by Marxologists, normally without awareness that the other positions are also *prima facie* coherent. Furthermore, these analytic possibilities are regularly confused with the question of whether the empirical referents of the concepts are perceptually separable, i.e. with the issue of whether the basis or superstructure is capable of being directly observed.

8 See G.A. Cohen (1979: 29, footnote 2) where he cites the following list of interpreters who have taken 'basis' to cover both productive forces and relations of production: Acton, 1955: 312 and 1967: 50; Calvez, 1956: 245; Duncan, 1973: 289; Eagleton, 1976: 5; McLellan, 1973a: 308; Mills, 1962: 82; Plamenatz, 1954: 24−5; and Therborn, 1976: 399.

Cohen's argument is that productive forces explain (account for, determine or shape) relations of production, more than vice versa. So is his complaint against these authors' undoubted error anything more than a quibble? Cohen's position is:

productive forces → basis (= relations of production) → superstructure.

He atttacks the idea that:

basis (= productive forces and relations of production) → superstructure.

His position is not a quibble insofar as productive forces are given primacy in explaining relations of production. But in terms of the role played by relations of production in explaining (accounting for, determining, shaping etc.) the superstructure, the significance of the differ-ences in defining basis do not amount to much, unless different conceptions of the super-structure are held, or unless the position Cohen attacks is taken to assert no priority at all in the causal relations operating between the analytical variables.

The remark in the Preface that 'The mode of production of material life conditions the social, political and intellectual life process in general' (Marx, 1970: 20−1) can be read in support of both Cohen's and Godelier's readings. However, material mode of production does appear to be Marx's meaning in this passage, and as there is no reference to basis (or infrastructure) within the sentence Cohen's reading again looks more exact.

9 They can also be expresssed more broadly as five logical possibilities by unpacking the third option that basis is 'imprecisely distinct' from the superstructure into the logical relations of overlap, intersection and inclusion. Thus we might have:

1   basis = superstructure; B = S, i.e. the set relation of identity; or
2   basis and superstructure are separate; they share no sub-sets; or
3   basis and superstructure overlap; B U S ‡ ø; i.e. the set relation of intersection; or
4   basis is included in superstructure; B is a sub-set of S (inclusion); or
5   superstructure is included in basis; S is a sub-set of B (inclusion).

Superstructure The disagreements over the way to define the basis (or infrastructure) are mirrored in disagreements over the definition of the superstructure. The first distinction is between those who define the superstructure broadly, to cover anything from a wide range to literally all features of human existence which are not basic (or infrastructural), and those who define its scope narrowly, so that not everything social is either basic or superstructural (or both). The narrower conception of superstructure is normally confined to matters pertaining to law and politics.[10] The vague phrase 'pertaining to law and politics' avoids prejudging the second distinction. Some define the superstructure as composed of institutions, as in 'legal and political institutions'. But others want to define the superstructure in terms of functions, as in 'legal, political and ideological functions'. The logical possibilities are fourfold, as the 2×2 matrix in table 1.1. illustrates. The vertical dimension captures the disagreement over the scope of the superstructure (which could, in principle, be subdivided infinitely), whereas the horizontal dimension captures the disagreement over whether superstructures are sets of functions or institutions. Cohen and Godelier's definitions fit into boxes 2 and 3 respectively. Boxes 1 and 4 remain unfilled, but as the definitions of 'functions' and 'institutions' are ambiguous in both Godelier and Cohen it is best to leave open the possibility that they are intellectually coherent Marxist positions.[11]

10 Apart from the famous sentence in the Preface which confines superstructure to the 'legal and political', the slight textual evidence − if it does anything − supports those like Godelier who give broad scope to the superstructure. Marx and Engels first used the terms base and superstructure (*Überbau*) in *The German Ideology*. They wrote of 'the social organization which develops directly out of production and social intercourse and which at all times forms the basis [*die Basis*] of the state and the rest of the idealist superstructure [*Superstrukter*]' (Marx and Engels, 1956, III: 36); and they indicted capitalism for destroying for the worker 'all natural and inherited family and political conditions ... together with their whole ideological superstructure [*Überbau*] (Marx and Engels, 1956, III: 36 and 56). In *The Communist Manifesto* the use of the term superstructure implies a narrower range for the concept: 'The proletariat, the lowest stratum of present day society, cannot stir, cannot raise itself, without blowing sky-high the whole superstructure [*Überbau*] of strata that constitute official society' (ibid., IV: 473). Blowing up the superstructure is here more or less equated with destroying the personnel in bourgeois legal and political institutions. Yet the usage of the term in *The Eighteenth Brumaire of Louis Bonaparte* implies that both institutions and ideas are included in its domain: 'Upon the different forms of property, upon the social conditions of existence rises an entire superstructure of distinct and characteristically formed sentiments, illusions, modes of thought and views of life' (Marx and Engels, 1969−70, I: 421).

11 Yet how one defines superstructure must relate to how one defines basis if there is to be a causal (let alone a dialectical!) relationship between the two concepts. Godelier consistently refers to both infrastructural and superstructural functions. Cohen defines basis as 'economic structure' rather than as 'economic institution' but there is no *prima facie* reason for supposing that Cohen regards these two descriptions as distinct concepts.

Note that the way basis or superstructure is defined is not necessarily linked to supporting or opposing functionalism, or functionalist explanations in social science. Both Cohen and Godelier endorsed functionalist modes of explanation at the time they wrote their texts (see G.A. Cohen, 1979: 248−89; and Godelier, 1980: 9−13) although they have slightly different conceptions of functionalism and functional explanation.

Table 1.1 A matrix of superstructures

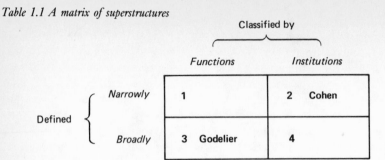

These ambiguities over the definitions of basis and superstructure create key problems for the coherence of the AMP (see pp. 182–4). However, it is premature to elaborate them here. Having briefly indicated the most obvious definitions of mode of production, and the range of definitions of basis and superstructure, it is time to advance a preliminary picture and begin discussion of the AMP.

THE ASIATIC MODE OF PRODUCTION

This preliminary definition is based upon the set of characteristics attributed to the AMP and gathered from systematic analysis of the collected works of Marx and Engels. These characteristics are fully supported by quotations from the works of Marx and Engels (Krader, 1975: 286–96).[12] This preliminary definition of the AMP is therefore what logicians call an extensive definition, derived from Marx and Engels's writings rather than from logical deductions from the premises of historical materialism.

Definition of the AMP

1   The AMP is a mode of production in which the level of development of the productive forces is greater than that of the primitive communist

12 Krader's citation of and commentaries on all the relevant works of Marx and Engels (1972 and 1975) are, despite their defects, an indispensable source to scholars interested in the AMP. Krader's work is principally exegetic but he does advance one mistaken argument. He believes that Marx and Engels's views on the characteristics and laws of motion of the AMP remained constant throughout their intellectual careers (or were sufficiently stable not to be of theoretical consequence). The argument is wrong, as two general and earlier survey essays demonstrate (Lichtheim, 1963; and Thorner, 1966). He also appears to believe that a textual 'treasure hunt' is sufficient to define the characteristics of the AMP. Yet with apparent inconsistency, he believes that Marx and Engels altered their views on the role of the AMP in the development of world history, and went through a series of stages in developing the AMP. (See also pp. 137–9).

mode of production but inferior to that of the capitalist mode of production.

2   Agricultural production overwhelmingly composes the largest portion of necessary and surplus production in the AMP. The vast majority of the population in a territory dominated by the AMP live in villages which are almost autarkic (in the sense that little inter-village trade takes place).

3   The level of development of the productive forces in the AMP is constrained for three reasons. First, as Adam Smith might have put it, the division of labour is limited by the extent of the market, which is limited by the size of the village community and the paucity of developed trade networks. Second, the village market in the AMP is limited by the fact that most production is for immediate consumption rather than for exchange. Accordingly, there is little requirement for money as a medium of exchange, and gold and precious metals are valued mainly for their scarcity and symbolic usages. Third, the productive forces of the AMP are constrained by its relations of production. The division of labour is developed upon a community (and/or caste) basis which blocks further developments in technological innovation and productive efficiency.

4   The development of the productive forces (and the production of means of subsistence in particular) within the AMP, under certain ecological conditions, necessitates the construction and administration of water supplies. The presence of such 'hydraulic' technology (as it is misleadingly called) is frequently empirically correlated with the AMP, although on its own is neither necessary nor sufficient for the genesis of an AMP within a given territory.

5   The AMP is a mode of production in which the principal social relations of production are as follows. The ruling class, which overlaps largely (or is identical) with the state officialdom, appropriates the surplus labour of the direct agricultural producers. Villagers pay a combined rent/tax to state officials, principally in kind, or in compulsory labour services for the state, rather than in money. The large number of villages ensures a surplus sufficient to sustain an affluent court aristocracy and a wealthy (on occasions, fabulously wealthy) monarchy. The urban population, centred on the court aristocracy and the monarchy, is thus parasitic upon the rural population. Limited manufacturing of products takes place in and for the court and administrative sites, and this sector depends for its maintenance upon the ruling class extracting revenue from the countryside. There is no large-scale merchant class, there being only limited capital speculation in long-distance trade, money lending and agricultural products. Within the villages, variations can occur in the extent to which relations of production are exploitative. On the one hand there are villages which are comparatively egalitarian in villagers' effective access to and possession of the land. On the other hand there are villages with internally developed class relations in which land access and relations of possession are exclusive and inegalitarian.

However, despite these variations, the bulk of the village population performs surplus labour for the state, although in the villages with internal class relations the dominant class is much less exploited.

6   It follows from our earlier discussion that the basis of the AMP is *either* the social relations of production just described in 5, *or* a combination of the relations of production and productive forces described in 3, 4 and 5.

7   The superstructure of the AMP, if defined narrowly and institutionally, has the following key traits. Legal institutions are developed, but do not recognize 'strong' private property rights in the means of production. 'Ownership' of the land is complicated by the communal claims of the village and by the claims of the state through the monarch. (It is a matter of debate whether or not the state − or the monarch − owns the land.) The political power of the monarch is 'despotic' and is exercised through an imperial officialdom which has both military and bureaucratic characteristics. The personnel who occupy the institutional roles in the superstructure of the AMP are subject to constant change, through monarchical control strategies, wars of dynastic succession, and wars of conquest by nomadic warrior tribes. However, the institutional structures of state control and coordination, in particular of revenue collection and corvée labour, remain constant (apart from when wars of succession or conquest occasion the collapse of the superstructure).

By contrast, when the superstructure of the AMP is defined widely it also encompasses, at the very least, all written and unwritten ideologies which venerate the monarchy, the imperial aristocracy and the state officialdom, and sanction or maintain production relations in the villages. At its most extensive the superstructure encompasses all religious, philosophical and cultural communications which consciously, or unconsciously, serve to sustain the social relations of production of the AMP.[13]

WHY IS THE ASIATIC MODE OF PRODUCTION SO CONTROVERSIAL?

At first glance it is difficult to see why the abstract picture of a pre-capitalist or pre-industrial social order presented in the definition on pp. 16−18 should be the source of so much political and scholarly controversy. Yet the furore generated by the AMP is obvious from the most casual acquaintance with the literature which feeds upon it. The AMP is

13 In this preliminary sketch the superstructure is not defined à la Godelier (see p. 15 and note 10 above) explicitly in terms of functions. Godelier's approach is in fact a response to the controversies generated within structuralist anthropological debates over basis and superstructure in the AMP and is dealt with in chapters 4 and 5.

an 'awkward appendage' to historical materialism (Caldwell, 1977). In the eyes of both loyalists and critics it is a subversive concept (Lefort, 1978: 631). It is often suggested that Marxists have died or have been imprisoned for adhering to a concept written out of history by Stalin.[14] 'The immense burden of theoretical distortions and contradictory ideologies which this concept has come to bear' (Godelier, 1978: 239) has been lamented with good cause since discussions on the AMP have led to the strangest insinuations. The most tendentious was the charge that Marx committed 'a sin against science' (Wittfogel, 1953: 350–9; and 1981: 386–88). The gravamen of Wittfogel's accusation was that Marx repressed his discovery of the AMP because the discovery was at odds with his revolutionary socialist politics. Wittfogel reasoned that the AMP was inconsistent with the Marxist theory of the state and was therefore 'blacked out' by Marxists because of its unwelcome suggestions about what might happen after a socialist revolution. The most comic insinuation about the formation of the AMP has been the suggestion that there was a connection between Marx's sexual activity in fathering the illegitimate child of Helene Demuth and his intellectual activity around the same time (the 1850s). Spawning the illicit theoretical pregnancy which we know today as the AMP took place at the same time as the spawning of Marx's bastard child (Gouldner, 1980: 300)![15] This example of dinner-table psychology is mildly amusing in comparison with the abuse heaped upon Wittfogel for his use of the AMP. He is called a 'renegade' with such regularity by Marxist critics that it appears to be a substitute for his forename. The New Left's best known historical sociologist preferred to damn Wittfogel with non-party and more academic contempt as 'a vulgar charivari, devoid of any historical sense' and as 'a more or less Spencerian survival' (P. Anderson, 1974b: 487). He prescribed a 'decent burial' for the AMP, aptly described as 'one of the most haunting and intriguing heresies' in Marxist thought (Gellner, 1983: 27). There is therefore widespread consensus that the AMP is 'the most controversial and contested of all the possible modes of production in the work of Marx and Engels' (Hindess and Hirst, 1975: 178).

There are scholarly, theoretical, political and ideological reasons for this controversial status. Detailed attention is paid to the scholarly causes of controversies in chapters 2 and 3, whereas the theoretical controversies are discussed in chapters 4 and 5. Here the task is to examine political and

---

14 See Mandel (1971: chapter 8) and Sawer (1979: 108–27). Stalin's *Dialectical and Historical Materialism* (1938) excluded the AMP from the received truth, *modo Tartarico*, as Wittfogel put it. See also note 2 in the introduction to this book.

15 Gouldner considered that Marx's 'anomaly fertile period began about the time he started *The Eighteenth Brumaire of Louis Bonaparte* in 1852 and intensified around 1853–4'. And he further observed, I believe without his having his tongue in his cheek, that 'Marx's disruptive illicit thoughts, were, like his illegitimate son, ordered from his house soon after its birth.'

ideological causes of controversy. There are five such causes: the small textual treasure left by Marx and Engels; the accusation that the concept is Eurocentric or Orientalist; its use in debates over the prospects for an 'Asiatic restoration'; its employment in debates over appropriate revolutionary Marxist strategy in non-European social formations; and finally the fierce debates which surround suggested parallels between the Asiatic and the socialist modes of production.

The Small Textual Treasure

In the introductory outline history, I suggested that when the AMP has not been controversial it has been neglected. One common cause of both the controversy and the neglect is the paucity of reference to, and elaboration of, the concept in the works of Marx and Engels. Apart from the occasional exaggeration,[16] and despite the immensity of the tomes published by Krader (1972 and 1975), Marx and Engels did not write at great length upon the AMP.[17] The relevant portions of the published writings of Marx and Engels can all be read in an afternoon. Of the writings published in Marx's lifetime, his political journalism − the 'muck',[18] as he described the columns he wrote for the *New York Daily Tribune* in the 1850s − is where to begin. Then there is the famous but unelaborated citation in the 1859 preface to *A Contribution to the Critique of Political Economy* (Marx, 1970: 21). Finally, there are some relevant asides and footnotes in Volume I of *Capital* (Marx, 1976a: 171, 452, 477−9). As for the published works of Engels there are pertinent passages in both *Anti-Dühring* (Engels, 1976: 223−36) and, more debatably, in *The Origin of the Family, Private Property and the State* (Engels,

16 In the course of criticizing some of the crude Cold War 'scholarship' of Black, Rostow and Schlesinger, Shlomo Avineri claims that Marx's discussions on modernization in Asia are expressed in dozens of articles (Avineri, 1969a: 174). It is true that there are dozens of articles by Marx and Engels, principally on India and China − as shown by Avineri's own edited collection (1969b). But there are only dozens of 'discussions on modernization' if one undertakes a particularly productive and imaginative 'symptomatic' reading.

17 Gouldner (1980, chapter 11) makes fun of Melotti and Sawer for overplaying their hands with the available writings of Marx and Engels. Melotti (1977: 11) took issue with Shapiro (1962: 282−4) who had stressed the small quantity of textual authority from the founding fathers for the AMP. Melotti's criticism of this accurate statement took the form of wheeling out an easily combustible straw man: Marx 'did not make just a single stray reference' to the AMP. Unfortunately arguing with phantom constructions is all too common in arguments about the AMP. Moreover, if we count published writings only and insist on literal exactness then Marx did indeed make only one stray reference to the AMP! Sawer's exaggeration was different, one appropriate for a surer scholar. In search of textual authority to support the argument that Marx regarded Western capitalist governments as potentially more oppressive than oriental despotisms she went to the extent of citing a scribble Marx made in the margin of H.C. Irwin's *The Garden of India* (Sawer, 1977: 49−50)!

18 'The continual newspaper muck annoys me. It takes a lot of time, disperses my efforts and in the final analysis is nothing' (Marx and Engels, 1956, XXVIII: 592, cited in McLellan, 1976: 284). The bulk of the journalism relevant to the AMP can be found in Marx and Engels (1959).

1978). If all these writings, published in Marx and Engels' lifetimes, with their express approval, were not collated and compared they might be missed, or, at most, strike the student of Marx as insignificant asides.

However, if one includes the pertinent unpublished writings of Marx and Engels an afternoon's reading will become a day's. Their earliest writings can be ransacked for apparently relevant asides (Marx and Engels, 1970). Their correspondence, especially with each other, must not be missed, especially for its value in illustrating their thought in progress (Marx and Engels, 1934). The 'Formen' passages in the *Grundrisse* are equally indispensable for the serious scholar (Marx, 1964: 67–120 and 1973e 459–79), especially since the *Grundrisse*, as Sawer has wittily put it, has earned the title of 'the Dead Sea Scroll of Marxism'. Marx and Engels's writings on Czarist Russia are arguably relevant.[19] Finally, there are salient passages in the unfinished Volume *III* of *Capital* (Marx, 1981) and fragments in the even more unfinished *Theories of Surplus Value* (Marx, 1978). However, the only way in which one can make an exhausting research project out of combing Marx and Engels's 'texts' for items relevant to the AMP is to include all their notebooks and marginalia. Needless to say that activity is now a fully fledged part of the Marxological industry (Krader, 1972).

The most straightforward and scholarly, respectable reaction to the textual paucity of Marx and Engels's writings on the AMP takes it as proof of its marginal significance both to themselves and to Marxism. This approach, in fact, has been employed by the best Marxist opponents of the Marxist credentials of the AMP ever since the 1920s.[20] In the 1920s and 1930s debates were conducted in the Soviet Union over the status of the AMP in Marxist political strategy and historiography. Although some Soviet 'scholars' tried to deny the existence of any textual authority whatsoever for the theses of those they dubbed the *Aziatchiki*[21] (Dunn, 1982: 9) it was not

19 Marx and Engels's writings on Russia are an embarrassment to good Bolsheviks. Affected by Czarist Russia's counter-revolutionary role in 1848–9, Marx and Engels were prone to classify it both polemically and anachronistically as an Asiatic despotism. Marx's writings on Russian history and society 'often lack balance or control' as one commentator has delicately put it (P. Anderson, 1974f: 492). Our reasons for not discussing them are given below (p. 143, n. 91). Engels's writings, *On Social Relations in Russia* (1875), and the afterword to *On Social Relations in Russia* (1894) – both, in Marx and Engels (1969–70) – and Marx and Engels's correspondence with Russian revolutionaries on the Russian commune (Marx and Engels, 1934; Shanin, 1983), illuminate their perspectives on pre-capitalist agrarian modes of production.

20 'Best' in the sense of having intellectual honesty and rational argumentation, rather than practical success. The 'right of the stronger' in Soviet debates on the AMP is not evident from the transcripts of the 1920s and 1930s debates, which seem to have been characterized by authentic debate (see Sawer, 1979; Dunn, 1982; and reviews of Dunn by Gellner, 1983; and O'Leary, 1984).

21 Supporters of the Marxist credentials and utility are known as the *Aziatchiki* in the Soviet Union; whereas their opponents are the *anti-Aziatchiki*.

a very compelling tack, given blatant evidence to the contrary.[22] It was obviously much better, more sophisticated and more honest to acknowledge the existence of writings by Marx and Engels pertinent to a putative AMP, but to claim that their very brief and underdeveloped character was proof of their lack of centrality to historical materialism. M.Ia. Godes, author of the main paper at the Leningrad conference of Marxist Orientalists in 1932, followed such an approach:

The statement on the Asiatic Mode of Production cannot be crossed out of Marx's works; our task consists not in blatantly repeating this statement but rather — since our contemporary ideas on the historical development of the countries of the East do not confirm the existence of a specific social order such as the Asiatic Mode of Production — in explaining how and why Marx at a particular stage in the development of his theory and at a particular stage of development of historical scholarship, expressed views on the social structure of the East, which in parts of them have not been confirmed. (Godes, cited in Dunn 1982: 9–10)

This approach is frank. The AMP, although authored by Marx, is wrong — in the sense of being empirically inaccurate and unhelpful; and its being wrong does no harm to historical materialism. Accordingly, all that is left of interest is to account for Marx's errors — which he attributed to Marx's being misled by 'bourgeois Orientalists'. In a different vein Godes argued that the AMP was at theoretical odds with historical materialism, and that the *Aziatchiki* were true to the letter of Marx rather than the essence of Marxism; they were citationists rather than social scientists:

A characteristic of this entire school is an acritical use of separate remarks of Marx on the Asiatic Mode of Production and the Orient, frequently out of context, and at any rate, out of the context of Marx's general teachings on social formations. It seems that the discussions of the Asiatic Mode of Production and the pronouncements of partisans of this theory have once more shown that quotations from Marx do not constitute Marxist teachings, and that not everyone who quotes Marx correctly applies his method, just as not everyone who repeats the Lord's prayer makes it to heaven. (Godes, cited in Bailey and Llobera, 1981: 101)

These arguments exemplify how the small textual treasures are capable of being dismissed, and *prima facie* very reasonably, on the grounds that they are brief marginalia not supported by subsequent historical and social scientific scholarship.

The scholarly basis for controversy is thus apparent. The weight we should attach not only to Marx and Engels's small amount of writings but also to their specific context is a matter of judgement likely to produce disagreement. It has often been pointed out that secondary commentators

22 Although salient unpublished writings of Marx and Engels such as the *Grundrisse* were unavailable for the beginning of the Soviet debate, there was no lack of availability of the Preface to *A Contribution to the Critique of Political Economy*.

on the AMP have treated all of Marx's writings as if they all were of equal theoretical status (Hindess and Hirst, 1975: 181−2).[23] Such slovenly scholarly practice was perhaps overdignified by being described as the product of the 'empiricist method' of reading, but the complaint against such practices is well taken. If the concept of the AMP is to make any sense it must, it seems, be free of scholastic debates: '[b]ecause the concept AMP is a general one it is neither necessary to look for it in, nor is it necessarily to be found in, the marxist writings on Asia' (Hindess and Hirst, 1975: 180). One can only agree with this desire to be rid of scholasticism and with the wish to ask whether the AMP is compatible with historical materialism. However, the problem is that the origins of the controversy over the AMP are in the first instance scholastic!

Strictures against writers on the AMP, like Wittfogel, who treat all of Marx and Engels's views and writings as if they have identical theoretical stature are apposite. Simply to sew together a theory from journalism, letters and incidental remarks is unsubtle. Users and abusers of the AMP regularly fail to stress the differential importance of Marx and Engels's published, as opposed to their unpublished, writings. Theoreticians do not publish everything they write, for good reasons. They may consider their materials undeveloped, repetitious, unoriginal or even both bad and wrong. Publication involves a commitment to defend, at least when it is not driven by financial or base considerations. These elementary propositions make the emphasis that Krader, for instance, has attached to Marx's 'ethnological notebooks' wholly implausible (Krader, 1972).[24] These 'ethnological notebooks' are not even unpublished writings, except in the most literal sense. They are notes, made in Marx's polylingual style, and at least at the level of intentionality are probably only intelligible to the deceased author. The attempt to oversell the importance of unpublished writings is often an excuse for authors to peddle their own distinct AMP with all the blessings that quotation-mongering is believed to confer.

In brief, the small textual treasure, debates over its context and fundamental disagreements over how to evaluate unpublished writings have all provided the stuff of literary controversy, which in discussions of Marxism are inevitably charged with politics and ideology. Moreover, most of the pertinent unpublished material of Marx and Engels was in fact either

---

23 Hindess and Hirst singled out Wittfogel's (1957) and Lichtheim's (1963) work as exemplifying this charge.

24 It is not difficult for the cynic to spot an interesting trend in fashion. In the wake of the vogue for the early Marx which dominated 1960s Marxologists, enthusiasm for the middle-aged Marx's unpublished *Grundrisse* developed in the 1970s, only to be displaced in the 1980s by the final craze for the writings of the late Marx. One might well ask: how do these trends relate to biographies (the same authors and readers growing older) or sociological realities (the youthful fervour of the 1960s; the crisis-ridden 1970s; and the retreat into private study in the 1980s)?

unknown or inaccessible to most European Marxists before World War I. The neglect of the AMP, outside of Russia, is partly accounted for by simple lack of knowledge of the idea amongst the practitioners of Marxism in its 'golden age' (Kolakowski, 1981).[25] Yet Plekhanov constructed a version of the AMP from the limited writings of Marx and Engels available to him, which suggests that the absence of much discussion of the AMP in the Second International, outside of Russia, is best explained by its lack of conceivable political or ideological relevance to the European Marxist movement. In retrospect there is no political or ideological reason why the AMP should have been so neglected in the Second International. The potential significance of the AMP in the arguments over the nature, and consequences of, imperialism has been verified by its re-emergence in early and late twentieth-century Marxist debates. What made the AMP become more visible and controversial in the time of the Third International?

Eurocentricity and Orientalism

Since the formation of the Third International, Eurocentricity has been the most frequent charge made against the AMP. The fact that the Russian Revolution took place on the Asiatic periphery of Europe engendered conscious awareness of the potentially explosive Eurocentric uses of the AMP amongst the theoreticians of the Comintern. And subsequently the concept has been resurrected for polemical purposes, to charge or absolve Marxism of Eurocentricity, in every decade of the twentieth century (with the exception of the 1940s).

The following sample of statements is instructive:

'In the early 1850s, Marx and Engels had still not freed themselves from the europocentric view of world development that imperialism itself had engendered' (Fernbach, 1973: 24).
'The modern Indian, or Uzbek, reader may feel that Marx did less than justice to some Asian dynasties ... He may feel that Marx's horizon was too Europocentric' (Kiernan, 1967: 163).
Marx had a 'europocentric vision of the world' (Carrère d'Encausse and Schram, 1969: 8).
Marx and Engels's writings on India were written 'from a European perspective' (Wielenga, 1976, chapter 1).
Marx's source material for the Asiatic mode of production was 'Eurocentric' (Gardezi, 1979).

25 The description 'golden age' is Kolakowski's term for the Marxism of the Second International and the Third International before Stalin (Kolakowski, 1981, volume 2). Major 'golden age' Marxists like Lafargue, Cunow and Luxemburg did employ — albeit incidentally — concepts like agrarian communism, oriental society and oriental despotism, without engendering any political argument. See chapter 3, appendix 2.

The revival of the AMP in the 1960s was not part of de-Stalinization, but a by-product of cultural imperialism, a new attempt to 'establish that the entire past history of social progress belongs to Europe alone' (Habib, 1975: 24).

These authors are all plainly hostile to the Eurocentricity of the AMP, but there are some non-Marxists who, in complete contrast, regard Eurocentricity as the supreme virtue of the concept (Lichtheim, 1963;[26] Wittfogel, 1957). However, the former response has been dominant in recent decades. In the eyes of both many Third International activists and contemporary Western Marxists (and of their critics), Marxism, like every other social theory produced in the nineteenth century imperialist metropolis, is vitiated by some its unacknowledged Eurocentric assumptions. The AMP is given pride of place in such criticism. Amongst Western Marxist historians the most frequent response is to regard the Eurocentricity of the AMP as sufficient warrant for the theoretical purge of a concept held to be a foreign – or rather bourgeois – intrusion into historical materialism.[27]

We can unpack the criticism of Eurocentricity into several interrelated components: racism, cultural chauvinism and Orientalism. Eurocentric racism displays the typical features of racism, assuming the innate superiority of European peoples when contrasted with their complement. Racists conveniently find sufficient racial homogeneity amongst Europeans to regard them as one race. Marx and Engels are intermittently found guilty of nineteenth-century stereotypical racism – indeed one author has gone so far as to write of the 'Prolet-Aryan' outlook of Marxism (C. Moore, 1974–5)! Examinations of Marx and Engels's correspondence have provided ample evidence for those who wish to level such charges at the founders of proletarian internationalism. Twentieth-century Marxists have regularly been embarrassed at the Victorian prejudices apparently shared by Marx and Engels. The AMP, distinguished from all the other modes of production by its telling geographical prefix, is often seen as symptomatic of such racism, and accordingly recommended for exclusion from a purified Marxist canon. Marxists who by contrast wish to uphold the utility of the concept have argued that its scientific content can be excavated from, and

26 Lichtheim's famous essay not only finds plausible Engels's notion that occidental liberties were born in the German forests, but also concluded with this flourish: 'this Hegelian-Marxist view insists upon the West's uniqueness; and to that extent, the present writer has no hesitation in calling himself an Hegelian.' Lichtheim was brazenly and proudly Eurocentric.

27 Anderson, for example, adopts this approach. He concludes that 'it is merely in the night of our ignorance that all alien shapes takes on the same hue' (P. Anderson, 1974b: 549). Nikiforov, the Russian Marxist, makes a similar point: the AMP is always located in places we do not know much about, and in times of which we know even less. (I am grateful to Ernest Gellner for this information.)

is analytically independent of, the racism, real or alleged, of Marx and Engels.

Eurocentric cultural chauvinism, unlike supposedly genetically grounded racism, manifests itself in assumptions about the (albeit acquired) cultural superiority of European civilization. The similarities between Marx's views on the progressive character of imperialism and the post-1945 social science literature on modernization are now commonplaces of theoretical discussion.[28] It is easy to regard the AMP as Marxism's own special brand of Eurocentric cultural chauvinism, especially if historical materialism is regarded as a variant of Hegelian historicism. In Hegel's philosophy the unfolding structure of conceptual thought, or Spirit, is 'demonstrated' to govern the development of all reality, but the privileged site of all world-historical developments, bar the first, is in the Occident (Hegel, 1956).[29] History begins in the despotic East but moves West, leaving in its wake the stagnant detritus of old social orders. If the AMP is simply part and parcel of Marx's undoubted Hegelian inheritance then the charge of cultural chauvinism is difficult to refute.

'Models' of social structures and their dynamics which have been 'abstracted' or 'inducted' from European historiography can also be culturally Eurocentric if applied uncritically to the evidence of non-European history. Here there is no deliberate racism or cultural chauvinism, but rather an unconscious blindness. However, defenders of the AMP claim that the concept's virtue lies in its explicit recognition of non-Europe, its different social structure and dynamics. In other words they argue that to *oppose* the use of the concept of the AMP in historical investigation, or strategic political calculation, is to be guilty of Eurocentricity. We can see the stuff of which controversy is made immediately. The paradox is that both *Aziatchiki* and anti-*Aziatchiki* can hurl the accusation of Eurocentricity at one another. It is, of course, not a strict logical paradox, as the premises of the opposing conclusions are strikingly dissimilar, but its presence serves to inflame both Marxist and non-Marxist debate on the AMP.

There is one variant of cultural Eurocentricity dubbed Orientalism by its critics (Abdel-Malek, 1981a: 73–96; Said, 1977; Turner, 1978). Eurocentricity is directed at the entirety of the rest of the globe, including the Americas, Africa, Australasia and Melenesia, whereas Orientalism is the ideological construction of the East. It is

a style of thought based upon an ontological and epistemological distinction made between the 'Orient' and (most of the time) the 'Occident' ... Orientalism is never far from what Denis Hay has called the idea of Europe, a collective noun

---

28 See Avineri (1969a and 1969b) and the furore surrounding the work of Warren (1981).
29 Here I use the term 'historicism' in the sense used by L. Althusser rather than K. Popper.

identifying 'us' Europeans as against all 'those' non-Europeans, and indeed it can be argued that the major component in European culture is precisely what made that culture hegemonic both in and outside Europe; the idea of European identity as a superior one in comparison with all the non-European cultures and peoples. (Said, 1977: 2 and 7).

In the oldest antecedents of Orientalist ideas the notion of the Orient extended into territorial Europe itself: it included both 'barbarian' and Islamic Europe. The Occident's home roots are thus found in the Europe of medieval Catholicism and the Occidental Roman Empire – with honorary membership conceded to Greece because of its glorious past. In the idioms of Orientalist ideology, successfully exposed by recent critics, there is a central contrast which it is not difficult to detect in Marx's adumbration of the AMP. In this contrast the Occident is unique. It is progressive, the zone of freedom, the time of times, the spur of humanity, the life of the world. The Orient is the Occident's other, equally unique, but a very different uniqueness is posited. The Orient is stagnant, the zone of despotism and sensuality, timeless, the prison of humanity, peopled by the children of darkness. Orientalism is shot through with such quasi-mystical contrasts, motifs and chiaroscuro effects. It has, in other words, the structures and antinomies of a myth. The myth is suffused with the language of poetry and art, rather than that of scholarship or social science, but any casual acquaintance with Orientalists and their writings will quickly persuade a reader of the ubiquity of the polarities which form the often unconscious framework within which the Orient is examined by Occidentals.[30] For many Marxists and non-Marxists this Eurocentricity, and its Orientalist variants, befog and damn the AMP; they exclude it *a priori* from social scientific discourse (P. Anderson, 1974b; Turner, 1978).[31] Eurocentric Orientalism shaped the birth of the concept and prevents its epistemic leap into the kingdom of scientific concepts. The dissensus on the AMP has some of its deepest roots in this vexed question of Eurocentricity.

The Prophetic Warning of an Asiatic Restoration

The problems posed by Eurocentricity in historical materialism and the AMP emerged in debates amongst Russian revolutionaries over the land question and the character of the Czarist social formation at the turn of the twentieth century. The 1906 Congress of the Russian Social Democratic Party (RSDP) was the site for an intense Bolshevik–Menshevik dispute

30 For instance, Elie Kedourie (1957) in his favourable review of Wittfogel's *Oriental Despotism* opened with the remark 'That despotism should be Oriental has always seemed a fitting sort of notion.'
31 Turner's (1978) arguments against 'Orientalists' are in places contradictory. He seems to accuse Orientalists of both expecting and not expecting non-Europe to be like Europe.

over Lenin's call for a programme demanding the nationalization of the land. Lenin's strategy was motivated by the desire to cement potential peasant support for the small Russian proletariat. Plekhanov, who had used the concept of the AMP, albeit under the name oriental despotism (in his then little known studies of Marxism and Russian history)[32] objected that Lenin's strategy might end in the disaster of an Asiatic restoration.

Plekhanov argued that Russian productive forces and relations of production were unripe for socialist revolution. A 'successful' 'socialist'-led revolution, incorporating land nationalization, would pave the way not for socialism but for an Asiatic catastrophe. By an Asiatic restoration Plekhanov meant the restoration of the domination of the AMP. The latter concept, on some interpretations, incorporates the notion of exclusive monarchial (or state) ownership of the land. Plekhanov believed that until very recently the social relations of production of the AMP had structured the social order of Czarist Russia. And the possibilities of a restoration of this old order were foreshadowed by the restorations which had befallen the English and French revolutions. They could not be wished away. Moreover, he warned that Lenin's strategy seemed almost designed to bring about this undesirable outcome.

In Plekhanov's understanding of the AMP its very structure prevented the development of urban democratic institutions — which were indispensable to both bourgeois democracy and the future of socialism. He reasoned that since many premature bourgeois revolutions had ended in 'restorations', notably several French revolutions, a similar fate might await an ill-advised, premature socialist revolution. He feared, in particular, a 'Chinese' system in Russia, a return to barbaric, 'semi-Asiatic' or Mongol rule, in which the state's monopoly of land precluded any form of self- or local government. Also, he explicitly feared a return to oriental despotism, and argued that to avoid such a possibility the RSDP should propose the municipalization of the land instead of following Lenin's programme. This alternative strategy would block the possibility of an immensely powerful, centralized and Asiatic system of government.

It is a matter of contention whether Lenin accepted the past existence of an AMP anywhere in the world.[33] But what is not in dispute is that he rejected firmly Plekhanov's fear of an Asiatic restoration. Lenin's *Report on the Unity Congress* included a rebuttal of Plekhanov's arguments. He agreed to accept, for the sake of argument, that the land had been nationalized in old Muscovy. However, Lenin then asked a rhetorical question:

---

32 See chapter, 3, appendix 2, p. 150.

33 See Wittfogel (1981: 389–400), Bahro (1981: 86) and Dunn (1982: 13–18) for contrasting positions. Bahro's contention that Lenin *never* mentioned the AMP is refuted by the quotation from Lenin in the text, on page 29.

What follows from this? According to Plekhanov's logic, it follows that nationalization would facilitate the restoration of Muscovy. But such logic is sophistry and not logic, it is juggling with words without analysing the economic basis of development, or the economic content of concepts. Insofar as (or if) the land was nationalised in Muscovy, the economic basis of this nationalization was the Asiatic mode of production. But it is the capitalist mode of production which became established in Russia in the second half of the nineteenth century and is absolutely predominant in the twentieth century. What then remains of Plekhanov's argument? He confused nationalization based on the Asiatic mode of production with nationalization based upon the capitalist mode of production. Because the words are identical, he failed to see the fundamental difference in economic, that is, production relations. (Lenin, 1965, 10: 331—2)

Although Lenin is alleged to have oscillated in his views on the AMP, and although it has even been suggested that in his last days the spectre of the Asiatic restoration re-emerged to haunt him, the above arguments against Plekhanov are free from doubt. There is no hint of oscillation, or psychological rationalization: Lenin's argument is based upon a rational appeal to Marxist logic — at least as he understands it. It is also based upon an empirical appeal: the idea that capitalism prevailed in the social relations of late Czarist Russia. There is no need to impute motives to Lenin's rejection of Plekhanov's arguments (Wittfogel, 1957: 389—400), especially when there is no further evidence to substantiate the imputation. Lenin's arguments are Marxist arguments — which is not to say that they compelling. They are merely the type of argument which one might have expected from a competent Marxist.

The case for Plekhanov's arguments did not surface again until the Russian Revolution was well under way, and by that time Plekhanov had become a heretic in the eyes of Soviet Marxists. But dissident East European Marxists have returned to the theme of an Asiatic restoration in the 1960s and 1970s with varying degrees of explicitness. Having experienced the political institutions of post-revolutionary societies in the Warsaw Pact bloc they have (unknowingly) addressed themselves to Plekhanov's nightmare. Their writings in effect have rehabilitated Plekhanov as a prophet, as Russian Marxism's Cassandra.[34]

Rudolf Bahro, when he was a utopian Marxist critic of 'actually existing' socialism in the DDR, provided the clearest illustration of the resurrection of Plekhanov's arguments. He did not dispute the Marxist rigour of Lenin's objections to Plekhanov. He assaulted the empirical foundation of Lenin's

---

34 The important writings are those of the Hungarian economist Varga whose testimony was such an indictment of post-revolutionary society, the writings of the DDR dissident Rudolf Bahro, and the censored text of G. Konrad and I. Szelenyi (Varga, 1968: 330—51; Bahro, 1981; and Konrad and Szelenyi, 1979). Tökei, a prominent Hungarian Sinologist and *Aziatchiki*, was the most influential figure in reviving the AMP in the wake of de-Stalinization.

argument: Lenin had erred in greatly overestimating the degree of capitalist development in Czarist Russia (Bahro, 1981: 86). According to Bahro the 'non-capitalist' road to industrial society had its origins in 'the legacy of the so-called Asiatic mode of production' (ibid: 13) because, *pace* Lenin, early twentieth-century Russia was a fused mosaic of several modes of production: the Asiatic, the feudal and capitalist. Bahro therefore revives Plekhanov's idea of an Asiatic restoration. Rather than interpret 'what went wrong' in the post-revolutionary development of the Soviet Union and Eastern Europe through 'romantic theories of deformation' – based upon the personal failings of key individuals – Bahro argues that Marxists should see the 'key in Asia ... in a past that is far behind our own European past' (ibid: 47–8). He thus provides a dissident Marxist account, extrapolated from the AMP, of the importance of pre-revolutionary, absolutist political culture in parts of Eastern Europe – a commonplace amongst non-Marxist scholars of the region.

Bahro's work is the most visible example to date of a self-consciously Marxist application of the concept of the AMP to the nature of post-revolutionary societies, an analysis which contributed to Bahro's incarceration and journey into exile.[35] His contention that not only does the AMP explain the form taken by the revolutions in Eastern Europe, but also that it 'exhibits an instructive structural affinity to our own epoch of the decline of class society' (ibid: 67), did not endear him to the authorities as it explicitly raised the question of non-class-based forms of exploitation in socialist societies.[36]

The controversial status of the AMP is now comprehensible. A fugitive Marxist concept, decanonized by Stalin, can be brandished by the heretic, who in any system of organized faith is always regarded as more dangerous than the unbeliever. The 'burden of Russia's past', 'the cult of personality' or 'bureaucratic deformation' are small theoretical beer in comparison with the ideological cleavages which can be opened by skilful deployment of the AMP. It is not the least of ironies that the Cold War arguments preferred in the 1950s by Wittfogel in *Oriental Despotism* should be found today, albeit restructured, in the language of Marxist dissidence in Eastern Europe.

The Asiatic Mode of Production and Revolutionary Strategy in Asia

However, it has not simply been the fear of an Asiatic restoration which has made the AMP controversial amongst Marxists, Soviet or otherwise. The

35 He has since become a leading figure amongst the West German Greens.
36 Other East European Marxist dissidents who have also gone into exile do not accept Bahro's arguments – see Fehér, Heller and Márkus (1983: 37–44) and the discussion on p. 37.

Comintern's debates over revolutionary strategy in China during the 1920s show that the concept can assume vital significance in Marxist discussions of policy formation.

Where and when the Third International's activists recognized the complexity of non-European social formations, they were aware that analysis of the non-capitalist components and legacies of such formations was indispensable to intelligent strategy. In particular, it could materially aid the identification of the principal lines of class cleavage which they believed served as the basis of a successful revolutionary strategy. Thus if it was assumed that the principal pre-capitalist facets of a social formation were feudal, then it seemed reasonable to conclude that feudal landlords were potentially in antagonistic class relations with a nascent 'national bourgeoisie', developing much in the manner of their older European brethren. If it was further assumed that the national bourgeoisie were 'progressive' — a synonym for anti-imperialist — it seemed to follow that the task of the proletarian vanguard in such social formations was to offer critical support and even an alliance to the national bourgeoisie. *Quod erat demonstrandum.*

However, if one did not believe these premises, in particular if one did not assume that the pre-capitalist facets of the social formation were principally feudal, then the 'deduction' of the correct revolutionary line was much more difficult. Those members of the Comintern and the Soviet *Aziatchiki* who contended that the principal non-capitalist facets of China resulted from the Asiatic rather than the feudal mode of production could be, and were, accused of being on route to Trotskyist conclusions.[37] Trotskyists after all opposed the strategy of alliances with 'progressive' bourgeoisies. The *Aziatchiki* were implying, in effect, that a progressive national bourgeoisie did not exist in China. The alleged absence of a salient, private, feudal, landowning class against which this national bourgeoisie was supposed to come into being made the strategic implications of the *Aziatchiki*'s analyses obvious. Moreover, one did not need to be very bright to see parallels between the Left Opposition's criticism of Stalin's disastrous advocacy of an alliance between the Kuomintang and the Chinese Communist Party (CCP) and the *Aziatchiki*'s attack on the theory that China was partially feudal.

However, the Trotskyists did not in fact analyse Chinese history in the same way as the *Aziatchiki* — as the more scrupulous of the anti-*Aziatchiki*

---

37 See Dunn (1982: 30–7). Dunn quotes Godes as concluding that 'the denial of feudalism in China always leads to political errors, and errors of an essentially Trokskyist order' (Dunn, 1982: 32). Varga comments that 'The opponents of the Asiatic mode of production declared that everybody (including the author of this book) who did not recognise the social order of China of the twenties as ordinary feudalism was a political enemy' (Varga, 1968: 349).

conceded (Dunn, 1982: 30–7).[38] The Trotskyists placed less emphasis upon China's pre-capitalist modes of production than upon China's involvement in the world capitalist economy and upon its consequent ripeness for a proletarian assault. Their arguments were based upon a generalization of Trotsky's model of permanent revolution (Knei-Paz, 1977; Trotsky, 1969). Whatever the particular conditions in a given social formation, Trotskyists have always distinguished themselves by their enthusiasm for the idea that the 'time is ripe', and by their rejection of popular fronts with the bourgeoisie. They did not need the AMP to reinforce this enthusiasm.

Comintern strategy in China thus provided the immediate political background to the Soviet discussions on the AMP which took place between 1925 and 1931. It is not essential to know the intricacies of these debates to understand how the AMP has become a hot potato in revolutionary discussions of Asia. The concept could be regarded, wrongly, as symptomatic of a Trotskyist disorder. But it could also be regarded as indispensable to 'correct' revolutionary analysis, if disaster was to be avoided. Such, at any rate, is the message of Tichelman's massive work on Indonesia, in which he intimates that the reason the Indonesian Communist Party (PKI) has been liquidated three times in his history is in part because of its neglect of the AMP in its strategic estimation of Indonesian social evolution (Tichelman, 1980). The AMP has entered discussions of revolutionary strategy not only in analyses of the CCP and the PKI but also in places as

---

38 The legend that the use of the AMP to analyse China was mainly the work of Trotskyists dies hard. So does the legend that Trotskyists used the idea of the AMP to criticize the Soviet Union. In fact Trotsky and his supporters in the 1930s did not accept the idea of a bureaucratic ruling class in the USSR. A recent guide continues the legend: 'The concept was used rather arbitrarily as a criticism of the USSR under Stalin, first by some Trotskyists, and then by K. Wittfogel' (Bloch, 1983: 113). This gloss is doubly inaccurate. The Trotskyists were not the first to use the AMP to criticize the USSR under Stalin because Trotskyists never used the AMP to do so, and because arguably Wittfogel was preceded by many Russian Marxists, including Bukharin, who compared Stalin's rule to that of Genghis Khan. As Wittfogel rightly notes (1957: 403–4), in the opening chapters of his books on the Russian revolutions of 1905 and 1917 Trotsky 'succinctly explained the managerial and exploitative quality of the Tsarist regime which, in his opinion, approached "Asiatic despotism"'. But in the 1920s and 1930s Trotsky did not discuss Chinese society in Asiatic terms, nor did he use the term 'Oriental despotism' when he criticized Stalin's bureaucratic despotism'

According to Sawer (1977: 95) 'Trotsky had never used the AMP concept.' From an inspection of the indexes of Trotsky's works this argument seems to be literally true, but Wittfogel is right to note the affinities between Trotsky's use of Asiatic despotism to describe Czarism and the concept of the AMP. For example, Pierre Vidal-Naquet quotes Trotsky's reply, published in *Pravda* in 1922, to the Stalinist historian Pokrovskij, who had insisted upon the non-uniqueness of Russian history: 'Notre retard économique [au XVIe siècle] se manifestait avant tout en ceci que l'artisanat, ne se disjoignant pas de l'agriculture, en restait au stade des petits métiers ruraux .... Ici, nous nous rapprochons plus de l'Inde que de l'Europe, de même que nos villes du Moyen Age tenaient plus a l'Asie qu'à l'Europe, de même que notre autocratie, placé entre l'absolutisme des monarchies européennes et les despotes asiatiques, se rapprochait sous maints rapports de ces derniers' (Vidal-Naquet, 1964: 542).

diverse as the Middle East, Egypt, Indonesia and India (Amin, 1974 and 1976; Rodinson, 1974; Sen, 1982), and as long as there are partially agrarian societies left in the world the concept can doubtless resurface to be used for similar arguments.

The Asiatic Mode of Production as Parable

It may still be difficult to see why the AMP should be such a taboo concept for Marxists, despite the scholarly disputes that surround its textual status, the charges of Eurocentricity which are levelled at it, its potential polemical incisiveness in accusations about an Asiatic restoration in the Soviet Union, and even its contentious role in Marxist revolutionary strategy. It is plain that the greatest source of controversy is where Wittfogel and subsequently others have chosen to draw blood. The heart of the controversy over the AMP is the theoretical vision suggested by its state apparatus. The state and society of the AMP is the ideological Achilles' heel of Marxism as an emancipatory doctrine, and as a doctrine which asserts the universal and primary significance of class struggle in human history.

Some authors, notably the late Alvin Gouldner, have seen the textual paucity which undergirds the AMP as proof of Marx's anxieties about the parallels between the AMP and socialism (Gouldner, 1980).[39] The small quantity of writing amounted to a 'significant silence', a mask which veiled an enormous anomaly for historical materialism. Using Kuhn's notion of a paradigm, Gouldner argued that Marxism's primary paradigm was historical materialism. Historical materialism's 'primary paradigm' had been developed by 1848: the unilinear theory of history based on the succession of five stages of economic development (primitive communism, slavery, feudalism, capitalism and socialism). In this paradigm each stage in history is governed by the development of class struggle which has as its objective basis a dialectical conflict between emergent productive forces and relations of production. The basis of each stage determines the superstructure which communicates ideological domination in a world in which social being determines social consciousness. The state in each stage is the tool of the ruling class. Yet Marx and Engels's research in the 1850s had uncovered a political phenomenon of immense duration and significance, not easily explicable within the primary paradigm, a major anomaly for historical materialism. (In Kuhn's philosophy of science an anomaly is an accepted observation or coherent idea at variance with the ruling paradigm.) This

---

39 Gouldner's position differed pointedly from that of Godes − compare p. 22 above. Gouldner argued that the small textual treasure was proof of the AMP's anomalous status, and explained its repression by Marx and Engels. Godes by contrast argued that the small textual treasure was proof of the undeveloped, incidental and incomplete nature of their writings.

anomalous research conclusion put into question the universal salience of class struggle and the idea that ruling classes must be based upon private ownership of the means of production. Above all, this anomaly threatened to let loose 'an even deeper dragon of the mind': Nightmare Marxism. In the sweat-drenched vision of Nightmare Marxism the archetypal Marxist dreamer fears that the lesson of history posed by the AMP and by Asiatic restorations is that in the modern world the existence of a propertied bourgeoisie is a necessary, if insufficient, guarantor for a civil society. In this nightmare, private property is recognized as the source of civilized freedom. The class based on private property, the bourgeoisie, can block, balance and deflect the ever-present threat of state bureaucratization. The Marxist in the grip of this nightmare believes that socialism, indeed Marxism itself, is an unwitting messianic religion of the damned, which when translated into revolutionary success brings about what it does not want: the chains of a totalitarian state. The small number of relevant texts which circle the AMP in 'only brief fugitive glosses' provide Gouldner's proof that Marx and Engels recognized the implications of this nightmare. Their refusal to examine the AMP in detail shows their retreat from its explosive implications.

With this virtually unacknowledged modernization of Wittfogel's arguments — albeit with a dose of customary northeastern American Freudian analysis — Gouldner accounted for the perilous status of the AMP amongst historical materialists. He claimed that buried in the 'texts' on the AMP is the semi-conscious recognition by Marx and Engels of the sorts of prophecy later made famous by Tocqueville and Weber. Socialism would not lead to the dictatorship of the proletariat; it would lead to the dictatorship of the official. Equality and classlessness would not produce greater freedom and the withering away of the state. Rather, equality and classlessness, as apparently suggested by the past history of the AMP, provide the social foundations of despotism. Marx in his heart may have been an anticentralist anarchist, but the consequence of his intelligence was to further an unprecedented centralization of authority in industrialized societies. His alleged decision to neglect (if not to repress) the AMP is considered symptomatic of his failure to address this conflict between his heart and his head.

Similar arguments, advanced without any of the sympathy for Marx which Gouldner displays, have been made by the Soviet mathematician and dissident Igor Shaferevich (1980). Drawing upon the work of the economic historian Heichelheim (1958) and Wittfogel (1981), Shaferevich argues that the AMP is proof that the 'socialist phenomenon' can occur at any time in human history. It is latent in the human condition and not something which can only occur after a certain level of productive development — as Marx and Engels insisted. When the latent socialist propensities of humanity are realized all individualistic and libertarian conditions are crushed by a despotic and stagnant egalitarian social order. The despotic regimes of the ancient Orient and South America — specimens of the AMP, according to Shaferevich — represent more than mere analogues of state socialism. They are concrete historical examples of the socialist regimes which now threaten everybody (Shaferevich, 1980: 132−92).[40] In his foreword to Shafarevich's virulent attack on socialism Aleksandr Solzhenitsyn sums up just how apocalyptically the AMP can be deployed in the discourse of the modern dissident:

Shafarevich has singled out the invariants of socialism … which depend neither on time nor place and which, alas, are looming ominously over today's tottering world. If one considers human history in its entirety, socialism can boast of a greater longevity and durability, of wider diffusion and of control over larger masses of people, than can contemporary Western civilization. It is therefore difficult to shake off the gloomy presentiments when contemplating that maw into which — before the century is out — we may all plunge: that 'Asiatic formation' which Marx hastened to circumvent in his classification, and before which contemporary Marxist thought stands baffled, having discerned its own hideous countenance in the mirrors of the millenia. (Solzhenitsyn, in Shafarevich, 1980: x−xi)

The warning that we all may live in the awful grip of the AMP by 2000 AD illustrates what causes most controversy: the use of the AMP as a parable for socialism *per se*. This causes greater ire than its use in arguments about the undesirable, and presumably remedial, legacies created by Asiatic restorations. Awkward questions multiply for the Marxist who accepts these parallels. If the AMP is the pre-industrial analogue of a centralized, state-directed economy, and if it is stagnant, despotic and unfree, does this parable foretell the present and the future of socialism? Was Max Weber correct to predict that socialism would be akin to the Egypt of the pharaohs? Must Marxist socialists produce polities and societies beside which the iron cage of bureaucratic capitalism appears like a pleasant play-pen? By Marxist reasoning the Asiatic and socialist modes of production share the feature that their bases and superstructures are analytically as well as observably indistinguishable, and perhaps this fact is a clue to the multiple unfreedoms experienced in both modes of production? Perhaps also the bureaucrats in the socialist societies are the industrial analogues, if not indeed the lineal descendants, of the exploitative bureaucracy of the AMP, and the socialist intelligentsia are like the priests and theocrats in the AMP? And if in some senses both the Asiatic and socialist modes of production lack classes, if they are both intrinsically state-centred, defined by despotic state autonomy, what do these anomalous occurrences imply for both historical materialism

---

40 Shaferevich's arguments are remarkably similar to those advanced in another attack on modern socialism that is indebted to Wittfogel: Baudin's *A Socialist Empire: The Incas of Peru* (1961).

and the promises of socialism? What prospects are there for an acephalous and free socialism if the parables and analogies are of any validity? Are bourgeois, or indeed anarchist, state theories empirically and theoretically correct? There is one further parable which combines the fear of stagnation with a critique of premature revolution: Marx 'did not consider the possibility that communism might occur prematurely, and like the Asiatic mode of production become a dead end of history' (Elster, 1985: 309). Contemporary dissidents in state socialist regimes suggest not only that Communism is a dead end but also that Marx repressed his knowledge that it would be so when he chose to 'circumvent' (to use Solzhenitsyn's expression) the AMP.

It should not be necessary to labour the questions and parables any further. They are plain, and are the most contentious cause of the Asiatic mode of production's controversial status. The sting of the 'Asiatic' parable for the student of Russian Marxism is nicely illustrated in the tale told by Vladimir Rybakov, a contemporary author of Polish and Russian extraction. Having described in a brief biographical note how he became an anti-Communist and a drifter when his parents had brought him to the Soviet Union after a childhood spent outside Russia, he continues:

I returned home like the Prodigal Son, mother welcomed me back, and I entered the Faculty of History at Chernovstsy University. Very soon, however, I started to play the fool. I didn't exactly smash any windows, but I drank a lot, horsed around and occasionally got into a fight. My real downfall occurred in my second year, when, again, I started to take a serious interest in history, in particular in Marx's theory of the so-called 'Asiatic Mode of Production'. This theory, I was to discover, was not only not recognised in Soviet universities, but was also taboo. In spite of that, I wrote an essay, showing how Marx himself had pointed out that in additon to his classic five stages of the development of production — primitive communism, slave owning societies, feudal societies, bourgeois societies, socialist societies — there was also a sixth and final category that applied to such Asian countries as China and India, whose historical development did not fit into the 'five stages' that were meant to be more typical of Europe and North America [*sic*!]. Marx called this sixth category — characterised by a uniform and repressive subjection of the working population to a vast, centralized bureaucracy (in other words an accurate prediction of the present state of affairs in the Soviet Union!) — 'The Asiatic Mode of Production'. I was summoned to the Dean of the Faculty, where I argued that I was only quoting Marx himself. This, it appears was no defence. In 1968 I was expelled from the university. (Rybakov, 1984: 78–9)[41]

41 I am grateful to Dr David Edgerton for the reference. It should be noted that Rybakov's claim that the AMP was unacceptable in Soviet universities is not compatible with the evidence of Dunn's book, which is replete with references to the acceptance of academic debates on the AMP in the USSR in the 1960s (Dunn, 1982). Chernovtsy History Faculty might have been a Stalinist backwater, or only privileged and trusted academics studying antiquity might have been able to use the controversial concept. Indeed Rybakov may have coloured his account of his expulsion a little, given that his description of what Marx says about the AMP includes a little literary licence.

What can dispassionately be said about the parables drawn between the AMP and state socialist regimes? There are basic objections which are often, and rightly made, to these analogies — whether or not they cause people to be expelled from universities, and whether or not they can be legitimately employed to foretell the fate of 'mankind' before 2000 AD. The use of the AMP to understand state socialist regimes may amount to using a version of Marxism to explain Marxist post-revolutionary regimes, and it may successfully draw attention to many of the parallels between pre- and post-revolutionary regimes, but there are compelling objections to the use of the AMP as a parable — whether or not one is a Marxist (Fehér, Heller and Márkus, 1983: 37–44). First, attempts to explain the features of 'actually existing socialisms' exclusively by reference to their backward origins seem grossly incomplete. Marxist regimes now represent integral social systems, organized according to a set of doctrines which are distinct from those found in any pre-capitalist systems. (Needless to say this argument is no defence of Marxist regimes.) Second, East European and Afro-Asian socialist systems exist in a great variety of national-historical environments which have little in common, even in terms of relative backwardness or extremely general characteristics of their socio-historical conditions. Third, the analogies between the AMP and 'actually existing socialism' are very loose. In important respects, the analogy does not hold. For example, in state socialist systems the state is the producer, and not simply the exploiter and redistributor of the social surplus; and socialist planning systems are based upon massive interdependencies between production centres, rather than upon atomized and autarkic villages. In the AMP the state's role is confined to facilitating production and exploiting the surplus; its personnel do not form part of the direct producers. However, needless to say, these pitfalls in the analogies between the AMP and 'actually existing socialism' have not prevented them from being articulated, or from being rejected with the utmost venom. The analogies remain the primary cause of the concept's controversial status.

SUMMARY: A SOCIOLOGY OF KNOWLEDGE OF THE ASIATIC MODE OF PRODUCTION

The sociology of knowledge is the study of how ideas or systems of thought are connected with social contexts. Its critics understandably have argued that while it may well be sociology it is not knowledge. The sociologist of knowledge is regularly and rightly accused of neglecting the cognitive content and truth or falsity of knowledge, and is held guilty of reductionism and of inventing spurious homologies between social contexts and patterns of ideas. But despite these valid objections to its vices, a brief sociology-of-knowledge sketch of the intellectual career of the AMP aids appreciation of the contexts in which it is discussed (or repressed).

In what contexts is the AMP favoured? And by whom? The answers to these questions have been suggested by the foregoing discussion. The AMP is upheld by Marxist intellectuals, in times of relative freedom of discussion within the Marxist party, movement, or regime, in three different contexts. The first, and least political, is one of genuine scholarly inquiry. Marxists are interested in the AMP to further scholarly research on social formations which cannot adequately be described as either feudal or slave-holding. The benefits of the AMP are obvious to the Marxist scholar who wishes to break free of the vice of Stalinist unilinealism, and the disturbing anomalies which Stalin's précis of history produced for educated historians, archaeologists and social theorists. As a concept articulated by Marx it also has the stamp of sacred authority. But sacred writings give priests greatest discretion when the writings are at their most ambiguous. The AMP's very underdeveloped character gives Marxist scholars greater freedom to 'revise' Marx in the direction of compatibility with the results of subsequent serious scholarship. Therefore the AMP allows a respectable Marxist account to be given of any social formation hitherto monopolized by the paradigms of the bourgeoisie. Perhaps these facets of the concept explain its attractive-ness to Marxist scholars in the 1920s and in the 1960s. In the periods before and after Stalinism there were Marxist archaeologists, anthropologists and historians keen to do, as they saw it, genuine scientific research, '*Unter dem Banner des Marxismus*', as a German journal of the 1920s put it, or '*à la lumière de marxisme*', as a post-Stalinization French journal expressed the desire. These intellectuals wanted to work under the banner of Marxism but not under the diktat of the General Secretary. The AMP offered them some intellectual flexibility.

The second political context in which Marxist intellectuals espouse the AMP is when revolutionary strategy in the less developed countries is under discussion. Here the benefits of the concept are sacred, but they are also strategic. The concept can be used not as a direct guide to action, but as a tool with which to reject orthodox Marxist characterizations of less developed social formations: as an alternative slogan to talk of 'feudal relics', 'semi-feudalism' or 'backward capitalism'. To suggest that a social formation has partly Asiatic features or legacies, or indeed that the AMP is 'articulated' with other modes of production, is to put question marks beside the nature and expected behaviour of any bourgeoisie, and to emphasize the potential for mobilization amongst village communities. While relatively rare in Marxist movements, support for the AMP in strategic analysis has generally been associated with a thoroughgoing revol-utionary enthusiasm. This propensity is partly based on the grounds that the impact of imperialism upon Asiatic social formations has created the objective conditions for revolution: all that is now required is the mobilization of the subject of history, and support for the AMP is normally associated with optimism about the fighting class qualities of the peasantry. But there seems to be little cognitive foundation for this correlation between *Aziatchiki* and revolutionary ardour and sectarianism.

The third and most intriguing context in which Marxist intellectuals espouse the AMP is in expressions of dissent. The concept's sacred authority is invoked to accuse a Marxist regime of being a bastard form of the Asiatic social formation, a modern-day analogue of oriental despotism. The dissident uses the language of the creed to accuse the Church of betrayal and treachery, of erecting evil (exploitation) while proclaiming its abolition (Communism). The parables and analogies are brandished to create embarrassment, to stir consciences, and to rally true believers to the recognition that the orthodox priests are heterodox, and that fulfilment of the faith requires yet one more revolution. In the absence of a liberal social-science milieu, without intellectual pluralism in universities, discussion of the AMP and its resonance for 'actually existing socialist' regimes is one way in which doubt can be engendered, with heretical or atheistic deviance usually following in its wake.

By contrast there seem to be only two contexts in which non-Marxist intellectuals are attracted to discussions of the AMP. The first, and most Cold War in character, is in intellectual and political combat, where the concept can be used pejoratively against Marxist regimes or as a political parable, a salutary tale to shake the thoughts of intellectuals contemplating espousing non-Western models and movements of modernization.[42] The second context is scholarly, the desire to study the development of a Marxist idea, the AMP, as a topic in the history of ideas, but also as a subject in comparative historical sociology and comparative politics, and to discuss the value of the idea in highlighting or explaining the phenomena which it is claimed to illuminate. This book is written in the second of these contexts.

42 Ernest Gellner has recently pointed out that in another cold war Russian critics have used the AMP to describe China under Mao, much in the way Wittfogel used it to describe Stalinist Russia (Gellner, 1986: 102–3).

2

The Antecedents of the Asiatic Mode of Production

History is prose, and myths fall far short of History.

Hegel, *The Philosophy of History*

This chapter examines the intellectual history of the best known conceptual antecedents of the AMP, oriental despotism and oriental society. The history of the idea of Oriental despotism is carefully traced. The stability and alteration in the meaning of oriental despotism is examined from its passage through Greece, Byzantium, medieval Europe and early modern Europe. The idea of oriental despotism is shown to be an elite-centred classification of the political systems alleged to exist in the agrarian empires of antiquity. The AMP, by contrast, focuses not just upon the organization of the ruling class but also on the economic, ideological and political relations alleged to exist in Asiatic societies. The claim that the AMP is simply the renaming of the concept of oriental despotism is therefore not sustainable. Two further arguments are advanced. First, a refutation is made of the description of Indian regimes as invariable specimens of oriental despotisms in the sixteenth and seventeenth centuries. The evidence of primary European sources does not fit easily with the stereotype; only the Indian regimes distinguished by being Islamic came close to the description of being oriental despotisms. Second, the concept of oriental despotism was incorporated and transformed in the philosophies of progress prevalent in the European Enlightenment. This late transformation of the idea was one prototype of the AMP. However, the idea of oriental society, developed largely by British utilitarians and political economists, has much better claims to being regarded as the key prototype of the AMP. The political and administrative preoccupations of the British as overloads of India produced reflections on oriental society which had a decisive impact upon the thought of both Marx and Engels.

ORIENTAL DESPOTISM

The historiographical consensus is that oriental despotism is the most significant conceptual forerunner of the AMP (P. Anderson, 1974b: 462–72; Bailey and Llobera, 1981: 13–23; Krader, 1975: 19–61; Lichtheim, 1963; Sawer, 1977a 4–39; and Wittfogel, 1957: 1).[1] This consensus is understandable but requires qualification. Marx and Engels drew more heavily upon accounts of oriental society than upon those of oriental despotism in their schematic adumbrations of the AMP. There is too much *post hoc ergo propter hoc* argument, the characteristic fallacy of political thought historiography, in the literature on oriental despotism and the AMP.

Despotism is one of the more obscure of the range of comparative politics concepts which were the common currency of pre-twentieth – century political thought. Today despotism is largely an archaic concept in academia. Like tyranny and absolutism it is used as political rhetoric rather than as part of the conceptual apparatus of contemporary political science. Totalitarianism, the closest modern conceptual equivalent, used to categorize regimes of total domination, is reserved for industrialized or industrializing societies. But as with totalitarianism, the history of the concept of despotism is one of almost uninterrupted controversy and polemic. The antonyms of despotism have varied slightly over many centuries, and have all been members of the cluster of concepts associated with freedom. The antimony between despotism and freedom reverberates throughout the history of occidental political thought.

The idea of oriental despotism, as opposed to mere despotism, has gone through multiple vicissitudes in the evolution of Western political thought (Koebner, 1951). Sophisticated analyses of continuities and discontinuities in its conceptual evolution (Stelling-Michaud 1960–61; Venturi, 1963) do not detract, however, from the general case that there are four core components of oriental despotism which recur with persistent regularity up to the eighteenth century. First, there is the idea of an untrammelled agrarian emperor; that is, the notion of a monarch or despot with power of such plenitude and autonomy as to be effectively free of political restraints. Second, there is the empirical belief that such despots were to be found principally in the Orient, in the land-based empires of Asia. Third, there is the associated assumption that the despot's apparatus of control was an administrative elite, dependent upon the despot for authority, office and revenue, in stark contrast to the independent European aristocracies. Finally,

1 All these authors draw heavily, indirectly or indirectly, upon a pioneering essay by Koebner (1951). So do I.

Krader's discussion of the antecedents of the AMP is entitled 'Oriental Society and its Sources' (1975: 9ff), but he blurs the distinction between oriental despotism and oriental society.

the subjects of such despots, especially the 'nobility', were regarded as
being, to all intents and purposes, slaves.

The following examination of the history of the idea of oriental despotism
avoids being wholly limited by three constraints which bind much contemporary political thought: the sociology − of − knowledge compulsion
which biases us towards the interests (real or imputed) of those who
deployed the concept of despotism; the contextualist compulsion which
counsels against the search for transhistorical stability in the meaning of
despotism and instructs us that all arguments about despotism were contemporary interventions in political debates; and the structuralist compulsion
which asserts that the logic of the arguments about despotism was invariant,
fixed by ideological premises, whether explicit or implicit. These three
compulsions downgrade, in different ways, the important consideration of
whether despotism was an empirically accurate description of historical
regimes. One of the contentions of this book is that the traditional concept
of oriental despotism is largely a mythical categorization of pre-industrial
regimes − the arbitrary power of the despot was largely restricted to
control over the immediate coercive apparatus, and even this power was by
no means secure.[2]

Ancient Greek Political Thought

The ancient Greeks first coined the concept of despotism as a tool of
comparative politics. As Voltaire pointed out in his *L'ABC*, the root
meaning of the Greek word δεσποτης (and its derivatives δεσποτικος and
δεσποτεια) is 'the head of the family', but it had a second meaning, 'the
master of slaves' (Voltaire, 1768: 323ff.)[3] These two meanings were combined
in the use of 'despotism' as a political concept to describe a form of
kingship. The monarch's relationship to his subjects was considered to be

2 This argument is much the same as that advanced in Mann (1984 and 1986: 130−78)
who distinguishes between *despotic* and *infrastructural* power. Despotic power encompasses the
range of actions that the ruler and the ruler's staff can implement at their discretion, whereas
infrastructural power is the capacity to penetrate and implement political decisions in the
wider society.

The infrastructural power of ancient despots of the Orient has been considerably and
anachronistically exaggerated. Such infrastructural powers as they had depended critically
upon their (relatively weak) capacities to control their nobilities. Their despotic power over
their aristocrats was what (allegedly) distinguished them from their occidental counterparts in
the eyes of pre-modern commentators. Subsequent authors have mistakenly extrapolated from
the thesis that elites were (relatively) centralized in the Orient to the thesis that oriental
societies had centralized political, cultural and economic systems (Wittfogel, 1981). See
chapter 6 below.

3 For some it is no accident that the Athenians adopted the word for a ruler of slaves to
describe the ruler of the Orient: Athenians, like orthodox Marxists, recognized the connections
between the nature of the state and the nature of labour exploitation (Wood and Wood, 1978:
39).

literally like that of a master's power over his slaves, but was also like the patriarchal authority of the head of the family, accepted by family members as traditionally legitimate. From Herodotus onwards Greek historians and philosophers contrasted their freedom with the despotism of barbarian peoples, especially the Persians whose emperors regularly threatened to conquer the Greek city states.

Aristotle's *Politics* contained the first comparative typology of political regimes (Aristotle, 1962: 115−16). He distinguished regimes along two dimensions, the degree of participation in government and the interests served by the government. On the first dimension he distinguished government by one, the few and the many. On the second dimension he distinguished right rule (in the common interest) from deviant rule (in the interest of the rulers). Aristotle's typology thus yielded six types of regime (see table 2.1). The sixfold classification was complicated by two features. First, actual regimes might contain elements of each government. Second, elaborating the classification, Aristotle contended that the three deviant forms of rule − tyranny, oligarchy and democracy − were characterized by despotic behaviour by the rulers.[4] For example, Aristotle argues that the demos of a democracy when uncontrolled by laws 'aims at absolute power and becomes like a despot' and that its behaviour is 'the exact counterpart of tyranny among monarchies' (ibid: 160).

However, several asides in the *Politics* suggest that Aristotle's typology was not meant to be universal; it was a typology of only Greek regimes. Certain 'non-Greek' kingships caused Aristotle some difficulties in classification. Were these despotisms forms of kingship or tyranny? They

have complete power equal to that of tyrannies but they are legally established and hereditary. Their rule, however, is as of master over slave, and it is because barbarians are by natural character more slavish than Greeks (and Asiatics more than Europeans) that they tolerate this despotic rule without resentment. Therefore, while they can be described as tyrannies for these reasons, they derive stability from their legality and hereditary succession. They can also be distinguished by the fact that the ruler has a royal, not a tyrant's bodyguard; a king's bodyguard is composed of citizens carrying arms, a tyrant's of foreign mercenaries. And the king rules over willing subjects according to law, the tyrant over unwilling subjects; so that the one receives protection from his citizens, the other needs it against them. (ibid: 136).

Aristotle's reasoning suggested that Asian kingships, whilst resembling tyrannies, were distinguished by their traditional legitimacy. Hereditary succession and the apparatus of a royal bodyguard were symptoms of this

---

4 'Tyranny ... is that form of monarchical rule which is despotically exercised over the political association called the state' (Aristotle, 1962: 116−17). 'Many oligarchies have fallen owing to their excessively despotic rule' (ibid: 205). He also argues in the same passage that both democracies and oligarchies can become unconstitutional (i.e. despotic − ibid: 205).

Table 2.1 Aristotle's typology of regimes

		Form of regime	
		Good (i.e. serves the interests of the community)	Deviant (i.e. serves the rulers' interests)
Participants in government	One	Kingship	Tyranny
	Few	Aristocracy	Oligarchy
	Many	Polity	Democracy

legitimacy. Compared with tyrannies he also believed that Asian kingships had fewer problems of succession. But they were despotisms because of the natural slave-like disposition of Asiatics.

Elsewhere in the *Politics*, Aristotle regarded Greek tyrannies as more degenerate than Asian kingships:

When dealing with kingship we also defined two forms of tyranny, both because the type of power exercised by a tyrant is almost interchangeable with that exercised by kings, and because both forms of rule can be according to law. But the two forms of tyranny differ from each other; in one, the more kinglike of the two, rule is both according to law and over willing subjects, the other is more 'tyrannical', rule despotically exercised according to decisions of tyrants. (ibid: 170).

Despite this more favourable comparison of Asian kingships with Greek tyrannies, Aristotle none the less maintained that 'Persian government offers many parallels' with the modes by which tyrants maintain themselves: the banning of free association, cultural deprivation, spying and the stirring up of strife amongst opponents of the regime (ibid: 225–6).

The interests, context and logic in which Aristotle constructed his typology are very difficult to determine. Aristotle's normative defence of polity, a 'mixed constitution', was plain enough. To go further and suggest that both his difficulties in including Asiatic monarchies in his classification and his analogy between Asiatic monarchical rule and slavery reveal Aristotle's interest in justifying a Greek conquest of Persia, such as that executed by his pupil Alexander the Great, is more than the evidence will bear.[5] The most sensible interpretation of Aristotle's typology and his empirical elaboration upon it is to regard it as a critical commentary upon Plato's *Republic*. Indeed Aristotle's opening of the *Politics* with the distinction

5 Aristotle advised Alexander to behave as a leader (*hegemon*) towards Greeks but as a

between *politikon* and *despotikon* is an explicit criticism of Plato's argument in *The Statesman* that household management, slave management and state management all require the same qualities (Koebner, 1951: 276).

After Aristotle there is no extant and extended discussion of the peculiarities of non-Greek kingships, or the specific characteristics of despotism in classical Greek philosophy. The Romans used the term *tyrannus* when expressing contempt for one-man arbitrary rule. Only in the Greek-speaking Eastern Empire was the term despot used of the emperor, and then as a functional equivalent for the Latin *dominus*. In the Roman Empire the term despot in Greek, and its Latin equivalent *dominus*, no longer had the odious connotations which Aristotle's philosophy had imparted to them.

Byzantine Uses of Despotism

After Aristotle Greek use of the term despot seems to have reverted towards the meaning of 'head of the family'. The term was used of the Byzantine emperor, and as the functional equivalent of the Latin *magister* in the official titles of the emperor (Murray, 1897: 256). It was also used as a vocative address (equivalent to the Latin *domine*, 'my lord') to the emperor, bishops and especially patriarchs. In the oriental parts of the Roman Empire and in the Byzantine Empire the term had the connotations of public functions, and was used of governors (Stelling-Michaud, 1960−1: 329). From the time of Manuel Commenus, despot became the formal title of princes of the Byzantine imperial house. Today, in modern Greek, despot remains the ordinary appellation of a bishop. And in the sense of 'lord' or 'prince' the title was borne, after the Turkish conquest, by the petty Christian rulers of dependent or tributary provinces, such as the despots of Morea or of Servia. Byzantine usage of despot (or its derivatives) thus had no apparent derogatory connotation.

---

despot towards the barbarians − see the discussion of Plutarch's *Moralia* 329b in Ehrenburg (1938: 62 ff).

Athenian intellectuals had advocated a Greek against the Persian King throughout the fourth century. Isocrates was the notable exponent of the cause (de Ste Croix, 1981: 295). It is interesting to note, in the light of the later use of the notion of oriental despotism to justify imperial conquests in the nineteenth century, that Alexander the Great and his successors claimed that whole *chora* of the Persian Empire, on the grounds that it had all ultimately belonged to the Great King. The *chora* was the whole of the vast area not included in the territory administered by any Greek polis, and was sometimes referred to as the *chora basilike* (royal *chora* − de Ste Croix, 1981: 97 and 10). That all land belongs to the king is often considered the defining feature of oriental despotism or the AMP. De Ste Croix is sceptical of the view that the Achaemenids 'claimed to be the actual owners of the land in their kingdom in a sense more real than the modern fiction of the ruler's "eminent domain"' (ibid: 150−1). He implies that the claim was the invention of the Macedonian conquerors. (De Ste Croix's objections to the AMP are critically discussed in chapter 4, pp. 189−90 and chapter 5, pp. 231−4.)

The Return of Aristotle in Early Medieval Europe

The *Politics* was 'rediscovered' in the western half of what had been the Roman Empire and translated into Latin in the thirteenth century. The rediscovery of Aristotle provided the framework for the political reflections of the educated of medieval Europe which decisively affected the occidental interpretation of the Orient.[6] In the fourteenth century the concept of despotism was used polemically by William of Occam and Marsilius of Padua in the course of their attacks upon the power of the medieval papacy. William of Occam tried to tighten up Aristotle's looseness in classifying monarchies, and distinguished *principatus regalis* from *principatus despoticus* and *principatus tyrannicus* (McIlwain, 1932: 400−3 and Koebner, 1951: 275−6). His distinctions are schematized in table 2.2.

Marsilius of Padua's *Defensor Pacis* (1324) by contrast accepted Aristotle's designation of Asian governments as despotic but used the term rhetorically to condemn papal absolutist ambitions. In the First Discourse, Marsilius (or John of Jandum according to some scholars) paraphrased Aristotle as follows:

Another method is that whereby certain monarchs rule in Asia; they receive their dominating authority through hereditary succession, and while they rule according to law, this law is like that of despots, being for the monarch's benefit rather than completely for the community's. The inhabitants of such regions endure such rule 'without protest' because of their barbaric and slavish nature and the influence of custom. This rule is kingly in that it is native to the country and is over voluntary subjects, because, for example, the monarch's ancestors had been the first inhabitants of the region. But it is also in a sense tyrannical, in that its laws are not completely for the common benefit but for that of the monarch. (Marsilius of Padua, 1980: 30)

Marsilius used many variants on *despoticus* in the course of a spirited attack on servility to the papacy and the unjust despotism established by the priests who had manipulated scriptural interpretation in their own interests.

The first translations of the Greek word for despot (and its derivatives) into the Italian and French vernacular took place in the fourteenth century. Nicolas Oresme's text *Le Livre de Politique d'Aristotle* (1371−4), which translated the passages in the *Politics* about the natural servility of Asiatics, glossed them with the suggestion that Asiatics had forgotten their birthright of liberty (Koebner, 1951: 281−2).[7] But just as the revival of Aristotle was

---

6 The difficulties the Greek concept posed for the medieval schoolmen Thomas Aquinas, Peter of Auvergne and Ptolemy of Lucca have been well documented (Koebner, 1951: 279−80). Ptolemy was perturbed by the Byzantine usage of despot which had none of the opprobrium attached to it by Aristotle.

7 Oresme also shared the same thoughts as Occam and Marsilius on the question of papal despotism. Indeed he was accused by the Inquisition of having been the French translator of *Defensor Pacis*.

Table 2.2 *Occam's classification of princes*

Form of regime	Interests served	Relations between rulers and ruled
Royal monarchy	Common good	Ruler bound by law and custom
Despotism	Ruler's	Ruled consent to ruler
Tyranny	Ruler's	Rule against will of ruled

complete and as despotism was acquiring currency in political thought the term was struck from the canons of acceptable discourse by the Humanist purging of the Latin language. Koebner's scholarly study charts the disfavour shown towards latinized versions of Greek words − in particular of *despotes* in the translation of Aristotle − and the attempt to replace latinized Greek with pure Latin terms (Koebner, 1951: 282). The Florentine Leonardi Bruni Aretino, who originated the concept of *humanitas*, translated both Plato and Aristotle into classical Latin. In his translation of the *Politics*, δεσποτεια was usually translated as *dominatio*. Subsequent political thinkers such as Bodin and Grotius who wrote in Latin as well as the vernacular, and who were to deploy the celebrated passages of Aristotle, followed the humanist's philological decree.

Turkey as the Other: Modern Political Thought

No one can quarrel with the judgement that 'Aristotle [had] opened the way to an unhappy confusion between despotic government and oriental monarchies which passed into the European intellectual milieu from the time of the crusades against the infidels' (Stelling-Michaud, 1960−1: 329).[8] This 'unhappy confusion' became especially evident in the interpretation of Aristotle in the late medieval era and the Renaissance. However, although the revival of Aristotle may have provided the terms despot, despotic and despotism, it was the contrasts (both real and imagined) between Christian and Turkish monarchies which formed the primary empirical basis for the distinctions made between occidental and oriental rule from the sixteenth century onwards.

8 My translation.

Machiavelli's *The Prince* (1514) did not contain the term despotism, but suggested a contrast between European and Turkish monarchies which was to become a central component in arguments about oriental despotism, especially in the hands of Montesquieu. Chapter IV of *The Prince* posed and answered a question: '*Why the Kingdom of Darius conquered by Alexander did not rebel against his successors after his death*'. Machiavelli explained that: 'all principalities known to history are governed in one of two ways, either by a prince to whom everyone is subservient and whose ministers, with his favour and permission, help govern, or by a prince and by nobles whose rank is established not by favour of the prince but by their ancient lineage' (Machiavelli, 1975: 44). A contemporary example of the first type was the Turkish Empire, and the French Empire was a specimen of the second. Machiavelli reasoned that a service nobility was more dependent than a hereditary nobility and hence more loyal to its king. It followed that: 'it is difficult to win control of the Turkish empire but, once it has been conquered, it can be held with ease ... the French state can be more easily seized, but it can be held only with great difficulty' (ibid: 45).

Machiavelli's contrast was meant to illustrate a political lesson: success in maintaining a conquest depended upon the type of state being conquered, not just upon the capacities of the conqueror (whence the ease with which Alexander's successors slipped into his shoes). Machiavelli also made clear that the freedman–slave contrast between Europeans and Asiatics applied to the respective nobilities – unlike Aristotle's more ambiguous writings which apparently applied the freedman–slave contrast undiscriminatingly to all Europeans and Asiatics. Machiavelli's portrayal of the Turkish nobility as slaves was to become an enduring motif amongst the European aristocracy, a prophecy on the depths to which their status could conceivably plummet.

Moreover, Machiavelli's contention that the form of the state had an impact upon the personal characteristics of the nobility also contained the germ of a key idea which would eventually transform the idea of oriental despotism. He associated the oriental empires with stagnation. He believed that the multi-polarity and constant warfare of feudal Europe favoured the development of *virtu* whilst the great land-empires of Asia disposed individuals towards inactivity and sluggishness. The founder of modern Western political thought thus has good claims to being the principal developer, after Aristotle, of the idea of oriental despotism.

In his 1568 annotated translation of the *Politics* into French, Loys le Roy decided to adopt the general expression for feudal lordship in translating despot. '*L'empire seigneurial*' was his rendering of despotic rule in French. He also argued that the Turkish, Moscovite and Ethiopian regimes were modern equivalents of the Persian form of rule described by Plato, Aristotle and Isocrates. The Moscovite and the Ethiopian, but especially the Turkish regimes, were also denigrated through the adaptation of Aristotle's classification.[9] At the beginning of the sixteenth century the Ottoman expansion into the Bulkans and the Danube plain was at full pitch, and the fear of the Turk which that inspired fostered the notion of an irreducible cultural and political chasm between the Islamic Orient and the Christian Occident.

Jean Bodin's *Les Six Livres de la Republique*, written in 1597, was so inspired by Le Roy's modernization of Aristotle that he devoted Chapter II of Book II to *la 'Monarchie Seigneuriale'*.[10] Bodin's typology of monarchies decisively influenced subsequent discussants of oriental despotism, especially Montesquieu, and his empirical illustrations of the geographical location of seigneurial monarchies profoundly affected future European investigation of Asia and Africa. Bodin distinguished royal, seigneurial and tyrannical monarchies:

Royal, or legitimate, monarchy is one in which the subject obeys the laws of the prince, the prince in his turn obeys the Laws of God, and natural liberty and the natural right to property is secured to all. Despotic[11] monarchy is one in which the prince is lord and master of both the possessions and the persons of his subjects by right of conquest in a just war; he governs his subjects as absolutely as the head of a household governs his slaves. Tyrannical monarchy is one in which the laws of nature are set at naught, free subjects oppressed as if they were slaves, and their property as if it belonged to the tyrant. (Bodin, 1955: 57).

He added that the distinctions legal, seigneurial and tyrannical could also be applied to aristocratic and popular regimes. Like Aristotle he believed that there was something intrinsic to Europeans which immunized them against despotism: 'The people of Europe are prouder and more belligerent than the inhabitants of Asia and Africa, and have never submitted to despotic rule since the Hungarian invasions' (Bodin, 1955: 58).

However, Bodin went significantly beyond Aristotle in two respects. First, he asserted that seigneurial monarchies were the first species of monarchy to appear in world history, and were rather rare in the contemporary world.[12] Second, Bodin asserted that the legitimacy of seigneurial monarchies derived from the right of conquest in a just war. His classification of the three types of monarchy is schematically set out in table 2.3. The 'empirical' evidence for the existence of seigneurial monarchies was frankly derived from the Bible and the Greek classics:

---

9 He thereby 'opened a chapter of political literature' (Stelling-Michaud, 1960–1: 330, my translation.)

10 In the Latin version of his book he used the term *dominatus*.

11 Tooley's modern translation anachronistically, albeit accurately, translates seigneurial monarchy as despotic monarchy (Bodin, 1955).

12 There was some philosophical, but scarcely empirical, warrant for this assertion to be found in Aristotle's suggestion that Persian-style kingship had been practised in an earlier epoch of Greek history.

Table 2.3 Jean Bodin's typology of regimes

| | Type of monarchy | | |
	Royal	Seigneurial	Tyrannical
Origins	Consent	Conquest: earliest form of rule	Usurpation
Location	Christendom	Turkey, Muscovy, Tartary, Ethiopia	(Possible everywhere)
Relations between rulers and ruled	King respects natural law	King is patriarchal, a master of slaves	King despises natural law; treats free as slaves

throughout the Scriptures the subjects of the Kings of Assyria and Egypt are always referred to as slaves. The Greeks too were convinced that whereas they themselves were free, the barbarians were enslaved, and by barbarians they meant the inhabitants of Persia and Asia. When the Kings of Persia made war, they always laid claim to both land and water, by way of indicating, says Plutarch, that they were the absolute lords of all property and all persons whatsoever. (Bodin, 1955: 57)

Bodin's development of the category of seigneurial monarchy was not primarily intended as a criticism of the Turkish monarchy. He was more preoccupied with avoiding some of the logical consequences which his theory of sovereignty seemed to imply. His doctrine of sovereignty appeared to make oriental monarchies indistinguishable from the Christian. His solution was simple. The doctrine did indeed imply that sovereignty was characterized by absolute discretion, but the way in which that discretion was practised allowed one to distinguish forms of rule. The discretion practised by seigneurial monarchs over their subjects' goods and lives was against natural law − either because natural law had never been valid in these countries, or because it had unfortunately been forgotten. His theory of sovereignty therefore did not preclude a normative comparative politics, but Bodin realized that it was problematic: 'if we can make no distinction between despotism and tyranny, we can make no distinction between rights of war against an enemy and theft, between the just and the brigand' (Bodin, 1955: 59). Quite so, argued later theorists, unpersuaded that the difference between despotism and tyranny was anything other than rhetorical.

The foregoing historical outline has shown that the idea of despotism went through several changes in the evolution of Western political thought up until the sixteenth century. However, the focus of all versions of the concept was primarily on the relations between the monarch and the aristocracy, rather than on the relations between the rulers and the mass of the population. The old idea of oriental despotism can therefore at best be regarded as anticipating two elements only of the concept of the AMP – the centralization of the ruling class and the idea of monarchical ownership of the land. From medieval times onwards, however, the concept of despotism was associated with specific oriental and especially Islamic empires. The validity of these descriptions is worth examining, especially with respect to India. If the travellers' tales told of India did not paint a uniform portrait of oriental despotism as applied to India this fact is of some consequence for us. Since the AMP developed primarily from Marx's study of India ambiguity in the historical evidence about Oriental despotisms is significant.

Travellers' Tales of India in the Sixteenth and Seventeenth Centuries

The sixteenth century has long been dubbed 'the century of discovery' and has retained this description despite the loaded Eurocentricity of the notion that Asia, Africa and America were only then 'discovered'. We have a very accurate picture of the European 'discovery' of Asia as recorded in the reports and narratives of the court ambassadors, maritime officers, naval adventurers, merchants and missionaries who travelled to Asia in the sixteenth century, thanks to Lach's *Asia in the Making of Europe*. The theme of many of these travellers' tales was that Asiatic political systems were despotic monarchies, extending in the extreme cases of Siam, Cambodia and Burma to royal ownership of all the land in the territory. However, the sixteenth-century European sources on India do not conform well with the imagery of oriental despotism as it had developed in occidental political thought up to the time of Bodin.

Lach's account of how India was appreciated by sixteenth-century Europeans provides a useful narration with which to compare the subsequent theories of Indian despotism constructed by Western philosophers from second- or third-hand versions of travellers' tales. Lach's text suggests that the picture of India in sixteenth-century European sources is more complex and differentiated than the eighteenth-century stereotypes of oriental despotism. The theory of oriental despotism was built upon less reliable and more simplistic seventeenth-century sources, but also upon the basis of a significant historical change. The subsequent consignment of India to the category of oriental despotism must be (charitably) explained by the fact that the European 'discovery' was coterminous with the rise and consolidation of the Mughal Empire. Oriental despotism, in plain words, was another way of describing Islamic government.

The sixteenth-century European literature can be classified into three categories (Lach, 1965): Portuguese commercial reports and chronicles of conquest, Jesuit newsletters and histories, and the *fin de siècle* reports of Italian, English and Dutch commentators who travelled to and resided in India.

Portuguese perceptions   The *Decadas* of Barros provided the first developed Portuguese geography of India, and described the region as divided into many kingdoms,[13] which were so bellicose and covetous that had it not been for the natural geographical barriers, the entire region would easily have fallen into the hands of one conqueror (Lach, 1965: 341). The great and numerous rivers, the mountains, lakes, jungles and deserts, and the proliferation of countless varieties of dangerous wildlife combined to make communications difficult and frustrate would-be conquerors.

Detailed accounts of the Indian kingdoms from primary Portuguese sources were informative. Ceylon was described as divided into several kingdoms, the king at Colombo deriving his revenues from his monopoly of cinnamon, elephants and precious stones. The king of another Ceylonese kingdom reportedly forbad his vassals to pass on their property from one generation to another and thus discouraged enterprise (ibid: 344).

The external trade of the Malabar coast from the eighth century to the advent of the Portuguese was described as having been in the hands of the Arabs. There were mixed and coexisting religions in Malabar. The *Zamorin* (emperor or sea-lord) was described as having vassals such as the 'king' of Cochin. The Nayar joint family in Malibar – based on matrilineal descent caused much comment. The king had no certainty about the identity of his father, and in summarizing the effects of this system the Portuguese traveller Barbosa commented that the kings of Malabar were always old. Lach argues he might also have added that this means that their reigns were uniformly short and always limited in constructive effectiveness. However that may be, short-lived and aged kings are not obvious candidates for powerful despotisms. The *Zamorin*, when sworn in, promised to preserve and enforce the laws, to pay the outstanding debts left by his predecessor, and to strive to regain what former rulers had lost. The *Zamorin*'s role in the administration of justice was critical (ibid: 357–8). But castes took responsibility for the misdeeds of their members, and the methods of trial and punishment differed depending on the caste of the offender or his status as native or foreigner. Nayars, for instance, were never imprisoned or fettered: if they did not turn up for trial before the king they were hunted by four peers, and tried by ordeal if they did. None of the Portuguese authors was clear on the political relations between the ruling families and the brahmins on the Malabar coast. The Nayars, however, lived in their

13 The Delhi sultanate had collapsed just before the Portuguese intervened in the economy and politics of the Indian Ocean.

own villages, in seclusion from others, and possessed their own palm trees and water tanks. Only the Nayars could remonstrate with the king and expect to receive a hearing and to see justice done. The Malabar political system was thus fairly clear in the Portuguese accounts. The king was by no means all-powerful; extreme caste segmentation and caste autonomy prevailed. And the king cooperated with traders in what was evidently an enlightened but self-interested revenue maximization strategy.[14]

The Hindu Empire of Vijayanagar (AD 1336–1565) was described as separated into five provinces, and Barbosa indicated that its towns enjoyed a high degree of independence (ibid: 372). In the capital merchants were encouraged. The king made it his business to ensure that they passed duty-free from the seaports to the capital. The city of Vijayanagar, as the entrepôt, administrative centre and royal residence, occupies the centre of the stage in all accounts of the empire. But in some respects the kingdom did partially resemble the stereotype of oriental despotism. The king left administration in the hands of governors – if they proved disloyal, royal vengeance was terrible and swift. Yet some of the nobles disciplined so severely were reputed to own more land than some kings in Europe (ibid: 375). The king's seraglio was described in graphic detail by the Portuguese, as was his fabulous wealth. Because each king was responsible for adding to the regime's wealth, and might not touch the accumulated treasures of his predecessors, the growth of imperial wealth was assured. Its rulers were at constant war with neighbouring rulers and a permanent army was maintained. The army was described as the population of the whole capital on the move – only the palaces, fortresses and temples remained behind (ibid: 380). The functional rationale behind the city-cum-away was explained by its impact on morale: the levies had no reason to want to return home.

The Deccan States and Goa were of particular interest to the Portuguese in the sixteenth century. Mohammed I, the sultan of Canar, which was renamed Decao, had established his independence recently from the Delhi sultanate. He decentralized his state into eighteen provinces in which each captain was charged with providing for the army from local taxation. To prevent them from becoming too independent they were not raised to the status of nobles, were forbidden to marry except with their own slaves, and had to maintain a capital city residence – with a son or relative resident if they themselves could not be (ibid: 383).

Gujarat (Cambay) was also ruled by Muslim sultans at the time of the Portuguese advent, but was said to have been independent for only a short time. They had originally been captains in the service of the Delhi emperor,

14 The Portuguese emphasized the imminent danger of a Moorish conquest of Malabar as a result of the sizeable resident community of foreign Moors.

and the hostility to Muslim rule is evident in the Portuguese accounts.[15] Gujarat was a great site for Muslim traders. There was a large, standing and mostly mercenary army, and the ethnically and religiously mixed population of the cities was ruled by grand viziers or captains. According to the Portuguese sources, before their arrival a centralization-feudalization political cycle seems to have operated for two centuries, Gujarat eventually seceding successfully from the Delhi sultanate. The towns of Gujarat (over 60,000) were administered by viziers, and freed slaves were reported capable of becoming governors (Lach, 1968: 401).

The political regimes of the east of India, from Cape Comorin to Bengal, were accorded less detail in Portuguese sources. However, certain features of Bengal's political structure attracted Portuguese attention. The ascendancy of the Muslims was noted, as was the wealth and military capacity of Husain Shah, who was constantly at war with the Delhi emperor (ibid: 415). Pires, the principal Portuguese source, vividly described the 'Pase practice'; that is, the institutionalization of regicide by successive Abyssinian eunuchs over a seventy-year period. They had become the rulers of Bengal after initially being hired as praetorian guards by Barbak Shah (reigned 1460—74). Pires' account is substantiated in Muslim sources. The traffic in slave eunuchs for all functions was also reported as being very extensive in Bengal.

On the rise of the Mughal Empire, and the conflicts within Hindustan, the Portuguese sources are uninformative, largely because the land interior of India mostly fell outside the scope of their trading activities. But what is clear from their accounts is that the picture of oriental despotism, in so far as it finds any confirmation, is most closely approximated in their descriptions of Muslim as opposed to Hindu regimes — with the exception of some limited features of the Vijayanagar Empire. Oriental despotism, if it existed, was imported to the whole of India by the Mughals — it was not its 'natural' condition.

Jesuit perceptions of India   In the sixteenth century these were more bigoted and less sensitive to the environment than those of Portuguese traders. 'A European reader of the earliest published newsletters would not receive a general perspective on Asia's political organization. Most of the missionaries are content merely to mention that the overlord is either a heathen or a Moor, and that he is either a friend or enemy of the Portuguese' (ibid: 433). They were especially superficial in their treatment of Hindu practices (ibid: 446).

15 Portuguese sources are responsible for the apocryphal story of Mahmud I (1458—1511), a Gujarati sultan who was reputedly reared on poison as a child to immunize him from attacks by enemies. The result was that flies and women perished on him! His successor was reported as lecherous and a lover of opium — but in all other respects regarded as a judicious ruler.

The history produced by the Jesuit Maffei, *Historiarum Indarum* (1588), was largely an account of the Portuguese conquests. The author regarded the political system of India as typified in Malabar. He describes the *Zamorin* as an emperor who governs four orders: magistrates (governors), priests (brahmins), the aristocracy (Naayrs) and finally the farmers and artisans. However, the Jesuit sources are more detailed than Portuguese accounts on the Mughal Empire, partly because they were inspired by the hope of converting Akbar, the greatest of the Mughal emperors. Three Jesuit missions (1580–3, 1591 and 1595–1605) to Akbar produced a widespread hope in Europe that the cultural conquest of the Mughal Empire and therefore the bulk of India, was imminent. The land-power of the Mughal emperor was emphasized in these sources, as was the number of kings who resided at Akbar's court. (Some kings served in his retinue, others were forced to reside at court.[16])

Akbar's selection of officials by merit, irrespective of social origins, was noted. However, commoners in high-status roles had to wear the insignia of their origins – presumably to remind them of their debt to the emperor. Akbar's judicial and administrative functions took up a large part of his time, although the essentially oral character of legal decision-making at the top was frequently observed. The Jesuit historian Peruschi (1525–98) summarized much of the primary European information on Akbar's kingdom and tells us that 'the king is lord of all and nobody owns anything of his own except that which is bestowed upon him' (ibid: 457). Akbar administered his empire through a service rather than hereditary nobility. The administrative and military nobility were moved around the empire, thus preventing them from establishing roots and their own political bases. Their estates passed to the king upon their death.

The application of the idea of despotism to India thus appears to be coterminous with European knowledge of the Mughal Empire rather than any other political system in India. This fact is still insufficiently appreciated. Whether or not it was a valid description of Mughal India, the subsequent facile application of the notion of oriental despotism to other, especially Hindu, regimes past and present in the subcontinent clearly was not warranted by the available historiography or primary sources.

Italian, English and Dutch perceptions of India   In the late sixteenth century these reflected trading and imperial interests. Much Indian travel literature was translated and circulated throughout Europe. The odysseys, diaries, memoirs and letters of Cesare de Fredrici, Gasparo Balbi and Filippo Sassetti do not tell tales of oriental despotism (ibid: 468–77). The accounts

16 This portrait, of course, suggests feudal hegemonic overlordship rather than the despotic imperial authority associated with the idea of oriental despotism.

of the English travellers Newbery and Fitch, who journeyed to Akbar's court, were more concerned with emphasizing the wealth and commercial activity in Mughal cities. Thus only in the seventeenth century did the description of India as an oriental despotism in travellers' tales became widespread. The political theories which based their interpretation of Indian political systems upon seventeenth-century sources clearly ignored the widely available and more differentiated accounts of sixteenth-century Europeans. It is true that were some elements in the sixteenth-century sources which could be manipulated to confirm the theory of oriental despotism, but the geographical variation in political systems within the subcontinent, the variable powers of monarchs over their nobles, and the constraints of religious customs and caste orders, would be neglected in any such reconstruction of sixteenth-century European sources. The theory of oriental despotism seems to have been an ideological response to the discovery of India; if it has any empirical foundations it was based upon the assumption that all Indian regimes had resembled the Mughal Empire.

Seventeenth-century travellers, whilst responsible for the dissemination of the idea of Indian history as the narrative of political despotism, are, however, noteworthy as much for their differences in emphasis as their agreements. Sir Thomas Roe (1581?–1644), an English ambassador to the Mughal court in 1615, kept a journal and wrote illuminating correspondence during his residence. He claimed in a missive sent to the Archbishop of Canterbury in January 1615 that the sovereign was the owner of all the lands in his realm, which is why his revenues exceeded those of 'any eastern prince', that the rule of law did not exist, and that 'The Moghul is heir to all those that die' (Churchill, 1732: 729).

Francois Bernier (1625–88), a French doctor, plied his trade at the court of the Great Mogul in the 1660s. The descriptions of the economic, political and cultural practices of the Mughal Empire contained in *Voyages, contenant la description des Etats du Grand Mogol* (1670) had a profound impact upon contemporary European intellectuals, and two centuries later were accepted without critical dissent by Karl Marx in his first writings on India.[17] Three features of Bernier's descriptions were widely circulated amongst the intellectual classes. First, he ascribed the comparative economic backwardness of the Mughal Empire to the absence of a legal system of strongly entrenched property rights such as existed in France. Weak property rights reduced the incentives to achieve prosperity. Bernier's comparison of the French and Mughal economies was about as sophisticated as modern popular journalism engaged in the task of comparative economic analysis, and like popular journalism Bernier's tales had a simple moral. He believed

17 See chapter 3, p. 87.

that monarchical contempt for private property rights spelled economic decline. He also thought that the cultural beliefs of non-Islamic merchants inhibited development: according to him they buried gold in the ground as an investment for the next life and not simply from fear of the despot. Bernier's tales had a contemporary political motive: to persuade Colbert, Louis XIV's finance minister, to dissuade the Sun King in his turn from declaring all French land to be royal property. The French nobility were terrified that such action was being contemplated and Bernier's Indian arguments were intended as useful critical ammunition.

Second, Bernier made the familiar distinction between the service no-bilities of the Orient and the feudal nobilities of the Occident (Bernier, 1914). Hindustan's political system, like that of the Turkish Empire, was based on grants of authority and land to governors, *jaghirs* and tax-farmers, but ultimate ownership remained vested in the emperor. The Mughal nobility were thus more dependent on their king than were the European aristocracy.

Finally, Bernier described the Mughal Empire as devoid of economically self-sustaining cities. Parallel to the centralization of authority in the emperor and his governors, the cities were sites of administrative imperialism. Indeed, quite fantastically, he described all the cities as wholly mobile military camps, composed of soldiers and artisans, who moved around Hindustan with the emperor. The Indian city, on Bernier's account, did not provide the appropriate environment for the development of industry or commerce on the model of the West European city. These three interrelated features of Hindustan as described by Bernier — monarchical ownership of all the land, a service nobility and parasitical cities — provided the core 'empirical' assumptions upon which future models of oriental society would be built by occidental political economists.[18]

Niccolao Manucci (1638?–70), a Venetian who settled in India in 1656, composed a history of Mughal India, *Storio de Mogor* (Irvine, 1907). Whilst accepting the thesis that all land was crown land and that hereditary property rights did not exist in the Mughal Empire, he gave a rather different explanation of the origins of despotic arbitrariness. He claimed that Hindu government was the most tyrannous and barbarous imaginable

18 The remarkable feature of Bernier's text is the extent to which his own interpretation of oriental despotism (and therefore that of his uncritical readers) is at odds with the evidence he himself provides in his narratives. For instance, he refers to hereditary rajas throughout and outside the Mogul Empire as sovereign within their own territories; he cites no laws or judicial verdicts which suggest that possession of the land by non-state officials was not hereditary; and he gives not a single example of the despot confiscating the property of a rich man upon his death during his time in India — and the incident he does discuss, from the reign of Shah Jahan, suggests that such practices were regarded as illegal! It is also not possible plausibly to reconcile his description of Indian cities as mobile military camps with the data he himself provides about Indian cities (S. Naqvi, 1973: 48–55). See also pp. 263ff.

because the rajas and kings were all foreigners and consequently treated their subjects worse than if they were slaves. Manucci's speculations were interesting because they locate the origins of despotism in conquest, and explain despotism's characteristics as the outcome of ethnic conflict – suggestive ideas to which we shall return.[19]

Like Bernier, Baron d'Aubonne – Jean Baptiste Tavernier (1605–89) – emphasized the great authority of the Mughal emperor over his aristocracy when contrasted with the influence of Western kings over their nobles: 'In the territories of this Prince, the nobles are but Royal Receivers, who render account of the revenues to the Governors of Provinces, and they to the Treasurers General, so that this Grand King of India, whose territories are so rich, fertile and populous has no power near him equal to his own' (Tavernier, 1676: 324). Tavernier's *Les Six Voyages qu'il a fait en Turquie, en Perse et aux Indes* was apparently directly influenced by Bernier but the historians' consensus is that Tavernier was a more factually reliable observer of the Mughal Empire. For that reason Tavernier's principal difference with Bernier is important. He believed that whilst the Great Moghul was indeed the absolute political power in the land he was not the sole or absolute landlord of his kingdoms.

Jean Chardin was another French traveller to Persia and India in the seventeenth century, and like Tavernier and Manucci he encountered Bernier in person. But his *Voyages en Perse et autres lieux de l'Orient* gave a more complex account of oriental despotism in Persia than Bernier's account of India. First, whilst despotism and caprice were fair characterizations of the king's relations with his court, the same could not be said of the monarch's relations with the people. The king was bound by customary law, and in any case, apart from tax collection, monarchical institutions barely affected the peasantry. Second, Chardin distinguished between land which belonged personally to the king and domanial lands which, although administered by the vizier, were the property of individuals. Political despotism did not rest upon the king's monopolistic ownership of all land. This more differentiated picture of oriental despotism was not widely communicated in Europe. It was Bernier's more sharply drawn model of Indian despotism which captured the imagination of the European intelligentsia. The descriptively more complex, and more accurate, travellers' tales of Chardin, Manucci and Tavernier were less exciting.[20]

19 See appendix 7.1.

20 Bailey and Llobera (1981: 18) mislead when they suggest that with 'few exceptions' there was agreement amongst seventeenth-century travellers that the ruler was the sole proprietor of the land. As they cite Krader's text in support (1975) it should be noted that the latter emphasizes that it was Bernier who was exceptional (and unreliable) in supporting this thesis in an unqualified way.

Despotism and Absolutism: English and French Political Thought

The popular use of 'despotism' in the English and French vernacular coincided with the great outpouring of political philosophy and pamphleteering in the seventeenth and eighteenth centuries. Its popularity had polemical rather than scientific origins as a term of comparative politics. The rise of 'despotism' in the political vernacular accompanied the drives for and against absolutism in England and France.

If, as has been suggested, Thomas Hobbes did not contribute to the development of the concept of oriental despotism (Sawer, 1977a: 13), it is true that his introduction of 'despotism' to the English language and his distinctive mode of interpreting despotism provided the opposing arguments against which both English and French political philosophers were to bring to fruition the idea of oriental despotism. Hobbes was distinctive because he universalized the applicability of the idea of despotism and removed its specifically Asiatic connotations. Hobbes, implicitly, was the most insightful of the early critics of the normative use of (oriental) despotism. Unlike his contemporaries, he regarded himself as a value-free scientist, and was at pains to point out that all political systems had identical structures of sovereign authority. There was nothing special about the power of a sovereign in a 'dominion despotical'. Hobbes did none the less differentiate political systems: they could be founded either by covenant (contract) or by conquest. However, since fear provided the common rationale for accepting either the covenant or the conqueror, Hobbes contended that there were no salient differences between despotisms and contractually founded systems. All regimes were despotic (founded upon fear), and the use of despotism as a term of opprobrium was simply emotive: it masked republican or feudalist sympathies. Hobbes's arguments in *Leviathan* (1651) self-consciously rejected the whole tradition derived from Aristotle of classifying regimes according to whether the ruler(s) ruled in the interests of the community or of the ruler(s) (Hobbes, 1968: 251–61). He believed that the use of 'tyranny' (the Latin equivalent of 'despotism') was simply emotive: 'they that are discontented under Monarchy, call it Tyranny' (ibid: 240).

Hobbes departed not only from Aristotle but also from Bodin, in other respects his closest precursor. Despotic monarchy was neither barbarian nor oriental. Its origins and scope were not goegraphically circumscribed. Moreover, *contra* Bodin, the legitimacy of despotism did not differ from that of a commonwealth founded on covenant, as both political regimes were rationally and legitimately founded on fear.[21] Nor were the consequences of despotism more harmful for its subjects than the effects of a covenant: in both cases the sovereign's power was untrammelled. Hobbes's

21 Bodin, as we have just seen, confined legitimate despotisms to those regimes constructed after just wars, a nicety that was irrelevant to Hobbes.

reflections on despotism were thus a logical corollary of his general theory that all sovereign authority was necessarily monist and established through the rational propensities of prudent beings concerned to avoid the 'war of all against all'.

Hobbes's most famous English critic was John Locke, whose *Two Treatises of Government* (1690) developed a theory of limited and legitimate government.[22] Consequently Locke could not accept Hobbes's contention that all sovereign authority was identical whether or not it was the result of conquest or contract. Locke restored the pejorative sense of despotism when he defined it as 'an absolute, arbitrary power one man has over another, to take away his life whenever he pleases'. But whilst Locke's repudiation of Hobbes's sophistry — that to enter a covenant and to accept conquest are equivalent activities — was critical in his own definition of despotism, nothing in his writings suggests a commitment to a theory of oriental despotism. Despotism in his hands is merely a general term for arbitrary and unconstrained rule, associated with conquest and slavery, but not specific to any part of the world.

Hobbes's arguments were better received in France, especially by Sorbière, who used them to defend absolute monarchy. Sorbière contended that the Ottoman Empire, and other Asiatic empires, enjoyed peace and prosperity in contrast with the constant feuds which bedevilled Western political systems (Koebner, 1951: 295). To Sorbière's mind the supposedly untrammelled authority of the sultan was responsible for the security and prosperity of his regime. His plea for absolutism provoked Pierre Bayle into a detailed repudiation in his *Réponse aux Questions d'un Provincial* (1703). Bayle's discussion of despotism at the turn of the eighteenth century marked the arrival in the French vernacular of the concept which was to become a watchword of the French aristocracy and the centre of one of the major debates of the Enlightenment.

French Absolutism, the Enlightenment and Asiatic Despotism

Voltaire, in the eighteenth century, articulated the correct opinion that it was only comparatively recently — that is, in the previous two centuries — that the terms despot, despotic and despotism had achieved widespread currency in political argument. The fame and frequency of the concept of despotism in polemic were largely due to the ideological efforts of Montesquieu, who gave full conceptual shape to the idea of oriental despotism. But the notion was already prevalent in the milieu of dissident

---

22 Locke explicitly attacked Sir Richard Filmer, author of *Patriarcha* and a defender of the absolute and arbitrary power of kings. Hobbes, by contrast, was an implicit target of Locke's treatises.

sections of the French aristocracy and exiled French Huguenots who had suffered from the revocation of the Edict of Nantes.[23] The rebellious nobility complained that the long reign of Louis XIV had resembled that of the sultan of Turkey because the aristocracy had effectively been excluded from intermediation in his absolutist conception of government. The idea of despotism had become a dissident code word amongst the French nobility. Huguenots had uncomplicated reasons for calling Louis's reign despotic, and the anonymous author of the pamphlets entitled *Les Soupirs de la France Esclave*[24] (1689–90) contended that the king's power had crushed the Church, the nobility, and the cities, like the Grand Seigneur of Turkey, in a manner hostile to both Christianity and reason.

Montesquieu's first major political writings, *The Persian Letters* of 1721, were composed during the regency of the Duke of Orleans after the death of the Sun King (Richter, 1977: 113–41). He used the literary device of having two Persian visitors to France composing letters home as a means to engage in political commentary. The device provided a means of making unsubtle criticisms of France under Louis XIV. French absolutism was condemned through mere comparison with Persian practices. *The Persian Letters* consist largely of psychological explorations of the logic of despotism, a system of rule centred on the whims and passions of a single ruler, the despot, who rules through subordinates. Montesquieu devised the seraglio sequence of the book, with its analysis of the laws of motion of the oriental harem, as a parable for despotic rule in general. Fear, jealousy, intrigue and boundless suspicion rule the seraglio: master, women and eunuchs alike. Montesquieu's work was meant, and received, as a sarcastic defence of limited monarchy against absolutism, through the parable of Persian despotism, but above all it was seen as a partisan defence of the political roles in the feudal social order of the increasingly redundant and threatened nobility.[25] The principal sources for Montesquieu's 'knowledge' of the Orient were Chardin's *Voyages en Perse et autre lieux de l'Orient* and Tavernier's *Les Six Voyages qu'il a fait en Turquie, en Perse et aux Indes* (Richter, 1977: 141). Needless to say Montesquieu's 'idea' of despotism

23 The pamphleteers of the Fronde revolt employed the concept of *monarchie despotique* against Mazarin — the chief minister during the regency of Loius XIV — arguing that the French monarchy had become like 'la tyrannie du Turc', a 'puissance arbitraire et despotique' (Koebner, 1951: 298–9). Mazarin's period of fame and infamy is tersely described in Stoye (1969: 77–106, 123–30 and 191–4).

24 Literally: 'The whispers of enslaved France'.

25 Louis Althusser's superb essay on Montesquieu emphasizes the baron's '*parti-pris*', and his locus in political thought as a paradoxical anachronism: a feudal enemy of despotism who 'became the hero of all the opponents of the established order. By a unique historical volte-face, a man who looked towards the past seemed to open the door to the future.' Althusser helps to explain why Montesquieu, the composer of feudalism's swan-song, is anachronistically regarded as a precursor of bourgeois liberalism (Althusser, 1982).

was based upon a selective and creative reading of these works rather than upon a scientific evaluation of the empirical reliability and consistency of these travellers' tales. As Althusser rightly emphasizes 'despotism is only a geographical illusion because it is a historical allusion. [A]bsolute monarchy ... is Montesquieu's target, or if not absolute monarchy in person, then at least the temptations to which it is prone' (Althusser, 1982: 82–83). Althusser cites the thirty-seventh Persian Letter as sufficient proof for his argument. There the visitor Usbek sketches a portrait of Louis XIV, for Persian – read 'French' – consumption, a picture which highlights the king's professed admiration for oriental government. The portrait of the seraglio and despotism are caricatures. Their 'object is to terrify and to edify' by their 'very horribleness', and thus aid the feudal nobility.

Montesquieu's second major work, *Considerations on the Causes of the Romans' Greatness and Decline*, published in 1734, makes even more plain the propagandistic intentions in his use of the idea of despotism. In an aside made in the course of discussing the causes of Rome's downfall Montesquieu remarks that

underlying the unanimity of asiatic [sic] despotism, that is, every government where power is not checked, there is always a more serious type of division. The tiller of the land, the soldier, the merchant, the magistrate, the noble are related only in the sense that some of them oppress the others without meeting any resistance. If this be union, it can be so not in the sense that citizens are joined to one another, but rather that sense in which corpses are united when buried in a mass grave. (Richter, 1977: Introduction)

Two things are of note in Montesquieu's polemical formulation. First, he qualifies despotism with the prefix 'Asiatic', but from the context it is evident that the definition 'every government where power is not checked' entails the merely incidental character of 'Asiatic'. His implied definition of despotism did not differ from that of Locke.[26] Second, Montesquieu prefigures his own argument in *The Spirit of the Laws* and the standard polarities of European conservatism when he implicitly contrasts the 'unity' of Asiatic despotism with that of European feudalism. Feudal unity is richly differentiated, its conflicts are ultimately socially beneficial, it is organic, to use the language of nineteenth-century conservative sociology. By contrast the unity of Asiatic despotism is mechanical, its social roles are like billiard balls which collide 'without meeting any resistance', it is disastrous – the unity of death. Such a chiaroscuro reverberates in the Orientalist literature after Montesquieu, and in a revamped form in the work of his most celebrated nineteenth-century disciple, Tocqueville.

26 Indeed Richter has established that in his original draft Montesquieu did not have 'asiatic' in front of 'despotism' in the above passage, and only decided to insert it to avoid problems with the censor (Richter, 1977: 317).

The Spirit of the Laws (1746) is famous for its combination of the traditional typology of regimes (despotism, monarchism and republicanism) with a theory of how geographical conditions predisposed societies towards each type of regime. It is the least polemical of Montesquieu's major writings, intended and received as a serious work of comparative political science; it was not mere apologetics for the feudal system. Two geographical features were singled out as independent variables causing different configurations of political power: size and climate.

The theory of size as an independent variable was simple enough: small territorial units have republics, moderately sized units have monarchies and large units have despotisms. Though simple, it is not easy to tell whether Montesquieu's theory was functionalist: the consequences of sovereign territory of a certain size explain the character of the sovereignty or intentional: rulers must change the organizational character of the regime as its size alters.[27] However, Montesquieu's elaboration of geographical determinism with respect to despotism seems mainly intentional:

A great empire presupposes despotic authority on the part of its ruler. Speed in executing his decisions must compensate for the distance separating him from his domains; fear must be used to prevent negligence on the part of the distant governor or magistrate; the law must be concentrated within a single person. And the law must change continually, as those accidents arise which multiply in a state in direct proportion to its size. (*The Spirit of the Laws*, Book viii, chapter 19, in Richter 1977)

This argument suggests that beyond a certain scale of territory a monarch must become a despot for administrative efficiency, and if his control over territory is not to disintegrate through logistical overload. Montesquieu further contended that the lack of extensive natural barriers (high mountains, internal seas and lakes) made Asia the perfect habitat for despotisms.

Montesquieu's second independent geographical variable was climate. The torrid climate of Asia predisposed the population to servility. The two variables (topography and climate) were employed to develop a tough-minded materialism: geography was destiny, and Asia's destiny was despotism. Montesquieu's geographical materialism, which was not wholly original, was denied by his own account of the importance of culture and religion. Unlike previous 'authorities' on despotism he contended that Ethiopia was not despotic. Christianity had spared it from its geographical fate. Islam, on the other hand, had an 'elective affinity' with despotism. Irrespective of the geographical environment Islam was associated with conversion by conquest. This startling supersession of geographical determinism by cultural determinism was not picked up by Montesquieu's contemporaries.

---

27 'To the extent that the state contracts or expands itself, its spirit will change as well' (*The Spirit of the Laws*, Book viii, chapter 20, in Richter, 1977).

Table 2.4 Montesquieu's typology of regimes

Polities	Republics	Monarchies	Despotisms
Nature of sovereignty	Part popular aristocracy / Popular democracy	Monistic but with powerful aristocracy	Monistic
Exercise of sovereignty	According to popular will	According to law	Capricious; religion a mild restraint on despot
Principle	Virtue	Honour	Fear

Social bases			
Size	Small territory, urban centre	Moderately sized agrarian territory	Large-sized territory in arid regions
Exemplars	Ancient Greek polis	Feudal monarchies	Asiatic empires

Montesquieu's typology of regimes is schematically presented in table 2.4. A distinctive feature of his analysis was the ascription of different organizing principles to each regime: virtue for republics, honour for monarchies and fear for despotisms. The contrast between honour and fear clearly reflected the respective positions of the aristocracy under monarchy and despotism. The implied contrast was made more extreme by Montesquieu's suggestion that there were no nobles in despotic systems: all were equally base, servile, eradicated from social ties, atomized and impotent before the despot. Despotism almost ceases to be associated with a society in Montesquieu's ideal type. There are only slaves, who by definition are not capable of society, and the despot is himself a slave of the logic of the system, given over to the indulgence of his meaningless passions.

Montesquieu was flexible enough to allow the caricature of a societyless system some internal variation. He believed that the worst form of despotism was one in which the monarch owned all the land, as Bernier had claimed was true of India. The implication was that there were other despotisms, or administratively centralized empires, in which the king did not own all the land, but had greater jurisdiction than a feudal monarch. However, even if there were variations in the extent of the despot's ownership of the land, Montesquieu believed that the logic of political relations between the despot and his administrative elite was always the same. A grand vizier was essential, both to distance the despot from the decisions of his administrators, and to give him a victim in the case of error.[28]

Montesquieu's Critics

The Enlightenment's best known historian, Edward Gibbon, criticized Montesquieu for having used and abused the relations of travellers in his theory of climatic determinism. But Gibbon himself contrasted the Occident and the Orient rather as Montesquieu had done. He compared the Roman Empire with Asiatic despotisms by arguing that the Roman emperors had pursued a sensible policy of incorporating non-Romans as citizens of the empire, and that

Domestic peace and union were the natural consequences of the moderate and comprehensive policy embraced by the Romans. If we turn our eyes towards the monarchies of Asia, we shall behold *despotism in the centre and weakness in the extremities*,[29] the collection of the revenue or the administration of justice enforced by the presence of an army, hostile barbarians established in the heart of the country, hereditary satraps usurping the dominion of the provinces, and subjects inclined to rebellion though incapable of freedom. (Gibbon, 1980: 66)

This passage from Gibbon comes early in his monumental history. His comparison is between the Roman Empire of the Antonines and the Asiatic despotisms of his own day − and in the latter respect his analysis scarcely differs from that of Montesquieu. Moreover, his analysis of the disorders and consequences of 'military despotism' in the Roman Empire, developed later in *The Decline and Fall of The Roman Empire*, is not very different from his description of Asiatic despotism in the passage cited above.[30]

However, Voltaire, rather than Gibbon, was Montesquieu's most detailed, polemical and celebrated critic. In several works, *Essai sur les mouers et l'esprit des nations* (1753−4), *L'ABC*, *dialogues curieux traduits de l'Anglais de*

---

28 Although Montesquieu was not especially well informed on this matter, it seems that he had some inkling of the political logic of slave bureaucracies in the Islamic empires. Illuminating remarks on the logic of Mameluke regimes can be found in Gellner (1981: 73ff).

29 My italics. This phrase accurately captures the logistical weaknesses of all pre-industrial empires.

30 Since Gibbon's time it has become more frequent to categorize the Roman Empire and Asiatic 'despotisms' as fundamentally similar systems − see *inter alia* Eisenstadt (1963) and Kautsky (1982).

Monsieur Huet (1768) and *Commentaire sur quelques principales maximes de l'Esprit des lois* (1777), Voltaire was witheringly critical of Montesquieu. The latter's defence of feudalism against enlightened despotism attracted Voltaire's distinctive venom.[31] Voltaire was a supporter of what became known as 'enlightened despotism' and a famous Sinophile. He first complained that despotism was unacceptable because it was not of good Latin parentage. Second, he noted that after Montesquieu's licence the range of the term was rapidly extended: 'Nous donnons aujourd-hui liberalement ce titre a l'Empereur de Maroc, au grand Turc, au Pape, a l'Empereur de la Chine' (Koebner, 1951: 275).[32] Third, he thought that Montesquieu's portrait of the despot was a fantastic caricature: 'Nous attachons a ce titre l'idée d'un fou feroce, qui n'écoute que son caprice; d'un barbare qui fait ranger devant lui ses courtisans prosternes, et qui, pour se divertir, ordonne a ses satellites d'étrangler à droite et d'émpaler à gauche'.[33] These three points were accurate if not decisive rebuttals of his contemporaries' usage of the concept.

Voltaire also distinguished despotism from tyranny, and argued that China was generally characterized by the former rather than the latter. Indeed he regarded China as an exemplary model of modernity in certain respects; especially its apparently meritocratic recruitment of the mandarinate. Moreover, like Gibbon, he cast aspersions on Montesquieu's practice of supporting his 'fantasies' with false and implausible citations from travellers' accounts, although his own Sinophilia was based upon an equally culpable reliance on travellers' tales. Finally, Voltaire disputed the ideological import of Montesquieu's distinction between royal monarchy and despotism. Voltaire did not deny that monarchy was and might be wholly abused. But to follow Montesquieu by arguing that the rights of a hereditary nobility are intrinsic to the meaning of monarchy was simply to apologize for feudal privileges and backwardness. The cry against despotism was evidently no more than a slogan employed by the declining feudal nobility to defend its interests.

Voltaire's assault on Montesquieu's empirical inadequacies was confirmed by Anquetil-Duperron, a French Orientalist whose writings in the late eighteenth century cast considerable doubt on the authenticity of travellers'

31 Hence, the dispute between Voltaire and Montesquieu over the nature and meaning of despotism is often regarded as an illustration of the class struggle between the declining nobility and the ascendant bourgeoisie in the plane of ideas. Whatever the validity of this class-reductionism Voltaire's attack on Montesquieu is worthy of consideration for its logic.

32 Literally: 'Today we give this title freely to the Emperor of Morocco, the Turkish Sultan, the Pope, the Emperor of China.'

33 Literally: 'We attach to this title the idea of a ferocious madman, who listens only to caprice; a barbarian whose courtiers prostrate themselves before him; and who diverts himself by ordering his agents strangle to the right of them and impale to the left of them' (Voltaire, *Commentaire sur quelques maximes de L'Esprit des Lois*, III).

tales of Asiatic despotism. His successive texts[34] were all directed at three targets: against Montesquieu's taller stories; against Nicolas Boulanger's *Recherches sur l'origine du despotisme orientale* (1761), which had popularized the concept of oriental despotism;[35] and against eighteenth-century British accounts of Indian history and customs. He contended that the legal system of the Mughal empire and of the Comorondel Coast was not adequately explained by the theory that the despot was the sole proprietor of the land. He also thought that the idea that the villages of the Comorondel Coast owned the land collectively was false. Private property had existed in the East.[36] The notion that it had not was a self-interested fabrication of the English, would-be conquerors of the subcontinent.

The Place of Despotism in Philosophies of Progress

Political thinkers of the early Enlightenment remained within the typological comparisons established by Aristotle — whether they believed in oriental despotisms or not — and were also constrained by the belief that the 'laws' of political forms were universal and immutable. Their political philosophies were still based on the essentially static milieu of agrarian societies. The move towards philosophies of history which embraced the idea of progress, characteristic of the late Enlightenment, shattered the empirical and normative framework of Aristotelian discourse. The typology of regimes survived in new guises but theoretical attention was now focused upon locating despotism and other political forms as stages in a scale of human progress. Philosophers of progress gradually came to share the rejection of the belief that all forms of government rested on stable, stationary orders, and also the rejection of simple cyclical theories of the rise and decline of regimes and empires. The thinkers of the late Enlightenment hovered between what have been aptly described as *episodic* and *world-growth* stories of progress (Gellner, 1964: 1–32).

In episodic conceptions of progress there is one episode, one transition from a bad state of affairs to one good state, whereas in world-growth or evolutionist theories progress is perpetual, whether it takes place continuously

---

34 *Législation Orientale* (1778), *Recherches historiques et géographiques sur l'Inde* (1786) and *Descriptions historique et chronologie de l'Inde* (1786–91).

35 Boulanger authored the idea that the existing oriental despotisms were the residual survivors of the theocratic phase of human development — anticipating, as we shall see, the ideas of Condorcet. Unlike Voltaire, Boulanger disliked all oriental despotisms including China. But like Voltaire he supported a rational, secularized monarchy in the West — not very different from the ideal of 'enlightened despotism'.

36 Anquetil-Duperron's motives have been debated. Althusser (1982), Venturi (1963) and Stelling-Michaud (1960–1) retrospectively endorsed him as a critic of colonialism. Anderson (P. Anderson, 1974b: 466) more convincingly portrays Anquetil-Duperron as a French imperialist criticizing British imperialism.

or discontinuously. In episodic conceptions despotisms, and oriental despotisms in particular, came to be regarded as states of evil, unenlightened, superstitious, tyrannous, primordial unfreedom, still in the pre-transition infantile condition. By contrast in evolutionist conceptions despotisms came to be regarded as a necessary steps on the ladder by humanity, a step up from barbarism on the journey towards freedom. The emergence of a changed philosophy of history, in which an idea of progress is pivotal, and consequently the outlook on despotism is transformed, is startlingly clear in the writings of Condorcet, Herder and Hegel.

The first inklings of this shift in intellectual orientation are evident in the writings of Turgot who, together with Adam Smith, is rightly credited with the independent creation of the 'four stages' theory of historical development (Meek, 1971). The four stages theory was based upon the idea of successive modes of subsistence − hunting, pasturage, agriculture and commerce − to which corresponded functionally appropriate political institutions, manners and morals. Turgot thought the Orient a backward and halted version of the agricultural stage. After some initial progress the Orient had stagnated at a low level of development (as we would express his ideas today). The Orient was a continent of despotisms, but Turgot distinguished two types of despotism: the political and the civil (Krader, 1975: 42−3). Political despotism was result of the establishment of great empires in the centuries of barbarism and nomadic conquests. Civil despotism was the product of slavery and polygyny. But what perturbed Turgot was the constraint on intellectual and scientific developments under political despotism. He did not explain why the Orient had stagnated after early promise, and simply suggested that the Orient had developed too early; it had not ripened slowly enough for the full moral, political, economic and scientific development which had taken place in the Occident.

Turgot's ideas were influential in France, feeding through into both Physiocratic and philosophical circles. The most spectacular, fideistic example of the *philosophes'* conversion to the doctrine of progress is found in a book which was partially indebted to Turgot, Condorcet's *Esquisse d'un tableau historique des progres de l'esprit humain* (1795),[37] which outlined ten stages of human intellectual progress. The accumulation of knowledge was the motor of history in this philosophy. If unimpeded by religious superstition, the sequential and ordered development of knowledge would bring virtue and freedom to all of humanity. In Condorcet's account the third stage in the mind's progress was represented in the despotic empires of Asia, notably China, where prejudice had halted scientific and technological growth. The backward political regimes of the contemporary world provided a visible archaeology in which human progress could be charted. Turgot

---

37 Literally: 'Sketch for an historical picture of the progress of the human mind'.

and Condorcet's philosophies of progress and their theories of stages of development became important components of French intellectual culture and were primary antecedents of the philosophies of Saint-Simon (and his disciple Comte) whose impact upon Marx and Engels is unquestionable.

Philosophies of progress and the location of despotisms as early stages in 'Man's' growth-story were especially prevalent in the German branch of the late Enlightenment, at the end of the eighteenth and turn of the nineteenth century – notably in the writings of Kant, Herder and Hegel. Kant described the various states of Asia as despotic and shared the emergent Sinophobia of the late German enlightenment, which was virulently expressed by Herder in his *Outlines of a Philosophy of the History of Man*. Herder's thought shared many of the presuppositions of Montesquieu, Turgot and Condorcet. He described Asiatic states as despotic and criticized Voltaire for his absurd admiration of Confucian China, which he condemned as an embalmed mummy wrapped in silk, a sleeping old ruin on the edge of the world where superstitious dogmatism had induced stagnation. But he also associated agricultural work, and the prevalence of the agricultural phase of human development, with despotism – the political and economic systems were symbiotically connected. And, like Montesquieu, Herder believed that climatic conditions in Asia were conducive to despotism. Thus, towards the end of the creative periods of the German and French Enlightenments, despotism and Asia had become firmly established as twinned concepts, tied together in geographical space, but also placed in time since they were situated as relics, fossils and reminders of humanity's first steps towards progress.

Nowhere is this emergent philosophy of history more dramatically expressed than in Hegel's *Philosophy of History*. Hegel's politics and philosophy are widely recognized as partially indebted to Montesquieu,[38] but two ideas dramatically differentiate the two thinkers: Hegel's belief in progress and his placement of Montesquieu's typology of regimes in the time-path of the journey of the world spirit. Today Hegel's philosophy is generally, and rightly, dismissed as incoherent, vitiated by fundamental logical flaws (Rosen, 1986). Yet despite its objective idealism, its historicism and its saturation with teleological and theological assumptions, his philosophy of history has retained its fascination for occidental political thinkers from Marx onwards.

Hegel's philosophy of history rests on the premise that history has meaning or purpose. The meaning of history is the development of the world spirit towards freedom. Human history is not the deliberate product

---

38 See, for example, Althusser's tribute: 'Hegel, who gave the category of totality enormous scope, well knew his own teacher when he expressed his gratitude for this discovery to Montesquieu's genius' (1982: 48), and also Mosher (1984).

of the intended actions of actors; rather it takes place behind their backs –
where 'the cunning of reason' operates. The suffering in the world is
explained as the by-product of the world spirit's dialectical evolution towards
freedom. The rhythm of the Hegelian dialectic is well known. In the
beginning is undifferentiated unity. Then there is the stage of conflict or
contradiction. And finally there is the stage of harmonious reconciliation,
of differentiated unity, when the contradictory stage is superseded and
unity is regained but with the knowledge and benefits derived from the
conflictual stage intact. Successive human cultures are the vehicles through
which the world spirit's progress can be charted.

The civilizations of the Orient mark the first irruptions of the journey of
the world spirit, but here, 'Since Spirit has not yet attained subjectivity, it
wears the appearance of spirituality still involved in the conditions of
Nature' (Hegel, 1956: 112).[39] History begins in the theocratic despotisms
of the oriental world. Hegel does, however, differentiate the Orient into
three separate realms: the Chinese, the Indian and the Persian. He was
least complimentary about the Indian realm, describing it as 'a wild chaos
of fruitless variation' (ibid: 113), and asserting that 'A state of things so
destitute of [distinct] thought is likewise imperishable, but it is in its very
nature destined to be mixed with other races – to be conquered and
subjugated' (ibid: 115). Hegel even equivocated over whether India and
China were in any sense part of the world spirit's journey towards perfection,
since they 'lie . . . still outside the World's History, as the mere presupposition of elements whose combination must be waited for to constitute their
vital progress' (ibid: 116).

Hegel's detailed description of India and Hindus is the most withering
hymn of hatred and contempt sung about the Orient in occidental social
philosophy. India for him was 'a region of phantasy and insensibility'
(ibid: 139). The dream was the generic principle of the Hindu nature, and
India was above all else a land of dreams, a world of 'voluptuous intoxication
in the merely natural' (ibid: 157), governed by a 'despotism without a
principle, without any rule of morality and religion' (ibid: 158). It is
therefore not surprising that the Hindu was deceitful and cunning: 'Cheating,
stealing, robbing, murdering are with him habitual' (ibid: 158). Given this
lack of dynamism and moral individualism it was not surprising that 'all
political revolutions . . . are matters of indifference to the common Hindoo,
for his lot is unchanged' (ibid: 154).

Hegel also asserted that India had no necessary role in the progress of
the world spirit, just about the worst charge in his philosophy, for to be
outside history is the fate of those who have never actually been animated
by spirit:

39 My understanding of this typical passage of Hegelese is that in the Orient individualism
is not yet developed, humanity is still partly in a natural state.

The spread of Indian culture is prehistorical, for History is limited to that which makes an essential epoch in the development of Spirit. On the whole the diffusion of Indian culture is only a dumb, deedless expansion; that is, it presents no political action. The people of India have achieved no foreign conquests, but have been on every occasion vanquished themselves. (ibid: 142)[40]

However, at least Indian empires were comforted by Hegel with the knowledge that they shared a common and necessary fate with other Asiatic empires – inevitable subjection to Europeans.

Hegel–was especially outraged by the Indian caste system, that 'most degrading spiritual serfdom' (ibid: 144) in which 'all the concrete vitality that makes its appearance sinks back into death' (ibid: 145). It marked, in pathological form, the failure of individualism to emerge in India. Hegel, like Montesquieu, admired regimes and societies in which disciplined individualism could flourish.[41] But the caste system constituted the complete negation of this ideal, the total submergence of the individual within a collective identity.

Hegel's portrait of oriental despotism closely resembles Montesquieu's. Only the despot enjoys freedom in this system albeit of a meaningless and arbitrary kind; whereas the rest of 'society' is in a state of abject and servile equality. There are no 'intermediary powers' to check the power of the monarch, and there are neither individual nor corporate rights which can be exercised in defence against the despot. Despite his generally optimistic philosophy of progress, it is intriguing that Hegel believed that despotism remained a general threat to modern societies. There was a potentially dark side to the dialectic. Progress was not a simple highway – many culs-de-sac were present. Hegel's critique of the Jacobins' political philosophy and the course of the French Revolution sharply demonstrated these beliefs. Modern societies could suffer disastrous setbacks when individualism and egalitarianism were pushed to their limits; despotism was a potential outcome of democratic enthusiasms. Hegel's themes, divested of their idealist expression, were to become standard components of conservative and liberal political sociology in the nineteenth and twentieth centuries.[42]

40 In fact south-east Asia was extensively colonized and conquered by south Indians.

41 Both thinkers, in Oakeshott's judgement, articulated a vision of a mode of association appropriate for 'the dominant moral disposition of the inhabitants of modern Europe: the historic disposition to be distinct' (1975: 251). To put it in a modern idiom both Montesquieu and Hegel were both concerned that individualism should be able to flourish within social constraints. Montesquieu believed that feudal monarchies provided the appropriate milieu whereas Hegel believed that the more centralized and rationalized monarchies of the Napoleonic period were superior cocoons for rational individualism.

42 There are also some references to despotism and oriental despotism in *The Philosophy of Right*. Hegel thought that the unity of church and state was found under oriental despotisms, 'but an oriental despotism is not a state, or at any rate not the self-conscious form of state which is alone worthy of mind, the form which is organically developed and where there are rights and a free ethical life' (Hegel, 1967: 173). However, he did regard both despotic and feudal monarchies as lacking in these 'organic' qualities (ibid: 188). Finally, he also uses despotism in one of Aristotle's senses, as a generic term for unconstitutional regimes: 'despotism means any state of affairs where law has disappeared' (ibid: 180).

Summary

This survey of the genesis and evolution of the idea of oriental despotism has shown the permanence of four central elements in its evolution in over 2000 years of occidental political thought before Marx and Engels were university students: the existence of emperors with absolute political autonomy; the location of these emperors in the land-based empires of the Orient; the absoluteness of the powers of oriental despots over their nobility by contrast with those of occidental kings; and finally, the slave-like 'equality' and lack of status differentiation amongst the emperor's subjects. The notion of oriental despotism was evidently a stereotype constructed from unreliable sources — or, worse, from a selective reading of sources — to serve as a parable for political sermons in the Occident. The evidence available in the Enlightenment (as well as the criticisms made of the concept by contemporaries of its enthusiasts) should have warned political thinkers that the concept did not adequately model, even as a first approximation, all the major political systems of the Orient. At best the Aristotelian notion of oriental despotism was a forerunner of the ideal-type contrast now frequently drawn between the political systems of occidental feudalism and the service nobilities found more frequently, if not exclusively, in the Orient. However, the despotic powers attributed to all oriental monarchs were highly questionable.[43]

The survey also compels us to question whether the negative stereotype of oriental despotism is merely reproduced in different words in the concept of the AMP. It is true that some of the authors who developed the idea of oriental despotism figure in Marx and Engels's references, and the ideas of the sovereign as sole landlord and the all-powerful ruler are present in Marx's sketches of the AMP. One further significant legacy of the idea of oriental despotism, albeit a historically recent theme, did appear in Marx and Engels's sketches of the AMP: the ranking of oriental despotism as a specimen of an early and now fossilized society. This idea stemmed from the philosophers of progress, especially Hegel, and not from the more remote occidental traditions of understanding the Orient which had been established by Aristotle. However, the key point is that Asiatic systems of production, economic class structures and ideological relations — especially those in the villages — were not elements in the older or more recent ideas of oriental despotism. The writers on oriental despotism focused on elite-level relations, not upon the texture of everyday life or upon the logic of economic and exploitation relations in the wider society — the features of a social order which Marxists emphasize. The problematic of the AMP, its theoretical focus, naturally centres on the typically Marxist concepts of

43 See chapter 6.

production and exploitation relations, concerns different from those addressed by the authors of the idea of oriental despotism. The problematic of oriental despotism, by contrast, centres on the relations between the monarchy and the nobility, on political institutions, or the lack of them, and upon the constraints placed by religion upon intellectual freedom.

ORIENTAL SOCIETY AND POLITICAL ECONOMY

The AMP, as a Marxist concept, owed more to the idea of oriental society developed by the classical political economists, the Physiocrats, the thinkers of the Scottish Enlightenment and the English Utilitarians. These thinkers of course drew upon the occidental discourse on oriental despotism, but their distinctive perspective, that of political economy, was novel. It was from their accounts of oriental society, as well as from the writings of British travellers, administrators and historians, that Marx and Engels formulated their idea of an AMP.

The Physiocrats

Voltaire's ideas were brought into political economy by several of the most famous Physiocrats who were also Sinophiles. However, their admiration for the Chinese Empire focused on its economic order which they believed confirmed the merits of their prescriptions. The Physiocrats were advocates of *laissez-faire* — especially the harmony of interests doctrine established by Mandeville and made famous by Adam Smith's 'invisible hand', namely the idea that the intentional pursuit of private interests unintentionally produces public benefits. The Physiocrats realized that to ensure the equilibrium of a *laissez-faire* system the interests of political rulers had to be integrated into its operations. Somewhat paradoxically, these enthusiasts of economic freedom commended a 'legal despotism' on the grounds that the ruler's interest in the growth of agricultural produce would guide the ruler towards the socially optimal economic policy.[44]

François Quesnay, the most famous of the Physiocrats, believed that a ruler who confined the tax base to direct taxation on the agricultural product made the ideal despot. Since in Physiocratic theory agricultural production was the basis of all economic activity — because all outputs depended upon this sector — it followed that a ruler persuaded by the

44 In our century the support rendered by Chicago economists to the Chilean regime of General Pinochet seems similarly paradoxical. The paradox is resolved only if one accepts Hayek's (and Bentham's) tendentious reconciliation of a regime governed by the rule of law (which 'appears' despotic, but is in fact 'constitutional') with a market order.
My account of Physiocratic doctrine depends upon Hirschman (1977).

theory would not tax agriculture beyond the optimal level for his own revenue maximization and the overall growth and output of the economy. Quesnay thought that China was an exemplary model of such a legal despotism – not the arbitrary caricature of Montesquieu – and by happy accident had enjoyed rulers who in practice followed the precepts of natural law.

One Physiocrat extended the meaning of legal despotism beyond the judicious, agrarian, fiscal regulation advocated by Quesnay. Linguet favoured complete ownership of all property by the ruler, praised the political power embedded in Oriental despotism, and attacked Montesquieu, largely by asserting the normative converse of all the latter's arguments. He accepted that structurally despotism was much as Montesquieu described it, but contended that it was a benign system both psychologically and economically. The Physiocrats thus portrayed oriental society as a 'positive model for Europe' (Sawer, 1977a: 18–24), in utter contradistinction to the negative conception of oriental despotism popularized by Montesquieu.

A later Physiocrat strongly dissented from this rosy portrait of Asiatic political economy. Baudeau assaulted the 'destructive policy adopted by the great arbitrary despots of Asia' and compared the subjects of the despot to a herd (Krader, 1975: 33–4). However, this Physiocratic revisionism was not an attack upon despotism itself; Baudeau wanted a legal order which protected private property rights and a despot who would play a similar role to that envisaged by Quesnay, namely a guardian of the private property system who through enlightened self-interest would not arbitrarily interfere with the subjects' rights. Baudeau's disagreement with the Physiocrats was empirical: the despots of Asia had not in fact been playing the role of enlightened legal despots.

The Scottish Enlightenment

The thinkers of the Scottish Enlightenment are perhaps the most neglected sources of historical materialism. Yet their accounts of stages in history and of modes of subsistence were strikingly similar to Marx's stages and his modes of production; their arguments were distinctively materialist; and Marx's writings are filled with copious references to their work. Ferguson, Hume, Millar and Smith, the key figures in the Scottish historical school, also commented upon both despotism and oriental society in ways which were to shape the arguments of Marx's more immediate sources as well as of Marx and Engels themselves.

David Hume's *Political Discourses* (1752) referred occasionally to ideas about Asiatic societies in *aperçus* which showed some indebtedness to Montesquieu although the empirical and normative thrust of Hume's essays was rather different. In his *That Politics May Be Reduced to a Science* Hume engaged in an implicit normative analysis of regimes — very much within the scope of the Aristotelian tradition.[45] Hume's political analyses were not pursued in any great depth by his fellow Scots. Adam Ferguson's *An Essay on the History of Civil Society* (1767) described despotism without specifically Asiatic connotations as the universal product of governmental degeneration. Evidently influenced by Gibbon's *Decline and Fall of the Roman Empire* Ferguson saw despotism as the end-stage of the life-cycle of political systems, but he also related despotism to the low state of commercial arts, an idea which anticipates historical materialism (Ferguson, 1966: 272ff).

However, Adam Smith's *Wealth of Nations* used Asian illustrations to warn of what might happen to a European society which did not follow the rules appropriate for a regime of natural liberty. He singled out the dire consequences of the caste system for the stultification of the division of labour[46] and in consequence the limitations placed upon size of the market. Political violence in Asia also had a negative impact upon 'the accumulation of stock'.[47] But by contrast, and consistently with his formulation of the theory of 'public goods', he noted that the sovereigns of Hindustan and China had played a positive economic role in developing communications,

---

45 Hume proclaimed as a universal axiom 'that a hereditary prince, a nobility without vassals, and a people voting by their representatives form the best monarchy, aristocracy and democracy' (Hume, 1953: 15). As one might expect of an Edinburgh philosopher well aware of the recent crushing of the native Scots aristocracy, Hume looked much less kindly upon the merits of feudal vassalage than did Montesquieu. He also commented critically upon Machiavelli's differentiation of occidental and oriental monarchies. While he conceded that Machiavelli had discovered 'an eternal political truth, he remarked 'Such is the reasoning of Machiavel, which seems solid and conclusive, though I wish he had not mixed falsehood with truth in asserting that monarchies governed according to Eastern policy, though more easily kept when once subdued, yet are the most difficult to subdue, since they cannot contain any powerful subject whose discontent and faction may facilitate the enterprises of an enemy. For besides that such a tyrannical government enervates the courage of men and renders them indifferent towards the fortunes of their sovereign — besides this, I say, we find by experience that even the temporary and delegated authority of the generals and the magistrates, being always in such governments as absolute within its sphere as that of the prince himself, is able with barbarians accustomed to a blind submission to produce the most dangerous and fatal revolutions' (Hume, 1953: 18). Hume's perspicacity is impressive. He anticipates the arguments made — notably by Max Weber — about the centrifugal characteristics of despotic or patrimonial regimes. Oriental despotism, far from being stable after its creation, as Machiavelli contended, had in-built contradictions which were always likely to generate endogenous collapse.

46 Smith believed the caste system was enforced by coercion. When discussing the enforcement of labour monopolies he remarks 'The police must be as violent as that of Indostan or ancient Egypt' to achieve their maintenance (A. Smith, 1976: 70).

47 '[W]here men are continually afraid of the violence of their superiors, they frequently bury and conceal a great part of their stock ... This is said to be common practice in Turkey, in Indostan, and, I believe, in most other governments of Asia' (A. Smith, 1976: 301). But Smith immediately comments that 'It seems to have been a common practice among our ancestors during the violence of feudal government' which suggests that Smith thought that oriental despotisms and occidental feudalisms were equally inhospitable to the accumulation and investment of stock.

especially water networks, a role which historically had not been as essential in Europe.[48] However, Smith observed that in the Orient − China, Egypt and Hindustan − the sovereign's public and private roles were still fused, in contrast to the differentiation of the occidental monarch's roles. The land ownership system was not differentiated from the family system. The oriental sovereign was both father of his people and owner of the land. In consequence the land tax and land rent were identical in the Orient − an idea Marx subsequently repeated in his sketches of the AMP. Smith, none the less, like the Physiocrats, thought this land tax or land rent made the sovereigns of these countries 'particularly attentive to the interests of agriculture, upon the prosperity or declension of which immediately depended the yearly increase or dimunition of their own revenue' (A. Smith, 1976: 204; and also 251−3).

The Utilitarians

The arguments of the Scottish historical school were directly influential in the formation of Utilitarianism, English 'philosophical radicalism', and it was from utilitarian political economy that Marx and Engels derived their portrait of oriental society. Textual evidence − elaborated in the next chapter (pp. 107−10) from Marx and Engels's writings, both published and unpublished, shows that the writings of the utilitarian political economists, especially the two Mills and Richard Jones, were the most important sources for their views of the Orient, especially their interpretations of Indian social formations.

James Mill's *History of British India* (1821) argued that the autarky of the Indian village community explained the stationary state of India before British intervention. Like the philosophers of progress with whom he held so much in common, Mill placed India low on the scale of civilized development, contending that it had been stagnant for millennia − its villages were open neither to trade nor to the beneficial consequences of a free division of labour. Mill was responsible for popularizing the image of India composed of stable villages and unstable political institutions (an image reproduced by Marx in a famous footnote in *Capital* Volume I).[49]

Although a scourge of traditionalism and a radical political philosopher, James Mill paradoxically argued for the retention of part of the legal structure of oriental despotism in India, but in conjunction with the establishment of private property rights. The explanation for this paradox

---

48 Smith's emphasis upon the sovereign's role in developing water networks was quite different from Wittfogel's emphasis upon the despot's importance in promoting hydraulic agriculture − see chapter 6.
49 See discussion on pp. 111−14.

is instructive. He feared that the creation of strong property rights in land would lead to the development of an unproductive (feudal) class of landlords – the principal defect in England and Ireland. He argued that if the state there calculated its share of the surplus according to the utilitarian theory of rent, and paid for public goods from this surplus, then India could be brought into the orbit of progressive society.[50] Consequently he advocated the retention of state ownership or, where this was at issue, the nationalization of the soil in India – an amazing step for a liberal and the executive head of India House. Mill's arguments echoed those of the Physiocrats on the merits of legal despotism. He entrusted a legal despotism to the British government rather than to an oriental emperor and replaced natural law with the doctrines of Utilitarianism.[51] However, Mill did break with one feature of the received prescriptions of Indian land revenue. Although prepared to accept the state as landlord of the soil he rejected the traditional method of land assessment – which had been based on the premise that the state should take a fixed share of the gross produce. Since the Ricardian theory of rent demonstrated to Mill's satisfaction that this procedure prevented all but superior land from being cultivated he favoured its replacement with an assessment which calculated the *net produce* after allowing the legitimate costs of capital and labour (Stokes, 1959: 92–110).

Marx was fully aware of Mill's acceptance of the idea that India before the British conquest had been an oriental despotism, and of Mill's engagement in debates over how Britain should rule India. He saw the debates amongst the British policy elite over Indian land tenure as symptomatic of the conflict of interests articulated by the apologists of the landlords on the one hand and the bourgeoisie on the other.[52] More importantly Marx imbibed from Mill and his fellow Utilitarians a picture of the political economy of the Indian village and oriental society which was far more detailed, albeit stereotyped, than that available in the theory of oriental despotism.

---

50 The utilitarian doctrine of rent and its implementation by well-educated administrative enthusiasts in the Indian Civil Service is excellently described by Stokes (1959: 81–139). Stokes's account of India as a site for the experiments of the Utilitarians is an excellent riposte to those historical accounts of British politics and policy-making which stress its fundamentally pragmatic, incremental, atheoretical and non-ideological nature. This description did not hold for many of Britain's colonies which, in the nineteenth century, were guinea pigs for applied philosophy and political economy.

51 Malthus, the defender of the functional economic role of landowners, opposed Ricardo and Mill's theory of rent and contended that if the British government adopted Mill's prescriptions in India then they would maintain despotism in India with all its undesirable consequences.

52 Mill's arguments are especially interesting in retrospect. During the triumphal beginnings of capitalist industrialization the philosopher of bourgeois political economy had no truck with the idea – now a received part of sociological wisdom – that the existence of a powerful, private, land-owning class had been indispensable to the genesis of capitalism in the Occident.

However, James Mill was not Marx's most important utilitarian source on oriental societies. To judge by explicit citations, the evidence of Marx's notebooks and the timing of Marx's reading in the early 1850s,[53] Richard Jones, a utilitarian disciple of Bentham and Ricardo, and lecturer at Haileybury — the college which prepared future Indian administrators — was Marx's primary source for his vision of oriental society. In successive publications, *Essay on the Distribution of Wealth* (1831), *An Introductory Lecture on Political Economy* (1851) and *Textbook of Lectures on the Political Economy of Nations* (1852), Jones synthesized the ideas found scattered in travellers' tales — notably Bernier's — with the analysis of utilitarian political economy.

There were four elements to Jones's model of Oriental society. First, he believed that Asiatic despotism, originating in the conquests of nomadic tribes, was characterized by the state's monopolistic ownership of the land. This monopoly of rent by the state inhibited capital accumulation and made all dependent upon the sovereign. Second, he believed that the Indian village was based upon an entrenched union of handicrafts and agriculture which inhibited economic trade and an advancement of the division of labour. Third, he believed that this rural stagnation was complemented by an urban system which also inhibited progress. The city was solely an administrative centre in which the surplus of the sovereign from rent was spent on servants and retainers. Fourth, he combined the second and third elements in order to produce a theory of the prevalence of unproductive labour in the Orient.[54] According to Jones labourers paid from revenue were essentially unproductive, their employment contributed nothing over the longer run to the accumulation of stock, whereas labourers paid out of capital were important for the accumulation of capital. The craftsmen of the imperial court in his opinion fell into the uproductive category and helped to explain the comparative lack of dynamism in the oriental city. As a parasitical and exploitative administrative apparatus it could not function as an engine of economic progress, and was entirely dependent for its prosperity upon the sovereign's fortunes and preferences for the location of his capital.

Jones's model was partially based upon a reconstruction of Bernier's account of India under the Mughals, and all its elements entered, without significant alterations, into Marx and Engels's descriptions and explanations of India and Asia. For example, Marx cited with approval Jones's explanation of the architectural achievements of Asiatic monarchies:

It has happened in ancient times past that these Oriental States, after supplying the expenses of their civil and military establishments, have found themselves in

---

53 See information in appendix 1 to chapter 3.
54 Smith's *Wealth of Nations* had made the famous distinction between productive and unproductive labour (Book II, chapter III).

possession of a surplus which they could apply to works of magnificence or utility . . . We see mighty coral reefs rising from the depths of the ocean into islands and firm land, yet each individual depositor is puny, weak, and contemptible. The non-agricultural labourers of an Asiatic monarchy have little but their individual bodily exertions to bring to the task, but their number is their strength . . . It is that confinement of the revenues which feed them, to one or a few hands, which makes such undertakings possible. (R. Jones, 1852: 77−8 − cited in Marx, 1976a: 451−2)

Therefore my claim that the idea of oriental society, as developed by the classical political economists, was more important than the idea of oriental despotism in the formulation of the AMP is now substantiated. However, while Jones's importance for Marx is now well recognized in the literature, J.S. Mill's *Principles of Political Economy* (1848) is a surprisingly neglected source of Marx's conception of oriental society. Since Marx regarded J.S. Mill as a 'cretin' − despite sharing (and taking) so many of his ideas − historians of political thought and Marxologists have been inclined to miss the many resemblances between Marx and Mill, one of which is their common understanding of the Orient. In Mill's 'Preliminary Remarks' to his famous text he sets out, five years before Marx wrote about the subject, a sketch of oriental society which bears an uncanny resemblance to Marx's later writings. Mill also adumbrated a theory of stages of economic progress which recalled that of the thinkers of the Scottish Enlightenment, and not significantly different from those found in *The German Ideology* and the Preface to *A Contribution to the Critique of Political Economy*.[55] In the beginning, Mill argued, all societies were made up of hunters and gatherers. The next stage of evolution was pastoralism, and then sedentary agriculture. Societies which reached this stage then bifurcated in their future development:

The first of these modes of appropriation by the government, is characteristic of the extensive monarchies which from a time beyond historical record have occupied the plains of Asia. The government, in those countries, though varying in its qualities according to the accidents of personal character, seldom leaves much to the cultivators beyond mere necessaries, and often strips them so bare even of these, that it finds itself obliged, after taking all they have, to lend part of it back to those from whom it has been taken, in order to provide them with seed, and enable them to support life until another harvest. Under the regime in question, although the bulk of the population are ill provided for, the government, by collecting small sums from great numbers, is enabled, with any tolerable management, to make a show of riches quite out of proportion to the general condition of the society; and hence the

---

55 However, the tension between *German Ideology's* stages and those in the Preface (discussed in chapter 3) is not present in Mill's sketch. Mill evidently believed in a bilinear theory of historical development.

inveterate impression, of which Europeans have only at a late period been disabused, concerning the opulence of Oriental nations. In this wealth, without reckoning the large portion which adheres to the hands employed in collecting it, many persons of course participate, beside the immediate household of the sovereign. A large part is distributed among the various functionaries ... and among the objects of the sovereign's favour or caprice. A part is occasionally employed in works of public utility. The tanks, wells, and canals for irrigation, without which in most tropical climates cultivation could hardly be carried on; the embankments which confine the rivers, the bazaars for dealers, and the serais for travellers, none of which could have been made by the scanty means in the possession of those using them, owe their existence to the liberality and enlightened self-interest of the better order of princes, or to the benevolence or ostentation of here and there a rich individual, whose fortune ... is always ... drawn ... from the public revenue. (Mill, 1848: 20–1)

Mill went on to describe other salient features of oriental political economy. The structure of the distribution of wealth in oriental society meant that manufacturing developed only for a narrow, albeit wealthy, market, and the direct producers lived directly as servants of the appropriators of surplus. The insecurity of the merchant classes led them to value liquid and mobile assets, like gold, rather than to pursue productive investments. The parasitic class of grain dealers and money dealers plied their trade largely upon that part of the national produce which formed the revenue of the government. 'Such in its general features, is the economical conditions of most of the countries of Asia, as it has been from the commencement of authentic history, and is still, wherever not disturbed by foreign influences' (ibid: 22). By contrast European agricultural communities had developed differently, autonomously from governments, and had eventually given rise to an urban economy. Perhaps more significantly, European feudalism developed in such a way as to facilitate capitalist development: 'The greater stability, the fixity of personal position, which this state of society afforded in comparison with the Asiatic polity to which it economically corresponded, was probably one main reason why it was also found more favourable to improvement ... feudal Europe ripened into commercial and manufacturing Europe' (ibid: 24). Here in a nutshell are two of the core themes in the theory of the AMP: both its defining productive forces and relations of production, and the implied contrast between the feudal mode of production and its Asiatic antonym as the explanation of occidental uniqueness. Mill, as so often, expressed Marx's ideas without sharing the same philosophical or ideological premises.

CONCLUSION

Marx and Engels's writings on India and Asia, in so far as they were explicitly organized around a model of an AMP, were more immediately and directly indebted to the writings of utilitarian political economists on oriental society than they were to the tradition of political theorizing and typologizing inaugurated by Aristotle. This conclusion is important not just for accuracy in the history of ideas but also because it suggests that much of the writing based on the theme that Marx and Engels repressed the alleged political implications which oriental despotism had for the future of socialism is both far-fetched and misplaced. Their concern with Asiatic societies stemmed from their interest in the applicability of historical materialism to the analysis of pre-capitalist societies, an interest which was itself almost wholly driven by their desire to demonstrate the uniqueness and genesis of capitalism. As most of Marx's life-work was based upon the critique of political economy it is not surprising that the main sources of his account of the Orient were the best known political economists of Victorian England.

3
Marx and Engels on the Asiatic Mode of Production and India

Marx's scattered pronouncements about India and/or Asia do not add up to a coherent view, so that the concept 'Asiatic mode of production' does not conceptualise much of anything and only causes endless problems for those who try to use it.

Lubasz, 'Reply to Kate Currie'

This chapter surveys Marx and Engels's 'texts' which refer to the AMP, explicitly, substantively or allegedly. It demonstrates three conclusions: that there is a lack of clarity and logical rigour in Marx and Engels's writings about the AMP; that many interpretations of these texts are erroneous and tendentious — the products of ideological or wishful reading; and that the evidence suggests that Marx and Engels's foci of attention on Asiatic societies, and beliefs about the historical location of the AMP, shifted in the course of their working theoretical lives. The argument is organized into two parts: a chronological analysis of Marx and Engels's writings relevant to the AMP followed by a systematic treatment of key problems in the interpretation of these texts.

THE TEXTUAL TREASURE: 1843–95

There is an unwritten rule of Marxology: to reduce controversy in the interpretation of Marx and Engels it is essential to quote in full any conceivably relevant passages which might prove important. Pedantry, unfortunately, is an indispensable safeguard against criticism in Marxology. This rule is all the more critical in the textual exegesis of the AMP — a concept which was explicitly mentioned by Marx, by that name, only on one occasion. The rule is followed in this chapter. However, fortunately, there is now agreement on where most of the Asiatic textual treasure is to be found, and barring the future discovery of more Marxist Dead Sea scrolls comparable to the *Grundrisse* and the *Ethnological Notebooks*, the 'texts' are limited in scope and easily identified. They are treated here largely in the chronological order in which they were developed, and to avoid the decontextualization of these writings their place in Marx and Engels's theoretical, political and ideological evolution is observed throughout.

Marx and Engels's Early Work: 1843–4

Marx and Engels's early work did not explore oriental despotism or society. However, before Marx became a Marxist, or as he became a Marxist,[1] he had contrasted the characteristics of political authority in Asiatic, ancient, feudal and capitalist societies in his *Critique of Hegel's Philosophy of Right*.[2] Marx referred twice to despotism in this unpublished text. In the first instance he merely transcribed section 278 of Hegel's *Philosophy of Right*, where despotism is defined as 'any state of affairs where law has disappeared and where the particular will as such, whether of a monarch or a people . . . counts as law, or rather takes the place of law' (Marx, 1975: 78). The second instance is both more revealing and more obscure. Here Marx criticized Hegel's defence of monarchy and his interpretation of the historical development of the state. In pre-modern times:

'Either the *res publica* was the real private concern of the citizens, their real content, while the private person as such was a slave – this was the case among the Greeks, where the political state as such was the only true content of their lives and aspirations. Or else the political state was nothing but the private caprice of a single individual so that, as in Asiatic despotism, the political state was as much a slave as the material state. The modern state differs from such states with a substantive unity between people and state not in the fact that the various moments acquire a particular reality, as Hegel asserts, but rather that the constitution itself develops a *particular* reality alongside the real life of the people and that the political state has become the *constitution* of the rest of the state. (ibid: 91)

1 Colletti argues that in the course of composing his unpublished *Critique of Hegel's Philosophy of Right*, Marx became a Marxist; that is, in 1843 (Colletti, 1975). Tucker assures us that Marx became a Marxist with the composition of *The Economic and Philosophical Manuscripts* (Tucker, 1961). Althusser (1969) places Marx's 'epistemological break' in 1846 – coterminous with the writing of *The German Ideology*. Gellner tells us that for V.N. Nikiforov, a contemporary Soviet Marxist, Marxism only emerges fully with Marx's readings of Morgan and Kovalevsky in 1881 (Gellner, 1986: 78–108). Gellner's gloss is apposite: 'tell me just when you think Marxism sprang from the head of Zeus – when the *coupure* took place – and I will tell you what your values are.'

2 S. Moore (1980: 215). Unfortunately, Moore does not paginate his source. There is a passage where Marx explicitly compares ancient, Asiatic and bourgeois political structures – see the discussion of Marx (1975: 78) in the text – but there is, to my knowledge, no passage where all four systems are compared side by side.

Interpreting the young Marx, or Hegel at any age, is difficult, especially interpreting the former commenting on the latter. However, two features of the above passage are clear when taken in the context of the *Critique*. Marx accepted, at least for the sake of argument, the existence of Asiatic despotism as a form of political rule. Second, he rejected Hegel's general theory that the modern state supersedes the conflict between private interests in civil society and is the expression of the universal interest. The modern bourgeois state had not resolved the contradiction between particular private wills and the universal or public interest, even if it differed dramatically from the polis of ancient Greece and the political system of Asiatic despotism.

However, Marx's main usage of 'despotism' in his early writings was unquestionably polemical rather than analytical. He used the term occasionally to condemn Prussian government. He wrote in this vein to Ruge in the *Franco-German Yearbooks* in March 1843: 'And the opinions of foreigners about the Prussian government! . . . the most repulsive despotism stands revealed for all the world to see' (ibid: 199). He also used the term, again writing to Ruge, in May 1843, to describe an alleged incident in Napoleon's gradual descent into megalomania, and to associate by implication the Prussian monarchy with these traits: 'Despotism's only thought is disdain for mankind, dehumanized man. In the eyes of the despot men are always debased' (ibid: 202). In the same letter despotism was used polemically, but with an intriguing phrase – italicized below – to compare the Hohenzollern and Romanov monarchies. Encouraged by the Czar, the Prussian king censored discussion of human rights, a decision which meant

a return to the old ossified, servile state in which the slave serves in silence and *the owner of land and people* rules as silently as possible over well-trained, docile servants. Neither one can say what he wishes, the one that he wishes to be human, the other that he has no use for human beings on his territory . . . for a despotism brutality is necessary and humanity impossible. (ibid: 205)

Two further passages in his writings of 1843–4 in which despotism occurs are of interest in the light of later controversies. First in a letter to Ruge of May 1843, when the composition of the *Critique of Hegel's Philosophy of Right* was under way, Marx attacked Montesquieu's theory of despotism:

The principle on which monarchy in general is based is that of man despised and despicable, of *dehumanized man*; and when Montesquieu declares that its principle is honour he is quite in error. He attempts to make this plausible by distinguishing between monarchy, despotism and tyranny. But these names refer to a single concept denoting at best different modes of the same principle. (ibid: 202)

At this time Marx saw no theoretical or morphological difference between feudal monarchy and oriental despotism. They were birds of the same feather. In Marx's eyes Montesquieu, like Hegel, was an apologist for monarchy.

The second passage is from the *Economic and Philosophical Manuscripts*. Here Marx criticized the primitive or crude communism of thinkers such as Gracchus Babeuf,[3] noting that such communism was '(a) still of a political nature, democratic or despotic, (b) with the abolition of the state, but still essentially incomplete and influenced by private property' (ibid: 347). The (obscure) context in which this passage occurs implies that there are two types of primitive, crude and egalitarian communism, namely the democratic and the despotic. Democratic communists were concerned to persuade people to communism in the manner of Fourier and Proudhon, while despotic communists were fundamentally coercive – in the style of Babeuf and the 'Conspiracy of Equals'. Marx differentiated his own communism from the crude, primitive levelling variety, but he did describe some utopian communists as despotic. At this stage of his life he did not have any inhibitions, *pace* Wittfogel, about using the term despotism in conjunction with certain types of communism.

The Formation of Historical Materialism: 1846–8

Marx and Engels's initial formulations of the doctrines of historical materialism cast important light upon their subsequent 'discovery' of the AMP. Despite their reading of Hegel, and their knowledge of the writings of the Enlightenment, the regimes and societies of the Orient did not figure in the texts in which historical materialism was first elaborated. In its first drafts historical materialism was essentially no more than a philosophical representation of the history of Europe. *The German Ideology* exemplifies this proposition (Marx and Engels, 1970). This text elaborated the theoretical premises of historical materialism for the first time – although it remained unpublished – and paid some attention to pre-capitalist societies and their modes of evolution. Marx and Engels asserted that the stages in the development of the division of labour corresponded with the development of different forms of property, and distinguished three forms of pre-capitalist property: the communal, the ancient and the feudal. The communal form corresponded to the underdeveloped production techniques prevalent amongst hunters and gatherers, nomads and some sedentary agriculturalists. Here the division of labour had not differentiated much beyond that of the family, and the social order simply involved a (patriarchal) extension of the family. Slavery, latent in the family, emerged in tandem with growing population, the expansion of social needs, and the growth of external intercourse – both war and trade.

---

3 Gracchus Babeuf (1760–97) was the leader of the *Conspiration des Égaux*, an authentic communist plot, during the French Revolution, and was the author of the memorable injunction 'Let all the arts perish that we may have fair equality!'.

The second 'communal and state property' of antiquity was the form which Marx and Engels believed to have developed from the unification of several tribes into a city[4] – through contract or conquest – and its genesis was accompanied by primordial slavery. While communal property relations persisted, real private property developed and eroded the anterior communalism. The emergence of private property was associated with a widening of the division of labour and increasing antagonisms between town and country. These processes culminated in the development of a systematic, class-divided social order which pitted citizens against slaves.

The third form, 'feudal property', like tribal and communal ownership was based on the community. But by contrast with ancient society, which sprang from the city, feudalism had its genesis in the countryside – subsequent to the decline and fall of the Roman Empire. Yet under feudalism the division of labour remained underdeveloped, despite evidence of an increasing differentiation between the town and the country. Only with the emergence of autonomous urban communities, the cocoons of the bourgeoisie, did the social preconditions of capitalism emerge in the West. In this first 'Marxist' account of the origins of capitalism we are given no comparative perspective on the non-European societies which did not autonomously develop capitalism, and we are treated largely to a description of occidental history rather than an explanation of the specific features which accounted for the emergence of capitalism in the Occident (Baechler, 1975: 11–12).

The *Communist Manifesto* was as Eurocentric as *The German Ideology*, which is hardly surprising given that it was nominally addressed to the modern industrial proletariat. The social formations of the Orient were not discussed. The famous assertion that the 'history of all hitherto existing society is the history of class struggles' was followed by a list of opposed classes whose inspiration was wholly derived from the history of Western Europe: 'Freeman and slave, patrician and plebeian, lord and serf, guild-master and journeyman'. Only after the defeat of the 1848 revolutions and Marx's journey into exile and research in London had he and Engels the opportunity and cause to investigate non-European historiography and ethnography.

Correspondence and Journalism

Between 1853 and 1858 Marx and Engels composed over forty brief articles for the *New York Daily Tribune*, largely on the political, social and military impact of British imperialism in India and China.[5] The most important of these articles for our purposes are 'The British Rule in India'

---

4 Their 'fusion theory' of the origin of the city was similar to that developed by Fustel de Coulanges in 1864 (Fustel de Coulanges, 1956).

5 To judge by the collection brought together in Marx and Engels (1959), thirty-seven of the thirty-nine articles were written by Marx, since his name appeared above them in the *New*

published on 25 June 1853, and 'The Future Results of the British Rule in India', published on 8 August 1853. But Marx and Engels wrote several articles on the Indian Mutiny in 1857, just at the time when Marx was composing the *Grundrisse* — parts of which would feature later in *Theories of Surplus Value* and *Capital*. Reflection on Indian society and history was therefore one of Marx's more significant intellectual diversions during his most creative intellectual phase.[6]

While researching his articles on India Marx reported his interim findings to Engels in a letter dated 2 June 1853. He began by rephrasing Hegel's question about the absence of history in the East. In his opinion what mattered was why the history of the East appeared to be the history of religions. He believed he had found his answer in the account of India given by Bernier (Marx and Engels, 1959: 311). He cited, without reservation, Bernier's account of the Mughal military system and his portrayal of Indian cities as mobile military camps, but was more concerned to emphasize that 'Bernier rightly considered that the basis of all phenomena in the East — he refers to Turkey, Persia, Hindustan — to be the absence of private property in land. This is the real key, even to the Oriental heaven' (ibid). In his reply, dated 6 June 1853, Engels wrote:

The absence of private property is indeed the key to the whole of the East ... But how does it come about that the Orientals did not arrive at landed property, even in its feudal form? I think it is mainly due to the climate, taken in connection with the nature of the soil, especially with the great stretches of desert which extend from the Sahara straight across Arabia, Persia, India, Tartary up to the highest Asiatic plateau. Artificial irrigation is here the first condition of agriculture and this is a matter either for the communes, the provinces or the central government. (ibid: 312)[7]

York Daily Tribune. However, several of the military pieces were almost certainly written by Engels.

6 The judgement that 'No theorization of any actually Asian patterns of social, economic or political life is to be found *anywhere* in Marx's writings' is extreme (Lubasz, 1984: 465 — my emphasis). This argument makes partial sense for the *Grundrisse* where Marx was at his most Hegelian, but is not plausible for Marx's writings in *Capital* or his *Ethnographic Notebooks* where he relies on and comments upon some of the best empirical sources of his day on Asian and Indian history and culture. Lubasz's provocative, well-argued but one-sided case would have been better made had he argued that Marx used his empirical sources on India selectively to produce his desired Hegelian conclusions. As we shall see, there is evidence that Marx abused his sources when analysing Indian history (see pp. 262–7).

7 Although Marx put virtually every thought and phrase from Engels's letter into his article 'The British Rule in India' he ignored Engels's point about artificial irrigation being the functional responsibility of either' the communes, the provinces or the central government'. In his subsequent article he asserts that irrigation is a function of the central government. Engels's careful qualification was apposite. He thereby avoids the censures levelled against both Marx and Wittfogel (see pp. 250–61).

From which source Engels derived his irrigation thesis is a mystery. Bernier, whom Marx cites as an authority for his ideas on India, did not subscribe to it. His travelogue is filled with accounts of the extent of rainfed agriculture in India, and his sole reference to irrigation is to 'ditches and channels' for the course of water — that is, small-scale, locally organized irrigation (S. Naqvi, 1973: 50–2).

Accepting Engels's central geographical materialist argument without dissent, plus many other substantive points made by his co-thinker, Marx completed his short essay on 10 June 1853. 'The British Rule in India' was an eloquent journalistic essay, simultaneously elegaic and cheerful. Here Marx used the expressions 'Asiatic despotism' and 'oriental despotism' for the first time to describe India before the British conquest. Marx began by comparing the geography of India to that of Italy, before remarking: 'in a social point of view, Hindustan is not the Italy, but the Ireland of the East. And this strange combination of Italy and Ireland, of a world of voluptuousness and a world of woes, is anticipated in the ancient traditions of the religion of Hindustan ... at once a religion of sensualist exuberance, and a religion of self-torturing asceticism.' (Marx, 1973a: 301). Marx rejected the then current opinion that there had been a 'golden age' in Hindustan, and ironically remarked that he preferred the authority of 'the Brahmin himself, who places the commencement of Indian misery in an epoch even more remote than the Christian creation of the world' (ibid: 302). But:

There cannot, however, remain any doubt but that the misery inflicted by the British on Hindustan is of an essentially different and infinitely more intensive kind than all Hindustan had to suffer before. I do not allude to *European despotism*, planted upon *Asiatic despotism*,[8] by the British East India Company ... [which] is no distinctive feature of British colonial rule, but only an imitation of the Dutch (ibid).

Rather, what was distinctive was that the British had imposed a social revolution upon India, something wholly novel in its history:

All the civil wars, invasions, revolutions, conquests, famines, strangely complex, rapid and destructive as the successive action in Hindustan may appear, did not go deeper than its surface. England has broken down the entire framework of Indian society, without any symptoms of reconstitution yet appearing (ibid).

However changing the political aspect of India's past must appear, its social condition has remained unaltered since its remotest antiquity, until the first decennium of the nineteenth century. The hand-loom and the spinning wheel, producing their regular myriads of spinners and weavers, were the pivots of the structure of that society ... England began with driving the Indian cottons from the European market ... and in the end inundated the very mother country of cotton with cottons ... [The] decline of Indian towns celebrated for their fabrics was by no means the worst consequence. British steam and science uprooted, over the whole surface of Hindustan, the union between agriculture and manufacturing industry (ibid: 304)[9]

Marx compared the pre-imperial and post-imperial political structures of India, but in an ironic rather than analytical vein: 'There have been in Asia,

8 The italics are mine.
9 Marx's argument had a hidden agenda. In his letter to Engels of 14 June 1853 he wrote:

generally, from immemorial times, but three departments of government: that of finance, or the plunder of the interior; that of war, or the plunder of the exterior; and finally, the department of public works' (ibid: 303).[10] Taking his cue from Engels, Marx argued that climate and territorial conditions 'constituted artificial irrigation by canals and waterworks the basis of Oriental agriculture. ... Hence an economical function devolved upon all Asiatic governments, the function of providing public works [the] artificial fertilization of the soil' (ibid). Marx further contended that the British in East India had accepted the departments of finance and war (that is, internal and external plundering) but had entirely neglected that of public works. These facts went far towards explaining the deterioration of Indian agriculture since it was not capable of optimal production in a regime guided by *laissez-faire* doctrines.

Marx also sketched what he regarded as the salient feature of the Indian social system besides the two elements of a government involved in public irrigation works as well as plunder, and the domestic union of agriculture and manufacturing in small centres, namely 'the so-called *village system*' (ibid: 304).[11] He did so by listing some of the twelve 'professions' detailed in an old official report of the British House of Commons (*The Fifth Report from the Select Committee on the Affairs of the East India Company*, 1812)[12] and he enumerated them, in full in his subsequent letter to Engels of 14 June 1853 (Marx and Engels, 1959: 313–14). While Marx conceded that it was 'sickening to human feeling' to witness the destruction of this village system he cautioned his readers to remember that

'Your article on Switzerland was of course a direct smack at the leading article in the Tribune . . . and its Carey. I have continued this hidden warfare in the first article on India, in which the destruction of the native industry is described as revolutionary. This will be very shocking to them' (Marx and Engels, 1959: 313). Carey was a radical American economist who espoused the union of industry and agriculture against the centralization of industry. Marx, as his Indian articles demonstrate, regarded both the destruction of the domestic unity of agriculture and manufacturing and the centralization of industry as progressive.

10 Marx's irony and analysis are copied directly from Engels's letter to Marx of 6 June 1853 – Marx and Engels (1959: 312).

11 The italics are Marx's.

12 According to Fernbach (1973: 305) Marx cited this report and list of 'professions' from Campbell (1852: 84–5), whereas Krader (1975: 83) suggests he took the list of village professions from Wilks's *Historical Sketches of the South of India*. Both are right according to Marx, who credits both Wilks and Campbell in an identical recitation in *Capital*, Volume I (Marx, 1976: 479, footnote 37). Hegel's *Philosophy of History* (1956: 154) also lists the same professions, and the Hegelian style of Marx's Indian essays is glaring. Richard Jones also cited the same passage, proof of its status as an established stereotype.

Marx may never have read the *Fifth Report* directly. Alternatively he may have done so very selectively. The *Fifth Report* includes other accounts of agrarian systems in India south of the Vindhyas, all of which suggest the atypicality of the account which Marx chose to highlight. The other accounts all clearly point to the existence of private ownership of land – including in the Vijayanagar Empire (S. Naqvi, 1973: 57–9).

we must not forget that these *idyllic village communities*, inoffensive though they may appear, had always been *the solid foundation of Oriental despotism*,[13] that they restrained the human mind within the smallest possible compass, making it the unresisting tool of superstition, enslaving it beneath traditional rules, depriving it of all grandeur and historical energies. We must not forget the barbarian egotism which, concentrating on some miserable patch of land, had quietly witnessed the ruin of empires, the perpetration of unspeakable cruelties, the massacre of the population of large towns, with no other consideration bestowed upon them than on natural events, itself the helpless prey of any aggressor who deigned to notice it all. We must not forget that this undignified, stagnatory, and vegetative life, that this passive sort of existence evoked on the other part, in contradistinction, wild, aimless, unbounded forces of destruction, and rendered murder itself a religious rite in Hindustan. We must not forget that these little communities were contaminated by distinctions of caste and by slavery, that they subjugated man to external circumstances instead of elevating man to be the sovereign of circumstances, that they transformed a self-developing social state into never-changing natural destiny, and thus brought about a brutalizing worship of nature, exhibiting its degradation in the fact that man, the sovereign of nature, fell down on his knees in adoration of Kanuman, the monkey, and Sabbala, the cow. (Marx, 1973a: 306).

Marx concluded with one of the most frankly teleological passages to be found in his writings. The social revolution in Hindustan was motivated by vile interests and implemented with stupidity, but whatever its criminality England was 'the unconscious tool of history in bringing about that revolution'. And whatever bitterness the spectacle of the crumbling of an ancient world may have for our personal feelings,

we have the right, in point of history, to exclaim with Goethe:
> *Sollte diese Qual uns quälen,*
> *Da sie unsre Lust vermehrt,*
> *Hat nicht Myriaden Seelen*
> *Timurs Herrschaft aufgezehrt?* (ibid: 307)[14]

Having terminated his article with the supremely confident assertion that the direction of Indian history was headed towards the long-run benefit of humanity, Marx replied to Engels on 14 June 1853. He summarized what he had written in 'The British Rule In India', and informed him that he had explained the stationary character of Asia by combining Engels's functionalist theory that irrigation was the business of the central government with his own theory of the village community's role in supporting 'stagnant

---

13 My italics.
14 Goethe's lines are from *Westöstlicher Diwan. An Sulieka*, and can be translated as 'Should this torture then torment us / since it brings us greater pleasure? / Were not through the rule of Timur / Souls devoured without measure?.' More simply put: we, the human race, are the historical beneficiaries of mass murderers, like Tamerlane and the English imperialists, but why should we torment ourselves if these developments are inevitable?

Asiatic despotism.'[15] Marx obviously regarded these two distinct arguments as mutually supportive, rather than as competitive or contradictory. Marx then listed for Engels's benefit the twelve stereotyped village professions of India before concluding his letter with two significant observations. He noted that there was disagreement amongst the British over the nature of the property system in land before the conquest of India, and stated that 'in the broken hill-country south of Krishna, property in land does seem to have existed' (Marx and Engels, 1959: 315). But he made no comment on the significance of this fact for any theory of Asiatic distinctiveness. He also suggested, as a result of his reading, that the origins of the idea that the state was the absolute landlord had arrived in India relatively recently: 'it seems to have been the Mohammedans who first established the principle of 'no property in land' throughout the whole of Asia' (ibid).[16] This promising idea was not one he was to follow up in his subsequent Indian articles.

Marx did follow up 'The British Rule in India' with articles on the history of the East India Company, its impact upon India, and British parliamentary debates on the government of India. In all these articles he regularly compared the British treatment of the Indians with their treatment of the Irish — the long-term results of which had been manifest in the Irish famine. In a brief essay, 'India',[17] Marx analysed the revenue extraction and landed property systems which the British had established in India, namely the *zemindari* and *ryotwari* systems.[18] He described the imposition of both systems by the British as 'agrarian revolutions', although they differed remarkably from each other. The *zemindari* system was an 'aristocratic' revolution albeit a caricature of 'English landlordism' — introduced by the British in the Bengal presidency. Here, following British authorities, Marx asserted that the British dispossessed the peasantry of their hereditary claims to the soil in favour of native tax-gatherers — the *zemindari*. By contrast the *ryotwari* system was a 'democratic' revolution — albeit a caricature of French peasant proprietorship — and was introduced by the British in the Bombay and Madras presidencies (Marx and Engels, 1959: 78). Here the native nobility 'were reduced with the common people to the

15 As we noted above (p. 87, n. 7) Marx has edited Engels's idea, and neglected the role of the provinces and communes in irrigation management. There is no known objection by Engels to this modification.

16 Here Marx was almost certainly relying on Campbell's *Modern India: A Sketch of the System of Civil Government* (1852). The latter also wrote that the tendency of the Muslims has always been to 'the formation of grand empires, having nothing feudal in their composition, but everything centralized — the only aristocracy being official, and the officials the creatures of the sovereign' — a passage which appears in Marx's notebooks of the period.

17 Written on 19 July 1853 and published in the *New York Daily Tribune* on 5 August 1853 — see Marx and Engels (1959: 77–80).

18 Marx's spellings.

holding of minute fields'. In both cases the implementation of the revolutions was motivated by a simple objective: the maximization of taxation revenue for the British, with predictably hyper-exploitative fiscal expropriations of the direct producers. Marx summarized the consequences in a graphic comparison:

Thus in Bengal, we have a combination of English landlordism, of the Irish middleman system, of the Austrian system, transforming the landlord into the tax-gatherer, and of *the Asiatic system making the State the real landlord.*[19] In Madras and Bombay we have a French peasant proprietor who is at the same time a serf and a *métayer*[20] of the State. The drawbacks of all these various systems accumulate upon him without his enjoying any of their redeeming features. (ibid: 79)

Marx's summary is intriguing for three reasons. First, he believed that the imposed British 'social revolutions' had not entailed the export to India of mature capitalist relations of production, but rather of pre-capitalist (and capitalist) exploitative relations which were not progressive by contemporary British standards. Second, he believed none the less that these systems marked a progressive step forward from 'the Asiatic system'. Finally, Marx also plainly accepted that the British India of his day still contained legacies, albeit caricatures, of pre-British production systems, including the Asiatic.[21]

None the less the enduring motif of Marx's Indian writings is the memory of his hymn to the progressive character of British imperialism, and its indispensable role in smashing what he would later call the AMP. As he put it in 'The Future Results of the British Rule in India', his final Indian article of 1853: 'England has to fulfil a double mission in India: one destructive, the other regenerating – the annihilation of old Asiatic society, and the laying of the material foundations of Western society in Asia' (ibid: 82). The English were creating the political unification of India through modern communication technologies, especially the railways; introducing a free press; creating a native intellectual class; and bringing mainland India into the orbit of European civilization.[22] Although the *zemindari* and *ryotwari* systems were 'abominable', Marx reasoned that they were progressive because they were two distinct forms of private property in land – 'the great desideratum of Asiatic society' (ibid).

In retrospect it is fascinating how rapidly Marx expected British industrial

---

19 My italics.

20 Marx's italics.

21 The passage thus provides some warrant for later Marxists who have tried to analyse Third World social formations as combinations or 'articulations' of different modes of production.

22 These passages should tempt every non-English modern liberal or socialist reader to make Gandhi's famous riposte: when asked what he thought about English civilization he replied 'I think it would be a good idea!'.

capitalism to transform India and Hindu civilization: capitalism would break up the 'self-sufficient inertia' of the villages and dissolve the hereditary divisions of labour 'upon which rest the Indian castes, those decisive impediments to Indian progress and Indian power'. However, Marx observed caustically that the British gifts, the destruction of Asiatic society and the regeneration of India, were not motivated by benign altruism. After all, he asked, have the bourgeoisie ever effected progress 'without dragging individuals and peoples through blood and dirt, through misery and degradation?' (ibid: 84−5). Marx confidently assured his readers that India's fate was both inevitable and that the rest of the world not yet in the capitalist orbit had a similar rendezvous with destiny. But on the bright side of the dialectic, history's invisible hand was at work: the fate of India was part and parcel of the realization by capitalism of 'the material basis of the new world', socialism. When capital had fulfilled its civilizing mission 'then only will human progress cease to resemble that hideous pagan idol, who would not drink the nectar but from the skulls of the slain' (ibid: 87).

The *Grundrisse*

Human progress is also a central theme of the *Grundrisse*. These notebooks, composed in 1857−8, were Marx's first extended analyses which prepared him for the writing of *Capital*. The *Grundrisse der Kritik der politischen Ökonomie* is a formidably dense and user-hostile text, but then it was not meant for publication. These features, inevitably, have made it popular amongst Marxologists, although it is difficult to see it as anything more than what its first editor's title suggested − a set of outlines for the critique of political economy. The claims made for the *Grundrisse* by its more scholastically intoxicated enthusiasts are unacceptable.[23] For our purposes the key passages are located in the 'Formen' a small segment of the *Grundrisse* devoted to the analysis of 'forms which precede capitalist production'. Since these texts are now widely available (Hobsbawm, 1964; Nicolaus, 1973) we can dispense with full citation except for the key 'Asiatic' passages and where a contestable point needs confirmation.

The 'Formen' have created much controversy. At one extreme they have been described as 'an historical essay on the nature, origin, and transformation of property in land' (Elster, 1986a: 188), and at another as an essay in

23 The pinnacle of *Grundrisse* hyperbole is the claim that: 'It is . . . the centrepiece of Marx's thought' and that 'In a sense, none of Marx's work is complete, but the completest of them is the *Grundrisse*' (McLellan, 1973: 14 and 25). These eccentric notions of completeness and of the location of intellectual centres ignore *Capital* Volume I, Marx's most complete work, both intellectually and aesthetically. The 'Formen' passages in the *Grundrisse* have also been described as 'the only coherent text written by Marx on the AMP', which entails notion of coherence even stranger than McLellan's notion of completeness (Skalnik and Pokora, 1966: 187).

'dialectical logic and retrospective reconstruction' (Lubasz, 1984: 465).[24] It is ironic that the first judgement is that of a philosopher while the second is that of a historian. Both judgements are insightful and yet simultaneously too generous and unfair. They are too generous because they credit these writings with an analytical coherence which they do not possess. They are unfair because one cannot neglect either the philosophical themes in these writings or the authentic historical data upon which Marx drew. The 'Formen' are notes in the philosophy of history. Examination of the pertinent 'Asiatic' asides in these passages supports this conclusion.

The first key 'Asiatic' passage in the 'Formen' occurs over three obscurely written pages. Discussing the presuppositions of capitalism Marx notes that the release of the worker from the soil as his natural workshop is required: 'hence dissolution of small, free landed property as well as of *communal landownership resting on the oriental commune*' (Marx 1973e: 471).[25] In both these forms of property there is a 'natural unity of labour with its material presuppositions': the labourer regards others in these circumstances as members of communities, and the purpose of labour is subsistence rather than wealth creation. The 'naturally arisen spontaneous community' — that is the family, or extended family (clan) — was a *'presupposition for the communal appropriation (temporary) and utilization of land'*. (ibid: 472).[26] Pastoral life preceded settled agriculture, according to Marx, and the original pastoral community was altered depending upon the 'various external, climatic, physical etc.' conditions under which it settled (ibid). Marx then commented on these communities in a series of disjointed notes. The least intelligible portions of these notes on the first form of landed property in the extended excerpt which follows are underlined and numbered.

The earth is the great workshop, the arsenal which furnishes both means and materials of labour, as well as the seat, the *base*[27] of the community. They relate *naïvely* to it as the *property of the community*, of community producing and reproducing

24 Support for Lubasz's rather than Elster's interpretation can be found in a typically obscure passage which precedes the 'Formen': 'In order to develop the laws of bourgeois economy, therefore, it is not necessary to write the *real history of the relations of production*. But the correct observation and deduction of these laws, as having themselves become in history, always leads to primary equations — like the empirical numbers e.g. in natural science — which point towards a past lying behind the system. These indications, together with a correct grasp of the present, then also offer the key to the understanding of the past — a work in its own right which, it is to be hoped, we shall be able to undertake as well' (Marx, 1973e: 460—1). This passage suggests that Marx believed that the history of pre-capitalist societies could be logically deduced from the knowledge of capitalist society, the results of which he promised to deliver at a later stage — which, given the context, may refer to the 'Formen'.

25 My italics.

26 Italics in original.

27 All italics in this passage are in the original.

itself in living labour. Each individual conducts himself only as a link, as a member of the this community as proprietor or possessor. The *real appropriation* through the labour process happens under these *pressupositions*, which are not themselves the product of labour, but appear as its natural or *divine presuppositions*. (1) This form, with the same land-relation as its foundation, can realize itself in very different ways. (2) E.g. it is not in the least a contradiction to it that, as in most of the *Asiatic* landforms, the *comprehensive unity* standing above all these little communities appears as the higher *proprietor* or as the *sole proprietor*; the real communities hence only as hereditary possessors. Because the *unity* is the real proprietor and the real presupposition of communal property, it follows that this unity can appear as a *particular* entity above the many real particular communities, where the individual is then in fact propertyless, or, property − i.e. the relation of the individual to the *natural conditions* of labour and of reproduction as belonging to him, as the objective, nature-given, inorganic body of his subjectivity − appears mediated for him through a cession by the total unity − a unity realized in the form of the despot, the father of the many communities − to the individual, through the mediation of the particular commune. The surplus product − which is, incidentally, determined by law in consequence of the real appropriation through labour − thereby automatically belongs to this highest unity. Amidst oriental despotism and the propertylessness which seems legally to exist there, this clan or communal property exists in fact as the foundation, created mostly by a combination of manufactures and agriculture within the small commune, which thus becomes altogether self-sustaining, and contains all the conditions of production and reproduction within itself. (3) A part of their surplus labour belongs to the higher community, which exists ultimately as a *person* and this surplus labour takes the form of tribute (4) etc., as well as of common labour for the exaltation of the unity, partly of the real despot, partly of the imagined clan-being, the god. Now, in so far as it actually realizes itself in labour, this kind of communal property can appear either in the form where the little communes vegetate independently alongside one another, and where inside them, the individual with his family work independently on the lot assigned to them (5a) (a certain amount of labour for the *communal reserves, insurance* so to speak, and to *meet the expenses of the community as such*, i.e. for war, religion etc.; this is the first occurrence of the lordly *dominium* in the most original sense, e.g. in the Slavonic commune,[28] in the Rumanian etc. Therein lies the transition to villeinage etc.); or the unity may extend to the communality of labour itself, (5b) which may be a formal system, as in Mexico, Peru especially, among the early Celts, a few clans of India. The communality can, further, appear within the clan system more in a situation where the unity is represented in a chief of the clan-family, or as a relation of the patriarchs among one another. Depending on that, a more despotic or a more democratic form of this community system. (6) The communal conditions of real appropriation through labour, *aqueducts*, very important among the Asiatic peoples; means of communication etc. then appear as the work of the higher unity − of the despotic regime hovering over the little communes. (7) Cities proper here form

---

28 This reference supports those who believe Marx regarded the Slavonic − commune as a variant of the Oriental commune − for example, Melotti (1977: 30).

alongside these villages only at exceptionally good points for external trade; or where the head of the state and his satraps exchange their revenue (surplus product) for labour, spend it as labour fund. (8) (ibid: 472–4)

This passage, taken as whole, is unclear, to be very charitable. Consider the underlined passages in order.

1   The real appropriation through the labour process happens under these presuppositions, which are not themselves the product of labour, but appear as its natural or divine presuppositions. Marx seems to suggest that in the earliest communities the appropriation of nature appears to the direct producers as natural or divinely ordained. The presuppositions of such production – that is, the notions the individual has of himself as a member of the community – are not the consequences of the past history of labour (or culture); rather they are the outcome of a primordial structure: the primitive communism of the clan.

2   This form, with the same land-relation as its foundation, can realize itself in very different ways. Marx suggests that the first form of landed property, based on the naturally arisen clan community, can be found in many variations. This idea is clear, but the import of its elucidation in the next two 'sentences' of Hegelese are anything but, and no claim to a definitive deciphering can be made here. All that can be said with confidence about this passage is that Marx apparently believed that examples of this community could be found in Asia and that the presence of hierarchical relations between a higher unity (or patriarchal despot) and the communes did not mean that such forms were examples of a systematically different type of communal form.

3   Amidst oriental despotism and the propertylessness which seems legally to exist there, this clan or communal property exists in fact as the foundation, created mostly by a combination of manufactures and agriculture within the small commune, which thus becomes altogether self-sustaining, and contains all the conditions of production and reproduction within itself. In this passage, of pellucid clarity by comparison with some of the others, Marx suggests that communal property relations exist in oriental societies, *despite* political or juridical appearances. He also suggests a 'relations of production – productive forces' relationship between the communal property relations and the production system of the autarkic village community based on a unity of manufacture and handicrafts.

4   [T]his surplus labour takes the form of tribute. Marx explicitly asserts that the characteristic of surplus labour – the defining feature of a mode of production for Marxists – in the Orient is that it is paid as tribute to the higher unity, a form of surplus labour which he later goes on to contrast with the forms typical of the ancient commune based on slavery, or the feudal manor.

5a and 5b   [T]his kind of communal property can appear either in the form where the little communes vegetate independently alongside one another, and where inside them, the individual with his family work independently on the lot assigned to them ... or the unity may extend to the communality of labour itself. Despite the lengthy and difficult parentheses which interrupt this passage its import is clear: Marx finds considerable variation within the first form of landed property. It is characterized either by total autarky with individual families labouring on separate plots or by communal agrarian production (which he thought was commonly found amongst Indian clans). However, this variation is within the same generic species of community.

6   Depending on that, a more despotic or a more democratic form of this community system. Moreover, the communes also have a further, political variation. Where the chief of the clan-family rules then the commune is despotic; where the elders govern it is more democratic. If we combine 5 and 6 we can construct a typology of four variants of this first form of landed property: the communal-despotic, the individual-despotic, the communal-democratic and the individual-democratic, as shown in table 3.1. However, Marx's notes are by no means as clear as this reconstruction might suggest, and my labelling of the elements of this typology, Community 1−4 is *not* intended to suggest that Marx himself said anything so explicit.

7   The communal conditions of real appropriation through labour, aqueducts, very important among the Asiatic peoples; means of communication etc. then appear as the work of the higher unity − of the despotic regime hovering over the little communes. This passage, with its references to water management, is the most Wittfogelian aside in the 'Formen' but it is also a denial of some of the inferences which Wittfogel wished to draw. The first part of the sentence indicates that the importance of aqueducts amongst Asiatic peoples is merely a particularly important version of the more general communal appropriation of nature found in examples of this

Table 3.1 The implicit typology of the first form

		Political form	
		Despotic	Democratic
Property form	Communal	Community 1	Community 3
	Individual	Community 2	Community 4

first form of pre-capitalist society — extensive water-management was not a necessary trait of the first form. Marx also suggests that these first forms are pervaded by an ideological illusion. The direct producers make a fetish of the despot, or higher unity, vesting the despot rather than themselves with the power and capacity which their works have demonstrated.

8 Cities proper here form alongside these villages only at exceptionally good points for external trade; or where the head of the state and his satraps exchange their revenue (surplus product) for labour, spend it as labour fund. Marx briefly described the key features of the cities which form on the basis of this first landed form. They are said to have the characteristics which he had — following Richard Jones and Bernier — attributed to the Indian city in his journalism. At most these cities were sites for limited inter-village trade and the luxury consumption of the ruler and his agents.

After this densely packed passage describing the first form of pre-capitalist landed property — which evidently contains many of the elements of what was subsequently referred to as the Asiatic mode of production — Marx then discussed other pre-capitalist forms. The second was the *ancient* or *classical* commune, and the third the *Germanic* commune. By contrast with the first, the second was described as the 'the product of a more active, historic life' (Marx: 1973e: 474). This second, ancient or classical commune, which Marx thought had manifested itself amongst the Greeks, Romans and Jews (ibid: 477), was more historically progressive because it contained one of the presuppositions of capitalism, namely private property. This second form combined private property rights for the citizen of the commune with collective or communal property. But Marx presented no clear explanation of why this commune developed differently from its Asiatic cousin. Nor did he provide an explanation of the evolution of the third major communal form, the Germanic. The latter differed from the other two communes, according to Marx, because the individual member neither shared in communal property as in the Asiatic form, nor was a private owner and shareholder in the collective property, as in the ancient form. The German commune, based on a primitive individualism, did not have the collectivist mentality of the Asiatic form, nor the political form created by the ancient city.

Marx then contrasted these three forms (the Asiatic, the classical and the Germanic) on the dimension of urban and rural social relations:

The history of classical antiquity is the history of cities, but of cities founded on landed property and agriculture; Asiatic history is a kind of *indifferent unity of town and countryside*[29] (the really large cities must be regarded here merely as royal

29 My italics.

camps, as works of artifice [*Superfötation*] erected over the economic construction proper); the Middle Ages (Germanic period) begins with the land as the seat of history whose further development then moves forward in the contradiction between town and countryside; the modern [age] is the urbanization of the countryside, not ruralization of the city as in antiquity. (ibid: 479)

In further asides Marx elaborated the distinctive features of the Asiatic form when contrasted with other pre-capitalist forms: 'In the Asiatic form (at least, predominantly), the individual has no property, only possession; the real proprietor, proper, is the commune – hence property only as *communal property* in land' (ibid: 484). By contrast with the other pre-capitalist forms the Asiatic commune is 'the substance of which the individual appears as a mere accident (ibid).

Marx then made his first attempt to sum up his discussion (ibid: 485–6). The key point was that all these pre-capitalist forms shared certain features in common, namely:

landed property and agriculture form the basis of the economic order;
the object of production is use-value rather than exchange-value;
appropriation occurs 'not through labour, but presupposed to labour (ibid: 485);[30] and
the 'individual's' relationship to nature is mediated by the 'naturally arisen, spontaneous, more or less historically developed and modified presence of the individual as member of a commune' (ibid: 486).

In parenthesis Marx argued that the survival of the first communes required the maintenance of their objective presuppositions, but they could be corroded by change, especially that induced by developments in productive and demographic systems:

Production itself, the advance of population (this too belongs with production), necessarily suspends these conditions little by little; destroys them instead of reproducing them etc., and, with that, the communal system declines and falls, together with the property relations on which it was based. The Asiatic form necessarily hangs on most tenaciously and for the longest time. This is due to its presupposition that the individual does not become independent *vis-à-vis* the commune; that there is a self-sustaining cycle of production, unity of agriculture and manufacture etc. (ibid: 486)

As in his Indian journalism, Marx was therefore committed to the thesis that the Asiatic was the most resistant to change of all pre-capitalist forms. But he did not say that it was wholly immune to the corrosive changes

30 This phrase is profoundly Hegelian/confusing/ambiguous. It seems, judging by the context, to suggest that nature is appropriated naturally in these forms and therefore that there is no exploitation of labour – which is curious given the references to 'tribute', 'slavery' and 'serfdom' elsewhere.

brought about by advances in production and population. Two further passages in the 'Formen' occur soon after which more or less elaborate the same theses.[31]

Having presented the most important 'Asiatic' and 'oriental' asides in the 'Formen' we must ask why they were there. What was Marx doing in the *Grundrisse?* First, Marx was reiterating his general emphasis upon the primacy of production, with which he began the *Grundrisse.* He wanted to establish both that the characteristics of production in pre-capitalist societies explained their general features, and that production in all these pre-capitalist forms differed from that which takes place in capitalist societies.

Second, the 'Formen' posed the issues of the origins and specificity of capitalism. But they were more directed towards elucidating the latter than the former. Marx emphasized that capitalism is distinguished from all previous modes of production by the complete separation of the direct producers from the means of production, and the monopoly of the means of production by one class: but the existence of wage-labour is the *differentia specifica* of capitalism. By contrast in all previous modes of production the labourer was still tied to the 'community' in patriarchal, tribal and feudal bonds. All previous modes of production are antonyms of capitalism because in them the direct producers are not separated from the means of production. It follows that addressing the origins of capitalism must involve explaining how the separation of the direct producers from the means of production, and the creation of capital and capitalists, occurred. Marx made a few gestures in the direction of explaining the origins of capitalism but this task

31 1 'Slavery and serfdom are thus only further developments of the form of property resting on the clan system. They necessarily modify all the latter's forms. *They can do this least of all in the Asiatic form. In the self-sustaining unity of agriculture and manufacture, on which this form rests, conquest is not so necessary a condition as where landed property, agriculture are exclusively predominant.* On the other hand, since in this form the individual never becomes a proprietor but only a possessor, he is at bottom himself, the property, the slave of him in whom the unity of the commune exists, and slavery here neither suspends the conditions of labour nor modifies the essential relation' (Marx, 1973e: 493 — my italics). This passage is relevant to Marx's remarks about 'general slavery' in the Orient.

    2 'The older and more traditional the mode of production itself — and this lasts a long time in agriculture; *even more in the oriental supplementation of agriculture with manufactures —* i.e. the longer the real process of appropriation remains constant, the more constant will be the old forms of property and hence the community generally. Where there is already a separation between the commune members as private proprietors (on one side), and they themselves as the urban commune and proprietors of the commune's territorium on the other, there the conditions already arise in which the individual can lose his property ... *In the oriental form this loss is hardly possible, except by means of altogether external influences,* since the individual member of the commune never enters into the relation of freedom towards it in which he could lose his (objective, economic) bond with it. He is rooted to the spot, ingrown. This also has to do with the combination of manufacture and agriculture, of town (village) and countryside' (ibid: 494).

did not become the central thrust of the 'Formen'. Indeed, as several critics have observed, all of Marx's *obiter dicta* on this question in the 'Formen' are circular. To 'explain' the origins of capitalism Marx describes the elements constitutive of capitalism, which obviously involves the use of elements of the *explanandum* in the *explanans* (Baechler, 1975: 13−19). The 'Formen' passages essentially do no more than contrast capitalism with pre-capitalist societies.

Third, Marx contrasts three pre-capitalist forms with each other in the 'Formen'. They all have their origin in a natural, spontaneous clan community. But because of a variety of material and geographical circumstances they have evolved differently. The Asiatic form is older than the other two. It has the greatest amount of surviving communal property and its individual members are the least conscious of themselves as individuals with juridical and political rights. It is also the most resistant to change, and has the least developed class relationships (although Marx does not use this expression in the 'Formen'). When Marx pointed elliptically to 'the general slavery of the Orient' (Marx, 1973e: 495) he was indicating that in the Orient, unlike the slavery of the ancient commune, or the serfdom of feudalism, the worker was not regarded as among the 'natural conditions of production for a third individual or community' (ibid). The 'general slavery of the Orient' described only a condition in which individualism was absent, in which the individual was conscious of himself only as part of the community; it did not describe a set of production relations:

In the self-sustaining unity of agriculture of manufacture, on which this form rests, conquest is not so necessary a condition as where landed property, agriculture are exclusively predominant. On the other hand, since in this form the individual never becomes a proprietor but only a possessor, he is at bottom himself, the property, the slave of him in whom the unity of the commune exists, and slavery here neither suspends the conditions of labour nor modifies the essential relations. (ibid: 493)

There is a fourth interpretation of what Marx was doing in the 'Formen' passages in the *Grundrisse*: the argument that he was seeking to provide a Hegelian demonstration of the origins of capitalism. This argument has found a recent persuasive advocate (Lubasz, 1984). Lubasz's 'genetic analysis' suggests that Marx arrived at his conception of the AMP through 'dialectical logic', through 'retrospective rational reconstruction'. In Marx's Hegelian language the capitalist mode of production is defined as a higher systematic unity, whereas the AMP is defined as an indifferent unity (that is, a non-systematically differentiated social order). The AMP was therefore not arrived at by Marx primarily in order to explain, describe or summarize the characteristics of ancient Asia, but rather was invented as a 'logical' solution in a Hegelian explanation of the origins of capitalism. It was conceptualized as an indifferent unity because all Hegelian 'explanations' of change and development start from indifferent unities which, through the working out of their internal contradictions, evolve into more complex and differentiated unities. The AMP is analogous to the family in Hegel's *Philosophy of Right*, the stage of felt reason, the natural, infantile condition of humanity. The genesis of the Asiatic form in the *Grundrisse*, what would later be called the AMP, is accounted for by Marx's need to define a starting point for the dialectical development of capitalism in history. It is therefore hardly surprising that it causes exceptional difficulties for Marxist historians. It was not a concept intended to aid the explanation of certain features of actual Asiatic societies. Indeed:

Having so very little knowledge of Asia as he did made it all the easier for Marx to impose upon the few data he did have the *shape* called for by dialectical logic and the *content* suggested by the categories of mid-nineteenth century, western European capitalism ... [But] why should Marx have identified primitive communism as specifically Asiatic ... The short answer ... is that Marx believed primitive communism to have been originally, but by no means exclusively, Asiatic. Marx thought primitive communism to have been a more or less world-wide phenomenon, with Roman, Germanic, Celtic, Slavic and other variants. The primitive communism of Asia was in his eyes simply the aboriginal form, the *Urform* from whose structure one could derive later patterns of communal and of private ownership. (Lubasz, 1984: 460–1)[32]

This 'Hegelian' reading of the 'Formen' passages is persuasive, precisely because it makes sense of these very obscure texts. However, two important qualifications must be made about Lubasz's thesis. First, asides elsewhere in Marx's writings suggest that systematically 'Asiatic' characteristics (particularly tributary structures of exploitation) are attributed by Marx to Asiatic societies and regimes. These comments, as we shall see, cannot easily be understood as suggestions that Marx thought that such social formations were simply specimens of primitive communism or of feudalism. Second, Marx's modifications of his assertions about pre-capitalist societies were the results of his critical encounters with mid- and late nineteenth-century history and anthropology. If he was attempting to fit his sources into the Hegelian schema he had devised in the 1850s then he conspicuously failed to achieve this fit satisfactorily. As with so much of Marx's writings

---

32 Lubasz's argument has the apparent merit of dissolving the problem diagnosed by Daniel Thorner (Thorner, 1966): how could the AMP be the first in a linear progression of modes of production and yet be incapable of change? Lubasz answers that the 'Formen' passages make it plain that the Asiatic form is merely one form of primitive communism amongst others. But, *pace* Lubasz, the nagging question remains of why Marx did not put primitive communism rather than the AMP first in the list he gives in the preface. (See below, pp. 104 ff.) The Preface has the Asiatic first in a list of 'progressive' formations – implicitly contrasting all these progressive formations with the non-progressive formation of primitive communism. Marx's lack of clarity, as usual, has generated endless possibilities for controversy.

the reader is left chasing loose ends and unravelling arguments which eventually lead nowhere.[33]

During the composition of the *Grundrisse* Marx penned a brief note for the *New York Daily Tribune* on 'Lord Canning's Proclamation and Land Tenure in India'.[34] When Canning, then the governer-general of India, annexed the statelet of Oudh, he proclaimed that the proprietary right in the soil of Oudh was confiscated by the British Government which would dispose of that right as it saw fit. This declaration revived

the discussion as to the land tenures of India – a subject upon which there have been great disputes and differences of opinion in times past ... The great point in this controversy is, what is the exact position which the zemindars, talukdars or sirdars, so called, hold in the economical system of India? Are they properly to be considered as landed proprietors or as mere tax-gatherers?

It is agreed that in India, as in most Asiatic countries, the ultimate ownership in the soil vests the Government; but while one party to this controversy insists that the Government is to be looked upon as a soil [sic!] proprietor, letting out the land on shares to the cultivators, the other side maintains that in substance the land in India is just as much private property as in any country whatever – this alleged property in the Government being nothing more than the derivation of title from the sovereign, theoretically acknowledged in all countries, the codes of which are based on the feudal law and substantially acknowledged in all countries whatever is the power of the Government to levy taxes on the land to the extent of the needs of

33 One ingenious solution to some of these problems, and one which supports Lubasz' reading of the 'Formen', has been suggested by Ernest Gellner (1986 and personal correspondence). The idea advanced here is that Marx and Engels did not have a theory of primitive communism before reading Morgan. It was late in their lives – after reading Lewis Morgan, the pioneering materialist anthropologist – that the idea hit them that there had been a conflictless, classless social order at the beginning of time – whence Engels's belated alteration of the text of the *Communist Manifesto* in 1888 to say that the history of all hitherto existing societies *in recorded history* is the history of class struggle. Until reading Morgan, Marx and Engels retained the Hegelian schema of history – history begins with Asiatic despotism. Post-Morgan historical materialism begins with primitive communism, as shown by the writings of the late Marx and *The Origins of the Family, Private Property and the State*. This solution to many of the textual problems which surround the AMP is inventive but is unfortunately empirically problematic. It is true that *The German Ideology* is vague about the nature of the first tribal societies, and bereft of references to anthropological studies. However, even this text refers specifically to 'tribal ownership' (Marx, 1977: 161). Moreover, Marx refers in *A Contribution to the Critique of Political Economy* (Marx, 1970: 33–4) and in *Capital* (Marx, 1976: 171) to forms of spontaneous primitive communal property – that is, to primitive communism – and both works were published before he had read Morgan. In the posthumously published *Theories of Surplus Value*, also composed before Morgan was available, reference is also made to 'the Asiatic communal system (primitive communism)' (Marx, 1978, III: 422–3). It seems fairer therefore to argue that Morgan enabled Marx and Engels to flesh out their sense of what primitive communism was like with some apparently hard empirical evidence. It is sounder to argue that Morgan enabled Marx to 'go public' on the 'Formen' – as opposed to suggesting that only with the arrival of Morgan were Marx and Engels able to renounce their Hegelian heritage.

34 Written 25 May 1858, published 7 June 1858 (Marx and Engels, 1959: 191–4).

the Government, quite independent of all considerations, except as a mere matter of policy, of the convenience of the owners. (Marx and Engels, 1959: 191)

Marx then described the controversy that ensued between those who held that the *zemindars* and the *talukdars* were the real owners of the land, and those who held that

> by the original Hindu institutions, the property of the land was in the village corporations, in which resided the power of allotting it out to individuals for cultivation while the zemindars and talukdars were in their origin nothing but officers of the Government, appointed to look after, to collect, and to pay over to the prince the assessment due from the village. (ibid: 192)[35]

These Indian passages are in distinct contrast with those in the 'Formen'. Here India is recognizably not a society of primitive communism or post-primitive communism; and, moreover, Marx did not deny the possibility that private property existed in this India. However, he plainly did not accept that contemporary India was obviously 'feudal'. These pieces of journalism fuel the controversy over whether the AMP refers to the epoch of primitive communism, or that just succeeding it (as suggested by the 'Formen'), or to a more progressive, or later, historical epoch, and also the arguments about the precise location of distinct Indian societies and regimes under such headings.[36]

A Contribution to the Critique of Political Economy

Only with the Preface to *A Contribution to the Critique of Political Economy*, published in 1859, did Marx invent the term 'Asiatic mode of production'. Having announced it to the world he subsequently never used the term publicly again.[37] However, the AMP made its debut in what is widely, and justly, regarded as the statement of historical materialism, the one occasion where Marx, as he said himself, summarized the general conclusions at

---

35 Habib misleadingly suggests that this opinion was firmly shared by Marx (Habib, 1983: 100). In fact Marx merely dispassionately reports both points of view.

36 Lubasz writes that Marx 'simply *ignored* information to the effect that in some parts of India "private" property did exist; he ignored − though he faithfully reported them − the current debates in Parliament about the nature and variety of Indian forms of land-holding; and he ignored what he had read, to the effect that the absence of private property in land had not been established in India until the coming of the Muslim conquerors' (Lubasz, 1984: 468). This mode of presenting Marx's arguments is contentious. Marx's 'Asiatic forms' in the 'Formen' referred to primitive communes in India, and not to (then) contemporary India in the immediate post-Mughal era. The information which he 'ignored' was therefore not relevant to a discussion of primitive communal forms in India.

37 There are only two other close-run mentions. In *Capital*, Volume I, Marx refers to the 'primitive oriental' system and in the unpublished *Theories of Surplus Value* reference is made to the 'Asiatic communal system (primitive communism)'

which he had arrived. This statement in the Preface was never subsequently altered, revised or criticized by either Marx or Engels. The AMP was named first in the list of the modes of production which Marx had identified as historically significant: 'In broad outline, the Asiatic, ancient, feudal and modern bourgeois modes of production may be designated as epochs marking progress in the economic development of society' (Marx, 1970: 21). This statement was not elaborated in the Preface, nor in the text of *A Contribution to the Critique of Political Economy*. Consequently it is uncertain whether Marx intended his list to describe *either* the necessary, programmed and chronologically ordered list of modes of production through which all societies (or alternatively, humanity as a whole) must travel; *or* the modes of production which have in fact existed in world history, sometimes simultaneously, but are distinguishable from each other by the degree of economic development which they facilitated.

The first interpretation has been Marxist orthodoxy for much of the twentieth century — whether or not the AMP has been accepted or dropped from the hallowed list. But there is no positive warrant for this interpretation in the Preface itself. Admittedly the Preface is not evidence against this interpretation. However, no creative interpolation is involved in accepting the second reading, which is the most reasonable contextual construal of the meaning of this key sentence. Much hinges on the choice between the two interpretations.[38]

There is a further difficulty with this list of 'epochs marking progress in the economic development of society'. The Asiatic is the first mentioned. It therefore seems reasonable to conclude that along with the other three the AMP is included in a group which is implicitly contrasted with an epoch which did not mark any progress in the economic development of society — that is, primitive communism.[39] But this reasonable construal of the text immediately raises two thorny problems. First, this interpretation is at odds with the passages in the 'Formen' which seem to take the Asiatic form to be a variant of primitive communism. And second, by implication, it generates the well-known paradox of a progressive mode of production which Marx elsewhere implies is stagnant and incapable of further development. In other words this interpretation places a severe burden on any unilineal interpretation of historical materialism.[40]

The term 'Asiatic mode of production' does not figure elsewhere in *A Contribution to the Critique of Political Economy*. However, in chapter 1, where Marx was concerned to define the nature of the commodity in capitalist society, he paused to compare the system of labour under capitalism

38 See pp. 162–75.
39 See footnote 33 above.
40 See pp. 176–82.

with patriarchal production, the services and dues in kind of the Middle Ages, and with

communal labour in its spontaneously evolved form as we find it among all civilized nations at the dawn of their history ... [41]

The communal system on which this mode of production is based prevents the labour of an individual from becoming private labour and his product the private product of a separate individual; it causes individual labour to appear rather as the direct function of a member of the social organization. (ibid: 33−4)

Some scholars have taken this passage to be an explicit reference to the AMP − and believe that Marx here demonstrates his conviction that communal property, which is the foundation of the AMP, is not restricted by his geographical prefix, and can be found outside of Asia as well (Bailey and Llobera, 1981: 31). This assertion is surely more than this textual evidence will bear. Marx did not name the AMP in this aside. Given its context, there is greater, or at least equal, legitimacy for the view that he was referring to primitive communism rather than the AMP. Yet this disagreement is symptomatic of a problem which bedevils Marxists and Marxologists alike: did Marx understand the AMP to be a sub-set (or indeed the primary and exemplary version) of the primitive communist mode of production; or did he regard the AMP as the mode of production which marks a or the transitional form out of primitive communism? These questions can be simplified: how old is the AMP? And how does it differ, if at all, from the primitive communist mode of production?

Marx did not answer these questions adequately, even by implication, in his subsequent writings. He gave birth to the AMP in the Preface but thereafter left it without a baptism, confirmation or indeed the last rites.

Theories of Surplus Value

Marx's voluminous (posthumously published) critique of the classical political economists known as *Theorien über den Mehrwert* or *Theories of Surplus*

---

41 In an accompanying footnote Marx wrote 'At present an absurdly biased view is widely held, namely that primitive communal property is a specifically Slavonic, or even an exclusively Russian, phenomenon. It is an early form which can be found among Romans, Teutons and Celts, and of which a whole collection of diverse patterns (though sometimes only remnants survive) is still in existence in India. A careful study of Asiatic, particularly Indian, forms of communal property would indicate that the disintegration of different forms of primitive communal ownership gives rise to diverse forms of property. For instance, various prototypes of Roman and Germanic private property can be traced back to certain forms of Indian communal property' (Marx, 1970: 33). This note was directed against populist and romantic agrarian anarchist ideas then emerging amongst sections of the European intelligentsia. It was also clearly based on Marx's writings in the *Grundrisse*. However, it is irritatingly unclear whether Marx regarded the primitive communal property under discussion as an element of the primitive communist mode of production, or of the AMP, or of both.

Value, was written between January 1862 and July 1863. There are two major passages of 'Asiatic' interest in these texts. The first comes in Marx's analysis, in Volume I, of the work of Simon-Nicolas-Henri Linguet, a critic of Montesquieu, and the second is in the concluding chapter of Volume III where Marx extensively discussed the theories of Richard Jones.[42]

There is also one important aside in Marx's discussion of the concepts of productive and unproductive labour in the work of Adam Smith which shows that he had not abandoned the ideas he had elaborated in his Indian journalism. Commenting on Smith, Marx wrote that unproductive labour is

labour which is not exchanged with capital, but directly with revenue, that is, with wages or profit ... Where all labour in part still pays itself (like for example the agricultural labour of the serfs) and in part is directly exchanged for revenue (like the manufacturing labour in the cities of Asia), no capital and no wage-labour exists in the sense of bourgeois political economy. (Marx, 1978, I: 127)

The argument that Asian societies were neither capitalist nor feudal in their economic relations is reiterated in the two important commentaries on Linguet and Jones.

Linguet's *Théorie des lois civiles, ou Principes fondamentaux de la société*, written in 1767, was directed against Montesquieu. Marx regarded Linguet as a reactionary critic of bourgeois society: 'He defends Asiatic despotism against the civilised European forms of despotism; thus he defends slavery against wage-labour ... The only statement directed against Montesquieu: *l'esprit des lois, c'est la propriété*[43] shows the depth of his outlook' (ibid: 345). Linguet held the harsh view that society is born of violence, and property of usurpation, but although anti-capitalist he drew no socialist inferences from his assertions. He even argued that the condition of wage-labourers under capitalism was worse than that experienced by slaves and serfs. Asiatic slavery[44] was 'a hundred times more preferable than any other way of existing, for men reduced to having to win their livelihood by daily labour' (ibid). However, Marx insisted on distinguishing slavery, in the Asiatic sense, from Graeco-Roman slavery, notably in an aside in his discussion of the work of Jones:

The original unity between the worker and the conditions of production (abstracting from slavery, where the labourer himself belongs to the objective conditions of production) has two main forms: the Asiatic communal system (primitive communism) and small-scale agriculture based on the family (and linked with domestic industry)

---

42 See chapter 2, pp. 78−9.
43 'The spirit of the laws is property' translates Marx's rendition of Linguet's idea. The Moscow edition glosses this apparent quotation with the remark that Marx puts the passage 'Leur esprit est de consacrer la propriété' in his own words (Marx, 1978, I: 487).
44 This expression is Marx's, placed in parentheses between excerpts from Linguet.

in one form or another. Both are embryonic forms and both are equally unfitted to develop labour as *social* labour and the productive power of social labour. (Marx, 1978, III: 422–3)

This aside is the clearest equation of the Asiatic communal system with primitive communism, and important evidence for those who hold to a 'primitive' interpretation of the AMP.[45]

Marx thought so highly of Jones that fifty pages of *Theories of Surplus Value* (ibid.: 399–449) are devoted to a critical engagement with his three texts (R. Jones, 1831, 1833 and 1852). His praise was considerable because he thought that Jones was free of the ahistorical economic ideology, prevalent amongst even the best of bourgeois economists, according to which capitalism was an eternal and natural feature of human existence. Jones, by contrast, was distinguished by

what has been lacking in all English economists since Sir James Steuart, namely, a sense of the historical differences in modes of production. (Marx, 1978, III: 399). Jones marks a substantial advance on Ricardo, in his historical explanation as well as in the economic details. (ibid: 402) What distinguishes Jones from the other economists (except perhaps Sismondi) is that he emphasises that the essential feature of capital is its socially determined form, and that he reduces the whole difference between the capitalist and other modes of production to this distinct form. (ibid: 424)[46]

Jones's sense of history was evident in his treatment of rent, his systematic comparisons between capitalist and pre-capitalist modes of production, and his extension of the distinction between productive and unproductive labour which Adam Smith had, in Marx's opinion, left underdeveloped. Jones treated rent not as an invariably capitalist category but rather as a social relation which had come into existence as a pre-capitalist form of coerced labour, that is, a form of surplus labour. Marx carefully excerpted those passages from Jones which categorized various forms of rent and took care to note Jones's argument that under systems of ryot rents the sovereign was the chief landlord and that the existence and prosperity of Asian towns depended upon the local expenditure of the rental revenue of the central government (Jones, 1831: 136–8; and 1852: 73–4; Marx, 1978, III: 410 and 435). The sudden rise and collapse of Asiatic cities, such as Samarcand and Candahar,[47] was attributed by Jones to the movements of the monarch, the fortunes of the central dynasty and the varying location of the capital

45 If primitive communism and the AMP are equated, Marxism is in terrible ideological trouble, because if primitive communism is compatible with political domination there is no reason to suppose that the same will not be true of advanced communism.
46 Marx was so impressed by Jones that he was moved to exclaim that 'The ministers of the English Church seem to think more than their continental brethren' (ibid: 428).
47 Nineteenth century spellings used as by Jones and Marx.

city of the empire (Jones, 1832: 48–9; Marx, 1978, III: 416). Commenting on a relatively detailed excerpt from Jones's analysis of the Asiatic city, Marx wrote without elaborating: 'See Dr. Bernier, who compares the Indian towns to army camps. This is due to the form of landed property which exists in India' (Marx, 1978, III: 435; Jones, 1852: 73–6). The absence of critical comment suggests that Marx accepted the thesis that the state in India was the chief landowner and rent collector.

The second feature of Jones's work which Marx emphasized was his assumption that the rapid accumulation of capital and of techniques distinguished the modern capitalist era from its predecessors. Marx commented that 'to a certain extent accumulation of wealth takes place in all stages of economic development, that is, partly an expansion of the scale of production and partly the accumulation of treasure, etc.' (Marx, 1978, III: 420). Marx agreed with Jones that economic development could take place in pre-capitalist systems[48] – including, by implication, the Asiatic system. But, by contrast, capitalist accumulation was systematic, and both deeper and faster. This qualitative difference stemmed from the facts that capital rather than revenue was the chief source of investment, that capitalists, unlike rentiers, had to accumulate to survive, and that free workers were obliged to sell their labour power to capitalists on pain of starvation.

Marx thirdly praised Jones for extending Adam Smith's distinction between productive and unproductive labour. The former is labour which is performed to obtain surplus value (profit) whereas the latter is paid for out of rent. To Jones, and Marx, the empirical predominance of the former over the latter marked the triumph of the capitalist mode of production, while the widespread prevalence of the latter belonged to 'earlier modes of production' (ibid: 426). Both men again agreed that Asian, and especially Indian society, was a specimen of one of these earlier modes of production.[49]

These passages excerpted from Jones in *Theories of Surplus Value*, together with Marx's commentaries, suggest that Marx continued to believe that Asian, and especially Indian societies, were different from European pre-capitalist social formations – in their rental forms of exploitation, in the pre-eminence of their states in revenue collection and distribution, in their urban structures and in their aboriginal communal conditions of labour. Indeed one of Marx's few substantive criticisms of Jones confirms that he still had 'Asiatic' convictions. He complained that Jones had overlooked the importance of the Asiatic communal system with its unity of agriculture and industry (ibid: 417).

48 He 'thus answers those asses who imagine that no accumulation can take place without the profit yielded by capital' (Marx, 1978, III: 421).
49 Marx cites a passage (Jones, 1852: 97) in which Jones comes close to describing Asia as stagnant (Marx, 1978, III: 444).

Capital: Volumes I and III

There are five pertinent Asiatic/Indian passages in *the* text of Marx, *Capital*, Volume I, which was published in 1867. Two are not important, and one, the most extended passage, repeats material we have already encountered in Marx's writings. The first of these passages is a repetition. In chapter 1, 'The Commodity', Marx reproduced the same footnote on primitive communal property which he had published in *A Contribution to the Critique of Political Economy* (Marx, 1976: 171). The second passage which is not important occurred in chapter 3, 'Money, or the Circulation of Commodities', where Marx asserted that at the commencement of the circulation of commodities only excess amounts of use-value are converted into monetary form; gold and silver are simply social expressions for superfluity or wealth. He also took the chance to make a joke:

This naïve form of hoarding is perpetuated amongst those peoples whose traditional mode of production, aimed at fulfilling their own requirements, corresponds to a fixed and limited range of needs. This is true of the Asiatics, particularly the Indians. Vanderlint, who imagines that the prices of commodities are determined by the quantity of gold and silver to be found in it, asks himself why Indian commodities are so cheap.

Answer: because the Indians bury their money. (ibid: 228)

The third and more significant passage occurred in the main text of chapter 13, 'Co-operation'. Here Marx referred to the colossal artefacts which were constructed with simple cooperation, without an advanced division of labour, by the ancient Asiatics, Egyptians and Etruscans. He quoted at length an excerpt from from Jones's *Textbook of Lectures on the Political Economy of Nations* on the prodigious constructions of ancient civilizations, before commenting

Co-operation in the labour process, such as we find it at the beginning of human civilization, among hunting peoples or, say, as a predominant feature of the agriculture of Indian communities, is based on the one hand on the common ownership of the conditions of production, and on the other hand on the fact that in those cases the individual has as little torn himself free from the umbilical cord of his tribe or his community as a bee has from his hive. Both of these characteristics distinguish this form of co-operation from capitalist co-operation. The sporadic application of co-operation on a large scale in ancient times, in the Middle Ages, and in modern colonies, rests on direct relations of domination and servitude, in most cases on slavery. As against this, the capitalist form presupposes from the outset the free wage-labourer who sells his labour-power to capital. (ibid: 452)

Marx thus distinguished, albeit loosely, three types of cooperation: that found in primitive communism, based on common ownership of the means of production; that found in pre-capitalist modes of production, based on domination, servitude and slavery; and that prevalent in the capitalist world, based on free wage — labour.

Given that Marx cited Jones on Asiatic empires in the preceding paragraph it is reasonable to read this passage as confirmation that Marx distinguished three independent pre-capitalist social orders — the Asiatic, the slave and the feudal. But he also seemed to be classifying the Indian communities as exemplars of primitive communism. Once again he blurred the distinction between the Asiatic and primitive communist modes of production, as he also did in an intriguing footnote appended to the paragraph from which the above passage is taken:

Peasant agriculture on a small scale and production by independent artisans, both of which, on the one hand, form the basis of the feudal mode of production, and, on the other hand, appear alongside capitalist production after the dissolution of the feudal mode, equally form the economic foundation of the communities of classical antiquity at their best period, after the primitive oriental system of common ownership of land had disappeared, and before slavery had seized on production in earnest. (ibid: 452–3, footnote 21)

This footnote deservedly enjoys a special and much discussed place in the scholarship of the AMP, for three reasons. First, it suggests that 'peasant agriculture on a small scale and production by independent artisans' is common to the feudal, slave and early capitalist modes of production, but not to the primitive oriental system of common ownership (is this the AMP?). Second, the passage explicitly suggests that the 'oriental' descriptor in the label 'primitive oriental system' was not a geographical prefix, at least in Marx's mind. He clearly believed that the 'oriental' form was prevalent at the dawn of history in the European cultures in which the slave mode of production developed. This belief in turn suggests that the AMP was not confined to Asia and was not everywhere incapable of development into a higher form, but that it was a necessary first stage in the unilineal pattern of the historical development of mankind. And third, the footnote was allegedly tampered with by Engels, for unexplained reasons. The 1887 English translation of *Capital* Volume I by Aveling, Moore and Engels removed the word 'oriental' from this footnote — although it remained in the German versions of *Capital*.[50]

The fourth relevant passage in *Capital* also leaves the reader confused because Marx is again seen to identify primitive communism with the modern Asiatic state. Marx seems to have believed that the social relations of primitive communism explained the political institutions of Asiatic states. He entered a two-page digression on the Indian village in the course

50 This editorial intervention was pointed out by R. Rosdolsky — see Thorner (1966). This intervention is sometimes cited in support of the thesis that Engels abandoned the idea of the AMP — see discussion on pp. 143–6.

of chapter 14, 'The Division of Labour and Manufacture'. He used the information he had gathered for his Indian articles and his writings in the *Grundrisse* in the 1850s to make an explicit comparison between the division of labour in the village and in the capitalist mode of production. In the latter 'anarchy in the social division of labour and despotism in the manufacturing division of labour mutually condition each other' (ibid: 477) whereas in earlier forms of society, in which the separation of trades has been 'spontaneously developed, then crystallized, and finally made permanent by law' we find 'on the one hand, a specimen of the organization of the labour of society in accordance with an approved and authoritative plan, and on the other, the entire exclusion of division of labour in the workshop or, at the least [sic], its development on a minute scale, sporadically and accidentally' (ibid:)[51]

Marx then continued:

Those small and extremely ancient Indian communities, for example, some of which continue to exist to this day, are based on the possession of the land in common,[52] on the blending of agriculture and handicrafts and on an unalterable division of labour, which serves as a fixed plan and basis for action whenever a new community is started. ... [E]ach forms a compact whole producing all its requires. Most of the products are destined for direct use by the community itself, and are not commodities. Hence production here is independent of that division of labour brought about in Indian society as a whole by the exchange of commodities. It is the surplus alone that becomes a commodity, and a part of that surplus cannot become a commodity until it has reached the hands of the state, because from time immemorial a certain quantity of the community's production has found its way to the state as rent in kind. The form of the community varies in different parts of India. In the simplest communities land is held in common, and the produce is divided among the members. At the same time spinning and weaving are carried on in each family as subsidiary industries. (ibid: 477–8)

Alongside the mass of the people 'thus occupied in the same way' Marx lists the same twelve professions mentioned in his letter to Engels of

51 This comparison is important to place Marx's discussion of the Indian village community in context, and is neglected by commentators. It effectively refutes Wittfogel's argument that Marx 'committed a sin against science' by suppressing his Asiatic discoveries. Here they are in the middle of *Capital* Volume I. Marx explicitly recognized that the villages, so to speak, operated according to 'an approved and authoritative plan' but he thoroughly disapproved of the consequences for labour productivity and human liberty. Marx rejected both the 'despotism' of the planned social division of labour in the ancient village and the 'despotism in the manufacturing division of labour' in the capitalist mode of production. He wanted communism as the highest form of individualism – not primitive, despotic and egalitarian communism – in preference to the despotism of capitalism. Marx was utopian, but he did not exhibit the bad faith suggested by Wittfogel.

52 What does this phrase mean? Marx, relying on Wilks's *Historical Sketches of the South of India*, spoke as if the phrase implied that the villagers in some place 'cultivated' the land 'in common' (Habib, 1983: 99).

14 June 1853 (see p. 89). Marx's point was that such a division of labour produced an entirely stationary village economy, incapable of achieving a division of labour akin to that developed in modern manufacturing. Marx cited as the exemplar of these stagnant village communities not the Indian village, but the village of Java as represented in Stamford Raffles's *History of Java* (1817). He considered the Javanese case, however, to be representative of the Asiatic generality,[53] and repeated the themes he had already spelled out in his Indian articles in the 1850s:

The simplicity of the productive organism in these self-sufficing communities which constantly reproduce themselves in the same form and, when accidentally destroyed, spring up again on the same spot and with the same name – this simplicity supplies the key to the riddle of the unchangeability of Asiatic states, and their never-ceasing changes of dynasty. The structure of the fundamental economic elements of society remains untouched by the storms which blow up in the cloudy regions of politics. (ibid: 479)

The fifth and final passage of Asiatic relevance concerns an aside by Marx on irrigation in chapter 16, 'Absolute and Relative Surplus Value', and shows Marx at his most Wittfogelian. Discussing the impact of the environment on the development of capitalism and the productive forces, Marx argued that development was most likely to occur where it was a nature-imposed necessity, since where 'nature is too prodigal with her gifts' she keeps Man 'in hand, like a child in leading-strings':

It is the necessity of bringing a natural force under the control of society, of economizing on its energy, of appropriating or subduing it on a large scale by the work of the human hand, that plays the most decisive role in the history of industry. Thus, for example, the regulation of the flow of water in Egypt,[54] Lombardy and Holland. Or irrigation in India, Persia and so on, where artifical canals not only supply the soil with the water indispensable to it, but also carry down mineral fertilizers from the hills, in the shape of sediment. The secret of the flourishing state of industry in Spain and Sicily under the rule of the Arabs lay in their irrigation works. (ibid: 649–50)[55]

There is therefore no evidence that Marx abandoned the ideas associated with the concept of the AMP in *Capital* Volume I, justly his most famous

---

53 Engels was later to use Java for a political parable in polemics over 'state-socialism' – see pp. 131–2.

54 Here Marx cited his source for Egyptian irrigation and commented that 'The necessity for predicting the rise and fall of the Nile created Egyptian astronomy, and with it the domination of the priests as the directors of agriculture' (Marx, 1976: 649).

55 In an accompanying footnote Marx asserted that 'One of the material foundations of the power of the state over the small and unconnected producing organisms of India was the regulation of the water supply. Its Mohammaden rulers understood this better than their English successors. It is sufficient to recall the famine of 1866, which cost the lives of more than a million Hindus in the district of Orissa, in the Bengal Presidency' (Marx, 1976: 650, footnote 7).

published theoretical work. There is of course much evidence of equivocation, ambiguity and uncertainty — in particular the reader is not left with
a very clear distinction between primitive communism and the AMP, nor
with a firm idea of the location of 'India', past or present, under either of
these classifications.[56]

Capital, Volume III, was largely composed in the 1860s but was unfinished
by the time Marx died, and was edited by Engels before publication in
1894. Several passages in this text also have passing asides on production
relations in Asiatic-Indian-primitive formations. The first occurs in chapter
10, where Marx was trying to argue that the values of commodities are not
only theoretically but also historically prior to the formation of prices of
production:

This applies to those conditions in which the means of production belong to the
worker, and this condition is to be found, in both the ancient and the modern
world, among peasant proprietors and handicraftsmen who work for themselves.
This agrees, moreover, with the opinion we expressed previously, [57]viz. that the
development of products into commodities arises from exchange between different
communities, and not between members of one and the same community. This is
true not only for the original condition, but also for later social conditions based on
slavery and serfdom, and for the guild organization of handicraft production, as
long as the means of production involved in each branch of production can be
transferred from one sphere to another only with difficulty, and the different
spheres of production therefore relate to one another, within certain limits, like
foreign countries or communistic communities.' (Marx, 1981: 277–8).

This excerpt suggests Marx believed in the existence of an original condition
of communistic communities which contrasted with the social conditions of
slavery and serfdom. However, he did not specify that Asiatic social conditions were the original condition of humanity.

By contrast, in a second passage in chapter 20, 'Historical Material on
Merchant's Capital', Marx explicitly identified the primitive community
with what appear to be 'Asiatic' social relations. Having listed four modes

56 Further evidence of ambiguity can be found in the *Results of the Immediate Process of
Production* (*Resultate*), a posthumously published draft of Part 7 of *Capital*, Volume I, where
Marx planned to analyse the accumulation of capital and which he chose not to publish. It was
not known to scholars until 1933. In the *Resultate* he wrote: 'The production of commodities
leads inexorably to capitalist production, once the worker has ceased to be a part of the
conditions of production (as in slavery, serfdom), or once primitive common ownership has
ceased to be the basis of society (India)' (Marx, 1976: 951) — a statement which apparently
equates India with primitive communism, or at least the basis of Indian society with primitive
communism.

57 Engels inserted a footnote at this juncture: 'At that time, in 1865, this was still simply
Marx's "opinion". Today, after the comprehensive investigations by writers from Maurer to
Morgan, it is an established fact scarcely anywhere contested' (Marx, 1981: 277–8). This
aside supports my argument in footnote 33 (see p. 103 above). Maurer and Morgan's influence
on Marx and Engels is discussed on pp. 124–5 and 130–2; and see notes 68 and 74 below.

of production – the primitive community, slave production, small peasant and petty-bourgeois production, and capitalist production – he specified the exploitative relations in three of them in parenthesis in a subsequent paragraph: 'In the case of the slave relationship, the serf relationship, and the relationship of tribute (where the primitive community is under consideration), it is the slaveowner, the feudal lord or the state receiving tribute that is the owner of the product and therefore its seller' (ibid: 442–3). It was Asiatic social relations which were synonymous with, or a sub-set of, tributary social relations, because in the same chapter Marx subsequently remarked that 'in those earlier modes of production the principal proprietors of the surplus product whom the merchant trades with i.e. the slaveowner, the feudal lord and the state (e.g. the oriental despot) represent the consumption wealth which the merchant sets out to trap' (ibid: 448). Here is a strong confirmation of Marx's coupling of the primitive community and the Asiatic/oriental state as components of a distinctive mode of production – in which tributary relations play the functional equivalents of slavery and serfdom in the slave and feudal modes of production.

The remaining discussion in the same chapter focused upon the impact of trade as a 'solvent' of pre-capitalist social orders. Marx made the point that the 'solvent' or revolutionizing consequences of trade are a function of 'the nature of the community of producers' and 'the solidity and inner articulation' of the pre-capitalist mode of production. He continued:

The obstacles that the internal solidity and articulation of pre-capitalist national modes of production oppose to the solvent effect of trade are strikingly apparent in the English commerce with India and China. There the broad basis of the mode of production is formed by the union between small-scale agriculture and domestic industry, on top of which we have in the Indian case the form of village communities based on common property in the soil, which was also the original form in China. (ibid: 449, 451)

Here once more the stagnant East is contrasted with Western Europe. The Orient was unchanging and stationary – with respect to its capacity for endogenous change to a new mode of production – even when exposed to the impetus for transformation provided by external trade. These asides were to illustrate and defend what Marx regarded as a core principle of historical materialism: new productive forces, and not distributive relations, were the prime movers in historical change. In the East only modern industry, brought from the West, could dissolve the anterior social formation dominated by the AMP.[58]

The next relevant passage in *Capital*, Volume III, occurs in chapter 23,

58 Marx repeated his analysis of the impact of commercial capital upon pre-capitalist social orders in his discussion of the impact of usury in chapter 36, 'Pre-Capitalist Relations', and once more distinguished the Asiatic from ancient and feudal forms by its resistance to

'Interest and Profit of Enterprise', and is of central importance to Marx's functionalist theory of the state in the AMP. Here the nature of the supervisory and managerial function in various types of labour process was analysed. Marx distinguished two forms: the role of the coordinator and the representative of the governing will in interdependent activities, such as the conductor of an orchestra, and the supervisory role which necessarily arises 'in all modes of production that are based on opposition between the worker as direct producer and the proprietor of the means of production' (ibid: 507). Both forms figure in the supervisory and managerial functions of certain regimes: 'In despotic states, too, the work of supervision and all-round intervention of the government involves both aspects: the performance of those common tasks that arise from the nature of all communities, and the specific functions that arise from the opposition between the government and the mass of the people' (ibid: 508). The universal managerial functions necessary to the maintenance of any state are here distinguished from the ill-defined [class?] 'specific functions that arise from the opposition between the government and the mass of the people', a conceptual distinction which poses severe problems for the conventional Marxist theory of the state.[59]

In Part 6 of *Capital*, Volume III, Marx discussed the 'modern form of landed property' in order, as he declared, to complete his analysis of capital. Although the analysis of landed property in its various historical forms lay 'outside the scope of the present work' (ibid: 751) Marx proceeded to make many points which shed light on his interpretation of landed property in pre-capitalist social orders. Most importantly, the legal notion of free private property in land was not universally present in the pre-capitalist modes of production: it 'arises in the ancient world only at the time of the dissolution of the organic social order, and arises in the modern world only with the development of capitalist production. In Asia, it has simply been imported here and there by Europeans' (ibid: 753). Moreover, in highlighting 'major errors which obscure the analysis of ground-rent' Marx distinguished various forms of rent that corresponded to different levels of development of the social production process:

Whatever the specific form of rent may be, what all its types have in common is the fact that the appropriation of rent is the economic form in which landed property is

transformation: 'Usury has a revolutionary effect on pre-capitalist modes of production only insofar as it destroys and dissolves the forms of ownership which provide a firm basis for the articulation of political life and whose constant reproduction in the same form is a necessity for that life. In Asiatic forms, usury can persist for a long while without leading to anything more than economic decay and political corruption. It is only where and when the other conditions for the emergence of the capitalist mode of production are present that usury appears as one of the means of formation of this new mode of production, by ruining the feudal lords on the one hand, and by centralizing the conditions of labour on the other' (Marx, 1981: 732).

59 See below, pp. 191–6.

realized and that ground-rent in turn presupposes landed property, the ownership of particular bits of the globe by certain individuals — whether *the owner is a person representing the community as in Asia, Egypt etc.*;[60] whether this landed property is simply an accidental accompaniment of the property that certain persons have in the persons of the immediate producers, as in the systems of serfdom and slavery; whether it is pure private property that non-producers have in nature, a simple ownership title to land; or finally, whether it is a relationship to the land which, as with colonists and small peasant proprietors, appears as directly implied, given their isolated and not socially developed labour, in the appropriation and production of the products of particular bits of land by the direct producers. (ibid: 772)

This passage demonstrates that on one fundamentally historical materialist criterion, property relationships, Marx continued to distinguish at least three sets of pre-capitalist landed property relations: Asiatic, slave and serf-based forms.

The same distinctions are again confirmed in some important passages which occur in chapter 47, 'The Genesis of Capitalist Ground-Rent'. Here Marx summarized his discussion of rent. He first pointed out that in a system of feudal labour-rent the identity between rent and surplus-appropriation is especially clear. He then continued:

It is clear, too, that in all forms where the actual worker himself remains the 'possessor' of the means of production and the conditions of labour needed for the production of his own means of subsistence, the property relationship must appear at the same time as a direct relationship of domination and servitude, and the direct producer therefore as an unfree person — an unfreedom which may undergo a progressive attenuation from serfdom with statute-labour down to a mere tribute obligation. The direct producer in this case is ... in possession of his own means of production ... he pursues his agriculture independently, as well as the rural-domestic industry associated with it. This independence is not abolished when, as in India for example, these small peasants form a more or less natural community, since what is at issue here is independence *vis-a-vis* the nominal landlord. Under these conditions, the surplus labour for the nominal landowner can only be extorted from them by extra-economic compulsion, whatever the form this might assume.[61] This differs from the slave or plantation economy in that the slave works with conditions of production that do not belong to him, and does not work independently ... If there are no private landowners but it is the state, as in Asia, which confronts them (the direct producers) directly as simultaneously landowner and sovereign, rent and tax coincide, or rather there does not exist any tax distinct from ground-rent. Under these conditions, the relationship of dependence does not need to possess any stronger form, either politically or economically, than that which is common to all subjection to this state. Hence the state is the supreme landlord.

---

60 My italics.
61 In a footnote at this juncture Marx cited Linguet, whom we encountered earlier as a critic of Montesquieu (pp. 107—8), for the opinion that the first deed of a conqueror is always to take possession of the conquered people (Marx, 1981: 926).

Sovereignty here is landed property concentrated on a national scale. But for this very reason there is no private landed property, though there is both private and communal possession and usufruct of the land. (ibid: 926–7)

This passage explicitly, and relatively clearly, contrasted the production and exploitation relations of feudalism, slavery and the Asiatic forms. The immediate producers in all cases experience direct domination and servitude but their lot differed in crucial respects. Asiatic small peasants and feudal serf producers were in possession of the means of production, unlike slave producers; but the taxes and rents of Asiatic peasants coincided, in contrast to those of feudal peasants. The state was their landlord and vice versa. Marx added in a subsequent paragraph that 'rent in kind', associated with the conditions of 'natural economy' – that is the fusion of domestic and agricultural industry and the almost complete self-sufficiency of the peasant family – was functionally appropriate for those 'static conditions of society that we can see in Asia for example' (ibid: 932).

The final salient passage for the AMP in *Capital*, Volume III occurs in chapter 51, 'Relations of Distribution and Relations of Production'. Here Marx criticized the bourgeois tendency to *naturalize* both relations of distribution and relations of production – a charge he levelled at J. S. Mill in particular. Marx said on the first part of the tendency:

The only bit of truth in this conception is this: once any kind of social production is assumed (e.g. that of the indigenous Indian communities or the more artificially developed communism of the Peruvians) it is always possible to distinguish between the portion of labour whose product is directly consumed individually by the producers and their dependants, and – leaving aside the portion for productive consumption – a further portion of labour that is always surplus labour, whose product serves to satisfy general social needs, no matter how this surplus product is distributed and who functions as the representative of these social needs. (ibid: 1017)

The salient item in this passage is Marx's identification of primitive Indian communities and 'the more artificially developed communism of the Peruvians' – once more putting in question the apparently restrictive geographical ambit of the AMP.[62]

---

62 Marx's knowledge of the Inca derived 'from Prescott's famous study, *The Conquest of Peru*, a remarkable book which came out in 1847 and whose instant fame had a dramatic impact on nineteenth-century thought. Marx, like his contemporaries, seems to have been much struck by the description of a huge empire run without the aid of literacy but held together by a mixture of ruthless military power and religion. Generally he seems to have synthesized the Inca to the oriental data, and he uses information from Prescott to explain the working of the "Asiatic" mode of production' (Bloch, 1983:38).

Engels: 'On Social Relations in Russia' (1875) and *Anti-Dühring* (1878)

The next major texts of Marx and Engels to be published in which 'Asiatic' references occur are found in the work of Engels, who composed several articles for the German journal *Der Volkstaat* in the early 1870s.[63] His article 'On Social Relations in Russia' was published there in 1875 (and reprinted in 1894 with an afterword). Engels, like Marx (although the latter equivocated several years later) expressed hostility towards the ideas of the Russian populists who were enthusiastic about the Russian commune or *obshchina*, both as a survival of primitive communism and as an embryonic or prefigurative version of future socialist organization. Far from being the harbingers of progress, Engels argued these communes were the foundation of despotism and stagnation. The 'complete isolation of the individual communities from one another, which creates throughout the country similar, but the very opposite of common interests, is the natural basis for Oriental despotism, and from Russia to India this form of society, wherever it has prevailed, has always produced it and always found its complement in it' (Marx and Engels, 1969–70, 2: 394).

Much the same ideas were expressed in Engels's major work of the 1870s, his tract against the rival socialism of Herr Eugen Dühring, composed during 1876–8. He read out the entire book to Marx – who also contributed an economics chapter to the collection. The key passages in *Anti-Dühring* of relevance occur in Part 2 – which was devoted to an exposition of Marx's political economy and a critical assault upon Dühring's 'force' theory of history. Engels was at pains to point out how Dühring's political economy was ahistorical. He asserted that:

The nature and mode of distribution of the products of a specific historical society are simultaneously given with the nature and mode of production and exchange in that society and with its historical preconditions. In the tribal or village community with common ownership of land, with which, or with the easily recognizable survivals of which, all civilized peoples enter history, a fairly equal distribution of products is altogether a matter of course; where a more marked inequality of distribution among the members of the community sets in, this is an indication that the community is already breaking up . . .

But with the differences in distribution, *class differences* emerge. Society divides into classes, the privileged and the dispossessed, the exploiters and the exploited, the rulers and the ruled; and henceforward the state, which the primitive groups of communities of the same tribe had at first arrived at only in order to safeguard their common interests (e.g. irrigation in the East) and for their protection against the

---

63 As we shall see on pp. 124–9, Marx continued to read and write on Asian matters – especially on Russia and India – but much of this material of the 'late Marx' remained unknown and unpublished before his death.

outside world, has the equal purpose of maintaining by force the conditions of existence and domination of the ruling class against the subject class. (Engels, 1976: 187–9)[64]

This is a fascinating passage in a book dedicated to the defence of the theses of historical materialism, because in it Engels unwittingly sold the Marxist pass. He allowed the reasonableness of the assumption that the primary origins of the state lay in the 'safeguard [of] common interests' and in the organization of communal defence; that is, he accepted, implicitly, that class differentiation came *after* the formation of the state. Class formation was therefore not the *primary cause* of the origin of the state. Engels gave collective organization for military defence (against force) equal primacy with functional and contractual explanations of the origins of the state. This passage is also important because, consistent with his 1853 correspondence with Marx, Engels singled out irrigation as a *differentia specifica* of state formation in the East.

In the following paragraph he also confirmed his belief in the stagnation of primitive communities, a fundamental theme in Marx's writings on India: 'The old primitive communities which have already been mentioned could remain in existence for thousands of years – as in India and among the Slavs up to the present day – before intercourse with the external world gave rise to the internal inequalities of property as a result of which they began to break up' (ibid: 189).

However, Engels's chief purpose was to criticize Dühring's theory of force.[65] In a direct challenge to Marx and Engels, Dühring had postulated the converse of the base – superstructure relationship: 'The formation of *political* relationships is the *historically fundamental factor*, and instances of economic dependence are only effects or special cases and are consequently always *facts of a second order*' (ibid: 201).[66] Engels sought to refute Dühring by arguing that the formation of private property in history was not the result of robbery or force:

On the contrary. It already existed, though limited to certain objects, in the ancient primitive communes of all civilized peoples. It developed into the form of com-

---

64 The full title of Engels' tract, *Herr Eugen Dühring's Revolution in Science*, was a parody of Dühring's *Carey's Revolution in Economic Theory and Social Science* – which was a hymn of praise to the ideas of Henry Carey, the very same Carey against whom the Marx had targeted some of his arguments in 'The British Rule in India'.

65 Engels was also concerned to emphasize the theoretical significance of Marx's investigations of pre-capitalist economies. He clearly did not regard them as incidental to their intellectual project: '[T]o carry out this critique of bourgeois economics completely, it was not enough to be acquainted with the capitalist form of production ... The forms preceding it or still existing alongside it in less developed countries had also to be examined and compared, at least in their main features. By and large, this kind of investigation and comparison has as yet been undertaken only by Marx' (Engels, 1976: 192).

66 Engels citing Dühring. Italics in original.

modities already within these communes, at first through barter with foreigners. The more the products of the commune assumed the commodity form . . . and the more the original natural division of labour was supplanted by exchange within the commune as well, the more unequal became the property status of the individual commune members, the more deeply was the ancient common ownership undermined, and the more rapidly did the commune move towards its dissolution and transformation into a village of small-holding peasants. For thousands of years Oriental despotism and the changing rule of counquering nomads were unable to injure these old communities; the gradual destruction of their primitive home industry by the competition of the products of large-scale industry brought them nearer and nearer to dissolution. Force was as little involved in this process as in the dividing up of the land held in common by the village communities (*Gehöfersschaften*) on the Moselle and in the Hochwald, which is still taking place today; the peasants simply find it to their advantage that the private ownership of land should take the place of common ownership. Even the formation of a primitive aristocracy, as in the case of the Celts, the Germans and the Indian Punjab, took place on the basis of common ownership of the land, and was not at first based in any way on force, but on voluntariness and custom. Wherever private property was instituted [it was] a result of economic causes. Force plays no part in this at all. Indeed, it is clear that the institution of private property must already be in existence before a robber can appropriate another person's property, and that therefore force may be able to change the possession of, but cannot create, private property as such. (ibid: 206–7)[67]

Two features of this part of Engels's critique of Dühring's theory of force raised problems more serious than the ones they solved. First, to make a convincing argument against Dühring Engels came very close to endorsing the Smithian theory of history. Trade and exchange, rather than force, class or production relations, were used to explain the foundations of private property in ancient primitive communes. Even the class formation of primitive aristocracies is said to have occurred through voluntary contract and custom rather than through military conquest – explanatory mechanisms which one would expect liberals to endorse more readily than Marxists. Second, Engels's use of the example of oriental despotism to score a point against Dühring was problematic. His argument, in a nutshell, was of this form: neither the 'force' of oriental despotism nor the 'force' of nomadic conquerors changed the ancient communities, rather competition from capitalist large-scale industry undermined them, therefore economics, and not force, is the motor of historical change. A nice counter to Dühring as an argument, but it had hidden costs. Engels had argued that trade and private property had developed endogenously in ancient primitive communes, but this argument leaves him without an explanation of the stagnation of the oriental village. Moreover, as Marx's journalism of twenty-five years

67 Italics in original.

previously had made plain, the dissolution of the village community was not just the product of 'free trade'. The 'force' of British imperialism had had something to do with the breakup of the Indian village. None the less Engels's conception of oriental despotism was not much different from Marx's AMP, and indeed shared the same problematic ambiguities – especially the same uncertainty over the degree of primitiveness of the social formations to which the term was confidently applied.

The final part of Engels's critique of Dühring's theory of force clarified some matters but clouded others. Dühring had argued that the cultivation of landed property in tracts of considerable size never took place anywhere 'without the subjection of man in some form of slave labour or corvée ... How could a large landed proprietor even be conceived without at the same time including in this idea his domination over slaves, serfs or indirectly unfree men?' (ibid: 223). Engels riposted that in the early history of all civilized peoples it was not 'large landed proprietors' who prevailed, but rather

tribal and village communities with common ownership of the land. From India to Ireland the cultivation of landed property in extensive tracts was originally carried on by such tribal and village communities (ibid: 224)[68] It is purely ... imagination on ... Dühring's part when he asserts that landed proprietors and serfs were required for the cultivation of landed property in extensive tracts. *In the whole of the orient, where the village community or the state owns the land*, the very term landed proprietor is not to be found in the various languages, a point on which ... Dühring can consult the English jurists, whose efforts in India to solve the question, who is the owner of the land? were [in] vain. (ibid: 225)[69]

Having elaborated further examples of Dühring's historical ignorance Engels presented his own theory of the origins of relations of domination and subjection. Engels's theses, long overlooked in most elaborations of the Marxist canon, are remarkable because they are an even more straightforward mix of the contractual and functionalist propositions suggested earlier. In primitive egalitarian communities.

there were from the beginning certain common interests, the safeguarding of which had to be handed over to individuals, true under the control of the community as a whole; adjudication of disputes; repression of encroachments by individuals beyond their rights; control of water supplies, especially in hot countries; and finally, when conditions were still very primitive, religious functions. Such offices are found in native communities in every period ... in the oldest German Marks and even today in India ... [they] constitute the beginnings of state power. (ibid: 229)

68 Engels cited Maurer's works on the ancient German Mark in support of his thesis that common ownership had existed amongst all the primitive antecedents of the civilized peoples of Europe and Asia.
69 My italics.

Despite their consensual origins such offices and functions became autonomous as the productive forces, population, conflicts of interest and external threats increased. But

> it is not necessary ... to examine ... how this independence of social functions as against society increased with time until it developed into domination over society; how when conditions were favourable, the original servant gradually changed into the master; how this master emerged as an Oriental despot or satrap, the dynast of a Greek tribe, the chieftain of a Celtic clan. ... how the individual rulers ultimately united into a ruling class ... [W]e are only concerned with establishing that the exercise of a social function was everywhere the basis of political domination; and further that political domination has existed for any length of time only when it discharged this, its social function. However many despotisms which rose and fell in Persia and India, each was fully aware that it was above all the general entrepreneur for the maintenance of irrigation throughout the river valleys, without which no agriculture was possible. It was reserved for the enlightened English to lose sight of this in India ... they have neglected the one activity which might have made their rule in India at least as legitimate as their predecessors. (ibid: 229–30)[70]

In this important passage Engels restates the argument that oriental despotism originated, at least partly, as a functionalist solution to the management of irrigation agriculture. He does so while presenting a general functionalist thesis of state formation in all primitive communities, and not just oriental ones. Although oriental despotism exemplifies this development, Engels did not apply one general label to this pristine social formation. However, the equation of the oriental despot with Greek dynasts and Celtic chieftains suggests the antiquity of what we now call the AMP.

In the immediately succeeding paragraph Engels explained the formation of slavery as a separate possibility, and then contrasted the dynamism of slave-holding societies with those based upon oriental despotism. Slavery was the outcome of societies in which state formation was well under way, facilitating the development of a social surplus. He also asserted – criticizing Dühring's pious dislike of slavery – that without the slavery of antiquity, modern socialism would have been impossible: 'our whole economic, political and intellectual development presupposes a state of things in which slavery was as necessary as it was universally recognized' (ibid: 231). Slavery was a great step forward by comparison with barbarism and the ancient communes:

70 This argument is another fascinating example of a self-defeating reply by Engels. By implication the origins of the state are found neither in class struggle nor in technical economic progress – because classes and economic progress emerge only *after* the state is in the process of creation. Rather the origins of the state lie in the acquisition of autonomy by those persons or organs initially charged with carrying out community functions and their subsequent enforcement of their autonomy in the form of domination. Surely Engels gave away the historical materialist position to non-Marxist theories of the state which emphasize the autonomy of political domination?

Where the ancient communes have continued to exist, they have for thousands of years formed the basis of the crudest form of state, Oriental despotism, from India to Russia.[71] It was only where these communities dissolved that the peoples made further progress of themselves, and their next economic advance consisted in the increase and development of production by means of slave labour. (ibid: 232)

This passage is imporant for three reasons. First, Engels associated oriental despotism with the crudest and earliest form of state, and with restricted, not to say retarded, development. But second, he stated that endogenous progress out of oriental despotism was possible, that is *progress towards the slave mode of production*. Oriental despotisms, at least on this characterization, were not intrinsically incapable of further development – an argument, whether made consciously or not, which amounted to a partial revision of Marx and Engels's earlier propositions on oriental stagnation. Finally, the implication of Engels's remark was that the historical road to progress passes from oriental despotisms through slaveholding societies to feudalism and thence to capitalism – one of the few passages which seem to repeat the unilineal theory of history articulated by Marx in the Preface.[72]

The Late Marx: India, Ethnology and the Fate of Russia

The works and writings of the late Marx (1868–83) have recently attracted much scholarly attention (Krader, 1972; Shanin 1983). Three points of interest are pertinent to the AMP: first, Marx had to confront his conception of Asian societies as a result of reading the latest history and anthropology; second, Marx shifted his unilineal and determinist conception of historical progress in favour of a multilineal and voluntarist conception of revolutionary endeavour as a result of his discussion with Russian populists; and finally, he seemed to change his mind over the nature of the village communities he had once described as the foundations of despotism and stagnation.

Marx's interest in primordial 'village communities' was reinvigorated by reading the work of the German jurist and historian, G. L. Maurer (1790–1872), whose researches demonstrated the longevity and primordialism of the institution of the German Mark. He wrote several enthusiastic letters to Engels:

His [Maurer's] books are exceptionally important ... Human history is like palaeontology. Owing to a certain judicial blindness even the best intelligences absolutely fail to see the things which lie under their noses. Later, when the moment has arrived, we are surprised to find traces of what we failed to see ... right in my own

---

71 My italics.
72 Alternatively, oriental despotism figures in Engels's account as a railway siding – where 'History' stops for lengthy periods. Certain societies enjoy the privilege of the express route.

neighbourhood on the Hunsrücken, the old Germanic system survived up till the last few years. I now remember my father talking to me about it from a lawyer's point of view ... what would old Hegel say in the next world if he heard that the general [*Allgemeine*] in Germans and Norse means nothing but the common land [*Gemeinland*], and the *particular, Sundre, Besondere*, nothing but a separate property divided off from the common land? Here are the logical categories coming damn well out of 'our intercourse' after all. (Marx and Engels, 1934: 235–7)

In his first letter to Engels on the subject Marx suggests that new proof had been provided for the view which he put forward in *A Contribution to the Critique of Political Economy*, that everywhere the Asiatic, or Indian, property forms constitute the starting point of civilization. The thesis of Russian originality in common property was exploded by Maurer's researches.[73] Since he equated Asiatic and Indian institutions with those of the German Mark, Marx's remarks on Maurer strongly suggest a primitivist interpretation of the AMP. They also look like a retrospective gloss on his previous work. Marx habitually argued that other people had discovered or confirmed what he had earlier suggested, and this habit was made easier by the vagueness with which he often formulated his ideas. However, the key point is that his enthusiasm for Maurer's research indicates no loss faith in the AMP.[74]

Consider now the late Marx's reading on India. The fact that Marx continued to maintain an interest in Indian history is shown by his extensive *Notes on Indian History* – published from a manuscript of Marx's by the Institute of Marxism-Leninism of the Central Committee of the CPSU (1959). The editors of these *Notes* unfortunately fail to date the manuscript. However, it is easy to calculate the period when at least some of the notes must have been made. We know that Marx's notes are mainly based on Elphinstone's *History of India* and Sewell's *Analytical History of India*. Sewell's book was published in 1870 so Marx's notes must postdate 1870. Since Elphinstone's book was published in 1841 (with a subsequent edition in 1874) it is difficult to judge exactly when Marx noted this text without the evidence of the manuscript. However, since Marx's notes on Kovalevsky's work on *Communal Landholding* (published in 1879) were placed between his notes on Elphinstone and Sewell, the *Notes on Indian History* can be confidently dated to the late 1870s and early 1880s.

73 Letter from Marx to Engels, 14 March 1868 (Marx and Engels, 1956, Volume XXXII: 42).

74 The Soviet scholar N. B. Ter-Akopyan, writing in the Russian journal *Narody Azii i Afriki* (1965, 2: 74–88 and 3: 70–85), argued that the disappearance of the term AMP from the discussions of the late Marx and Engels was explained by Maurer's researches: 'once they found that the community and the collective forms of property were universally spread in the past, Marx and Engels gave up the previous term' (cited in Skalnik and Pokora, 1966: 179–87). The Asiatic term may have disappeared, but not the concept.

These notes confirm that Marx's knowledge of Indian political history was mainly confined to that of the 'Mussulman' conquest, the Mughal Empire and the British conquest and exploitation of India.[75] He noted the details of the successive Islamic invasions of India and the turbulent military and court politics of the Mughal era without making any substantive comments. However, he carefully noted the nature of the Indian revenue system under Akbar as portrayed by his sources – including the details of the assessment and collection which showed that the revenue was paid in cash (Marx, 1959: 42). Judging by these notes Marx had little knowledge of or interest in the history of the Hindu regimes which had prevailed before the Turkish invasions. He repeated without comment the erroneous statement of Elphinstone's that Alexander the Great was the last invader of India before the Mohammedans (ibid: 66). But in a parenthesis he remarked that:

(*Kingdom of Magadha* was a most interesting one. Its *Buddhist kings* wielded extensive power; they belonged for many years to the *Kshatriya caste*, until one of the Sudra caste – the fourth lowest of Manu's four castes – named *Chandragupta* – called Sandrocottus by the Greeks – murdered the King and made himself sovereign; he lived in Alexander Magnus' time . . .). (ibid: 67–8)[76]

But this was all Marx had to say on the regime which looked like the most promising historical specimen of the AMP in Indian history – or at least was so regarded by his follower and critic Wittfogel.

The inference may plausibly be drawn that Marx regarded the AMP as a primitive formation, rather than an appropriate concept for understanding the major empires in Indian history. In any case the chronological notes on Indian political history are of less theoretical import for the AMP than are Marx's notes on Kovalevsky. Marx's interest in the Indian village community and India's social and political structures was revitalized by M. M. Kovalevsky, a Russian legal historian, in the late 1870s and early 1880s. Kovalevsky's *Communal Landholding, The Causes, Ways and Consequences of its Disintegration*, published in Moscow in 1879, contained ample factual material to whet Marx's appetite, and he paid particular attention to the chapter which focused upon communal landed property in India. The book also included a chapter on the 'Process of Feudalization of Landed Property in India under Muslim Rule'. Kovalevsky believed that India had been feudalized under Mughal rule. Although he recognized that the maintenance of the imperial claim to the ownership of the land made Indian feudalism less developed than that of Western Europe, none the less:

---

75 According to my calculations the ratio of notes on pre-British India to the British conquest and after is 7:11, with most of the notes on pre-British India being confined to Islamic invasions and Mughal civil wars.

76 Italics in original.

Of all the four factors usually, though unjustly, acknowledged by medieval historians to be the sole aspects of Germano-Roman feudalism, three – the beneficial systems, farming out and commendation – may be said to exist in India conquered by the Muslims. Only of patrimonial justice, at least so far as the civil code is concerned, it is possible to say that it was absent in the empire of the Great Mogul. (cited in Gamayunov and Ulyanovsky, 1960)

Marx's marginal comments on this passage indicate his disagreement with the judgement that Mughal India had been feudal:

On the grounds that the 'beneficial system', 'farming out' (the latter, though, is by no means purely feudal – the proof – Rome) and commendation occur in India, Kovalevsky sees here feudalism in the West European sense. But Kovalevsky forgets about serfdom which is absent in India and which is of the greatest importance. As to the individual role of protection (cf. Palgrave) not only of the bonded but also of the free peasants by the feudals (who functioned as *vogts*), this was in India of little importance, with the exception of the *wakufs*. The idealization of the Land (*Boden-Poesie*) characteristic of Germano-Roman feudalism (see Maurer) is as of little interest to India as it is to Rome. In India land is nowhere so noble in the sense of being, for instance, inalienable for the benefit of those outside the nobility. However, Kovalevsky himself sees the basic difference – the absence of patrimonial justice where civil law is concerned in the Empire of the Grand Mogul. (ibid:)[77]

Marx also rejected Kovalevsky's argument that the Islamic conquest of India which led to the imposition of the Muslim land tax (*kharaj*) on the peasantry had entailed the transformation of absolutist land ownership into feudal landownership.

However, this straightforward interpretation of Marx's notes on Kovalevsky – widely accepted by reputable scholars as proof of Marx's continued support for the idea that India had not been feudal but 'Asiatic' or 'oriental' (P. Anderson, 1974b: 405–7; Krader, 1975: Part 2) – has reportedly been challenged by the orthodox Soviet Marxist Nikiforov (Gellner, 1986: 93–8).[78] Nikiforov contends that it was Marx's reading of Kovalevsky that finally persuaded the old man to abandon his commitment to the AMP. His argument is that (1) Kovalevsky provided evidence of private ownership of land coexisting from ancient times with communal landownership in Indian history. (2) This evidence was incompatible with the categorization of India as a specimen of the AMP. (3) Marx does not comment on (1). Silence means consent and therefore (4) Marx accepted the errors of his previous 'Asiatic' thinking.

If this construction fairly represents Nikiforov's arguments it is open to

---

77 Italics and underlining as in original.
78 Gellner avoids substantive comment on the merits of Nikiforov's Marxology – being more concerned with the reasons for the latter's interpretation of the late Marx.

obvious objections. First, silence does not always mean consent. Second, Marx had recognized long ago, notably in his correspondence with Engels in 1853, the truth of (1), but had nonetheless formed the concept of an AMP. Third, conclusion (2) is unwarranted if one accepts that any post-primitive social formation might be an articulation of several modes of production. Finally, Marx's explicit commentary on Kovalevsky shows that he was highly critical of the latter's liberal use of the term 'feudal'. The only valid inference that one can draw is that Marx thought that many pre-capitalist societies were neither feudal nor primitive communisms. The case for suggesting that Marx retained his Asiatic beliefs after reading Kovalevsky is more plausible than Nikiforov's thesis.

The evidence of what are grandly called Marx's *Ethnological Notebooks* confirms the error of Nikiforov's interpretation (Krader, 1972).[79] These notebooks comprise Marx's excerpts and comments on Lewis Morgan's *Ancient Society* (1877), Sir John Budd Phear's *The Aryan Village in India and Ceylon* (1880), Henry Maine's *Lectures on the Early History of Institutions* and John Lubbock's *The Origin of Civilization* (1870). These notes show that Marx became very interested in the empirical details of contemporary anthropology and ethnography of primitive societies and in discussions of the social and legal characteristics of primordial village and tribal communities. More importantly here, the notebooks show that Marx's reading of Budd Phear if anything reinforced his views on the Indian village community and his rejection of the thesis that India had ever been feudal: 'That ass Phear describes the organization of the [Indian] rural community as feudal' (Krader, 1972: 256). This specimen of marginalia seems plain enough in meaning, although Nikiforov thinks otherwise and has suggested that Marx was simply disagreeing with Phear's particular description of the Indian village as feudal: he had in fact been persuaded by Kovalevsky that the Indian social formation was feudal. Nikiforov's suggestion is certainly creative, but implausible for the reasons already given.[80]

The ethnological readings of the late Marx were driven by a theoretical concern − how to integrate the materials of anthropology and ancient history with the theses of historical materialism − and by a practical concern − how revolutionary socialists ought to approach societies with archaic survivals of the 'Asiatic' village community. The theoretical task was accomplished by Engels after Marx's death, in *The Origins of the*

---

79 Krader's commentary is obscure and disorganized although filled with interesting information. His subsequent essay on Marx's ethnological notes has the same traits (Krader, 1982).

80 See above, pp. 127−8. Marx did, however seem, to accept the thesis that the Indian village communities had been self-governing: 'In the East, under the village system, the people practically governed themselves' (Krader, 1972: 284, Marx's Conspectus on Budd Phear).

Family, Private Property and the State, partly on the basis of Marx's notes (see below, pp. 131–2). The practical question produced considerable equivocation on Marx's part, manifested by his correspondence with Russian populists. Marx first commented on the debate over the nature of the Russian *mir* in a letter to Engels in 1868:

> Borkheim is translating the chief passages from the Russian book on the disintegration of agriculture for me, and has also given me a French book about it by the Russian, Shédo-Ferroti. The latter makes a great mistake … when he says the Russian communal system first originated from the law prohibiting the peasant from leaving the land. The whole thing, *down to the smallest details*, is absolutely identical with the primitive Germanic communal system. What the Russians have added (and this is also found in a section of the Indian communal system, not in the Punjab but in the South), is (1) the non-democratic but patriarchal character of the commune leadership, and (2) the collective responsibility for taxes to the state, etc. [So] the more industrious the Russian peasant is, the more he is exploited for the purposes of the state … The whole foul mess[81] is in a process of collapse. (Marx and Engels, 1934: 253)

Marx obviously accepted the controversial thesis that this commune was a primordial relic rather than a comparatively recent administrative creation of the Czars. He evidently believed that the Russian commune was merely one specimen, albeit with its own peculiarities, of the archaic commune which he had referred to in *Capital* and *A Contribution to the Critique of Political Economy*.

He was first required to give a practical revolutionary advice on the commune when Russian intellectuals asked him whether the apparently unilineal theses of *Capital* meant that Russia would have to undergo the full transition to capitalism before the liberation of socialist revolution. The *Narodnik* theorist Mikhailovsky had criticized the theses of *Capital* precisely because its determinism suggested that Russia could not by pass capitalism. In his letter to the editor of the *Otyecestvenniye Zapisky*, written towards the end of 1877, Marx begged to differ, and, to the subsequent embarrassment of Russian Marxists, sided with the Narodniks: 'If Russia continues to pursue the path she has followed since 1861, she will lose the finest chance ever offered by history to a nation, in order to undergo all the fatal vicissitudes of the capitalist regime' (ibid: 353) In the several drafts of his letter to another Populist, Vera Zasulich, composed in 1881,[82] Marx experienced some difficulty in providing a theoretical defence of this position, but it is evident that he had only partially revised his conception of the revolutionary potential of the peasantry and the socialist potential created by the presence of archaic survivals of communal village structures.

81 A very delicate English translation of the German for 'shit-heap'.
82 Four drafts of this letter exist (Shanin, 1983).

The Origin of the Family, Private Property and the State

Engels's anthropological text, first published in 1884, and written from Marx's conspectus on Lewis Morgan's *Ancient Society* (1877), enjoys a controversial status in the debate about the AMP precisely because it does not mention the concept. Engels accepted the unilineal periodization of history set forth by Morgan, namely savagery, barbarism and civilization, and asserted that slavery, serfdom and capitalism were the three forms of exploitation of the three great epochs of civilization (Engels, 1978: 213). Since Engels argued that Morgan had independently discovered the results of Marx's materialist conception of history and since Morgan did not mention an independent Asiatic road of historical development or stagnation, the anti-*Aziatchiki* make much of the silence of *The Origin of the Family, Private Property and the State*.

Indeed, since there is nothing on the AMP in this famous text we need not dwell upon it. However, the inferences which anti-*Aziatchiki* draw from this absence are insupportable (see below, pp. 143−6). For the moment it is worth remarking upon two facts. First, Engels nowhere explicitly repudiated the AMP (or oriental despotism). Second, there is a so far wholly unobserved fact in the Marxological industry which surrounds the study of Marx, Engels and Morgan. Morgan's early work, as was well known to his contemporaries, was directed towards demonstrating that the American Indians had Asiatic (that is Indian), origins! In his previous book, *Systems of Consanguinity and Affinity of the Human Family* (1860), Morgan had demonstrated this thesis to his satisfaction. He even remarked of the famous mistake of the discoverers of America, who believed they had circumnavigated the globe to reach India, that his research had shown that their 'error was truth' (Boorstein, 1983: 636−46). Morgan's kinship researches, in so far as they confirmed the similarities between American Indian and Asiatic Indian kinship, family and social structures, therefore could not have been seen by Marx as a falsification of his previous 'Asiatic' beliefs. If Marx understood the AMP to be the original form of the transition from barbarism to civilization (or the higher state of barbarism), Morgan's work could not have caused any shock to his previously articulated notions about 'Asia'. Indeed if anything Morgan's research confirmed the 'primitivist' reading of the AMP, by demonstrating the existence of a shared origin of all societies in a communal form of barbarism (which in the American version was also stagnant). The fact that Engels regarded slavery, serfdom and capitalism as the three forms of exploitation in civilization is compatible with the notion that Asiatic (read 'primitive communist') relations prevailed in the era of barbarism. The mystery of the missing mode of production in *The Origin of the Family, Private Property and the State* dissolves if we accept the significance of these facts.

Further proof that there is no mystery is established by Engels's correspondence in the same year as the publication of *The Origin of the Family, Private Property and the State*. Reading J. W. B. Money's *Java, Or How to Manage a Colony* (published in 1861) persuaded him that Dutch imperialism differed materially from that of the British in India. The Dutch had made no attempt to modernize Java – through the introduction of private property in land or through destroying the old village community. Rather they had chosen to maintain the pre-capitalist system of tribute collection and had simply siphoned off the surplus through what Money called the native aristocracy – chieftains and village headmen. Engels regarded this situation as a useful political parable to criticize the 'state socialism' of Bismarck. In a letter to Bebel sent on 16 January 1884 he wrote ironically:

If you wish an example of state-socialism then take Java. On the basis of the old communistic village communities, the Dutch Government has there organized all production in so 'socialistic' a fashion, and has so nicely taken all sales of the products into its hands, that, aside from about 100 million marks in salaries for officials and the army it receives an income of some 70 million marks a year to pay interest to the luckless states which are creditors of the Dutch. In comparison Bismarck is an innocent child.' (Marx and Engels, 1959: 344)

More corroboration that Engels regarded Java as a specimen of what Marx had once called the AMP, but what Engels generally called oriental despotism, comes from a letter written a month later (16 February 1884), this time to Kautsky:

It would be a good thing for somebody to take the pains of elucidating the state socialism now rampant by using the example of it in *Java* where its practice is in full bloom ... Here it will be seen how on the basis of the old community communism (*Gemeindekommunismus*) the Dutch organized production under state control and secured for the people what they considered a quite comfortable existence ... This case is highly interesting and can be turned to practical use. Incidentally it is proof of how today primitive communism furnishes there as well as in India and Russia the finest and broadest basis of exploitation and despotism (so long as it is not aroused by some element of modern communism)[83] and how in the conditions of modern society it turns out to be crying anachronism (to be removed or further developed) as much as were the independent mark associations of the original cantons.' (ibid: 345)

These letters confirm two important facts. First, despite the alleged silence of *The Origin of the Family, Private Property and the State*, Engels persisted in describing certain Asiatic societies in the terms of the AMP – albeit with a primitivist reading of that concept in which despotism coexists with primitive

83 Engels's parenthetic remark mirrors the late Marx's equivocation about the socialist potential of oriental village communities.

communism. Second, far from being embarrassed by the parallels between the AMP and state socialism, Engels was pleased by them. He wanted to emphasize rather than hide these parallels, *pace* Wittfogel, precisely, because he was opposed to state socialism, and believed that advanced communism would entail something altogether different.

KEY SCHOLARLY PROBLEMS IN INTERPRETING MARX AND ENGELS'S TEXTS ON THE ASIATIC MODE OF PRODUCTION

There are obvious difficulties in interpreting Marx and Engels's texts on the AMP, written over fifty years and in many languages. Some were published in books and articles as digressions − all with varying and multiple theoretical and ideological purposes. Some were drafted for publication, some were uncompleted and some were never even intended for publication. To lump all these texts together and expect a consistent model/concept/theory of the AMP to emerge painlessly, or like Athena from the head of Zeus, is a fundamentally unrealistic project. The problems which the early Christian Church faced in producing consistency and coherence from the sayings of Matthew, Mark, Luke and John bear an uncanny resemblance to the problems faced by Marxist fideists, reluctant to accept that the masters could ever be wrong, let alone apparently contradict themselves.

Three key problems of interpretation of the texts on the AMP and Marx and Engels's Asiatic writings are evident: their alleged dependence on the idea of oriental despotism; the precise status of the AMP in relation to primitive communism and other modes of production; and the issue of whether they retained the same views on the AMP, or modified them significantly, or even completely changed them.

Post Hoc Ergo Propter Hoc

The foregoing survey of Marx and Engels's writing relevant to the AMP has established that the study of despotism *per se*, let alone the study of bureaucracy, was not by any stretch of the imagination their prime concern. When they used the terms 'Asiatic despotism', 'oriental despotism' or 'despotism' after the 1850s, they were interested in describing social orders with the economic features of the AMP (especially village communities with traces of primitive communist relations of production and autarkic divisions of labour, urban centres bereft of embryonic capitalist production, and agrarian systems in which taxes and rents coincided) rather than the political system made famous by Montesquieu.

Their interest in Asiatic societies stemmed from two principal theoretical concerns. First, as scholars, analysts and critics of capitalism they were interested in Asiatic societies because of widespread beliefs held about Asia which were pertinent to the historical materialist conception of capitalism. They believed that within Asia primordial exemplars of primitive communism still existed, and that in India stagnant versions of the first social orders to replace primitive communism were still in being, albeit contaminated by the existence of political despotism. To judge by their writings and bibliographical citations, Marx and Engels's empirical beliefs were based more upon the Victorian historical and anthropological scholarship available to them than upon the past speculations of philosophers in occidental political though about despotism.

There is little point in denying the selectivity of Marx and Engels's historiographical and anthropological sources: Marx and Engels's beliefs about Asia and India were certainly bolstered by wishful thinking. They wanted to find evidence of primitive communism and communal ownership in non-capitalist economic systems. Marx and Engels's fundamental thesis that capitalism was historical and not natural − that it had birthmarks as well as a future rendezvous with death at the hands of the proletariat − was by implication supported by the evidence of Asian and Indian historiography and ethnography. They reasoned that such research confirmed that social orders had existed in which private property had either not been present or not been predominant. If these facts had once been possible, it followed that they might again be possible, albeit at a higher level of social organization. Communism was therefore not incompatible with human nature; in fact it constituted humanity's original nature.[84]

Second, Marx and Engels were interested in explaining the origins and development of capitalism. The contrast between occidental and oriental societies, especially in the early communal forms discussed in the *Grundrisse*, served the function of allowing Marx to construct a story which, for all its problems, explained why and how capitalism had first come into the world, 'dripping with blood', in the heartlands of European feudalism. Moreover, Marx was preoccupied, especially later in life, with the spread of capitalism outwards from its European and North American 'heartlands'. What would happen to the ancient and 'democratic' village communes which he believed,

---

84 Of course their ideological argument left itself open to a rejoinder which they failed to spot: if the primitive communist regimes of the past were natural, and compatible with political despotism, then perhaps advanced communism will be equally naturally compatible with political despotism. This ideological counter to Marxist claims about the naturalness of communism now has a long pedigree. The work of Alexander Zinoviev (for example, 1984) is merely one of a series of books which have agreed with the assertion that communism and despotism are the natural condition of humanity and have contended that Western civilization is unnatural, artificial and novel.

in common with many nineteenth-century socialists, existed throughout the world? More importantly, he was interested in the question of what should happen to them. How should socialists in agrarian societies conduct themselves? The issue that Marx was confronting towards the end of his life was not the issue of political despotism, but rather 'the fate and history of the Asiatic communal village' (Levine, 1977: 76).

It is therefore for many reasons an example of the *post hoc ergo propter hoc* fallacy to argue that the AMP was simply a renaming of the idea of oriental despotism. Moreover, to compound the error, many analysts have read back into the ancient idea of oriental despotism the concept of the same name later articulated by Wittfogel (1981). It is both anachronistic and inaccurate to suggest, as Wittfogel did, that the idea of oriental despotism was understood by Marx to include personal autocracy *and* bureaucratic centralization. Studying Marx's contemporary sources for his ideas on India shows that not only were they were not concerned to describe India as bureaucratic, but, moreover, they did not associate despotism with bureaucracy.[85] Even Patton's *The Principles of Asiatic Monarchies* (largely a crib of Montesquieu's *L'Ésprit des Lois*) which Marx read in 1853, did not mention the notion of bureaucracy. Further confirmation is provided by Marx's *Notes on Indian History*, which suggest an appreciation of Akbar's administrative system as one which remained fundamentally rooted in its militaristic and warrior origins rather than as a prototype of a civilian bureaucracy.

It is true that Marx's English sources on India were concerned, as he was, with the issue of landownership in a pre-capitalist system. It is equally true that monarchical ownership of the land was a prominent theme in the (pre-Wittfogelian) idea of oriental despotism. However, the protagonists of the idea of oriental despotism were primarily concerned with contrasting the power of feudal landowners under occidental monarchs with those of service nobles under oriental despots. Marx and Engels's theoretical concerns and emphases were different. They were more interested in whether the peasants owned or possessed the land individually or collectively, and how the mechanism of surplus extraction in the Orient differed from that of the Occident. They were more interested in the villages of oriental society as sites of production and exploitation than in the relations between the monarch and the aristocrats. Therefore even where the idea of the AMP overlaps with that of oriental despotism there are significant differences of emphasis and conceptual purpose.

---

85 The one author whom Marx used in his Indian studies who used the word bureaucracy to describe the Indian political system was referring to post-British conquest India and *not* to pre-British India (Dickinson, 1853). See appendix 3.1. for a full list of Marx's sources on India.

The Age and Status of the Asiatic Mode of Production

Is the AMP identical with primitive communism? Is it a distinctive mode of production of its own? Is it a concept which elucidates the transition from primitive communism to class-divided societies? Is it a concept which explains the workings of social formations outside Europe as late as the eighteenth century? The simplest answer to these questions is that we do not know, and perhaps can never know because Marx and Engels's texts are multiply ambiguous. Throughout this chapter passages have been presented which confirm that Marx and Engels thought of the AMP as:

1 the form of primitive communism;
2 a form of primitive communism;
3 a transitional order from primitive communism to class-divided society, which non the less become a historical *cul-de-sac* (or alternatively a historical railway siding)
4 an independent social order partly coterminous in time and level of development with the other major pre-capitalist social orders.

Figure 3.1 sketches these four possible interpretations of the status of the AMP in relation to other modes of production. Since Marx and Engels never reviewed their writings on these issues we cannot know whether this ambiguity reflected changes in context, in their views, or indeed straightforward and unresolved confusion.[86] However, in my judgement the weight of the textual evidence suggests that Marx's position – after his journalistic writings on Mughal India – shifted towards understanding the AMP as one form of primitive communism and/or a transitional form, in which the transition from primitive communism to class-divided society occurs. That this shift was tentative is evidenced by writing in *Theories of Surplus Value* and *Capital*, Volume III, which would seem to describe an independent Asiatic social order coexisting in time with Western feudalism. Moreover, as there is textual evidence to support all four interpretations and no definitive statement by Marx and Engels supporting one and rejecting the other three, my judgement must remain contestable. However, I shall seek to demonstrate that it is not contestable that Marx and Engels retained their belief in the idea of an AMP from the 1850s until their deaths.

Discontinuities, Silences and Alleged Crippling

The small textual treasure on the AMP provides a beanfeast for those who like textual exegesis and hermeneutic controversies. However, the fault

---

86 There are plenty of unresolved confusions in Marx – see Elster (1985) for an unsparing dissection of most of them.

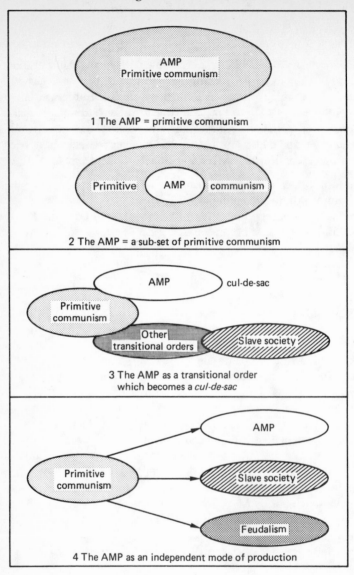

Figure 3.1 Four ways of understanding the status of the AMP in Marx's writings

lines of interpretation which separate scholars and polemicists run along three questions. First, did Marx and Engels maintain fundamentally the same views on the AMP from 1853 until their deaths? Second, did Marx abandon the AMP? And finally, did Engels abandon the AMP?

Did Marx and Engels maintain a stable concept of the AMP?   The idea has been defended that Marx and Engels' conception of the AMP remained stable right from its birth in Marx's Indian articles of 1853 until the deaths of Marx and Engels:

Marx never added very much to the model of Oriental society he derived from the political economists, apart from his explanation of the origins of the system, which he had already arrived at through Engels in 1853. In *Capital* Marx simply adds some points of detail to the model ... The continuity of Marx's thought about Asiatic society stemmed from the fact that in political economy Marx found an explanation for the backwardness of the orient which fitted in completely with his life-long anti-étatist views. The monopoly of economic initiative by entrepreneurial state power resulted in stagnation, as would be argued by any nineteenth-century liberal, including Marx who shared the views of the liberals about the role of state power. (Sawer, 1977a: 51)[87]

There are several problems with this position. First, the concept was not named by Marx until 1859, after he had written the *Grundrisse*, and some six years after his Indian articles of 1853. Second, even accepting that the 1853 articles are a first elaboration of the concept, it is evident that the age and status of the AMP compared with other modes of production becomes increasingly uncertain between 1853 and 1858, and remains so thereafter. In 1853 the concept is being applied to pre-conquest India, the India of the Mughal Empire, but in the *Grundrisse* it seems to be be located in a much more primordial social formation – the point of transition from primitive communism or indeed within primitive communism itself. Third, there is no warrant for the view that Marx's explanation of the foundation of despotism by the combination of isolated village communities and an entrepreneurial interventionist state is wholly derived from the ideological concerns of the classical political economists. (It is also contradictory, as I shall argue in chapter 4.) Arbitrariness, the state's monopoly of land revenue and the absence of the rule of law in oriental societies concerned the classical economists rather more than state entrepreneurial activity. They had recognized the need for certain public goods to be provided by the state. In any case, after the 1853 articles, Marx's primary emphasis in explaining oriental stagnation rested upon the structure of the self-sufficient village community and not upon the allegedly entrepreneurial role of the state. The former was supposed to explain the latter. Moreover, it is contentious, to say the least, that Marx shared the same views of state power as those held by nineteenth-century liberals. Therefore there are difficulties with both the assertion that there is essential continuity in Marx's texts and the explanation for this alleged continuity.

87 While Sawer concedes some minor discontinuities in Marx's understanding of the AMP she holds firmly to the view that the AMP was a fully fledged concept in 1853.

By contrast other authorities distinguish 'stages' in the development of the 'theory of the Asiatic mode of production':

Before he developed that theory he swiftly recapitulated the steps which European social thought had taken: in his youth Marx made a fleeting reference to the oriental despotism, but this characterization was a mere rhetorical flourish. In the second state, or the first actual one, he addressed himself to the concept of oriental society as a whole. In it he brought out the economic factors at work, but paid most attention to the political and social characterization of the society, and it remained at a distance from the subject matter. This stage is represented by his articles written in 1853 ... and his correspondence with Friedrich Engels ... In the next stage, which was begun in 1857–8, he formulated the theory of the AMP in a general way; there he initiated the inquiry into the internal economic relations in a specific way, and at the same time, he set forth the legal and political forms in their economic relations ... [but] he had not yet found the characterizing term to be applied to this conception; this he introduced in 1859 ... This theory was further developed in the 1860s, in the writing which culminated in the first volume of *Capital*. There the theory is found in a strict sense but it is not yet systematized, being expressed here and there in the text. (Krader, 1975: 1–2)

This evaluation does not imply fundamental and discontinuous stages in the evolution of Marx's thought on the AMP, in which each stage entails a complete rejection of the previous one. Rather, it amounts to an add-on model of conceptual development. At each stage Marx is alleged to have made the concept more Marxist than before until finally the strict theory appears in *Capital* – albeit not yet systematized. There are difficulties with this position also. First, to describe the young Marx as having 'swiftly recapitulated' European social thought on the Orient is an exaggeration. Whatever knowledge of the Orient Marx acquired in the 1840s was purely incidental, a by-product of his more research-directed reading. Second, the economic, legal and social dimensions of the AMP do not vary sufficiently and systematically enough in Marx's writings between 1853 and 1867 to warrant the designation of clearly demarcated stages. It is easier to suggest that the same concept was being used in different contexts – which is why, if at all, different dimensions seemed to be salient at different times. Finally, the idea that the theory of the AMP is present 'in the strict sense' only in *Capital*, the Holy of Holies, is an amusing example of pure fideism. Perhaps with 'the sixth sense' it can be appreciated.

Other authorities have even found different 'models' of the AMP in the work of Marx and Engels (Lowe, 1966; Hobsbawm, 1964). The first, developed in the 1853 articles, was a political model, which sought to explain the phenomena associated with oriental despotism. The second, developed in *Capital*, was an economic model which explained the under-development of commodity exchange in certain social formations. The third, developed in *Anti-Dühring*, was a stage in a model of historical progress, the demarcation of a transitional stage from communal to individual small-peasant ownership. These demarcations are also unconvincing. The 1853 articles were not directed at developing a political model of oriental despotism, a prototype of the agrarian analogue of totalitarianism articulated in Wittfogel's *Oriental Despotism*. There is no systematic economic 'model' of the functioning of the AMP in *Capital*[88] and what there is of one has its place in a typology of all pre-capitalist production relations, which explains how profoundly capitalism differs from pre-capitalist social systems.

The textual evidence obliges me to conclude that Marx and Engels's texts are so ambiguous that no thesis of continuity or discontinuity can be confirmed. This very ambiguity supports both schools of interpretation. A poorly articulated concept can be maintained consistently and continuously precisely because it is poorly articulated; but equally, definitional laxness allows considerable modification to be stipulatively introduced into a concept by an interpreter, thereby creating the impression of discontinuity. My agnostic judgement on this matter does not suggest, however, that Marx and Engels were ambiguous about the very idea of an AMP.

Did Marx abandon the AMP?   Three answers are given to this frequently posed question: 'yes', 'no' and 'maybe' – or as the more elegant Scottish verdict puts it, 'not proven'. I shall consider the arguments of those who answer 'yes' and those who sit on the fence, before firmly supporting the 'no' verdict.

The most famous or notorious positive answer is Wittfogel's argument that Marx committed a sin against science by repressing his discovery of the AMP. The subtitles of the chapter which Wittfogel devoted to his theme convey the flow and flavour of his case:

Marx, Engels, and Lenin Accept the Asiatic Concept . . . Marx follows his classical predecessors with regard to the institutional structure and the developmental position of the Orient . . . Marx's Asiatic Interpretation of India, China, and Post-Mongol Russia . . . Marx warns against confusing the state-controlled agrarian order of Asia with slavery or serfdom . . . Retreat from truth . . . Marx mystifies the character of the ruling class . . . Marx and Engels's sin against science. (Wittfogel, 1957: 370–7 and 380–9)

Under the first four of these subheadings Wittfogel made the unanswerable case that Marx at one stage accepted the Asiatic concept – although as Marx invented the term AMP, 'accepting' is an ungenerous description. The last three subtitles contain the juicy polemical contentions. Wittfogel

---

88 A serious attempt to construct an economic model of the AMP can be found in Diviçioglu (1967).

accused Marx of retreating from the truth through 'crippling' the AMP 'by dropping the idea of a bureaucratic ruling class' (ibid: 380). This charge implies that Marx once articulated the idea that a bureaucratic ruling class existed in the AMP and that he subsequently dropped it. However, Wittfogel's charge is even stranger. He argues that having read Mill, Jones and Bernier, Marx *should* have described the ruling class of the AMP as bureaucratic: 'Marx's interest in the class issue, the data at his disposal, and his objection to the mystification of social relations point to one conclusion, and one conclusion only. They all suggest that from his own standpoint Marx should have designated the functional bureaucracy as the ruling class of Oriental despotism. But Marx did nothing of the kind (ibid: 381) Marx regressed even further, in Wittfogel's view. He became increasingly reluctant 'to discuss the managerial aspect of Oriental despotism' (ibid:) In other words Marx did not emphasize, as Wittfogel did, the agro-managerial/hydraulic role of the oriental agrarian bureaucracy. Rather Marx 'obscured the specific managerial functions of the despotic state of the Orient, which in the '50s had intrigued him so greatly'. (ibid: 382).[89] Having marshalled his case Wittfogel asserted that Marx's 'retrogressions' were a sin against science. Obviously

the concept of Oriental despotism contained elements that paralyzed his search for truth. As a member of a group that intended to establish a total managerial and dictatorial state and was ready to use 'despotic measures' to achieve its socialist ends, Marx could scarcely help recognizing some disturbing similarities between Oriental despotism and the state of his program. (ibid: 387)

Wittfogel's argument is both tendentious and false. When charging somebody with suppressing incriminating evidence there must be a *prima facie* case for the prosecution, but Wittfogel's charge has no supporting material evidence. His argument is not built upon even one quotation in which Marx recognized that the AMP had sombre implications for socialism. It is debatable whether or not Wittfogel even has circumstantial evidence. Neither J. S. Mill nor Richard Jones, let alone Bernier, explicitly designated a functional bureaucracy as the ruling class of oriental despotism. Therefore Marx can scarcely be charged with dropping an idea which he did not come across! Wittfogel performed this designation, and then creatively interpreted asides from Mill, Jones and Bernier to suggest that his own theory of oriental despotism had venerable antecedents, which Marx had very conveniently ignored. Wittfogel's argument was roughly along the

---

89 This argument neglects the fact that the idea originated with Engels (see pp. 87−9 above) and that it was Engels in *Anti-Dühring*, rather than Marx, who emphasized the managerial functions of the despotic state in their later writings, and did so as late as 1878 (see pp. 119−23 above). Moreover Engels, unlike Marx or Wittfogel, thought irrigation functions were capable of being performed by local communities.

following lines: 'If a reasonable social scientist is confronted with the evidence that confronted Marx he must come to the same conclusions to which I, Karl A. Wittfogel, have come.' This appeal not only rests on the dubious merits of the assumption that all good social scientists should reason like Wittfogel, but also neglects more reasonable explanations of Marx's responses to his Asiatic 'discoveries'. For a start Wittfogel's conclusions might never have occurred to Marx, as seems to have been the case. He was after all concerned with matters other than the possibility that a man called Joseph Stalin would do extremely brutal things in twentieth-century Russia. Marx may have suffered from 'wishful thinking', as he seems to have done on regular occasions in his life. But proof of wishful thinking requires that the thought to be wished away, or wished into existence, must have occurred in the first place. We have not a shred of evidence that Marx had the sorts of thoughts which Wittfogel thinks should have occurred to him. It is even possible that Marx lacked Wittfogel's perspicuity.

Wittfogel's charge, that Marx deliberately suppressed evidence and committed a sin against science bypasses all the more reasonable interpretations of Marx's failure to come to Wittfogel's conclusions. We do, it is true, have evidence that Engels saw parallels between oriental despotism and state socialism (see pp. 131–2 above); but, first, this evidence post-dates Marx's death and, second, it is is wholly at odds with Wittfogel's contentions because Engels *welcomed* the parallels, which he saw as useful ammunition for an attack on Bismarck's state socialism – very strange behaviour from somebody who should have been paralysed, or at least embarrassed, by the association.

None the less, orthodox Marxists have agreed in some respects with Wittfogel. Nikiforov concurs with him that the concept of the AMP is fundamentally at odds with key tenets of Marxism, and that Marx and Engels initially supported the idea of the AMP. However, Nikiforov argues that they rightly repudiated it. Nikiforov's case, as reported in Gellner (1986), is that historical materialism was not completely put on a materialist footing until Marx had read and digested the works of Morgan and Kovalevsky. These authors allowed Marx to place historical materialism on a firm and empirical basis and to divest the theory of residual Hegelian errors. Both Morgan and Kovalevsky placed communal ownership in the primitive community and not in a more developed social formation, thereby compelling Marx to re-evaluate his position. The evidence of some of his last notes and marginalia are invoked by Nikiforov to suggest he had concluded that the idea of oriental despotism – and *a fortiori* the idea of the AMP – was a by-product of imperialist fabrication. The idea of 'despotism + primitive society' was 'John Bull's main and favoured doctrine, as he became intoxicated with primitive "despotism"' (Nikiforov, cited in

Gellner, 1986: 93). But as we have made plain enough throughout this chapter, from the 1850s onwards Marx's writings were ambiguous as to the 'primitiveness' of the AMP. Therefore even if one were persuaded by his argument that Morgan forced Marx to tidy up historical materialism, Nikiforov's thesis would have to be qualified: Morgan and Kovalevsky become important in helping Marx to resolve an ambiguity rather than in changing his mind.

Nikiforov's thesis that historical materialism was furbished up at a late stage also rests upon the more dubious assertion that Marx's notes on Kovalevsky imply that he had come to accept that the idea of private property in land had existed in pre-conquest India. This reading of Marx's reading of Kovalevsky is especially forced because, as we have seen (pp. 126–8 above), Marx's conspectus on Kovalevsky is mostly a catalogue of disagreements with the latter's description of India as feudal. And if it wasn't feudal, or capitalist or slaveholding, then what was it? Nikiforov further contends that Kovalevsky's impact in revising historical materialism is present in Marx's letters to Zasulich. In these drafts there is no mention of the AMP, but instead, these are references to an 'archaic formation'. However, the weight of this argument is vitiated by the fact that one of Marx's drafts mentions despotism existing above the communes (Gellner, 1986), which fundamentally weakens Nikiforov's case that Marx had abandoned the coupling of the political institution of despotism with the socio-economic relations of the primitive oriental village. Nikiforov finally bolsters his argument with the assertion that Engels abandoned the AMP, pointing out that Engels intended to write a monograph on *Three Basic Forms of Enslavement* which he never managed to commence. According to Nikiforov the fact that Engels neither elaborated nor apparently had any intention of elaborating a fourth form of exploitation, and the fact that a fourth form of exploitation has never been subsequently been found by the *Aziatchiki*, confirm the proposition that the AMP was abandoned in the final, mature versions of historical materialist arguments, polished up after Marx's encounter with Morgan and Kovalevsky.

The generally orthodox Indian Marxist historian Irfan Habib provides the best example of the development of the Scottish verdict on whether Marx abandoned the AMP. He argues that 'there seems to be good reason to believe that Marx developed considerable reservations about the "Asiatic" concept after 1867' (Habib, 1983: 111). His reasons are instructive. First, he points out that the AMP was problematic for historical materialism: it left many issues unresolved – for example, did the AMP precede slavery or not? Second, by the late 1870s historical evidence against Marx's initial impressions of India was starting to accumulate: evidence of the development of private property in Indian land prior to the British conquest put a question mark against the thesis that India had been in a state of primordial stagnation. Kovalevsky's evidence also put in doubt the general idea that the state had been the landed proprietor throughout Asia: this institutional arrangement was a by-product of Islamic conquests rather than intrinsically Asiatic. Moreover, Habib points out that, from Elphinstone's *History of India*, Marx could have drawn the conclusion that under the Mughals the exploitative surplus was paid in money and not in kind – a fact which implied a far more monetized and developed pre-conquest economy than Marx's journalism or asides in the *Grundrisse* or *Capital* had suggested. Habib also suggests that the contradiction between Marx's understanding of despotism standing above society, as articulated in the *Grundrisse*, and his general theory of the state as a product of social contradictions must have been glaring. In fact, in his notes on Maine's *Lectures on the Early History of Institutions* Marx had rejected Maine's idea of a state standing above society – an implicit element of the AMP – and had insisted that it arose out of social contradictions (Gunawardana, 1976: 387).[90] Therefore Habib concludes that there is 'enough evidence that Marx's continued reading on India after 1867 led him to reconsider the force of a number of his earlier ideas on pre-colonial India' (Habib, 1983: 115).

However, Habib is a good enough historian to recognize that the case for full abandonment of the AMP is not proven. He admits that Marx still refused to call India feudal, and therefore did not place it under the most obvious alternative classification to the AMP. Like many scholars and polemicists he places a great deal of weight on the case that Engels abandoned the concept. One's judgement on this contention is decisive in evaluating whether or not the founders of historical materialism abandoned Marx's bastard child.

Did Engels abandon the AMP?   There are three well-known Engels pastimes amongst Marxological scholars. The first uses Engels to absolve Marx of blame for something discreditable.[91] This pastime is exemplified in the attempt to confine to Engels the view that the functional requirements of

90 Gunawardana argues that Marx's notes on Maine explicitly reflect his dissatisfaction with the theory of the oriental state that he had developed, but not published, in the *Grundrisse*.

91 On this stratagem all scholars must concur with Anderson's measured verdict: 'It has long been fashionable to depreciate the relative contribution of Engels to the creation of historical materialism. For those who are still inclined to accept this received notion, it is necessary to say calmly and scandalously: Engels's historical judgements are nearly always superior to those of Marx' (P. Anderson, 1974b: 23, footnote 12). In line with this verdict I have ignored Marx's 'Asiatic' historical writings on eighteenth-century, Czarist Russia, because they are abusive and frankly rubbish. My argument that Marx did not abandon the AMP is 'supported' by these wild writings (Marx, 1954, 1969 and 1972; Marx and Engels, 1952). These texts do not tell against any of the arguments advanced in this book, because they do not tell anything very much – except that Marx could be paranoid and foolish.

irrigation have anything to do with the AMP. The second, more rarely deployed and only used in cases of dire emergency, uses Engels to correct Marx. In discussions of the AMP it is suggested that Engels dropped the concept after Marx's death in the light of subsequent historical discoveries and ethnographic and historiographical surveys. The third finds Engels guilty of some offence and finds Marx guilty by association. Wittfogel's charge that Engels committed 'a sin against science' is a specimen of this pastime.[92] What substance is there in these games? Did Engels abandon the AMP?

There is no positive evidence in the form of an explicit statement by Engels rejecting the concept. There is, however, some circumstantial evidence. Neither the term AMP nor that of oriental despotism appears in Engels's published writings in the twelve years between the death of Marx in 1883 and his own death in 1895. In *The Origin of the Family, Private Property and the State*, published in 1884, not only does neither term appear, but it has been suggested that Engels implicitly excludes the AMP from historical materialism by making slavery, and only slavery, the first type of class society. Godelier even explains this change with the suggestion that Engels abandoned the AMP because neither Morgan nor he could find evidence of powerful monarchical regimes amongst the Greeks, and therefore, since the AMP did not appear to be universal, Engels felt obliged to leave it go (Godelier, 1964: 17−23).[93] Finally, there is the evidence that Engels edited a key 'Asiatic' footnote in the English translation of *Capital*, Volume I (see p. 111).

There are several lacunae in these detective stories. First, since Engels played little part in the development of the idea of the AMP in Marx's lifetime it is scarcely compelling to suggest that his silence after Marx's death speaks rejection of Marx's ideas. Engels's role in the development of Marx's asides on the AMP was minor, with the important exception of his correspondence with Marx in 1853 and his own writings on Russia in 1875. He displayed small interest in Asian socio-economic history, as opposed to interest in the military history of Asian wars, reflecting a standard intellectual separation of interests between Marxism's two founding

92 There are even more fanciful Marx−Engels games, such as the argument that *Anti-Dühring* is a work of 'anomaly-containment' since here the origins of a ruling class are allowed to be state-generated rather than society−generated. In this text Engels allegedly downplayed the dramatic contrasts between the Western feudal system and the Eastern Asiatic system. His contrast between the functional and exploitative origins of the state was a more generalized version of the contrast between Eastern and Western systems of stratification − and deliberately prevented the difficult ideological questions posed by the AMP from coming to the fore (Gouldner, 1980: 327). Needless to say this 'reading' rests upon 'a symptomatic' intuition.

93 This creative argument allows Godelier to argue that the discovery of the Mycenean civilization, which he thinks was a specimen of the AMP, has removed the anxieties allegedly faced by Engels.

fathers. The one occasion when Engels wrote in public on the substantive subject matter of the AMP, oriental despotism or oriental society, was in *Anti-Dühring*, the text of which was carefully reviewed by Marx, and to which Marx contributed a chapter. Therefore, these exceptions aside, Engels failed to mention oriental despotism or the AMP between 1853 and 1883, a fact which makes his public silence after 1883 less than surprising. Surely here silence must be construed as consent to Marx's ideas if it is to imply anything at all? In any case this alleged 'silence' is questionable, as we shall see.

The silence of *The Origin of the Family, Private Property and the State* on the AMP should also not be a matter of surprise. The task of that book, based upon Marx's notes on Morgan, was to show that Morgan's anthropology had independently confirmed historical materialism. Morgan, Marx and Engels based their materials on North American Indian sources, as well as materials from Greek, Roman and German history, and thereby excluded Asia from the study of gentile institutions. Silence about Asia and the AMP was therefore to be expected. None the less, Engels referred to 'the traces of these institutions in the ancient history of civilized peoples of Asia' (Engels, 1976: 156). And he gave Indian examples in his discussions of the origins of the family: citing the cases of the Waralis, Magars and Munniporees. But the problem lies less in this empirical material than in Engels's concluding arguments. Engels's theoretical summary suggested that 'Slavery is the first form of exploitation, the form peculiar to the ancient world; it is succeeded by serfdom in the Middle Ages, and wage labour in modern times. These are the three great forms of servitude characteristic of the three great epochs of civilization; open, and in recent times disguised, slavery always accompanies them' (ibid: 213). What, we might well ask, has happened to the AMP in this schema which harks back to those of *The German Ideology* and *The Communist Manifesto*?

Several arguments counsel against the hasty conclusion that Engels abandoned the AMP. First, Engels's summary, like his book, may have referred to the history of Europe alone. The suggestive if unsupported argument has also been made that 'Engels' interests appear to have been slightly different from Marx's. He was probably preoccupied rather less with the survival or disintegration of the primitive community, and rather more with the rise and decline of feudalism' (Hobsbawm, 1964: 52), an idea that might help explain Engels's lack of apparent enthusiasm for the AMP in this text. A textual explanation for the absence of the AMP in *The Origin of the Family, Private Property and the State* has even been offered: Engels's 'main object was to show the nature and form of the notion that led to the establishment of the slaveholding mode of production of antiquity. He did not at all claim to be describing the extreme diversity of world history' (Parain, 1964: 5 — my translation). Second, Marx and Engels's use of the term 'slavery' often extended to any form of intensive or despotic exploitation, and consequently no inference of abandonment of the AMP can be inferred from Engels's schema. Finally, it has been argued that the AMP does indeed figure in the text of *The Origin of the Family, Private Property and the State*, albeit without the dignity of its own name. The late Marx's AMP may be identical with the general social form of primitive tribal communalism which in his 1881 draft letters to Zasulich he termed the 'archaic formation'. Accordingly, Engels's references to the village community, the German Mark and the *naturwüchsiges Gemeinwesen* are references to this archaic formulation (Draper, 1977: 559–60). This argument finds further support in Engels's writings after 1884, in the letter about Java's 'old communistic village communities' and in what he wrote in the 1894 afterword to his *Social Relations in Russia*, having left the main body of the text unaltered:

Communal ownership of land was a form of tenure which in the primitive epoch had been prevalent among the Germans, the Celts, and the Indians, in short, among all the Indo-European peoples, which still exists in India, which was only recently forcibly destroyed in Ireland and Scotland, and still occurs here and there in Germany even today, and that it is a disappearing form of tenure which is, in fact, a phenomenon common to all peoples at a definite stage of development. (Marx and Engels, 1969–70 2: 389–90).

There is indeed a lack of integration between the theses of *The Origin of the Family, Private Property and the State* and the arguments of *Anti-Dühring*. However, contextual explanations of this malintegration are surely preferable to those of Gouldner and Wittfogel, because they make no unwarranted appeal to psychology.

In any case, there is an additional trumping argument which suggests that neither Engels nor Marx abandoned the AMP, and makes up for any weaknesses in my battery of counter-arguments to this notion. This trump card is decisive in answering the question of whether the founding fathers abandoned the concept. Engels spent much of the 1880s editing *Capital*, Volume II and Volume III. He had almost total discretion in the editing of *Capital*, Volume III, and the opportunity to indicate in footnotes precisely where he or later scholarship had rejected or superseded Marx's arguments. That Engels did not excise or qualify Marx's detailed remarks on oriental despotism and tributary social relations in *Capital*, Volume III, must count as sufficient proof that Engels, like his co-theorist, not only did not repudiate the AMP, but was happy to affirm its existence in the last and most serious intellectual task of his life. Perhaps just as significantly, in subsequent editions of *Anti-Dühring*, including one published in 1894, Engels did not delete or qualify the Asiatic or oriental passages in his own work. Neither Engels nor Marx, it may safely be concluded, abandoned the substantive conceptual commitments suggested by the AMP.

CONCLUSION

There was a lack of clarity and rigour in Marx and Engels's writings about the AMP and India, fuelling the many erroneous interpretations of their implications. However, no serious scholar can now question that Marx and Engels believed in the existence of a separate and in some respects distinctive Asiatic social order, mode of production or social formation. Whether they were right or consistent to do so is a separate question, addressed in subsequent chapters on both theoretical and empirical grounds.

APPENDIX 3.1   MARX AND ENGELS'S READING RELEVANT TO THE
ASIATIC MODE OF PRODUCTION AND INDIA, 1843–95

This appendix lists all the relevant sources, primary and secondary, to which Marx and Engels referred explicitly in their published and unpublished writings and which can reasonably be construed as having informed their understanding of India and their conceptions of the AMP, oriental despotism and oriental society. Research for this appendix was aided by Rubel (1957), Hobsbawm (1964), Krader (1972) and Levine (1977). However, it was mainly built up by following the relevant references in Marx and Engels's works.

Author	Text	Date read	Cited in
Addington, S.	*The Advantages of the East-India Trade to England*	1850–60s	C
Aristotle	*Politics*	#	C
Bernier, F.	*Voyages*	1853	SC, NYDT, CCPE, C, TSV
Brougham, H.	*An Inquiry into the Colonial Policy of the European Powers*	1850s–60s	C
Campbell, G.	*Modern India: A Sketch of the System of Civil Government*	1853	NYDT, C
Chapman, J.	*The Cotton and Commerce of India*	1853	NYDT
Child, Sir J.	*A Treatise wherein it is demonstrated that East India Trade is the Most National of All Foreign Trade*	1853	NYDT
Dickinson, J.	*The Government of India under a Bureaucracy*	1853	NYDT

Elphinstone, M.	*History of India*	> 1870?	NOIH*
The Select Committee on East India Affairs	*Fifth Report of the Select Committee on East India Affairs*	1853	NYDT
Hegel, G. W. F.	*The Philosophy of History*	#	GI, C
Hegel, G. W. F.	*The Philosophy of Right*	1843–4	CHPR, C
Irwin, H. C.	*The Garden of India*	1881	EN
Jones, R.	*Essay on the Distribution of Wealth, and on the Sources of Taxation*	1851	G, C, TSV
Jones, R.	*An Introductory Lecture on Political Economy*	1851	C, TSV
Jones, R.	*Textbook of Lectures on the Political Economy of Nations*	1852–	C, TSV
Jones, W.	*Manusmriti*	1853	SC, NYDT
Kovalevsky, M.	*Communal Landholding*	1879–80	EN
Linguet, S. N. H.	*Théorie des lois civiles, ou principes fondamentaux de la société*	1850s	TSV, C
Lubbock, J.	*The Origins of Civilization and the Primitive Condition of Man*	> 1880	EN
Mackinnon, W. A.	*History of Civilization and Public Opinion*		
Maine, H. S.	*Lectures on the Early History of Institutions*	> 1880	EN
Mill, James	*The History of British India*	1853–8	NYDT
Mill, J. S.	*Principles of Political Economy*	1851	NYDT, TSV, C
Morgan, L. H.	*Ancient Society*	1878–83	EN, OFPP & S
Money, J. W. B.	*Java, Or How to Manage a Colony*	1883–4	OC
Montesquieu C.-L. de	*De l'Esprit des lois*	#	CHPR, C
Mun, T.	*A Discourse of Trade, from England unto the East Indies*	1853–	NYDT
Mun, T.	*England's Treasure by Forraign Trade*	1850s–60s	C

Murray, H. and Wilson J.	*Historical and Descriptive Account of British India*	> 1858	C
Papillon, T.	*The East India Trade a Most Profitable Trade to the Kingdom*	1850–60s	C
Patton, R.	*The Principles of Asiatic Monarchies*	1853	
Pollexfen, J.	*England and East-India Inconsistent in their Manufactures*	> 1853	NYDT
Budd Phear, J.	*The Aryan Village in India and Ceylon*	1881	EN
Raffles, S.	*History of Java*	1853	SC, C, CCPE
Forbes Royle, J.	*Essay on the Productive Resources of India: An Inquiry into the Causes of the Long Continued Stationary Condition of India*	1853	
Saltykov, A. D.	*Lettres sur l'Inde*	1853	NYDT
Sewell, R.	*The Analytical History of India*	> 1870	NOIH*
Smith, A.	*The Wealth of Nations*	#	EPM, G, TSV, C
Wilks, M.	*Historical Sketches of the South of India*	1853	SC, CCPE, C

Key

\# = texts that Marx and Engels read throughout their working lives, and/or it is uncertain when they first read the text.

> = after

* = I assume Marx's *Notes on Indian History* were taken at the same time as he read Kovalevsky's book (that is, *c.*1879–80). His abstract of Kovalevsky is found in between Marx's chronological notes on Indian history taken from Elphinstone and Sewell – see (Marx 1959b: 66). They cannot have been taken before 1870 as that is the year of publication of Sewell's work.

Abbreviations

Texts or collections of Marx and Engels – see bibliography for full references.)

C	=	*Capital*, Volumes I–III
CCPE	=	*Contribution to the Critique of Political Economy*
CHPR	=	*Critique of Hegel's Philosophy of Right*
EN	=	*Ethnological Notebooks*
EPM	=	*Economic and Philosophical Manuscripts*
G	=	*Grundrisse*

GI   =   *German Ideology*
NOIH   =   *Notes on Indian History*
NYDT   =   *New York Daily Tribune* articles
OC   =   *On Colonialism*
OFPP&S   =   *Origin of the Family, Private Property and the State*
SC   =   *Selected Correspondence*
TSV   =   *Theories of Surplus Value*

Note: Where a date is specified for when Marx read a work but there is no citation in his published writings, I am relying on Marx's *Exzerpte*.

APPENDIX 3.2   THE ASIATIC MODE OF PRODUCTION IN THE
SECOND INTERNATIONAL

The AMP, or oriental society — as it was more often called by classical Marxists — did not drop out of the Marxist lexicon in the Second International in the Marxist 'golden age' (Kolakowski, 1981, Volume 2). The Marxist tradition retained the concept of a separate AMP until Stalin excised it. The understanding of the history of the concept created by Wittfogel is erroneous. Marx must have failed to 'cripple the concept' if it was employed by his most famous and immediate disciples. Second International Marxist luminaries like Lafargue, Cunow and Luxemburg did employ — albeit incidentally — concepts like agrarian communism, oriental society and oriental despotism, and without engendering any political argument, let alone controversy.

Kautsky employed the concept of oriental despotism in an article he wrote on *Die moderne Nationalitie* for *Die Neue Zeit* in 1887 (Draper, 1977: 662—4). He used the concept to criticize anarchists, reminding them that agrarian communism had been the basis upon which a despotic superstructure had been erected. And he referred without embarrassment to an aristocracy as the ruling class in oriental despotism.

Plekhanov's use of the concept was more controversial. Plekhanov analysed the development of the Czarist state explictly as a specimen of an oriental despotism, a state stronger than society, a despotic superstructure established upon an agrarian communist economic base (Baron, 1958). Plekhanov also applied the notion outside of Russian contexts, and was concerned to express its importance for the Marxist theory of the state:

According to Labriola, the state is an organization for the rule of one class over another or others. That is so. But it scarcely expresses the whole truth. In states like China or ancient Egypt, where civilized life was impossible without highly complex and extensive works for the regulation of the flow and overflow of big rivers and for irrigation purposes, the rise of the state may be explained largely by the direct influence of the needs of the social productive process ... the above must not be lost sight of if an incorrect and one-sided idea of the historical role of the state is to be avoided. (Plekhanov, 1969: 117—8).

The key point is that the practice of these Second International Marxists shows a complete lack of inhibition about using the AMP — or rather a term with the same substantive intellectual content. The burial of the AMP was not carried out by Marx or Engels or the theorists of the Second International. Nor even Lenin explicitly repudiated the concept: he simply rejected the empirical appropriateness of Plekhanov's application of the idea to Czarist Russia (see pp. 27–9).

4

The Theory, Dilemmas and Contradictions of the Asiatic Mode of Production

In a number of ways, the idea of the Asiatic Mode of Production constitutes a conceptual canker which, once introduced into the Marxist belief-system, ends up by corroding it fatally.

Gellner, 'Stagnation without Salvation'

This chapter analyses the theoretical location of the AMP in standard interpretations of historical materialism. An outline of the tenets and principal variants of historical materialism precedes an account of the general dilemmas and problems posed by the AMP for all historical materialism. The arguments developed here are analytical, not historical. They appraise and develop ideas from diverse sources: the writings of classical, Western, Soviet, East European and Indian Marxists, as well as those of non-Marxist commentators and critics. The conclusion of this chapter and the one which follows can be summarized in a formula: *historical materialism is damned if it retains the Asiatic Mode of Production, and damned if it doesn't.*

HISTORICAL MATERIALISM

'Historical materialism' is the established shorthand expression for Marx's theory of history even though Marx did not use the phrase himself, preferring to describe his approach as the materialist conception of history. Marx claimed his theory of history was scientific, and rejected many of the charges brought against it which suggested otherwise. He denied that his theory was supra-individual, or a theory of some impersonal, hypostatized and disembodied subject, 'Man'. In a famous passage in the jointly written *The Holy Family*, Marx and Engels remarked that 'History does nothing: it does not possess immense riches, it does not fight battles' (Marx and Engels, 1975: 93). Towards the end of his life Marx counselled the editors of a Russian newspaper against reading *Capital*, Volume I, as a 'general historico-philosophical theory, the supreme virtue of which consists in being supra-historical' (Marx and Engels, 1934: 355). He regularly affirmed that he did not think of the study of history solely as the transformation of structures beyond the control of human actors. In the introduction to *The Eighteenth Brumaire of Louis Bonaparte* he wrote that 'Men make their own history, but not of their own free will' (Marx, 1973d: 146). The same statement implies that Marx's theory of history was not a radical voluntarism — as Maoists later suggested. There are constraints on human choice, imposed by past developments and by current structures, which limit the discretion of historical actors. A new and better world cannot be created *ex nihilo* by idealistic action. But such activity might lessen the 'birth-pangs' felt in the transition to a new social order (Marx, 1976: 92).

The objections which he anticipated and attempted to repudiate were, none the less, very reasonable construals of certain of his major writings. To use the title of a recent and deservedly influential text, *Making Sense of Marx* is not easy (Elster, 1985).[1] Marx was a fertile, but confused and confusing, theorist of history, just as he was fertile, confused and confusing in his economic and methodological discussions. These facets of his work have facilitated the generation of multiple Marxes, and apparently infinite variatons on what are alleged to be the central tenets of historical materialism. The dispute over what were Marx's underlying epistemological and methodological assumptions dramatically confirms this luxuriant variation. The Hungarian Lukács once argued that orthodox Marxism was defined exclusively by method (Lukács, 1967: 1). The trouble with Lukács's dictum is that there is no consensus as to what precisely is Marxist method. Engels described it as dialectical materialist, which remains orthodoxy in the Soviet Union (Engels, 1964). Max Adler thought it consistent with Kantianism (Adler, 1978). Karl Löwith thought it a secularized theology and many contemporary theologians of liberation have found it possible to combine Marxism and Christian theology (Löwith, 1948). Lukács himself regarded orthodox Marxism as Hegelian. Della Volpe described Marxism as 'moral galileism' (della Volpe, 1980). Various Western Marxists have proved to their satisfaction that Marx was a historicist (Gramsci, 1971), and that he was not (Althusser and Balibar, 1970); that Marx was at his methodological best as a structuralist (Althusser, 1969; and Godelier, 1972), and, on the contrary, as a methodological individualist (Elster, 1985; and Roemer, 1986b); that Marx was a realist (Bhaskar, 1978), the originator of a 'scientific research programme' (Callinicos, 1982), a critical liberation theorist (Jay, 1973), and so on *ad infinitum*. As with methodology so with historical materialism. There is no consensus amongst Marxists, or non-Marxists, about its principal assumptions, methods and predictions.

1 For a critical survey of Elster's work see O'Leary (1987).

However, beneath the bewildering variety of alleged versions of historical materialism three major variants are dominant in contemporary academic discussion, and these I shall label the productivist, the structuralist and the Hegelian respectively.[2] They are sufficiently rigorous to merit sustained analysis.

Productivist Historical Materialism

Productivist historical materialism is often described as the 'technicist' or 'technological determinist' reading of Marx and Engels's theories. It has been the dominant interpretation of Marx's theory of history, for both Marxists and critics of Marxism. In the Second International it was ably expounded and defended by Plekhanov and Kautsky (Baron, 1963; and Salvadori, 1977). In the Third International both Bukharin and Stalin shared its assumptions while differing politically from the theorists of the Second International, and eventually with one other (Bukharin, 1926; and Stalin, 1938). Trotsky, the founder of the Fourth International, was also a gifted exponent (Knei-Paz, 1977).[3] Productivist historical materialism has therefore been the background theory of all major Marxist movements since the late nineteenth century – with the notable exception of the voluntarist theories associated with Chinese Marxists. Amongst Western academic Marxists it fell out of favour during de-Stalinization. Subsequently it has revived, however, notably through the efforts of Isaac Deutscher and various historians and academics inspired by Trotskyism, as well as the scholarly work of self-styled 'Analytical Marxists', notably Gerry Cohen, John Roemer and William Shaw (G.A. Cohen, 1979; Deutscher, 1966a and 1966b; Roemer, 1986; and Shaw, 1978).[4]

Productivist historical materialists share three tenets. First, the textual authority for their readings of historical materialism is predominantly de-rived from Marx's Preface to *A Contribution to the Critique of Political*

2 This classification is open to challenge. Nicos Mouzelis assures me that there is a fourth version of historical materialism which is more open, less technologically determinist, less structuralist, less teleological and less historicist than the three versions I shall discuss below. He cites as examples the work of Laclau (1977) and Laclau and Mouffe (1985). However, in my judgement such species of Marxism are not recognizably Marxist, and certainly not historical materialist in any important sense. The fact that the authors of such ideas retain some lingering sentiment for the Marxist label – or indeed the post-Marxist label – tells us something about their desire not be identified with so-called 'bourgeois' social theory. It tells us nothing about the substantive intellectual content of their ideas. Indeed the 'discourse Marxism' (or 'disco-Marxism' as I like to call it) of Laclau and Mouffe largely consists of the pretentious inflation of sensible statements which are unexceptionable to pluralist social scientists when they are translated into clear propositions.

3 The multiple sectarian fragments of the movement he founded still embrace productivist doctrines (Hodgson, 1975).

4 Boastfully (but fairly) the Analytical Marxists describe themselves as the '*Marxismus sine stercori tauri*' group.

Economy. Second, they share the general assumption that history is the story of the development of the productive forces, or the successive, cumulative and revolutionary conquest of nature by the human species in pursuit of its needs. Third, they claim that a scientific theory of history was developed by Marx, which is empirical, can be tested against historical evidence, and stands or falls on its empirical validity whatever its philosophical or normative appeal. The scientific claim is that this theory can be used to demonstrate how the development of the productive forces explains the transformation of property systems, state systems and the ideas about social organization held by human agents.

These three common tenets of productivist historical materialists mask important differences amongst them. There is little consensus on the definitions of key concepts, namely mode of production, relations of production, basis, superstructure, state and ideology. However, there is, implicitly at least, a consensus that three law-like relations hold between some of these concepts. First, there is the development thesis: the productive forces tend to develop throughout history (G.A. Cohen, 1979: 134). This thesis assumes that human beings, in conditions of scarcity, are sufficiently rational to attempt to improve their welfare. It also assumes that the acquisition and dispersal of technical knowledge are cumulative. Second, there is the primacy thesis: the nature of the productive relations of a society is explained by the level of development of its productive forces (ibid). This thesis is the heart of productivist historical materialism. To show that it is false or incoherent is to shatter the overall theory. Third, there is the economic functionalist thesis: the superstructure of any society is functionally explained by its economic base. This thesis is the best known law of productivist historical materialism.

The primacy thesis is rejected, or revised, by structuralist historical materialists, who are also more cautious about the development and economic functionalist theses.

Structuralist Historical Materialism

Structuralism is a concept which describes a multitude of intellectual ideas and movements but can be simplified into two overlapping meanings. First, there is structuralism as a method of inquiry, the characteristic presupposition of which is that knowledge of a system is best acquired through investigation of the relations between its objects and the discovery of their reciprocal interconnections and rules of transformation (Piaget, 1971).[5] Second, there is structuralism, or *structuralisme*, as a Parisian intellectual

---

5 As a description of a method of inquiry structuralism in this sense has a long philosophical pedigree. Its twentieth-century reputation was established in linguistics by Saussure, and more notably by Noam Chomsky.

fashion of the 1960s and 1970s. Structuralist Marxism, as articulated by the French philosopher, Louis Althusser, exemplified both types of structuralism. Although Althusser was highly critical of what he described as the 'structuralist ideology' of Levi-Strauss and other French intellectuals, he shared many of the *structuralistes'* assumptions, especially their assault upon humanism and empiricism.

Structuralist historical materialism was defined by Althusser primarily through a series of denials (Althusser, 1969; and Althusser and Balibar, 1970). It is easier to list these denials than to state coherently his positive theory. First, historical materialism is not a humanism. It is a theoretical anti-humanism. It is not concerned with individuals' motivations, volitions, natures or meanings. Rather, Marx's theory of history recognizes that 'individuals' are bearers of structurally determined social relations.[6] Second, historical materialism is not a historicism. By this formulation Althusser wished to distance historical materialism from the charge that it was teleological. Some of Althusser's most suggestive writing consisted of his demonstration of the simple metaphors and similes which lie behind historicist interpretations of historical materialism. Hegelians, he suggested, think of each historical epoch as an expressive totality in which each of the social practices of the era (economy, culture, religion, art and politics) is an expression of a single essence, which in turn corresponds to a stage in the development of the world spirit. But, Althusser argued, since there is no subject of history in historical materialism, the notion that history has an end has to be repudiated.[7] Third, historical materialism is not an essentialism. It is the science of social formations and modes of production. These social formations and modes of production are not 'centred', or composed of an essence. Indeed they are 'decentred'. But, none the less, social formations are a combination of invariant practices (economic, political, ideological and theoretical), arranged in a hierarchy in which each practice is relatively autonomous of the others, and the economic is dominant only 'in the last instance'. Fourth, as the previous formulation suggests, historical materialism is not an economism; that is, it is not what productivist historical materialists say it is. Althusser and Balibar suggested that economic determination in

---

6 According to Althusser, Marx had travelled an intellectual road to Damascus in the 1840s and experienced an 'epistemological break' from the humanist Hegelian problematic (Althusser, 1969). Therefore so-called Marxists who read Marx as a Hegelian humanist were pre-Marxist in their thinking.

7 He believed that Marx had shown that 'history was a process without a subject.' Marx therefore could not have wanted to contend that the culmination of that process was known already, or indeed that the notion of the culmination of history made sense. As, *contra* Hegelian historicism, reality is overdetermined − that is, subject to multiple causation − it followed that the Marxist totality should not be identified with the Hegelian. The Marxist totality was rather a complex 'structure in dominance'.

the last instance amounted to no more than the determination of which practice was to be dominant in any given social formation.

Althusser's *mélange* of injunctions about what was not historical materialism and what was the science or problematic of historical materialism became known as structuralist historical materialism.[8] His 'interpretation' of Marx was constructed through a controversial 'symptomatic' reading which seemed to permit him arbitrary freedom in designating which of Marx's texts were genuinely Marxist. This reconstruction of historical materialism played a significant role in intellectual debates amongst Western Marxists in the 1960s and 1970s, but by the late 1970s and the early 1980s it was widely discredited even amongst its erstwhile enthusiasts (Cutler, Hindess, Hirst and Hussain, 1977; and Benton, 1984). However, the interventions of many of Althusser's adherents in debates on pre-capitalist modes of production, and their attacks on productivist historical materialism, did sometimes raise the level of debate in arguments about the AMP. For these reasons the problems posed for structuralist historical materialists by Marx's texts on the AMP merit attention.

Hegelian Historical Materialism

Hegelian Marxists provide the most speculative and least scientific reading of historical materialism. There are many passages in Marx which show his indebtedness to Hegel and his style is littered with Hegelian language and motifs. These dimensions of Marx's writings, present even in *Capital*, are a permanent embarrassment to productivist and structuralist historical materialists. However, since the collapse of the Second International many theorists have based their reading of Marx upon the many Hegelian themes in his work. Lukács, Kojève, Sartre and the theorists of the Frankfurt school, Adorno, Horkheimer, and Marcuse are amongst the most notable Western Marxists to have read Marx through Hegelian spectacles.[9]

Hegel's philosophy of history, as Marx himself suggested, was reconstructed by Marx in materialist language.[10] For both Hegel and Marx the goal of history, its meaning, was freedom for the subject of history. The subject in Hegel's case was the World Spirit (God), in Marx's case the human species. The freedom was two-sided: the positive freedom to achieve self-realization on the part of the subject of history, and negative freedom

---

8 Althusser's description of what was not historical materialism comes very close to describing what historical materialism had always been understood to mean − especially by critics such as Popper (1957, 1962) and Acton (1955).

9 An excellent account of Marxism as a soteriology derived from Hegelian philosophy can be found in Kolakowski (1981). Much of Western Marxism has in fact been a return to Hegel (Merquior, 1986).

10 See, for example, the preface to the second edition of *Capital* (Marx, 1976: 102).

from the constraints and frustrations which had prevented its full self-realization in the past. For both Hegel and Marx, history was a theodicy, an explanation of the existence of evil in the world. Hegel's teleological conception of history was an elegant solution to the perennial theological problem of evil. The problem is the one every atheist poses the Christian believer.[11] Hegel's answer to this dilemma of the problem of evil was to transcend it by refusing its premises. The World Spirit was not yet perfect, nor yet omnipotent and omniscient. The evil in the world was the by-product of the World Spirit's estrangement and alienation from his future perfection. Evil, so to speak, was a by-product of God's adolescence. Human societies are the vehicles of the World Spirit's successive transformations towards objective freedom. As the World Spirit reaches harmonious integration and perfection so human societies will become integrated and perfected, and evil will wither away.

Marx's transformation of Hegel's teleological theology into a more secular theory preserved the shell of Hegel's theology but removed the actor, the World Spirit, as the subject of history. Althusserians describe this transformation by suggesting that Marx took from Hegel the idea of history as a 'process without a subject'. However, they are wrong on two counts. First, Hegel's theory of history had a subject, the World Spirit; and second, Marx's theory of history substituted a new subject, 'Man', a hypostatized conception of the human species as a unitary actor in place of the World Spirit. In Marx's speculative theory of history, exploitation is the evil in the world. The evils of class-division and exploitation are necessary to the attainment of the final end of history, human self-fulfilment in advanced Communism. Marx's functionalist mode of historical explanation has its deepest roots in an eschatological theodicy which structured his thinking long after his formal abandonment of Hegel's philosophy.[12]

The fundamental teleological and eschatological assumptions in Hegelian historical materialism are captured in figure 4.1. The set of stages represents the destined evolutionary path of the human species. Each separate phase of the lower half of the staircase is travelled by a different ethnicity (Semenov, 1980). The overall upward path of the staircase illustrates the

---

11 If God is all-perfect, omnipotent and omniscient why does evil exist? There is a dilemma here: *either* God is not all-perfect (alternatively 'perfection' includes 'malevolence'), *or* God is not omnicompetent and omniscient. This thorny problem for Christian, Jewish and Muslim conceptions of God can be transcended in three ways. The Hegelian way transcends the dilemma by putting God's perfection into the future. God is not yet perfect, but will be. Evil is a necessary by-product of God's perfection. The Pascalian trick transcends the dilemma by suggesting that if humans can set themselves obstacles which bind their freedom, why cannot God do the same by creating human choice but abstaining from intervening against its consequences? The rational transcendence of the dilemma is to reject the notion of God as an infantile and illogical superstition.

12 The passage in Marx's *Critique of Hegel's Philosophy of Right* where the proletariat is

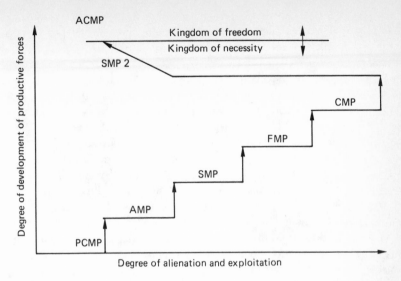

Key

PCMP   Primitive communist mode of production
AMP   Asiatic mode of production
SMP   Slave mode of production
FMP   Feudal mode of production
CMP   Capitalist mode of production
SMP2   Socialist mode of production
ACMP   Advanced communist mode of production

Figure 4.1 The Hegelian historical materialist staircase

assumption that the evolution of modes of production marks humanity's progressive conquest of nature – the development of the productive forces. The fact that the path traces a staircase which reverses direction rather than following a straight path suggests that Hegelian historical materialism is a secular theodicy. Humanity begins in primitive communism: the garden

heralded as the subject and object of history confirms the indelible imprint of Hegelian theodicy in Marx's thought. 'Where, then is the *positive* possibility of German emancipation? *Answer*: In the formation of a class with *radical chains* . . . a class of civil [*bürgerlich*] society that is not a class of *bürgerlich* society . . . an estate [*Stand*] which is the dissolution of all estates . . . a social sphere which has a universal character because of its universal suffering, and lays claim to no *particular right* because no *particular wrong*, only wrong in general, is committed against it . . . a sphere which can no longer invoke a historical title but only a *human* one; which does not stand in one-sided opposition to the premises of the German political system; a sphere, finally, which cannot emancipate itself at all without emancipating itself from all other social spheres, thereby emancipating all those other social spheres; a sphere, in short, which is the complete loss of the human being, and hence only by *fully regaining the human being* can it regain itself. This dissolution of society in the form of a particular class is the proletariat' (Marx and Engels, 1956, I: 379).

of Eden. The self-realization of the species dictates that humanity must experience increasing alienation, exploitation and class-divisiveness: purgatory. The successive modes of production after primitive communism are, ever more intensively, alienating and exploitative, right up until the turning-point of history, the transition from capitalism to socialism. Here humanity reaches the landing. After socialism has been achieved the final threshold on the road to paradise can be traversed. The kingdom of necessity ends and the kingdom of freedom begins. Alienation, exploitation and class-divisiveness are gradually reduced, until the culmination of history is reached. The staircase suggests the characteristic rhythm of the Hegelian dialectic which beats beneath the theory of historical materialism. In the beginning there is always undifferentiated unity (primitive communism). The world is one. Then there is fragmentation (class-divided society). The world is many. Finally, there is differentiated unity (advanced communism) which supersedes the contraditions of the second stage but attains the unity of the first stage yet at a more profound level because it has subsumed the experience of the second. The world is one again but wholesome.

The relevance of Hegelian historical materialism to the AMP, as we have seen, is that there is a remarkable reproduction of certain features of Hegel's portrait of the Orient and India in Marx's writings.[13] Was the AMP part of Marx's Hegelian heritage with which he failed to settle accounts? There is in Hegel's philosophy of history an empirical story of which cultures have carried the progress of the World Spirit and of the order in which they have done so. Did Marx accept, implicitly, Hegel's empirical narrative while divesting it of its idealist shell? After all, Marx's 'texts' on the AMP are heavily indebted, to the point of plagiarism in some cases, to Hegel's writings on the Orient. Madi'iar, a Hungarian cadre who became a Comintern agent in China, widely recognized as the most persuasive of the *Aziatchiki* in the Soviet Union in the late 1920s, contended that the AMP exemplified Marx's practice of turning Hegel on his head and extracting the rational kernel from Hegel's mystical shells: historical materialism was the materialist version of Hegel's *Lectures on the Philosophy of World History*. However,

[i]t is interesting to note that one finds far fewer germs of historical materialism in Hegel's writings on ancient (Greek and Roman) society, feudal (German), and bourgeois society than in those on the Orient. We cannot pursue this point here. For our purposes, it suffices to note that Marx began from Hegel, surpassed Hegel, and put the Hegelian teaching aright in developing his concepton of social formations. (Madi'iar, 1981: 79)

The first point is correct, but the assertions that Marx 'surpassed' Hegel

13 See pp. 69–71 and 86–104.

and put his 'teaching aright' are more contestable. Marx did differ from Hegel in that he tried to base his arguments about an AMP upon empirical evidence, but he did not surpass Hegel because he never fully rid himself of his mentor's teleological premises.[14]

THE GENERAL THEORETICAL PROBLEMS OF THE ASIATIC MODE OF PRODUCTION

The fundamental point of this book is that the AMP creates insuperable theoretical difficulties for whichever version of historical materialism is accepted by Marxists, whether productivist, structuralist or Hegelian. Six major questions arise in assessing the compatibility of the AMP and historical materialism:

1 Can the AMP be made compatible with the unilineal model of evolution associated with historical materialism, especially in its productivist and Hegelian variants?
2 If the AMP describes a social order incapable of evolving into a higher mode of production, what happens to the plausibility of any historical materialist theory of transition from one mode of production to another?
3 Can the basis of the AMP be conceptually distinguished from its superstructure, and a law-like relationship established between its basis and superstructure?
4 Are there classes in the AMP, and are there classes which can be defined in conventional Marxist categories?
5 What is the historical materialist explanation of the state form of the AMP?
6 What is 'Asiatic' about the AMP?

These six general theoretical questions matter to all the variants of historical materialism I have outlined, and the problematic answers they inspire are discussed in order below.

---

14 There are other Hegelian/theological facets to the AMP. In the Judaeo-Christian religions the myth of the Fall explains the cause of humanity's suffering and also the source of its redemption. All class-divided societies represent Marxism's functional equivalent of the Fall. However, the AMP seems more akin to a special section of purgatory. Societies trapped in it can be saved only by a messiah operating in another world, the proletariat, born of the capitalist mode of production, the 'subject and object' of history whose genesis was foretold as necessary to the achievement of paradise.

There is also an interesting tension between the Darwinian element in historical materialism (emphasized by productivist historical materialists) which suggests a continuous evolutionary progression in human forms, and the eschatological element (emphasized by Hegelian Marxists) which suggests an initially satisfactory state, a fall into alienation and exploitation, and a return to an (improved) satisfactory state.

Unilinealism and Multilinealism

Unilineal historical materialist models assume that history proceeds along a single developmental path. Multilineal models by contrast assume that history proceeds by diverse paths to the eventual goal of history: advanced communism. Since the de-Stalinization of Marxism in the 1950s, elaborations of both of these interpretations of historical materialism have multiplied, and precursors of both positions have been eagerly sought amongst classical Marxists, including the founding fathers.

Unilinealism   After Lenin and Stalin were granted canonical status there was little overt doubt amongst Western and Eastern Marxists that historical materialism meant that human history was the unfolding of a single 'pre-programmed' developmental sequence. Modes of production superseded one another in an ordered series of stages which the Marxist historian could find in the development of any country's history. This interpretation, vulgar unilinealism, is shown as figure 4.2. The authority for vulgar unilinealism primarily derived from texts which gave Marxists little cause to believe otherwise: Marx's Preface to *A Contribution to the Critique of Political Economy* as well as from Engels's *The Origin of the Family, Private Property and the State*. The early writings of Marx and Engels, especially in *The German Ideology* and *The Communist Manifesto*, as we have seen, were also filled with straightforward unilineal assumptions about historical development.

The vulgar model of unilinealism allows Marxist politicians and Marxist historians some discretion to make the theory compatible with both the known facts of history and their strategic perspectives on the future. Some concessions were necessary for rational Marxists because '[t]here never was a society which was once Asiatic, and then became ancient, and then feudal, and then at last bourgeois capitalist' (Plamenatz, 1954: 38). Three concessions are made by Marxists to make the vulgar model more supple. First, there can be 'long and variable' time lags between countries' speed of transition from one mode of production to another. They do not all develop in the same way or at the same speed. The class struggle and the development of the productive forces are allowed to take varying forms in different social formations. Second, there can be telescoped transitions. The transformation of one mode of production into the one after next can take place within the space of a year, as Trotsky argued in *The Permanent Revolution* (Trotsky, 1969). Third, a country can skip a mode of production entirely if compelled by imperialism or guided by socialist development. Thus for some Soviet analysts India was force-marched by British imperialism from an Asiatic social order into a semi-feudal and semi-capitalist order (Clarkson, 1979). However, vulgar unilinealists insist that no country

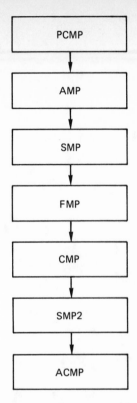

Key

PCMP	Primitive communist mode of production
AMP	Asiatic mode of production
SMP	Slave mode of production
FMP	Feudal mode of production
CMP	Capitalist mode of production
SMP2	Socialist mode of production
ACMP	Advanced communist mode of production

Figure 4.2 Vulgar unilineal historical materialism

can escape the necessary costs of transition altogether, whether those of primitive capitalist accumulation or those of primitive socialist accumulation. Lessening the 'birth pangs' is the most that revolutionaries can administer by way of political placebos. However, some Marxists after the Bolshevik revolution argued that the lower the level of development of the productive forces in the country that was skipping the 'natural' endogenous sequence of development, then the greater would be its costs of transition. History was a rigorous accountant.

The second version of unilinealism, the Stalinist, is ultra-vulgar (figure 4.3). It omits the AMP from the ordained sequence of stages, is much less

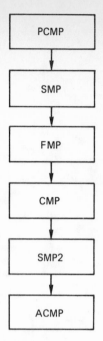

Key
PCMP   Primitive communist mode of production
SMP   Slave mode of production
FMP   Feudal mode of production
CMP   Capitalist mode of production
SMP2   Socialist mode of production
ACMP   Advanced communist mode of production

Figure 4.3 Stalinist unilineal historical materialism

generous in the scope given to party strategists or historians to accept different rhythms in transitions, and rejects Trotsky's ideas of the possibility of telescoped transitions — although it retains the possibility of skipping modes of production[15] — and the associated costs. The Stalinist model also forces its adherents to describe all the class-divided societies of the pre-capitalist world as either feudal or slaveholding.

The third version of unilinealism, the Hegelian (figure 4.4), is the most

15 'Stage-skipping' is, however, a privilege bequeathed by the presence of a socialist regime. The Stalinist five-stage model remains the orthodox Marxist-Leninist position, especially in Soviet primers. For example, a pamphlet entitled *The Logic of History* is a primer aimed at potential recruits outside the Soviet Union by the then chief editor of Progress Publishers. As in a catechism he poses the question and provides the answer: 'What modes of production are known in history? The history of mankind knows five modes of production' (Neznanov, 1978: 10–11).

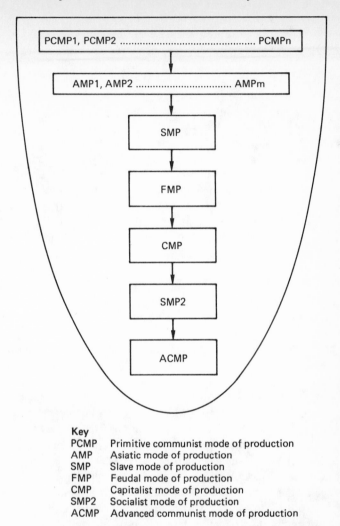

Key
PCMP   Primitive communist mode of production
AMP   Asiatic mode of production
SMP   Slave mode of production
FMP   Feudal mode of production
CMP   Capitalist mode of production
SMP2   Socialist mode of production
ACMP   Advanced communist mode of production

Figure 4.4 Hegelian unilineal historical materialism: 'the funnel of history'

sophisticated and allows the greatest scope for discretion to Marxist historians to make the model fit historical facts. It does not assume that the teleological evolution of modes of producton must necessarily take place in one country, as both the vulgar and Stalinist models suggest. Rather, the world − or the human species − is the site or centre of the developmental programme. The Hegelian model, as constructed by Semenov, allows for the possibility that some primitive communisms will never endogenously produce an AMP (Semenov, 1980). Rather, some peoples will remain at this stage until the triumph of socialism. Moreover, it follows that some Asiatic social formations will never produce a slave mode of production, that some slave societies will never endogenously produce a feudal mode of production, and so on. Large numbers of primitive communist modes of production (PCMP1, PCMP2 ... PCMPn) have existed in world history but only some develop Asiatic modes of production. (Many are called but few are chosen.) Large numbers of Asiatic modes of production have existed in world history (AMP1, AMP2 ... AMPm – where m<n), but apparently only one autonomously developed into the slave mode of production. (Many are called but only Greece is chosen.) The survival of specimens of primitive communism and the absence of Asiatic survivals in the modern world is explained by the isolation of primitive communist tribal formations – less attractive and less exposed to absorption by superior modes of production. The key theme of the Hegelian unilineal model is simple and ingenious. Each transitional sequence specified in Marx's Preface must necessarily occur, but at the level of world history rather than within each territory or ethnic group. Eventually the world will be covered by one mode of production, the socialist, but until that time, specimens of all pre-socialist modes of production in principle can survive as living museums testifying to the historical progress of humanity.

The Hegelian model of unilinealism also assumes that the most peripheral social formations will be the site of transitions from one mode of production to another. Thus the transition from the AMP to the slave mode of production took place in the peripheral and underdeveloped hinterland of an Asiatic social formation. Ancient Egypt and/or ancient Persia was the Asiatic core, and ancient Greece the periphery which developed a slave mode of production. Similarly, the transition from the slave mode of production to the feudal mode of production took place in the most backward part of the former Roman Empire, ancient Gaul. The transition from the feudal mode of production to the capitalist mode of production took place in the most peripheral of the feudal societies, those of North-western Europe. The transition from the capitalist mode of production to the socialist mode of production took place in the most backward of the major capitalist societies, Czarist Russia. This theme also smacks of secu-larized theology. (The first can be last, and the last can be first.)

Table 4.1 simplifies, summarizes and contrasts these three unilinealist models and the position of the AMP within them. The vulgar and Stalinist models assume that capacity for development to a higher mode of production is generally endogenous in each society, whereas the Hegelian model assumes that development is generally exogenous to each particular society, determined by the leading society which is the current standard bearer of development. In the Hegelian model development is of course endogenous to the human species as a whole, with different cultures being the vehicles of progress.

Table 4.1 Comparing unilineal historical materialisms

Unilineal model	Development	Focus	Anomalies
Vulgar	Endogenous	Societies	Transition from AMP to SMP
Stalinist	Endogenous	Societies	Cyclical dynamics in pre-capitalist societies
Hegelian	(a) Endogenous	Human species	Transition from PCMP to AMP
	(b) Exogenous	Societies	Transitions from PCMP to AMP are multiple and endogenous; other transitions are exogenous

Each model also has its own anomalies. The Hegelian model faces a key anomaly with respect to the AMP. The transition from the primitive communist mode of production to the AMP occurred endogenously several times, whereas in every other transition development is exogenous to each society. The transition from the AMP to the slave mode of production occurred once only, in ancient Greece, leaving open the suggestion that the development of human history may well be open to wholly exogenous influences (that is, non-historical materialist influences) which altogether preclude historical progress from occurring in certain societies. It suggests therefore that some ethnicities dominated by the AMP are doomed to stagnation. Only lucky, wholly fortuitous accidents spur the transition of one or two societies out of the AMP (an argument which jeopardizes the philosophical premises of Hegelian historical materialism, because that rests on the assumption that the development of humanity towards perfection is necessary and not contingent).

The Stalinist model avoids the vulgar model's anomalies and the many problems of the AMP by excluding the AMP by fiat from the accepted canons of historical materialism. However, it merely displaces these anomalies. A whole range of ancient agrarian societies is difficult to describe as either slaveholding or feudal, and in the course of fitting data into either of these conceptual strait-jackets, Soviet analysts have been forced into presenting implicitly cyclical rather than linear evolutionary models of pre-capitalist history. This problem has proved particularly acute in Soviet Marxist analyses of Near Eastern, Chinese and Indian history. Most of the historical social formations in these regions could not plausibly be described as examples of the slave mode of production. But the exclusion of the AMP from the canonical stages reduced Stalinist historians' typological choices to two:

either they had to accept that the feudal mode of production had persisted throughout the history of these regions, which reduced the explanatory value of the category, and obliged them to understand feudal social formations as inherently cyclical rather than dynamic;
or they had to accept that the slave mode of production had existed in these regions. (Aside from the fact that in many cases this classification was empirically implausible, it also produced the awkward and anti-unilineal result that in some regions of the world feudalism preceded *and* succeeded slavery!)

It was therefore 'no accident' that one of the reactions to the problems imposed by Stalinist historiography and the five-stage model, particularly the problem of describing Near Eastern societies as 'slaveholding', was the rehabilitation of the AMP amongst Soviet scholars in the early 1960s (Dunn, 1982).[16]

The vulgar model has remained the most popular academic version of historical materialism, and the one most frequently found in the works of Marxist and non-Marxist historians. The vulgar model is capable of further adaptation. The most popular contemporary form of adaptation appeals to the notion of 'the advantages of backwardness' (Veblen, 1915; Elster, 1986b). Trotsky's theory of 'combined and uneven development', which uses this notion, is an adaptation of the vulgar unilineal model, not a denial of it as some have contended (such as Elster, 1986b). Trotsky's theory of the advantages of backwardness presupposed that the peripheral social formation which would become the first version of the next ordained mode of production would go through all the stages allotted to societies in the vulgar model, albeit very rapidly. Trotsky did not argue that Russia would go from feudalism to socialism and skip capitalism. Rather he argued that partially capitalist Russia would undergo the transition to socialism before the full development of capitalism. The bourgeois and proletarian revolutions would follow one another in rapid and continuous, but not instantaneous, succession.[17] Consequently Trotsky's arguments were an adaptation of the endogenous unilineal model. The key theoretical assumption was that the least developed social formation dominated by a particular mode of production could become the site of the next epochal transition because it had

    16 Dunn's account of Soviet debates suggest that Soviet scholars now challenge the reality and/or 'typicality' of the slaveholding society (which, as we shall see, in effect transfers the dilemmas posed by the AMP to a different mode of production). According to Dunn the term 'pre-feudal society' − that is, a reconstructed AMP − now has many Soviet exponents.
    17 Better translations of the Russian title of Trotsky's work known in English as *The Permanent Revolution* apparently would be *The Uninterrupted Revolution* or *The Continuous Revolution*.

only recently developed. The social formations in which the current mode of production has long flowered are somehow impeded from rapiJ transition to the next mode of production. They suffer the penalties of being the best exemplars of the existing mode of production first. They develop rigidities which make transition much more difficult. There are many illustrations of this style of reasoning amongst classical Marxists (Cornforth, 1953, vol. 2; Gramsci, 1971; and Trotsky, 1969).[18]

This adaptation of the vulgar model of unilinealism, to my knowledge, is not explicitly extended to the AMP by any Marxist. A reconciliation would have to take the following form: the AMP does possess the internal dynamics (or contradictions) to generate within itself the slave mode of production, and every empirical instance of a social formation dominated by the AMP was capable of such development. The fact that this transition occurred rarely (or once only) in most of the historical manifestations of the AMP was because these societies were such strongly developed versions of the AMP. Moreover, the advent of globally dominant modes of production, namely capitalism and socialism, precluded the eventual endogenous transition to superior modes of production which otherwise would have occurred naturally. This reconciliation of adapted unilinealism and the AMP rests on various counterfactuals, such as 'had India been left outside the development of capitalist imperialism — which *ex hypothesi* could not have happened — then eventually it would have embarked upon the vulgar transitional sequence of its own accord.' This way in which the vulgar model might be adapted to fit in with the AMP, as we shall see, pushes it towards the unfalsifiable Hegelian version of unilinealism.

18 Gramsci argued that the transition to socialism was easier in Russia because the superstructural elements and hegemonic culture of advanced capitalism were not well developed there, which made feasible an early socialist capture of the state apparatus (Gramsci, 1971). Trotsky argued that socialist ideas (generated against capitalism in the West in the site of the most advanced developments) were disseminated immediately with the onset of capitalism in Russia, an underdeveloped capitalist society (Trotsky, 1969). The proletarian movement therefore might triumph more quickly than in the West, as in fact proved the case (at least for a few months). The British Marxist philosopher Maurice Cornforth summarized the flavour of these adaptations of the vulgar model succinctly. Having discussed the five stage vulgar unilineal model he contended that the

new system does not necessarily appear first in that place where the old one has been most strongly entrenched and most fully developed. Indeed, in those communities where the old system has become most strongly entrenched it may be hardest to get rid of, so that the breakthrough of the new system is effected in the first place elsewhere. As we know, this is what happened in the case of the first breakthrough of socialism, which was effected in Russia, 'the weakest link in the chain of imperialism', and not in the more advanced capitalist countries. (Cornforth, 1953, vol. 2: 65).

Cornforth's argument has been classified as Hegelian (Sawer, 1977a: 199). However, as Cornforth did not believe that the transition must take place on the periphery, and also believed that each society was endogenously capable of evolving into the higher mode of production (given time and freedom from external intervention), his arguments clash with our understanding of the Hegelian model, best articulated by the Soviet author Iu. Semenov (1980). Sawer and I are operating with differing conceptions of Hegelian historical materialism.

The Stalinist model of unilinealism was explicitly adopted to avoid some of the ideological problems which the AMP posed for the vulgar model (see pp. 24–37). These ideological embarrassments apparently were decisive in Stalin's decision to exclude the AMP from historical materialism in the infamous party tract, *Dialectical and Historical Materialism* (1938). Stalin had the authority of Lenin's lecture on *The State* posthumously published in 1929, which also did not mention the AMP. Lenin's lecture was in fact a précis of Engels's *The Origin of the Family, Private Property and the State* (where the AMP did not appear). Stalin could have relied on some logical arguments made by Soviet academicians against the AMP, many of which depended upon the AMP's inconsistency with the unilineal model, but he chose not to do so. However, arguments as opposed to decrees were made. Godes argued for the rejection of the AMP because of the problems it posed for the vulgar model. He did not deny that Marx wrote about an AMP. 'The statements on the Asiatic mode of production cannot be expunged from the work of Marx' (Godes, 1981).[19] Godes simply thought that Marx had been wrong, and that his errors were misleading his comrades in important contemporary political analysis, namely, the course and prospects of the Chinese revolution. He noted major theoretical defects in the *Aziatchiki's* arguments. First, they had no theory of transition out of the AMP. Marxism required a theory of how class struggle in the AMP must inevitably create the transition to the next form of society. A mode of production which has no internal laws of motion cannot be integrated into historical materialism. Consequently arguments based on such a 'mode of production' have to be rejected. One reason for this theoretical rejection was to confirm that 'the Orient, in a very unique fashion, went through the same stages of social development as Europe' (Godes, 1981: 103).[20] The *Aziatchiki* had simply failed to understand feudalism, and once they had understood it, the problems posed by their belief in the AMP would disappear. Feudalism had four defining features: landownership was the basis for the accumulation of the surplus product; the direct producer conducted his own indpendent economic operation; in the relations between the owner of the means of the production and the direct producer extra-economic coercion prevailed; and finally, the hierarchy of landownership corresponded to the hierarchy of political power (ibid). While there was variety in feudal systems these four features defined it as a mode of production. By comparison the four characteristics of the AMP emphasized by the Soviet *Aziatchiki* – namely, nationalization of the land, agrarian

19 Stalin of course did try to expunge them!
20 As I cannot read Russian I do not know whether the notion of 'a very unique fashion' is a poor translation or a faithful rendering of poor thought in the original. Whichever it is, the equivocation indicates Godes's difficulties.

communes, artificial irrigation and a centralized despotic state – could not define a mode of production, because they did not specify a set of production relations, and because they could not have existed in a pure form. If these features had existed in the Orient, Godes submitted that their significance was greatly exaggerated.[21] However, his critical point was theoretical: the AMP was not a mode of production, because it was incompatible with unilinealism and because it was poorly specified.

Modern defences of the five-stage Stalinist model which follow or renew Godes's line have been articulated in the Soviet Union in recent years, by authors who believe that the five-stage model is an empirical issue rather than a matter of faith and that the AMP is incompatible with Marxism (Kachanovskii, 1971; and Nikiforov, 1975).[22] Their decision to exclude the AMP from historical materialism illustrates that neo-Stalinists merely displace the difficulties posed by this awkward concept for the unilinealist interpretation of historical materialism. Orthodox Soviets try to incorporate the facts of 'Asiatic' features in many oriental and Eastern societies by suggesting that they point to 'survivals' of primitive communism – just as the peasantry in capitalist societies point to the 'survivals' of feudalism. But they have great difficulty in presenting plausible empirical evidence to support the thesis that oriental societies went through the canonical stages of the vulgar model, and similar problems in excluding the possibility that some Near Eastern and European societies went through the wrong stages at the wrong time! One Soviet author has identified the fundamental problem with neo-Stalinist five-stage unilinealism: there are in fact more deviations and exceptions than cases which fall under the 'rule' of uni-linealism (Danilova, 1971: 269–328).

The Hegelian version of historical materialism, nicely described as a 'torch-relay model' of development (Gellner, 1980: 64), is the best adapted of the unilineal models. Its appeal has recently revived in the Soviet Union but has well-established roots in Russian discussions of the AMP. For example, in reviewing Metchnikoff's *Civilisation and the Great Historical Rivers* Plekhanov opened his discussion with distinctly Hegelian questions:

What causes affect the internal development of human societies? Why do some races remain almost at a standstill while others unite into great state bodies, with the beginning of a political presence, where learning, literature, applied and fine arts and great productive forces, in a word, where everything which we call civilisation develops? And why, at different times, are different peoples the bearers of civilisation? (Plekhanov, 1981: 58)

21 Godes omitted to discuss the class formation of the AMP, which was dear to the *Aziatchiki* – a matter of some importance for those who believe that what is not said is as salient as what is said.
22 I am relying on the précis of Kachanovskii's work in Dunn (1982: 109–20), and of Nikiforov's work in Gellner (1986).

The current bearers of civilization, when they accept Hegelian historical materialism, have a (temporarily) flattering answer to Plekhanov's question. The theory requires that if one ethnicity is the first to arrive at a given stage in the ordained sequence of modes of production then necessarily another ethnicity will be the first to arrive at the subsequent stage. The Soviet bearers are thus told that they can best advance humanity at this time. Their past backwardness belongs to that period in which others advanced civilization before handing over the title deeds. Since they are also charting humanity's journey into the kingdom of freedom they will be the last people to fill the role of history's guardian angel. Hegelian Marxism thus gels comfortably with both Marxism and Russian nationalism.[23] Hegelian historical materialism also solves the best known anomalies in productivist historical materialism by making the theory easier to reconcile with historical facts. However, the problem with the Hegelian defence of unilinealism, as demonstrated by Gellner (1980), is that it makes Marx's theory of history a *redescription* rather than a *falsifiable explanation* of the development of world history. It saves the baby by throwing out the bathwater. However, the hidden price is that the baby's legitimacy becomes an issue. There is no serious sense in which Semenov's reconstruction of historical materialism passes muster as a contribution to a positivist science of history.

The fundamental problems faced by unilinealist interpretations of historical materialism, whether vulgar, Stalinist or Hegelian, and whether defended with or without the AMP, explain the recent popularity of multilineal models of historical progress amongst Western and Soviet Marxists.

Multilinealism   The Preface to *A Contribution to the Critique of Political Economy* of 1859 has generally been interpreted as endorsing a unilinealist view of history. But the key sentence is ambiguous: 'In broad outlines Asiatic, ancient, feudal and modern bourgeois society can be designated as progressive epochs in the economic formation of society' (Marx, 1970: 21). It tantalizingly suggests both a temporal sequence of modes of production in historical development and an analytical ranking of these modes of production on a criterion of progress. It has led to the harsh suggestion that the ambivalence stems from thoughtlessness: 'What was Marx thinking of when he said what he did about the "progressive epochs in the economic formation of society"? Indeed, we may ask, without impertinence, was he thinking at all?' (Plamenatz, 1954: 39). However, whether it was thoughtless or deliberate this ambivalence has allowed certain Marxists to emphasize

---

23 However, there is a thorny problem. Surely a different ethnicity must have the privilege of charting the transition from socialism to advanced communism? Several Soviet interventions in Eastern Europe might be interpreted as designed to prevent such a prospect.

the *analytical* ranking of pre-capitalist class-divided modes of production rather than the *temporal* sequence accepted as part of the Marxist canon by the unthinking faithful. Those who follow this analytical interpretation and make a multilineal interpretation of Marx's theory of history also normally rely heavily on the evidence of the *Grundrisse*, which formed the notebooks from which Marx drafted his *A Contribution to the Critique of Political Economy* and parts of *Capital*.

One awkward problem for these multilinealists is that the 'Formen' suggest that Marx regarded all pre-capitalist class-divided modes of production as roughly on the same level of development of the productive forces. Thus the 'Formen' leave no apparent room for an analytical ranking of these pre-capitalist modes of production — save on one criterion. Since part of the purpose of the 'Formen' was to explain the distinctiveness of capitalism, the important analytical ranking of pre-capitist modes of production for Marx may not have been the quantitative level of development of the productive forces but rather the capacity of a given mode of production to produce capitalism; that is, its capitalist fertility.

The 'Formen' certainly suggest a mundane multilinealism in that they accept that many post-primitive societies developed all over the world. They also suggest that different formations, if not modes of production, developed from the same primordial primitive commune. Indeed the best defence of a multilinealist interpretation of historical materialism has been advanced by Umberto Melotti, who relies heavily on the 'Formen' (Melotti, 1977) and argues that a unilineal interpretation is on balance less compatible with Marx's texts. He points out that nowhere did Marx explicitly suggest that the AMP was a precursor of the slave mode of production. Whilst Marx discussed the transitions from the slave to the feudal and from the feudal to the capitalist mode of production, in many places and with specific geographical references, he never discussed a society which autonomously underwent the transition from the AMP. This alleged fact is anomalous for both the vulgar and Hegelian versions of unilinealism.[24]

Melotti's reconstruction of the *Grundrisse* and Marx's model and periodization of history are sketched in figure 4.5. On this reading the 'Formen' show that Marx believed that four communes developed out of the primordial commune. (This interpretation, which creates a stage intermediate between primitive communism and the Asiatic mode of production, solves at a stroke the problem of the temporal placement of Asiatic mode of production discussed in pp. 135–6.) These four communes in turn were the seedbeds of four different societies (the semi-Asiatic, Asiatic, slave and feudal), with Japanese feudalism emerging from an implicit but undiscussed

24 In fact, a footnote in *Capital* does suggest that the slave mode of production developed out of the primitive oriental community — see p. 111.

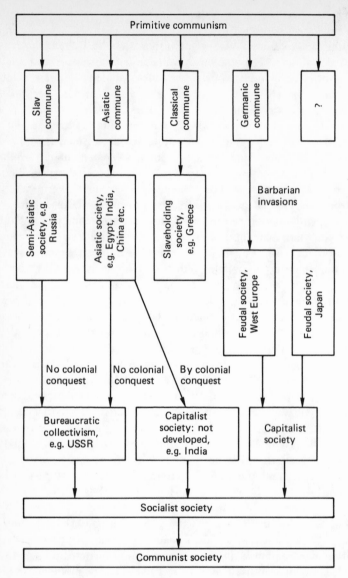

Figure 4.5 Melotti's multilinealist reconstruction of historical materialism

commune. The 'Formen' not only suggest that historical development was multilineal but also that several societies (Asiatic and semi-Asiatic) developed along *culs-de-sac.* They were incapable of further development unless transformed from the outside by capitalist societies. Melotti's reconstruction respects this textual constraint. He also respects the assumption in the

'Formen' that all pre-capitalist societies throughout the world were transformed by the expansion of capitalism.

Melotti's reconstruction of Marx's periodization of development is wholly original in two respects. First, he argues that capitalism transformed feudal societies into advanced capitalist societies (the First · World), prompted semi-Asiatic societies and independent Asiatic societies to undergo bureaucratic collectivist revolutions (the Second World) or through colonial conquest transformed Asiatic societies into underdeveloped capitalist societies (the Third World). Second, he introduces a new mode of production, 'bureaucratic collectivism'. This mode of production is not just Melotti's neo-Trotskyist way of describing Communist regimes. It also enables him to revise the concept of the AMP. For on Melotti's account the AMP is capable of evolving into a higher mode of production. True, the AMP cannot develop endogenously into capitalism, and thereby Melotti remains faithful to Marx's notion that it was stagnant. The trick is that the AMP can develop into a mode of production which Marx did not anticipate. Moreover, Melotti argues there is a natural affinity between regimes with Asiatic pasts and bureaucratic collectivism. This novel multilineal version of historical materialism merits the name 'left-wing Wittfogelism'.

Any multilineal reading of Marx's theory of history does avoid some of the difficulties central to the unilineal reading. It is easier to reconcile with historical data, and unlike Hegelian unilinealism it is not simply a philosophical schema which is immune to falsification, since its descriptions may be false. Equally, however, any multilineal historical materialism poses new problems and trivializes others. On the basis of textual evidence it remains unclear whether the AMP was one route out of the primordial commune (Melotti's argument) or the most widespread specimen of the primordial commune (Lubasz, 1984). The multilineal schema is also so open to revision as to remove its Marxist distinctiveness. A theory apparently compatible with every description of historical diversity explains nothing. Multilineal schemas may be superficially 'empirical' but they are philosophically banal. So far, they remove necessity from Marx's theory of history, converting it into redescription rather than explanation. Thereby historical materialism ceases to be a philosophy of history which tells why what has happened did happen, or which can be extrapolated to what will happen. Multilinealism also puts in jeopardy the Marxist believer's faith about the unification of humanity under some putative advanced communism.[25] If the world has been 'many' until now, why must it become 'one' in the future?

25 One of Sawer's multilineal schemata is a bifurcated world-growth story which ends with two different socialisms, a Western socialism and an Eastern socialism. This seems unintentionally analogous to the Dave Allen joke about two heavens: the Protestant heaven and the Catholic heaven. (See Sawer, 1977a, chapter 5.)

The Permanently Stagnant Mode of Production?

The locus of pre-capitalist modes of production in historical development was not Marx's most pressing theoretical problem. It has, however, progressively acquired greater importance for Marxists. Marxist historians' focus on the transformation of the 'epoch' as the time horizon of their explanations accounts for the rising importance of pre-capitalist modes of production in their work (Dunleavy and O'Leary, 1987: 342). Marxist social scientists with a professional interest in the development and underdevelopment of pre-capitalist societies have been keen to elaborate and if possible integrate general Marxist ideas in their specialist fields. The AMP has played its part in the expansion of Marxist anthropology, historiography, geography and sociology. However, this part has been problematic because of the stagnant character of the AMP.

Many passages in Marx and Engels's texts suggested that they considered Asiatic societies, especially Indian village communities, as inherently stagnant. The implications of an inherently stagnant mode of production are deadly serious for historical materialism. The most straightforward difficulty is well known. All vulgar unilineal schemata face the logical contradiction that a schema of stages predicated upon endogenous linear evolution contains one stage which is incapable of internal transformation into a higher stage. If Marxists accept the AMP then either the schema of endogenous linear evolution is false, or the stagnation thesis is false. One can only believe both on pain of contradiction, or by accepting Hegelian dialectical propositions (which amount to the same thing).

Second, all multilineal schemata face the problem that their acceptance of the stagnation thesis converts world history into a contingent set of developments. They threaten to make Marxist historiography indistinguishable from the bourgeois variety. They remove the necessity and the universal scope of historical materialism. They also create the possibility of 'stagnation without salvation', to use Gellner's graphic expression (Gellner, 1983). A mode of production from which there is no exit except through the contingent intervention of another fits ill with the ruggedly optimistic Marxist assumption that historical developments are necessarily progressive, even if only in the very long run. Furthermore, the systemic contradiction which is believed to be 'the motor of history', namely the dialectic between productive forces and relations of production, is jeopardized if one mode of production is incapable of unfolding into another mode of production.

These implications are recognized by Marxists. Even the most firm advocates of the utility of the AMP in historical materialist analyses, and supporters of the thesis that the AMP was stagnant, are careful to leave room for doubt about whether the AMP is a historical blind alley. Plekhanov in his polemic against the Narodniks stated that: 'Were Russia isolated from the economic and political influences of West European life, it would be difficult to see when history would undermine at last the economic foundation of the Russian political set-up' (Plekhanov, 1961: 275). A more equivocal formulation is difficult to imagine. The demiurge history, whilst predictable in other respects, might never have begun its work in Russia, although the qualifying phrase 'at last' also suggests that the redemption of Russia by endogenous historical development was not *a priori* impossible.

There is another side to the issue of stagnation: the theoretical argument − let alone the empirical confirmation − that the AMP was stagnant remains to be demonstrated. It is not demonstrated in Marx; it is merely asserted. Despite the acceptance of the stagnation thesis by both Marxists and non-Marxists, the definition of stagnation and the mechanisms by which stagnation is maintained are by no means self-evident. Stagnation must mean the incapacity to evolve into a higher mode of production.[26] However, as unilinealists are uncomfortably aware, we know that this thesis must have been falsified at least once, or else we would all still be inhabiting the 'Asiatic' condition. Leaving this insuperable objection to one side there is still the difficulty that allegedly stagnant Asiatic societies may have had capitalist potential. Their 'natural' evolution was pre-empted by the expansion of capitalist imperialism from Western Europe and North America. Therefore, it might fairly be reasoned that at best the stagnation hypothesis is a counterfactual assertion which can never be falsified. There is no 'Asiatic society' sitting in a historical laboratory, isolated from the capitalist world economy, available for us to inspect to see how it reproduces itself and whether or not it is capable of transformation into a higher mode of production.

What textually warranted materials would be required to convert Marx's assertion that oriental society is stagnant into an argument? The mechanisms which might be invoked to explain the stagnation of the AMP and which are features of the AMP include:

---

26 Stephen Dunn, (1982: 120) apparently expounds an even stronger version of Asiatic stagnation. Having told us that the 'pre-feudal stage' (a catch-all category intended to incorporate both the slaveholding and Asiatic modes of production) 'is not capable of giving rise to a higher stage out of itself, and that the revolution to which it is subject is a purely destructive one', he suggests that the Asiatic version of the 'pre-feudal stage' could be destroyed only by European imperialists. Barbarian conquests could not destroy it − the Asiatic mode of production was both incapable of development and incapable of regression. Dunn does not elaborate this conjecture (reminiscent of interpretations of the patterns of Chinese history) which suggests that the AMP was both stagnant and possessed of immense and immediate powers of resuscitation: every barbarian conquest could be absorbed and eventually the barbarians would preside over a new social formation dominated by the AMP. If we recall Marx's remarks on Indian history before the British we can find textual warrant for Dunn's strong version of stagnation: 'All the civil wars, invasions, revolutions, conquests, famines, strangely complex, rapid and destructive as the successive action in Hindustan may appear, did not go deeper than its surface' (Marx, 1973a: 302).

village autarky;
the strength of communal ownership and production; and
the power of the despot over any potential bourgeoisie.

However, each of these explanatory mechanisms is deficient.

First, the imputed notion of village autarky is problematic. Marx in his 'Asiatic' sketches recognized what Asian historians have long known, namely that Asiatic villages traded with each other, that merchants travelled between villages, that the monarch often taxed the village communities in cash rather than in kind, and that the monarch and his officials participated in long-distance trade in luxuries (Chaudhuri, 1985). These conditions were not those of total autarky, and in several respects resembled those prevalent in pre-industrial Europe. Moreover, the juxtaposition of autarkic villages and a state which taxes such villages in cash is a contradiction in terms. A well-reconstructed argument would have to emphasize that the 'Asiatic' village was in some clear respect more autarkic than its slaveholding or feudal counterpart. Such an idea seems to have been at the heart of Marx's repeated references to the 'union of manufactures and handicrafts' in the Indian village. However, the idea remains obscure and undeveloped. Marx gave no theoretical account of what makes such a union persist in a stable equilibrium in a zero-growth economy. Moreover, Marx did not make much of one plausible mechanism for explaining the stability of the union of handicrafts and manufactures in the Indian case, namely the importance of caste as an impediment to economic progress. His successors have been at pains to reduce caste to an ideological epiphenomenon or to class (Meillassoux, 1973). Alternatively, but with similar implications, they stress the similarities between Indian castes and the feudal castes of Western Europe. They therefore deprive themselves of the potential benefits of this explanatory mechanism by regarding the invocation of caste as a Weberian rather than Marxist mode of explaining agrarian stagnation.

Second, the thesis that the strength of communal ownership and production made the AMP stagnant, quite apart from its closeness to circularity (given that these traits define the AMP as an antonym of capitalism), faces an awkward problem. This feature of the AMP is also integral to primitive communism, or the primordial commune. Therefore, on the several occasions in which class-divided modes of production emerged from primordial communism, communal ownership did not act as an insuperable barrier to the development of a higher mode of production. Why communal ownership should have different consequences for a higher mode of production is mysterious.

The third thesis, which helps solve the foregoing mystery, faces a different objection. The idea that the power of the despot over any potential bourgeoisie maintained stagnation in the AMP, in so far as it is a plausible thesis, is not very Marxist. In standard historical materialist accounts, conflicts between members of the ruling class are supposed to provide opportunities for subordinate classes to advance the next mode of production rather than to seal off the prospects of historical progress.[27] Moreover, this thesis explains the stagnation of the AMP by reference to the predatory nature of its political institutions. A state-centred explanation of stagnation rather than an economic explanation is being offered. Without an account explaining why the economic basis of the AMP required such a dysfunctional state, Marxists cannot easily imbibe such a story. State-centred explanations of the operations of a mode of production are the hallmark of non-Marxist social theory.

The plausibility of the thesis that despotic predatory behaviour curtailed the prospects of autonomous capitalist growth is also open to challenge. The pre-industrial state apparatus everywhere had to rely on merchants to ensure the supply of luxury goods and to centralize and monetize the taxation system. 'Enlightened despots' had systematic reasons for not curbing all the incentives for capital accumulation. Moreover, capitalist development took place in absolutist Western regimes (and in Japan) which had despotic core executives as fundamental features of their state apparatuses. Therefore the cultural absence of 'enlightened self-interest' becomes more important than despotic arbitrariness in contrasting the Orient with the Occident. The explanation of occidental development and oriental stagnation must, it seems, move to cultural rather than institutional comparisons, a task which many analysts have embarked upon (Hirschman, 1977).

However, it should also be noted that explanatory problems with stagnation are not exclusive to the AMP. In *Capital*, Marx described all earlier modes of production (that is, pre-capitalists ones) as essentially conservative (Marx, 1961: 486). Moreover, in *The Communist Manifesto* Marx and Engels contrasted the revolutionary nature of the bourgeoisie with the conservatism of all pre-capitalist ruling classes:

> The bourgeoisie cannot exist without constantly revolutionizing the instruments of production, and thereby the relations of production, and with them the whole relations of society. Conservation of the old modes of production in unaltered form, was, on the contrary, the first condition of existence for all earlier industrial classes. Constant revolutionizing of production, uninterrupted disturbance of all social conditions, everlasting uncertainty and agitation distinguish the bourgeois epochs from all earlier ones. (Marx and Engels, 1967: 83)

These assertions are problematic for productivist historical materialists, since there is a *prima facie* case that the alleged conservatism of all pre-capitalist modes of production fits very uncomfortably with the notion that

27 The idea that the 'mutual ruin of the contending classes' is always on the agenda of history was not much emphasized by Marx, even though the phrase was mentioned in *The Communist Manifesto* (where Marx seems to have had the slaveholding society of the Roman Empire in mind).

these modes were structured as they were because such structures were functionally optimal for the development of the productive forces.[28] However, there are special problems with the conservatism of the AMP. If it is inherently stagnant, it decisively weakens vulgar and Hegelian unilineal schemata of historical materialism, since they must accept that one mode of production was a historical dead end from which humanity miraculously escaped. Moreover, even multilineal schemata must concede the wholly contingent nature of historical progress — thereby jettisoning the ideological benefits of Marx's philosophy of history.

The only way to make the stagnation thesis partially compatible with historical materialism is to suggest the relative stagnation of the AMP by contrast with other modes of production. Figure 4.6 sketches the development of the productive forces under various modes of production against time, and aims to show the following:

First, it is coherent for Marxists to portray all class-divided modes of production as inherently limited in their development capacities. With the exception of socialism (and advanced communism, which will succeed it), the stylized development path of each mode of production must eventually reach a maximum where the first derivative of the development of the productive forces with respect to time must be zero.

Second, it is coherent for Marxists to portray all pre-capitalist modes of production as 'conservative' by comparison with capitalism. The relevant comparison is the quantitative extent to which they are capable of developing the productive forces. Under capitalism a dramatic leap in the development of the productive forces takes place before it starts to approach its stagnation limit.

Third, specimens of one mode of production (such as the capitalist) can remain at higher levels of development than specimens of their successors (in that case, than examples of the socialist mode).

Fourth, *ceteris paribus*, it is coherent for Marxists to argue that all pre-capitalist modes of production tend towards a developmental limit, or stagnation (even if particular social formations dominated by any given mode of production never reach this limit, and experience revolutionary transformation before stagnation sets in).

Finally, the AMP can be shown to approach its stagnation limit comparatively earlier than all other modes of production, and social formations dominated by the AMP can remain at that limit longer than social formations dominated by other modes of production.

28 One answer suggested by G.A. Cohen, (1979: 171) is that although pre-capitalist modes of production were inherently more conservative than capitalism they were, none the less, optimal for the productive forces as then developed. His analogy is interesting: 'sports cars are faster than jeeps, but jeeps are faster on boggy land.' The AMP of course has no obvious analogue since it seems to keep humanity glued to the pre-capitalist bog.

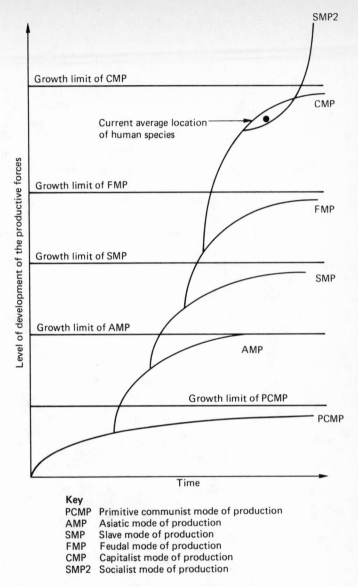

Key
PCMP Primitive communist mode of production
AMP   Asiatic mode of production
SMP   Slave mode of production
FMP   Feudal mode of production
CMP   Capitalist mode of production
SMP2 Socialist mode of production

Figure 4.6 Developmental paths of modes of production

This reconstruction of Marx's arguments about the stylized developmental paths of modes of production, the stagnation of the AMP and the conservatism of pre-capitalist societies makes his thought compatible with the development thesis suggested by productivist historical materialists.

However, it does not resolve the problem posed by the absolute stagnation of the AMP[29] — that is, its incapacity endogenously to develop into another mode of production. This facet remains fundamentally anomalous for historical materialism.

Basis and Superstructure

Some Marxists — notably Lukács, Balibar and Anderson — have suggested that the relations between basis and superstructure differed in pre-capitalist from those in capitalist societies (P. Anderson, 1974b: 404—5). This suggestion implies that the determination of the superstructure by the base is a theory confined to the capitalist mode of production, rather than a transhistorical general law in Marx's theory of history. Many non-Marxists have expressed similar ideas (Finley, 1973: 50; and Giddens, 1981).[30] However, whilst these suggestions may or may not be true, they are not authorized by Marx. In a footnote to *Capital*, Volume I, Marx rejected any such correction of the theory he had set out in the Preface to *A Contribution to the Critique of Political Economy*.[31]

Let us assume that Marx believed that the basis of the AMP determines its superstructure. Recall the two definitions of basis and of superstructure (and the sub-definitional debate about the scope of the superstructure):[32]

basis 1 = production relations; or
basis 2 = mode of production; and
superstructure 1 = (a) legal and political institutions, and or (b) ideology + (a); or

29 Marx refers in the *Grundrisse*, albeit obliquely, to one system-inducing mechanism which affected all pre-capitalist societies, namely the impact of population growth (Marx, 1973e: 486 — see also pp. 99—100). He indicated that the Asiatic form of the primordial commune, although tenaciously resistant to change, could be affected by population growth. This apparent denial of the stagnant character of the AMP (if it is the AMP as opposed to primitive communism) is not repeated elsewhere. Moreover, the change-inducing mechanism invoked by Marx is problematic for historical materialism. Population growth cannot be an unambiguous specimen of the devolopment of the productive forces which then somehow induces changes in the relations of production, since population growth may be accompanied by declining or increasing productivity. Finally, the invocation of population growth as an important explanatory mechanism for social change is problematic for Marx's periodization of history. The AMP, at least in unilineal accounts, must be succeeded by the slave mode of production. But historical evidence suggests that the origins of slave modes of production are more plausible in conjunction with population shortages rather than population surpluses.

30 It is now even becoming conventional to argue that the classical functional relationship between basis and superstructure applies only to classical capitalism (Habermas, 1974: 195).

31 This point is made by Elster (1985: 238). Whilst the overall import of Marx's objection is unclear, it is evident that he was objecting to the idea that the causal relations between base and superstructure differed in pre-capitalist societies from those which obtain in capitalist societies.

32 See pp. 13—16.

superstructure 2 = (a′) legal and political functions, and or (b′) ideological functions + (a′)

Consider first the institutional reading; that is, basis 1 determines superstructure 1 (a). The key problem here is that it seems impossible to separate production relations from superstructural institutions, either analytically, or empirically.[33] The AMP exemplifies the problem. The production relations must take the form, primarily, of a ruling class which appropriates villagers' surplus labour through taxation; but the superstructural legal and political institutions must be the same. Basis and superstructure are fused − or confused. This 'problem of legality' is created by the fact that since the basis is constituted by property or ownership relations it is indistiguishable from the legal superstructures which it is supposed to explain (G.A. Cohen, 1979: 88).[34] The contention that the basis − superstructure distinction only makes sense in capitalist society is understandable in light of this analytical difficulty. There are also ideological difficulties. Not only must the primacy of the economic be questioned, but it becomes plausible to argue that the fusion of basis and superstructure is the source of Asiatic stagnation, and indeed, by creative extension, of socialist stagnation. The autonomy of political and legal institutions becomes an alternative candidate for motoring (or retarding) historical progress. Rather than the dialectic between production relations and productive forces, it is political, juridical and cultural institutions which enter independently into any serious account of technological progress.

Furthermore, if we take any institutional reading of basis and superstructure (basis 1 and superstructure 1(a) and 1(b)) then there is a fundamental problem with the meaning of the 'determination' of the latter by the former. If, as vulgar Marxists insist, there is a one-to-one correspondence between basis and superstructure, then the apparently wide variations in the superstructures of such divergent systems as ancient Mesopotamia, Achaemenid Persia, Mughal India and imperial China create problems (Dunn, 1982: 11−12). Historical materialists face a simple dilemma. Either such social formations did have different bases, in which case the taxonomy of economic bases developed by Marx and Engels is radically insufficient to capture the range of relations of production in pre-modern societies; or the same economic base is compatible with very wide divergences in political,

33 A determined effort to argue otherwise can be found (G.A. Cohen, 1979: chapter VII), but it has been effectively refuted (Lukes, 1983).

34 Cohen's attempt to solve the problem by distinguishing *rechtsfrei* descriptions of production relations from superstructural property relations − that is, 'powers' from 'right' − is unconvincing. First, any attempt to derive a *rechtsfrei* definition of production relations is contestable (Lukes, 1983: 112). Second, 'powers' are affected by 'rights' in ways which cannot be reduced to powers, so the functional relations between powers and rights posited by Cohen are implausible. For instance, there are always norms behind contracts, as Durkheim suggested.

legal and ideological superstructures. The first horn of the dilemma saves the one-to-one correspondence theory, but at the price of rejecting the taxonomic adequacy of Marx's list of pre-capitalist modes of production. But the alternative option destroys the explanatory power of the law-like determinaton of superstructure by basis both in the AMP and in all other modes of production. At most it leaves Marxists with the rather loose thesis that the superstructures which exist at any time are generally not incompatible with their bases. They are satisfactory, even if they are not optimal. 'History', it seems, tolerates great inefficiency.

The functionalist account of relations between basis and superstructure suggests that the superstructure ($2(a')$ or $2(b')$) is as it is because it is functional for the base (2). However, this account also faces the difficulty of distinguishing the functions of production relations from the functions of superstructures. Moreover, the key problem posed by basis 2 is exactly the same as the one posed by the stagnant character of the AMP. The superstructure is explained functionally as beneficial for the development of the productive forces, but simultaneously it must be described as a dysfunctionally permanent brake on their development. This problem exists independently of the dubious merits of functionalist explanations. However, on productivist historical materialist accounts the characteristics of basis 2 at time t must be functionally explained by their optimality for developing the productive forces at time $t -$ otherwise the theory becomes so flexible as to be compatible with all historical evidence.

The AMP therefore exposes the key weaknesses in the theory of basis and superstructure, one of the core beliefs of historical materialists. This problem is, however, a general one in Marxist accounts of pre-capitalist social formations, and explains why Western Marxists as distinguished as Perry Anderson, Etienne Balibar, György Lukács and Jürgen Habermas have sought to relieve historical materialism of this embarassing pair of concepts.

Classes and the Asiatic Mode of Production

Whether or not classes exist in social formations dominated by the AMP has continually taxed Marxist theoreticians. Their dilemma is straightforward: on the one hand if there are no classes Marxists cannot explain the existence of the state in the Asiatic mode of production, but on the other hand if there are classes then these classes cannot be based on private ownership of the means of production.

The arguments in favour of the theory that the AMP is a class-divided mode of production are of two kinds: textual arguments from the authority of Marx, and, second, substantive theoretical and empirical arguments based upon the imputed relations of production and exploitation in the

AMP. The textual evidence for Marx's own views on the class structure of the AMP is slender. Even an enthusiast for the AMP confesses 'it cannot be said that the class structure of Asiatic society emerges with full clarity from Marx's analysis' (Melotti, 1977: 59). The identity of the exploited class is clear enough: 'almost all the inhabitants of the village community, reduced to "general slavery" by the higher power' (ibid). But what is obscure is who makes up the exploiting class. Melotti has a fairly clear answer: 'State officials, mandarins, bureaucrats, the military . . . constitute the real privileged class of the Asiatic system, the group of people outside the productive communes who appropriate the rent from the land, equivalent to a tax on it' (ibid: 61). However, this definition reconstructs Marx's silence.[35]

The *Aziatchiki* in the Soviet Union in the late 1920s and early 1930s were in no doubt that substantive theoretical and empirical arguments could be made to identify the principal line of class contradiction in the AMP:

the basic class division of oriental society is between the fundamental masses of the peasants, joined together in communes, and the former servants of the commune, who have separated themselves from the commune and formed themselves into a ruling class. (The priests in Egypt, the literati in ancient China, and so on) . . . [I]n oriental society the conduct of class war was confined to the struggles between the peasants of the commune and the state of rent and tax collectors. (Madi'iar, 1981: 93)

The *Aziatchiki* were not shy about defining the ruling class as a bureaucracy whose class characteristics were determined by their exploitation of the communes. The Soviet Sinologist M.D. Kokin (1906–39) argued thus:

The surplus labour or product was extracted by the bureaucrats from the direct producer. I cannot call this group of people other than bureaucrats, although it would be possible to find another name for them. But this is not important. The term is not important. Marx and Engels did not give a name to this class. When mention is made of the ruling class in Asiatic society, Marx speaks of the state. That is why I chose the word bureaucrat as, in my opinion, the most appropriate name. (Kokin, 1981: 96)

---

35 Melotti is puzzled by the fact that in his estimation Marx seems very aware of the problem of bureaucracy, yet does little to theorize its importance. The best answer is that Marx was not aware of the 'problem of bureaucracy'. Melotti confesses 'that in this case there may have been some resistance on his part to openly recognizing the class nature of bureaucracy in a State that was not based on private ownership of the means of production – or at least, to use his own words, a certain "judicial blindness" on his part' (Melotti, 1977: 61). The reference to 'judicial blindness' is misleading, because it implies that Marx used it in direct connection with the AMP – in fact it stems from a letter to Engels on the significance of the German Mark (see pp. 124–5).

This solution posed difficulties, as Kokin was aware. For example: was every bureaucrat a member of the ruling class? He answered in the affirmative. His argument, based on the Chinese example, was that recruitment to the bureaucracy was hereditary. Moreover, the job qualifications demanded literacy in hieroglyphics – credentials which no non-exploiter could conceivably obtain. But answering in the affirmative entails a *prima facie* problem for Marxist class theory. The normal Marxist orthodoxy assumes that 'legal position is only a result of the position in the process of production' (ibid). Kokin skirted this theoretical difficulty by suggesting that bureaucratic and production roles were fused in the AMP. He had no empirical doubts: Chinese historical sources unequivocally suggested that every bureaucrat was a member of the ruling class. However, there is a problem in generalizing the class relations in the AMP from the Chinese case. No other Oriental pre-industrial society had such a well developed bureaucracy – if that term is not an anachronism even in the Chinese case. Who constituted the ruling class elsewhere in social formations dominated by the AMP? There is, after all, in Marx's writings also warrant for a classless interpretation of the AMP. The *Grundrisse* sketches essentially classless villages communities, at most emergent class-divided communities, presided over by the 'imaginary unity', the despot.

Assume, however, for the sake of argument that Marx thought that there were classes in the AMP. The critical question is: can the relations of exploitation within the AMP be described, and if so, what are the relations between exploitation and class relations? Marxists have generally defined exploitation, when they use it as a technical term, as circumstances in which one class produces a 'surplus' over and above that necessary to reproduce itself, but another class controls the use of that surplus. They have also generally assumed that this definition produces a binary class structure of exploiters and exploited, and that production relations are directly related to exploitation relations, since productions relations specify relations of ownership (or control) over of means of production.

The key question for the AMP is whether taxes are a form of exploitation. The anarchist or libertarian capitalist always answers this question in the affirmative, irrespective of the mode of production, because taxation involves the coerced extraction of another's labour or property (Nozick, 1974). Marxists seem obliged to take the same line; but this equivalence raises all sorts of thorny issues about exploitation under socialism. The question 'who benefits?' matters more to the Marxist than to the anarchist or libertarian capitalist in evaluating whether or not taxation is exploitative. Taxes can be used to finance the production of what economists call public goods (Samuelson, 1954). Irrigation systems might conceivably be public goods if they are non-excludable and display jointness of supply. Consequently everybody who benefits from the production of goods and services in which state-managed irrigation features as a necessary input is a beneficiary of the expenditure of the revenues raised from taxes used for such purposes. The exploitative character of taxation here is not apparent, if anarchist objections are left to one side. The provision of services like irrigation is financed through coercion but it is a rational and legitimate solution to a problem of 'collective action'. If the AMP operated as this reasoning suggests, then its state structure is identical to the guardian state of liberal theory – an understandably discomforting result for Marxist fundamentalists.

In the case of a social formation dominated by the AMP, the Marxist concerned to analyse taxation as an indicator of class exploitation has to show not only that taxation was coercive, but also that only the class of direct producers paid taxes (even though they were not the only beneficiaries of public expenditure or public services), and that the benefits of state expenditures were distributed differentially, as private goods, for members of the exploiter class. In historical social formations alleged to be exemplars of the AMP the confirmation of this style of argument may not be difficult. The Asiatic state, it might be suggested, provided public goods, but exploitatively: the state was the manager of both a positive-sum and a zero-sum game, both functional and exploitative. However, even when it is demonstrated that state officials siphoned off some of the proceeds of taxation allegedly raised for public goods, to finance consumption or luxury goods, the question remains: are the principal beneficiaries of such exploitation a class – that is, a class by Marxist criteria? After all, they enjoy the proceeds of exploitation as state officials, rather than as landowners.

There are three Marxist answers to this question, and as for all good questions, they come in the customary triad: yes, no, and yes and no. Each answer also creates its own problems. 'Yes' is the answer made by Marxists happy to define state officials as a collective exploitative class. The same people are also generally inclined to accept both the concept of the AMP and the suggestion that state socialist or 'bureaucratic collectivist' or 'state capitalist' regimes may contain a collective exploitative class (Draper, 1977: 484–590; Melotti, 1977; and Sweezy, 1980: 55–84 and 113–33). This position, associated mostly with neo-Trotskyists, utopian Western Marxists and dissident East European Marxists, suggests that the 'betrayal of the revolution' carried out on behalf of the proletariat is more or less inevitable this side of material abundance for all. 'No' is the answer of orthodox Marxists, especially members of ruling communist parties, who insist that state officials cannot be exclusive members of a class. They are always instruments of class rule, at most a sub-set of another class. 'In the last instance' they are employees of the primary exploiters in society who control the state. Orthodox Soviet Marxists are generally hostile both to the AMP and to the idea that socialist societies have class divisions.[36] This position rules out by definitional fiat a class-divided AMP from acceptable Marxism. The AMP is only compatible with this Marxism if it is reduced to a specimen of primitive communism. 'Yes and No' is the answer of those Marxists who argue that state officials constitute a distinctive and demarcated class in the AMP, but do not do so in state socialist regimes (Mandel, 1971). Everybody is a state official in state socialist regimes so there is no identifiable collective exploitative class – the state is the instrument, deformed or otherwise, of the collective non-exploitative class, the proletariat. This position, while sophisticated, rests upon empirical assertions about the 'dictatorship of the proletariat' which fly in the face of the most cursory inspection of the evidence available about the stratification of state socialist regimes.

These three answers do not analyse the full gamut of possible relations between the state officialdom and exploiter class in a social formation. There are four, or perhaps five, important logical possibilities:

1 *Identity* – the state officialdom and the exploiter class are indistinguishable. This is how class relations in the AMP have been generally understood.

2 *Separation* – the state officialdom and the exploiter class are composed of separate people. The Marxist presumption is that the former are the instruments of the latter.

3 *Intersection* – the state officialdom and the exploiter class intersect. The presumption is that key state roles are occupied by members of the exploiter class.

4 *Inclusion.* Here there are two sub-possibilities: (a) the exploiter class is a sub-set of the state officialdom, or (b) the state officialdom is a sub-set of the exploiter class. The former, like 3, suggests the possible existence of non-exploitative state officials; whereas the latter suggests that exploitative state officials act on behalf of the rest of the exploiter class.

These four (or five) logical possibilities exhaust the possible relations between the state and the exploiter class. In the AMP three of these possibilities, 3 and 4(a) and (b), are difficult to specify because non-state

36 The argument of the Soviet Marxist Iu. V. Kachanovskii exemplifies this orthodoxy:

the state in and of itself never was a class and never could be. A class is a group of people occupying a particular economic position ... As for the state, it is also a group of people, but with other traits – organized and armed, united in an apparatus for the support of political power ... Let us admit now that both groups coincided – that the ruling class was completely merged with the personnel of the state apparatus. May we say that 'the state itself as a unit ... actually receives benefit from exploitation? We think not. The 'actual benefit of the state itself' ... is an illusion. Behind the benefit to the state or even to an individual organ of it, there always stands in the final analysis the interests of certain concrete living persons. (Cited in Dunn, 1982: 114–5.)

exploiters are not specified in the concept. Possibility 1 creates an even greater problem. The exploited are indistinguishable from the dominated, the exploiters from the dominators. The Marxist theory of the state is jeopardized by such a fusion precisely because there seems to be no pre-existent class which brings the state into being, and therefore the emergence of the state cannot be explained in the proper Marxist way — through the operation of class struggle (see also pp. 191–6).

These problems are symptomatic of general difficulties historical materialists encounter with the theory of class and exploitation in pre-capitalist societies, both in achieving operational definitions and in advancing the thesis that some, let alone all, history in such societies is the history of class struggle. More importantly they have difficulties in linking exploitation relations, production relations and modes of production. Consider the illuminating typology of forms of exploitation in pre-capitalist societies implicit in the work of a very hostile Marxist critic of the AMP (de Ste Croix, 1981: 205–6). It is reconstructed in table 4.2. This 2 x 2 matrix captures de Ste Croix's typology of forms of exploitation in classical antiquity, and differentiates both exploited and exploiters as individual and collective subjects. All these forms of exploitation existed in the Roman or ancient Greek world.

De Ste Croix's reasons for classifying more than the dyadic relations between slave and slaveholder as forms of exploitation were obvious. He wanted to include under the classification of relations of exploitation the whole gamut of economic and political relations between subjects in the Roman Empire outside of the sphere of personal slavery. If he did not follow this strategy then his claims for the importance of class struggle in the ancient Greek world would have been much less convincing. But his desire to extend the scope of Marxist exploitative relations in the world of classical antiquity ironically, and unintendedly, reintroduces the exploitation relations often attributed to the AMP. Consider in turn each cell in table 4.2. It is apparent that de Ste Croix has unwittingly reintroduced all of Marx's pre-capitalist modes of production into his forms of exploitation. Cell 1, the slaveholder/slave dyad, is the form of exploitation associated with the slave mode of production, while cell 3, the landlord/villages dyad, clearly summarizes exploitation in the feudal mode of production. Cell 4, the state/villages dyad, by contrast, corresponds with intuitive notions of exploitation in the AMP. Cell 2 is less easily classified, as it is intended to cover state exploitation of individuals, whether as slaves or peasants. It seems to be a cross between exploitation in the Asiatic and the slave modes of production.[37] However, a second interpretation is possible. Since for

---

37 Judging by Dunn's (1982) survey much of the controversy in Soviet historiography of the 'archaeological empires' of the Near and Middle East centres on whether the forms of exploitation in cell 2 should be described as Asiatic or slave exploitation.

Table 4.2 A representation of de Ste Croix's forms of exploitation

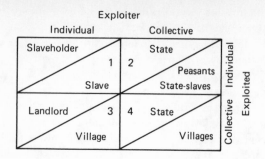

most Marxists the state is an instrument of the exploiter class it follows that taxation is designed to distribute the proceeds of collective exploitation to individual members of the exploitative class. Consequently orthodox Marxists are inclined to see the exploitative taxation implicit in cell 2 as a variant of feudal exploitation. The ambiguous relationships between exploitation relations and the production relations which are supposed to define a mode of production are starkly illustrated by cell 2.

The general strategy taken by Marxist historians, anthropologists and archaeologists who wish to omit the AMP as class-divided exploitative mode of production from historical materialism is straightforward. They seek *either* to deny the existence of the forms in cells 2 and 4 in a given social formation, or to reduce specimens of cells 2 and 4 to empirically salient variants of cell 1 or of cell 3. Even if they grant the existence of the form in cell 2 they argue that whatever its empirical salience in a particular social formation it is never so critical as to raise the issue of defining the mode of production. The frequently unstated premise (empirical, and therefore in principle falsifiable) is as follows. In pre-capitalist societies the bulk of exploitation, – that is the greatest mass of surplus extraction take place under the exploitative forms described in cells 1 or 3. Consequently the issue of defining an exploitative class-divided pre-capitalist mode of production always reduces to a binary choice: either a feudal or a slaveholding society.

A final and critical problem with the vexed issue of class and exploitation in the AMP is whether class struggle exists in this mode of production. The point arises because all other modes production are defined by fundamental class divisions which are the mechanism through which social change is supposed to occur. It is through class struggle that the dialectical contradiction between the development of the productive forces and production relations is realized. The AMP, if it is stagnant, must therefore be characterized either by a muted class struggle which is incapable of ever revolutionizing society, or by the absence of class struggle. The former position is anomalous for Marx's theory of history, whereas the latter requires the reduction of the AMP to a specimen of primitive communism. The class or classless character of the AMP is therefore fundamentally problematic in several respects, an impression which will be strongly reinforced by our examination of the state of the AMP.

The State and the Asiatic Mode of Production

Marxist theories of the state can be divided into three types (Dunleavy and O'Leary, 1987: 236−58). The first is that of the instrumentalist model, in which the state is regarded as the instrument, or the organization, of the exploitative class. The state is staffed, at its highest echelons, usually by members of the dominant exploitative class who ensure that state outputs reflect their interests. The second is that of the arbiter model, in which the state is held to be an organization whose personnel can acquire a certain degree of autonomy from the interests of the dominant exploitative class when there is a (relatively) evenly matched class struggle between the exploiters and the exploited. The third is that of the functionalist model, in which the state is identified with all the institutions in a social formation which contribute to the maintenance of the existing mode of production. The functionalist model is both *ex ante* and *ex post*. The state is conceptualized as existing in order to fulfill certain universal and class-specific functions − that is, it is both functional and exploitative − and at the same time it is identified with all those activities which have the consequences of preserving existing relations of production.

These three basic variants on Marxist theories of the state are capable of being internally subdivided and developed for historical and political analysis. For example, the instrumental account is also compatible with what has been described as an 'abstentionist control' model in which the exploitative class allows the state to be formally run by personnel who are not part of the exploitative class (Elster, 1985). They do so intentionally, in order to disorganize the exploited class by making them engage in a two-front struggle, against the state and against the exploitative class. The arbiter model can also be extended to cover transitions from one mode of production to another. Modern Marxists no longer confine the arbiter state to periods of short, sharp and fairly equally balanced class struggle, as in *The Eighteenth Brumaire of Louis Bonaparte,* but also assert its existence in regimes which have lasted for centuries. There is warrant for this revision in Engels who, in *The Origins of the Family, Private Property and the State*, portrayed the absolutist regimes of Western Europe as arbiter states which presided during a long, balanced war of attrition between the bourgeoisie and the nobility.[38] Many subsequent Marxists have endorsed Engels's picture of the absolute monarch as relatively autonomous of the aristocracy because of the fairly evenly matched struggle for power and influence between the nobility and the bourgeoisie. The functionalist model naturally is the easiest to extend, as in principle any activities which sustain a given social order can be made into state functions, whether or not these activities are intended to serve such functions.[39]

There are many, mostly valid, objections to all these Marxist models of the state (Dunleavy and O'Leary, 1987). However, here the important question is how the state of the AMP fits into these models. The answer is that it does not fit at all well. Consider the instrumentalist, arbiter and functionalist models in order.

The instrumentalist model of the state   In the AMP, this model must identify the state as the instrument of the exploitative class. But there are some doubts in Marxist accounts of the AMP as to whether an exploitative class exists at all in any social formation dominated by this mode. Moreover, even when the existence of an exploitative class is asserted, or conceded, it is not clear that its members are distinguishable from the personnel who staff the state apparatus. If the first, 'classless' interpretation of the AMP is correct then the instrumentalist model collapses. Class antagonisms are supposed to generate a need for a state apparatus on the part of the exploitative class, but if that class does not yet exist there can be no instrumentalist rationale for the state. To parody Engels's remark about socialism, there is no state, only administration in this version of the AMP.

On the other hand, if there is a class of exploiters, not all of whom are members of the state apparatus, then on conventional Marxist logic they must be either feudal lords, slaveowners, capitalists or even peasants. Yet, by definition, these groups cannot count as members of the ruling class in any concept of the AMP. To construct an instrumentalist model of the state in the AMP we must suppose for the sake of argument that there exists a class of exploiters in the AMP who do not hold official state postions, and who are not private landlords, slaveowners or capitalists, and we must suppose that state officials act on their behalf if not at their immediate behest.[40] In principle it makes sense to regard the state (composed of other members of the exploitative class) as the instrument of this

38 By contrast Anderson (P. Anderson, 1974b) seems to regard the absolutist states of the early modern era as instruments of the aristocracy.

39 It has become habitual amongst Western Marxists to describe any organizational, ideological or policy development as a functional response by the state to the contradictions of advanced capitalism (Offe, 1984).

40 These arguments and those which follow apply with equal force to the 'tributary' reconstructions of the AMP which I discuss on pp. 197–200.

exploitative class, provided that members of this class recognize, implicitly or explicitly, that the state is a solution to their collective action problems. Yet for the state to be regarded as the instrument of this class it has to be shown that the members of this exploitative class have potential controls over their state officials, and that they are the principal beneficiaries of the functioning of the state organization. But neither condition can be met without radically redefining the AMP. All accounts of the AMP in which exploitation is acknowledged agree in representing the state as the principal exploiter in the social formation in which it is prevalent, and in describing state officials and the emperor as the principal beneficiaries of such exploitation. Even aside from the taboos of religion and customary law the Asiatic ruler is portrayed as far more powerful, and far less constrained by high-status social strata, than a feudal king.[41] Supra-class accounts of the state in the AMP are prevalent amongst *Aziatchiki* and are not compatible with an instrumentalist Marxist account of the state. In any case, the conditions necessary for the confirmation of the instrumentalist model in the AMP cannot be met if the social formation analysed resembles Marx's — since state officials are the principal beneficiaries of tributary exploitation.

The arbiter model of the state   This model has never been explicitly extended to the AMP. The reasons are obvious. The arbiter model rests on either of two premises, which are normally combined:

that in civil society there are social classes engaged in struggle in which the contestants are evenly matched, and
that the social formation in question is poised at a potential point of transition from the dominance of one mode of production to another.

The problem is that neither of these premises is consistent with any of the images of the AMP current in Marxist literature. First, there are difficulties in identifying the relevant classes, let alone in accepting the assumption that they are engaged in equally matched class struggle. And second, by most definitions, the AMP is incapable of development into a higher mode of production, and therefore cannot ever be at a transitional conjuncture between modes of production (except, of course, under the impact of capitalist imperialism and intrusion).

---

41 As the heterodox Russian writers Bogdanov and Stepanov put it in the 1920s: 'as the new centralized bureaucratic mechanism develops ... the authoritarian principle is pursued ever more mercilessly in the form of completely unlimited subordination of the lower to the higher, in which the only link in the chain — the despotic monarch who has replaced the supreme suzerain — acquires absolute power over all without exception' (cited in Dunn, 1982: 131).

The only way an arbiter style argument can be constructed is to follow Godelier's manoeuvre (Godelier, 1978).[42] He suggests that the Asiatic state arises in response to the breakdown of primitive communism and reflects the tensions between communal property and nascent private property. However, this argument, while stretching Marxist orthodoxy considerably, still faces the problem that the Asiatic state seems to retain its autonomy long after the point of transition from primitive communism has occured. The arbiter model, after all, is still a theory of the relative autonomy of the state from the dominant social class. The state of the AMP, on the other hand, seems to be either one in which there is a literal identity, a fusion of roles, between the primary exploitative class and the ruling class (which returns us immediately to the problems faced by intrumentalist accounts of the state of the AMP); *or* one which enjoys absolute autonomy from the exploitative classes outside the state, because its members run the state apparatus in their own interests. However, neither of these assumptions is consistent with the Marxist arbiter model, and therefore no arbiter-reconstruction of the theory of the state of the AMP seems possible.

The functionalist model of the state   Marx, as have seen, suggested that dual functions were performed by the tributary or despotic state. One set of functions was universal, indispensable to all complex societies; the other set was exploitative. This possibility, that a state might be both functional (that is, beneficial for all) and simultaneously exploitative (that is, supervising or facilitating the expropriation of surplus labour by one class at the expense of another) is conceded by the more sophisticated of Marx's disciples. (It is only Marxist fundamentalists who are prone to see state activity and class relations as a zero-sum game between exploiters and exploited.) The main difficulty with applying a functionalist account of the state of the AMP ironically is that it is the only plausible explanation offered by Marx for this particular phenomenon. In the 'Asiatic' state the universal functions of the state triumph over its exploitative functions. The best 'Marxist' account of the origins of the Asiatic state is therefore identical with the accounts of the origins of the state prevalent in liberal social contract theory or liberal sociology. Theoretical contamination from bourgeois fall-out is not small scale for Marxists concerned to save the AMP.

    The only obvious distinctive and universal function for the state of the AMP, as opposed to those performed in other modes of production, and one that is consistent with Marx's texts, is the function of organizing irrigation. However, this function cannot serve as an *explanation* of the origin of the state of the AMP because it is open to the very simple

---

42 Godelier's position is made more consistent by his explicit abandonment of the hypothesis that the AMP is stagnant.

objection of circularity. This objection stands whether or not one accepts functionalist explanations as legitimate and whether or not the organization of irrigation by states was of historic importance. On the functionalist model, the organized irrigation system develops *after* the state is formed because the state is necessary to its development. But this suggestion leads into a vicious circle because, short of invoking teleological arguments, the question of the origins of the state immediately re-emerges. To be acceptable, explaining the state's emergence to serve the irrigation function requires the belief that the origin of the state was planned (or contracted for) by village communities. This type of explanation once more rehabilitates the liberal theory of the social contract, a Marxist *bête noire*.

There is a further and even more fundamental problem with any functionalist account of the state of the AMP. There is a logical incompatibility between two elements in the concept: the notion that the state performs a universal and necessary function and the notion that the village community is independent or self-sufficient. If the villages of the AMP are genuinely autarchic, self-sufficient, self-maintaining and stable, then what indispensable universal functions can the state possibly be required to fulfil? The notion of an indispensable universal function suggests that the communities are in some sense dependent upon the state, but the notion that the village is self-sufficient rules out the possibility that the village community can be economically dependent upon the state. If it is accepted that the villages are not self-sufficient then one of the intellectual pillars for the argument that the AMP is both stagnant and self-reproducing collapses (as does at least some of the explanatory utility of the AMP in accounts of the failure of capitalism to emerge in the Orient). The alternative is equally painful. The idea that the state in the AMP does not perform some universal and economically necessary function leaves the origins of this state problematic – short of invoking militarist or anarchist theories of state formation. There is no dilemma for 'bourgeois' theorists, since the origin of the state can be explained by non-economic universal functions – for instance the Hobbesian theory of the state as a solution to 'the problem of order' is not incompatible with the idea of economically self-sufficient villages. But there is a painful dilemma for Marxists who wish to maintain some functionalist account of the state of the AMP.

The functionalists compound their portrait of the state in the AMP by arguing not only that it is functional, in the sense that its interventions are necessary to the reproduction of the economic base, but also that it is, simultaneously, 'ideologically fetishised', because 'real relations are expressed ideologically in an inverted form' (Taylor, 1975: 137). The problem here is that to make a fetish of something, for Marxists, is to attribute to it powers which it does not possess (G. A. Cohen, 1979: 155); so if the state is being fetishized then *prima facie* it does not possess the powers which the functionalist model suggests it must have. It may be that these theses are reconcilable. It may be that what Marxists want to suggest is that religious veneration of the state in social formations dominated by the AMP falsely attributes to the monarch the ability to produce the harvest, sow the seed and so on, when in fact it is peasant labour which produces these results. However, the fact remains that an economically functional state must play a role in agrarian production, and that therefore the 'fetishization' must be founded on some facts rather than a complete inversion of reality. The monarchy, if not the monarch, is indispensable for the successful organization of production on the functionalist account. Either wholesale ideological fetishization of the state is false or the functionalist account of the state is false. There is only one sensible way to transcend this dilemma: the state must indeed necessarily intervene in communal production, but it is 'the ideological representation of this intervention that permits an extraction of surplus labour beyond what is required for the maintenance of communal village production' (Taylor, 1979: 138).

This argument moves towards combining a functionalist and exploitative (instrumental) conception of the state. (It also leaves it entirely uncertain whether the ideological representation is a dominant ideology, propagated for purposes of manipulation, or whether it is the spontaneous product of the fetish-prone peasants of the AMP.) Indeed most contemporary Marxist defenders of the AMP want to work simultaneously with an instrumentalist and a functionalist conception of the state. But this tendency merely compounds two unsatisfactory accounts. The state may well be both functional and exploitative, but the former assertion cannot serve as an explanation of the origin of the state without contradicting Marxism, and the latter assertion poses the difficulty of state-based rather than class-based exploitation. The conclusion is unavoidable: whichever theory of the state Marxists operate with, whether instrumentalist, arbiter or functionalist, there are fundamental peculiarities, anomalies and inconsistencies between the state of the AMP and historical materialism.

What is Asiatic about the Asiatic Mode of Production?

Marx's discussions of the AMP referred mainly to India, although he and Engels made arguably 'Asiatic' references to China, Persia, Java, ancient Peru and the Etruscans.[43] Since Marx's time the concept has been applied most frequently and famously to China, by Soviet Marxists both before the AMP was proscribed and after its partial rehabilitation in the early 1960s, and by Wittfogel both when he was a young Marxist Sinologist and later as a Cold War colonel. However, since World War II both Marxists and anti-

43 Citing 'The British Rule in India' as his authority, the Hungarian Varga argued that:

Marxists have massively expanded the number of historical regimes classified as either dominated by the AMP or containing significant 'Asiatic' elements. Wittfogel's *Oriental Despotism* (discussed in detail in chapter 6) applied this category to an immense plethora of non-Asiatic and non-oriental empires. Neo-Marxists have found the AMP in many periods of history, and in many geographical areas beyond China and India. Aztec, Babylonian, Cambodian, Cretan, Egyptian, Etruscan, Ghanian, Incan, Imerinanian,[44] Korean, Laotian, Malian, Mesopotamian, Tibetan and Veitnamese civilizations were all considered as candidate-specimens of the AMP in a collection of Marxist essays published in Paris in 1969 (CÉRM, 1969). The *Centre d'Études et de Recherches Marxistes* took the concept on a tour through world history and found it applied almost everywhere – except to Western Europe. Subsequently other Marxists have extended the applicability of the AMP even further, notably to the histories of Indonesia (Tichelman, 1980), Turkey (Islamoglu and Keyder, 1977), Iran (Abrahamian, 1975) and Thailand (Reynolds and Lysa, 1983).

The first major problem with the 'Asiatic' label of this mode of production is obvious. There are no structural elements of the AMP which might explain why the label 'Asiatic' should be applied to the overall configuration. This mode of production is distinct from all the others mentioned by Marx because it is the only one which has a geographical tag. These reasons, as well as Marx's many passing remarks about Asiatic societies, explain why the concept is regarded as Eurocentric or Orientalist. It is therefore not surprising that contemporary Marxists, who believe that a postive theory of the AMP can be excavated from whatever undesirable normative origins it may have had, have offered at least three different labels. These labels are intended to 'de-Asiatize' it. The best known are the 'tributary mode of production', 'politocracy' and the 'archaic mode of production'.

The 'tributary' label was first suggested by a Japanese Marxist, Jiro Hoyakawa, but was independently advocated by Ioan Banu, a Hungarian Marxist philosopher, and by Samir Amin, an African Marxist political

---

From Marx's . . . remarks it clearly follows that:
1) the term 'Asiatic mode of production' *should not be interpreted in a geographic sense*, since he includes vast areas of Africa [*]. For this reason he sometimes uses not only the term 'Asiatic society' but also 'Oriental society';
2) *Marx did not extend the concept 'Asiatic mode of production' to the whole of Asia*, but only to those regions where the rainfall was insufficient for agricultural production. It would follow that it would be useless to attempt to solve the problem of the Asiatic mode of production on the basis of conditions in China, as was done by our sinologists. In most regions of China there was enough rainfall to carry on agriculture without irrigation. (Varga, 1968: 332–3)

* The basis for Varga's African interpolation is Marx's references to Egypt and the Sahara in 'The British Rule in India'.
44 Now the Malagasy Republic.
45 Amin (1980: 68) tells us that Hoyakawa coined the term in a Japanese controversy – in what context he does not say.

economist (Amin, 1980b; and Banu, 1967).[45] Amin argues that there are only three major formations in world history before socialism: the communal, the tributary and the capitalist. Slavery, for him, is the exceptional socio-economic structure because of the small number of societies it affected (Amin, 1980: 59). The matrix in table 4.3 captures Amin's three formations. To each formation corresponds a given level of organization of the productive forces and a functional ideological system. The tributary formation corresponds to a centralized state which engages in the organization of the production of use values and the management of limited markets and major construction works, and is associated with a universal world religion (Islam, Christianity, Hinduism) which cements the formation. So far Amin's reasoning is that of a conventional Marxist. Functionalist basis–superstructure assumptions frame his account.[46] However, his tributary formation is revisionist. He has replaced the universal feudalism of Soviet Stalinism with a universal tributary formation.

The tributary mode of production, as defined by Amin, has four central features: the surplus product of the direct producers is extracted by non-economic means; production is mainly for use-value rather than exchange value; the superstructure, with a centralized state and a great religion, is dominant; and finally, it has the appearance of stability and even stagnation, but it is not in fact stagnant. This tributary formation is in part a reconstructed version of the AMP. However, it also includes the feudal mode of production. Amin argues that

The feudal mode is simply a primitive, incomplete tributary mode ... Feudal property is not radically different from tributary property. Rather, it is a primitive form of tributary property, a form resulting from the weak and decentralized character of political power ... [T]he absolute European monarchies became very similar to complete tributary forms ... [T]he primitive feudal mode evolved towards the tributary mode; the tributary mode is not the exception but the general rule and the feudal mode is not the exception but the general rule and feudal mode is a particular and exceptional variant of the tributary set. (ibid: 61–2)

The class struggle in the tributary formation takes the form of conflict between the tributary class (state officials or the feudal aristocracy) and the peasantry, a conflict which the peasantry can win but without winning the long-run benefits. Theirs is a tragic fate. Any successes of the peasants in weakening the tributary formation can benefit only the bourgeoisie – as a by-product – who will form the ruling class under the next formation, capitalism.[47]

---

46 Amin's is also a three-stage philosophy of history (tribalism, agrarian society and industrial society) in which slavery and socialism are awkward past and future appendages.

47 If it was true that in this formation the victorious peasant class did not inherit the next formation, why should things be any different for the proletariat in that next formation? Amin does not address this question.

Table 4.3 *Amin's three social formations*

Formation	Key unit for production	Ideology
Communal	Village, clan, tribe	Kinship
Tributary	State	Great religions
Capitalist	Universal market	Nationalism

The tributary formation is clearly not a trivial renaming of the AMP. It is both a theoretical attempt to avoid some of the dilemmas associated with the AMP and an ideological intervention against Eurocentricity and Orientalism. Amin's tributary formation is clearly situated in time: it is post-primitive communism and pre-capitalist, and is not an awkward primitive/transitional mode of production.[48] The tributary formation has a clear state, it has a class structure (albeit one which looks Weberian rather than Marxist) and it has a (rather looser) specification of the level of development of the productive forces. As an ideological intervention Amin's reconstruction is also a *tour de force*.[49] Rather like the Hegelian Marxist Semenov he argues that capitalism developed first on the periphery of the tributary formation. Europe's privileges rested upon Europe's comparative backwardness: 'precisely because of its poor origins, European society traversed the tributary period more quickly. This is the thesis of unequal development: European society was more flexible because it was peripheral' (ibid: 63). However, his argument remains an ideological intervention, because Amin does not make the theory of unequal development precise and leaves his assertions exposed to the same flaws which critics have detected in Trotsky's theory of combined and uneven development (Elster, 1986: 54–63), and in Semenov's Hegelian Marxist theory of development on the periphery (Gellner, 1980: 59–82). The major problem in Amin's account is that he has displaced to the slave mode of production all the key

48 Amin attacks the type of reconstructed AMP advocated by the Hungarian Marxist Ferenc Tökei and the French Marxist Maurice Godelier. First, he considers it absurd to use the same term (Asiatic or other) for lineage (clan or tribal) and state formations. Such formations differ radically in their degree of development of the productive forces. (This argument is also made by the Soviet orientalist L. B. Alayev [in personal correspondence].) Second, he considers the notion of a continuous privileged development for Europe to be false. For example, centralized tributary formations in Asia and North Africa were far more advanced in production, knowledge, civilization and market development than early feudal Europe. Third, the notion that collective ownership of the land persisted throughout millennia in Asiatic empires is false (Amin 1980: 48, 54, 59, 62).

49 For an argument indebted to Amin see Wickham (1985).

anomalies, dilemmas and contradictions that I have suggested characterize the AMP. Amin's slave mode of production is difficult to fit in a unilineal schema, is stagnant, historically meaningless, confined to one geographical area and so on. None the less, Amin has at least succeeded in mustering an argument which is as superficially compelling as its antithesis: the ideologically Eurocentric account which sees the development of capitalism in Europe as a teleological process from which Asia was excluded by virtue of inherent stagnation.

By contrast with Amin, Draper and Semenov see no fundamental problems with the 'Asiatic' label, but agree that it would avoid confusion and unnecessary controversy if the mode of production were to be renamed. We have it on Gellner's authority that Semenov has reformulated the AMP with a new and non-geographic name, 'politicocracy' (Gellner, 1986: 80), a name which conveys the significance of centralized institutions in this formation. (Semenov also argues that Marx ceased to use the Asiatic label because he recognized that politocracy existed outside Asia, and not, *contra* Nikiforov, because he had abandoned the idea of the AMP altogether.)

Draper, by contrast, professes not to be embarrassed by the Asiatic prefix in the controversial mode of production. He thinks that Marx's choice of the term was in no sense Eurocentric or Orientalist. As he puts it: 'Just as the discovery of Peking man did not mean that only the Chinese had prehuman ancestors, so too the survival of living-fossil social forms in Asia did not mean that the "Asiatic" mode of production was an Oriental monopoly' (Draper, 1977: 539). But he too seems to have a marginal preference for a new, less controversial and less confusing label − albeit one with impeccable textual credentials. The expression 'archaic formation', used in one of Marx's letters to Vera Zasulich of 1881, was developed as a result of Marx's new-found knowledge of a European version of such a formation. Marx's reading of Maurer's work on the German Mark confirmed that the 'Asiatic' mode of production had existed in Europe − indeed, perhaps it had even come into existence there as long ago as it had in Asia. Draper therefore concludes that the concept 'archaic formation' conveys Marx's intended meaning without any geographical 'Asiatic' confusions arising − even though such confusion is, in his opinion, utterly unwarranted. Moreover, he counsels his readers that Marx's change in label 'should not obscure the identity of substance' with the AMP (ibid: 544). This renamed AMP is therefore different in scale and time to Amin's. It can exist in small-scale tribal, clan and lineage systems, and its time span extends from its origins in the transition between primitive communism and the formation of class-society, right up until the advent of capitalism.[50]

---

50 Semenov's positioning of the AMP is the same: 'from the birth of class society right up to the eighteenth and even nineteenth century, the asiatic mode of production continued to

The AMP, it seems, faces the problems which used to face every bastard child dumped on another's door: who were its parents, where does it come from, what is its real name, and does it matter what name it has?[51] However, unlike some such children it does not seem destined ever to find a happy home with the friends of its real parents.

CONCLUSION

The foregoing discussion of fundamental questions in the AMP has revealed five theoretical dilemmas and two problems which the AMP poses for historical materialism.

The first dilemma is that the AMP is either part of a unilineal schema, in which case it contradicts the theory of historical progress; or it is part of a multilineal schema, in which case historical materialism ceases to be a theory of history and becomes instead a redescription of world history. The second dilemma is that the AMP is either stagnant, in which case it does not fit the general Marxist theory of historical progress (and also lacks a developed theory of what makes it stagnant); or it is not stagnant, in which case its role in Marxist explanations of the origins of capitalism is redundant. The third is that the basis of the AMP either cannot be conceptually or empirically distinguished from its superstructure; or, if it can, there appears to be no law-like relationships established between its basis and its super-structure. The fourth is that either there are no classes in the AMP, in which case the general Marxist theory of the state breaks down or there are classes, in which case the Marxist theory of class has to be considerably modified to incorporate state and corporate classes. Similarly, there is a fifth dilemma over whether exploitation exists in the AMP: either it does not exist, in which case a liberal theory of the state is true of the AMP; or it does exist, in which case exploitation derives from the state rather than society.

There are two fundamental problems in addition to these dilemmas. First, general Marxist theories of the state (whether instrumentalist, arbiter or functionalist models) cannot be satisfactorily reconstructed to fit the Asiatic case. Second, there is an unresolved debate over whether the 'Asiatic' in AMP should be replaced by a more geographically neutral term, and over whether the AMP can be incorporated as a special case of a

exist in certain countries of the East ... these countries remained at the stage of the first class-endowed socio-economic formation' (Semenov, 1980: 55).

51 Immanuel Wallerstein, a Neo-Marxist 'world systems' theorist, has also, arguably, rechristened the AMP (Wallerstein, 1974). He argues that wherever there was an empire which was coextensive with the areas of a world economy then economic development was blocked. This 'world-empire' is defined by the extraction of tribute by a central authority, and according to Wallerstein its superstructural characteristics blocked infrastructural developments.

more general mode of production.

These five fundamental theoretical dilemmas, two thorny problems, and the ideological and political controversies already outlined, serve to explain why the AMP is one of Marx's most awkward legacies to Marxists.

5

The Asiatic Mode of Production
and
Varieties of Historical Materialism

[H]istorical materialism remains the only intellectual paradigm capacious enough to be able to link the ideal horizon of socialism to come with the practical contradictions and movements of the present, and their descent from the structures of the past, in a theory of the distinctive dynamics of social development as a whole ... it will not be replaced as long as there is no superior candidate for comparable overall advance in knowledge.

Anderson, *In the Tracks of Historical Materialism*

The theory of productive forces and relations of production – perhaps the most important part of historical materialism – is dead.

Elster, *Karl Marx: An Introduction*

Chapter 4 outlined the general problems posed by the AMP for some of the most general canons of historical materialism. It might be supposed that some better-specified reconstructions of historical materialism can cope more successfully with this anomalous mode of production. However, the AMP poses extreme difficulties for each of the more rigorous variants of historical materialism sketched in pp. 152–61. The specific problems encountered by the productivist, structuralist and Hegelian versions of historical materialism are elaborated below. They serve to confirm that the AMP, however reconstructed, causes acute and insoluble theoretical anomalies for historical materialism. For these reasons, amongst others, historical materialism seems best described as 'dead', as Elster puts it, rather than as the capacious paradigm linking past, present and future in an ideal and scientific whole, which Anderson would have us believe.

PRODUCTIVIST HISTORICAL MATERIALISM AND THE
ASIATIC MODE OF PRODUCTION

Productivist historical materialism has four major difficulties which bear upon the theoretical utility of the AMP. First, there are problems of conceptual ambiguity; second, problems in operationalizing concepts; third, problems with functional and teleological explanations; and finally, problems with the primacy thesis.

Ambiguities in Productivist Historical Materialism

The ambiguities in productivist historical materialism are centred on its key concepts – mode of production, productive forces and relations of production – and also in the meaning of its central hypothesis: the development thesis. First, the very term 'mode of production' is itself ambiguous: one intriguing challenge to the Marxist credentials of the AMP rests on the premise that the whole debate which surrounds the concept stems from the misleading consequences of Marx's ambiguous use of this expression. The German term *Produktionweise* is not the straightforward equivalent of the theoretical concept of mode of production with which we have worked in this book. It can mean simply the very broad notion 'circumstances of production', a relatively atheoretical and imprecise notion by comparison with the systematicity, albeit problematic, I have so far associated with the concept of mode of production. 'If the term "Asiatic mode of production" is considered in this light, we obviously come to the conclusion that Marx could understand under this heading not necessarily a distinct system, but the circumstances of production in the lands of the East. Such an attitude is quite close to the truth' (Lentsman, 1966: 28).[1] However, this ingenious attempt to kill the entire discussion at a stroke must fail. The sole occasion in which Marx publicly used the expression AMP was in the famous Preface to *A Contribution to the Critique of Political Economy*, where he defined the core concepts of historical materialism and named the Asiatic along with other modes of production. The list of progressive modes of production defined there was obviously intended as a set of systematic examples of modes of production in a systematic statement of Marx's key theoretical beliefs. The modes of production referred to in the Preface cannot reasonably be read as a reference to a vaguely situated set of 'circumstances of production', and therefore Lentsman's attempt to downplay the 'MP' in AMP is unconvincing.

There are, none the less, fundamental ambiguities in other core historical materialist concepts which impair the clarity of the AMP, especially the productive forces. Productive forces can be defined by productivist historical materialists both intensionally and extensionally. Intensionally a productive force 'must be capable of use by a productive agent in such a way that production occurs [partly] as a result of its use, and it is someone's purpose

---

1 Lentsman's article was translated from the Soviet journal of classical scholarship, *Vestnik drevnei istorii*, 1965, No. 3.

that the facility so contributes towards production' (G.A. Cohen, 1979: 32). Extensionally productive forces are defined to include means of production, labour power, spaces and premises.

The major difficulty with the intensional definition is its potential ambit. Cohen's definition is meant to tidy up Marx's profligate tendency to use 'productive forces' to include everything related to increased productivity or output. Marx's wider usage makes the productive forces indistinguishable from relations of production — and many other processes. For example, if religion is related to increased productivity then on Marx's looser usages it must be counted as a productive force. The stipulation of intentionality by Cohen is meant to circumscribe what can be counted as a productive force. The distinction between material work relations and social relations illustrates this attempt to narrow the ambit of the productive forces: 'On our account, knowledge of ways of organizing labour is a productive force, part of managerial labour power, but the relations established when that knowledge is implemented are not productive forces. It is necessary to distinguish the blueprint for the set of relations from the relations themselves, and it is the first which is a productive force' (ibid). However, this solution still seems to allow far too many social processes into the classification of productive forces. For example, if we conclude on the basis of analysis that religion is deliberately employed to organize production, as is arguably the case with the caste division of labour in the Indian village, surely we must then affirm that Hinduism or the ideology of caste, in so far as they are intentionally employed to organize production, must (at least partly) be productive forces?

The extensional definition of the productive forces is also ambiguous. Here the problem is the place of knowledge as a candidate member of the productive forces (Elster, 1983 and 1985). Marx asserts that science is, amongst other things, a productive force. Accordingly, productive forces can be either spiritual or material. But the extensional definition also makes it clear that productive forces are things which can be owned. (If they cannot be owned, the standard Marxist fall-back ploy is that they can be 'effectively controlled'.) This criterion, 'ownability', seems to offer a way of excluding the Hindu religion or caste ideology from the ambit of the productive forces. As the Hindu religion cannot be owned, *ergo* it cannot be a productive force. However, as Marx (and Cohen) want science to be a productive force, there is a dilemma. In what way is science distinguishable from religion?[2] Even if we accepted for the sake of argument that science

2 This question concedes nothing to the playful relativism of those who argue that there are no important epistemological differences between science and religion (for example, Feyerabend, 1975). The question refers solely to the status of science and religion as potential members of the class of elements included in the definition of productive forces.

can be owned through professional exclusion and through the use of patents, there is a difficulty in arguing that organized religion is not 'ownable' in the same way. For instance, in the India of the AMP it might be argued that exclusion through caste, through the monopoly of sacred language and literacy, and through control of caste designation, rendered religion the property of the dominant social caste. There is an easy objection to this analogy: religious knowledge relevant to production was not individual, but collective, and the knowledge could easily be acquired by members of exploited classes. However, the objection also applies to science: much scientific knowledge relevant to production is collective and is relatively easily disseminated. The specification of the productive forces of the AMP is thus rendered ambiguous.

The relations of production are also conceptually ambiguous. In productivist historical materialism, relations of production are relations of effective control over productive forces. Following Marx's Preface, property relations are but the 'legal expression for' relations of production. Accordingly productivist historical materialists have been content, at least initially, to define relations of production in the language of ownership and non-ownership of productive forces. This understanding of relations of production faces the difficulty of deciding what is owned (and what is not owned) that is intentionally relevant to increasing production. But deciding these matters may not be easy, as we have just seen. Furthermore, the difficulties in separating basis from superstructure emerge with a vengeance when we try to disambiguate production relations (pp. 182–4). Understanding the complex gradation of producers' rights with respect to the means of production is notoriously complex in agrarian societies. Finally, there is considerable imprecision in the relations between exploitation and production relations (Roemer, 1982, 1986b and 1988).[3] The former is not a function of the latter, nor vice versa. The concept of production relations, the twin of the productive forces, is therefore as ambiguous as its sibling.

The linchpin of productivist historical materialism, the meaning of the development hypothesis, is also multiply ambiguous (Elster, 1985: 300). For example, Marx's texts warrant both an extensive and an intensive interpretation of the development of the productive forces. Extensive development occurs if population growth occurs and if population is counted as a productive force; whereas intensive development occurs if surplus per capita rises. Further ambiguities in this thesis have been fully and adequately explored by others (ibid: 243–53), and there is no need to duplicate this work here.

3 Roemer demonstrates that (Marxist) exploitation can take place in a classless economy, and that exploitation is analytically independent of the configuration of the ownership of the means of production. These results demonstrate rigorously the absence of systematic relations between exploitation and production relations (Roemer, 1986b).

Productivist historical materialism is impaired by these ambiguities in its key concepts. In its defence it might be contended that these puzzles are those which any social scientific theory throws up, and that their resolution is feasible through careful disambiguation and operationalization of the concepts. However, the ambiguity which surrounds the meaning of the development thesis is a great handicap to the coherence of any productivist version of historical materialism. I believe that while the AMP is a canker in the flawed theory of historical materialism, it is merely one of many concepts which, when unpacked, lead to the unravelling of the theory of which they are a part.

Operationalizing Productivist Historical Materialism

The problems of operationalizing the key concepts of productivist historical materialism are related to but independent of the ambiguities I have just discussed. If historical materialism is to be a genuine scientific theory, capable of verification or falsification in principle, we must be able to confirm or disconfirm its central hypotheses. This requirement demands concepts which are capable of being operationalized. The major problems associated with operationalizing historical materialist concepts are of direct relevance to the social scientific utility of the overarching theory and one of its offshoots, the AMP.

The first problem is to operationalize the productive forces. Having surmounted, or ignored, the ambiguities in the meaning of the productive forces discussed above, we must be able to construct an index of their level of development. Such an index is required so that we can be confident that certain modes of production are more *progressive* than others[4], that certain countries are more developed exemplars of a mode of production than others, and that the productive forces are (or were) fettered by production relations from developing further. Without such an index, historical materialism can be no more than a very crude heuristic device, fettered by its own internal limitations from developing into a social scientific framework.

How might we measure the level of development of the productive forces? Several criteria have been offered in Marxist historiography and political economy. They include:

the degree of intensiveness of the division of labour;
the character of the inputs of raw materials and means of production employed in the production process;
the organization of the labour process (Sawer, 1977a: 206; and Welskopf, 1981: 242−8);

---

4 'Progressive' must be understood here exclusively in the sense of advancing the level of development of the productive forces.

the size of the actual (or the maximum feasible) social surplus in the mode of production (G.A. Cohen, 1979: 198);[5]
the free labour-time available for the direct producers;[6]
the population which can be sustained by the existing productive forces.

Marx and Engels themselves never rigorously compared differences in the level of development of the productive forces in pre-capitalist social formations. The difficulties involved in creating an index for the development of the productive forces, and the immense labour in finding reliable data with which to compare pre-capitalist economies, are not difficult to spot, but modern economists have none the less made some pioneering efforts in these directions (E. Jones, 1981; Pryor, 1977). Marx and Engels's neglect of the problems involved suggests dogmatism, ignorance or simple lack of recognition of their importance. More generously, it seems likely that they did not consider as very significant the differences between pre-capitalist modes of production on the index of levels of development of the productive forces. This interpretation is plausible, since many passages on pre-capitalist modes of production can be found in the 'Formen', *Capital*, *Theories of Surplus Value* and *Anti-Dühring* where Marx and Engels's attention is primarily focused upon comparative relations of production rather than levels of technological progress, and where all pre-capitalist economies are treated as specimens of natural economies dominated by production for use-value rather than exchange-value.

However, this interpretation of the past masters' neglect poses immense difficulties for productivist historical materialism. The productive forces are supposed to determine the relations of production, yet on the generous interpretation of Marx and Engels's texts the same level of development of the productive forces seems to be correlated with at least three diverse sets of production relations (Asiatic, slave and feudal). Second, any unilinealist version of historical materialism requires an index of levels of development in order to show that historical progress has occurred in the transition from one mode of production to another. If pre-capitalist modes of production do not differ on an index of progressive development of the productive forces then the explanatory power of productivist historical materialism is considerably diminished. Third, the possibility that the same productive forces are compatible with very different relations of production creates

5 Cohen (1979) distinguishes four societies (pre-class, pre-capitalist class, capitalist and post-class societies) according to their levels of productive power. He suggests that the size of the surplus is the appropriate indicator for classifying such societies. He omits to mention whether he is referring to potential or actual surplus, but one suspects he means the former.

6 This criterion produces awkward problems for Marxists. Humans in the stone age lived, and still live, in an affluent, leisurely society. By this index − the free labour-time available for the direct producers − all post-stone-age societies mark a decline in living standards (Sahlins, 1972).

further problems for the notion that the 'motor of history' depends upon contradictions between relations of production and the development of the productive forces. Finally, a correct productivist Marxist taxonomy of social orders should define and test levels of development of the productive forces and deduce from these indices the functionally appropriate relations of production. But productivist historical materialists make ownership rather than technology the key criterion in defining social orders, despite their emphasis on the primacy of the productive forces (Gellner, 1964: 132–3).[7]

Cohen tries to reply to this last objection by suggesting that Gellner's query is misguided 'It is often appropriate to classify entities by their form, not their content, and formal classification is correct in the present case, for individualisation by productive forces would not yield social types' (G.A. Cohen, 1979: 98). However, this attempted riposte is self-defeating. To those who say that to mean something the primacy thesis should make productive forces the key variable in the construction of Marxist taxonomies, it is no reply to contend that such a procedure is fruitless. It is true that Cohen's conflation of all pre-capitalist orders into one social form, discussed below (pp. 212–15), is an attempt to do what Gellner suggests a consistent Marxist should do. But it does so at the cost of abandoning what has always been regarded as a core element of historical materialism – namely, the belief that there was more than one social form intermediate between primitive communism and capitalism.

Yet even if historical materialists were to develop an agreed index for the level of development of the productive forces, they would then face a second major crisis of operationalization. Could they measure the level of development of the productive forces independently of the relations of production? This question poses a twofold snare for productivist historical materialists. First, there may be no transhistorical and invariant measure of the level of the development of the productive forces. This difficulty would make each mode of production incommensurable because we would not have an agreed general index. (This problem is similar to some of the objections raised against GNP indicators as guides to comparative studies of cross-national economic welfare.) Second, if the productive forces can be defined only in relation to the relations of production then we have good reasons to be sceptical of the causal relations which are alleged to hold between them.

---

7 The primacy of the productive forces was expressed most crudely by Marx in the famous statement in *The Poverty of Philosophy* that 'the hand-mill gives you society with the feudal lord; the steam-mill, society with the industrial capitalist' (Marx, 1977: 202). Max Weber, discussing the 'Indeterminate Economic Preconditions of Patrimonialism and Feudalism', decisively rebutted this assertion as 'at most correct in its second part, and then only partially. The steam-mill fits without any difficulty into a state socialist economy. The first part of the statement, however, is entirely incorrect: the hand-mill has lived through all conceivable economic structures and political "superstructures"'. (Weber, 1978: 1091).

The reason for believing that production forces cannot be measured independently of production relations is simple. To measure labour productivity in a social formation, as opposed to labour productivity in a particular activity, we need an index which aggregates inputs and outputs so that we can proceed to calculate input/output ratios. In capitalist societies Marxists face severe problems in operationalizing the labour theory of value for such tasks (see, *inter alia*, Steedman, 1977), but in pre-capitalist societies there is not even such a highly contestable measure. Cohen suggests that we measure the free labour-time available for the direct producers — that is, the ratio between necessary and surplus labour (G.A. Cohen, 1979: 134) — in order to determine the level of development of the productive forces. But this 'solution' does not measure the level of development of the productive forces independently of the relations of production, since the ratio of necessary to surplus labour is a measure of the rate of exploitation, which must be related to, *inter alia*, the length of the working day, the means of production owned or not owned by the direct producers and so on, all of which are indirectly, if imprecisely, connected with the relations of production (Callinicos, 1982: 142–5).[8]

There is a final problem in the operationalization of the level of development of the productive forces, of especial importance for the AMP. Suppose that, through an appropriate mix of ingenuity and perspiration, all of the above conceptual and operationalization problems have been solved. There might then be a fundamental empirical problem: what would happen to the plausibility of productivist historical materialism if the evidence of a productive forces index showed that social formations dominated by Asiatic modes of production were regularly higher on scales of development than social formations dominated by slave or feudal modes of production? For example, on the basis of population supported under one mode of production compared to another, both India and China had far more populous cities and more rural inhabitants per hectare of cultivated land than Western Europe at the point of transition from feudalism to capitalism. Such evidence, *prima facie*, would not be good news for the productivist historical materialist hypothesis that 'no social order is ever destroyed before all the productive forces for which it is sufficient have been developed, and new superior relations of production never replace older ones before the material conditions for their existence have matured within the framework of the old society' (Marx, 1970: 21).

---

8 Alex Callinicos and Michael Rosen, who taught me at Oxford University in 1980–1, were helpful guides on these matters.

Functionalist and Teleological 'Explanations' in Productivist Historical
Materialism

Productivist historical materialism is also open to methodological charges
which go beyond the difficulties of presenting it as a form of positivist
social science capable of operationalization. The accusation is often made
that historical materialism is essentially functionalist in its mode of explanation, and that it is also radically impaired by its teleological character
(Elster, 1982; and Giddens, 1981). Some productivist historical materialists
embrace these charges without shame; and are happy to defend both
functionalist explanations and historical materialist functionalist explanations
(G.A. Cohen, 1979, 1982; Wright, Levine and Sober, 1987).

This is not the place to resolve the issues at stake in accepting the
validity or otherwise of functionalist explanations.[9] However, the AMP
does pose straightforward problems for historical materialism even if we
accept, for the sake of argument, the validity of functionalist and teleological
explanations. The *telos* of history is radically jeopardized by the existence of
a mode of production which is incapable of endogenous development. This
mode of production can have no historical meaning; at best it testifies to
the contingent nature of the royal march of history to advanced communism.
For the more secular Marxists, who distinguish teleological from functionalist
explanations and defend the latter rather than the former, an equally severe
problem is created by a mode of production whose production relations
cannot by definition be explained by their role in developing the productive
forces. However, Cohen has so often and ingeniously defended functionalist
reasoning in Marxism that one has to be cautious. A Cohenite who wanted
to save the AMP might reply as follows: 'Asiatic production relations are
indeed functionally explained by their role in promoting the productive
forces. However, Asiatic production relations never in fact reach the point
at which they become dysfunctional for the development of the productive
forces.' This reconstruction would save a functionalist and stagnatory account
of the AMP, but its the costs would be twofold. First, the thesis is untestable
and open to all the objections to which functionalist objections are open.
And second, we would need an account of why Asiatic production relations
are peculiar in never reaching the point at which they become dysfunctional
for the development of the productive forces.[10]

9 In a debate will one of my colleagues I have explicitly attacked the value of functionalist
explanations in Public Administration (Dunleavy, 1982; and O'Leary, 1985), elaborating the
arguments advanced by Elster (1983) and Barry (1978).

10 Cohen, as I shall discuss in a moment (pp. 212–15), does not want to save the AMP.
Indeed he is now equivocal about his defence of historical materialism (G.A. Cohen, 1983).

Primacy and the Asiatic Mode of Production

Productivist historical materialism is often challenged on the meaning and validity of its core claim: the primacy thesis (Plamenatz, 1954). In what sense are the productive forces more important, more primary, than production relations? And (especially significant for multilineal versions of productivist historical materialism) if productive forces do have primacy in history, in what sense are they 'explanatory' of so many diverse sets of pre-capitalist production relations? Are not technologically determinist 'explanations' dependent upon spurious correlations and illustrations rather than causally developed accounts of the relationships between technologies and property relations? I need not elaborate these questions here. It is sufficient to note that challenges to the primacy thesis are especially acute for the AMP. If productive forces really do have primacy in history why then are they incapable of developing to the point of rupturing Asiatic production relations? What makes certain production relations immune to a technological breakthrough?

To Kill the Asiatic Mode of Production?

The most revisionist strategy for productivist historical materialists concerned by these problems with the AMP is to adopt Stalin's strategy and exclude it altogether from a reconstructed historical materialism. Stalin presented no argument for his strategy. Subsequent Marxists have made up for Stalin's bad manners and have provided arguments, as we saw in chapter 4, for excluding the AMP from the conceptual apparatus of historical materialism.

One strategy is to reduce the substantive social structural features alluded to by the use of the term AMP to mere internal variations within either feudalism or slavery. The major rationale here is the contention that where Asiatic features are present in a social formation they are never so important as feudal or slave aspects. This strategy must be based upon appraising empirical evidence, and so far I have suggested that it is not possible to render a firm empirical verdict on such arguments. The criteria for operationalizing productive forces, relations of production and social surpluses are so underdeveloped and unpromising as to make empirical pronouncement dogmatic.

The second form of argument cuts the knot. The problems posed by all pre-capitalist modes of production (between primitive communism and capitalism) for productivist versions of historical materialism are excised by one stroke, or rather absorbed through one swallow. Cohen, for example, chooses to conflate the Asiatic, slave and feudal modes of production into one general category which he calls 'pre-capitalist class society'. It is perhaps debatable whether he includes the AMP in this conflated new category. After all, Cohen states in a footnote: 'We shall not discuss the "Asiatic Mode" of production, which is difficult to classify. See the illuminating treatment by Shaw, *Productive Forces and Relations of Production*, pp. 326—35, and the superb critique of the concept by Anderson, *Lineages of the Absolutist State*, pp. 426—96' (G.A. Cohen, 1979: 199). This note strongly suggests that Cohen is persuaded by Anderson that the AMP should receive an intellectual burial. However, two pages later Cohen argues that 'Distinct agricultural societies ... at much the same level of productive power, could have needs of different kinds of irrigation, and this might help to explain differences in economic structure they displayed' (ibid: 201). A more concise version of Wittfogel's functionalist version of the AMP is difficult to imagine! But whether Cohen does or does not include the AMP under the classification of 'pre-capitalist society' is not of substantive consequence. It is his overall strategy, very representative of neo-Marxist reconstructions of historical materialism, which is important.

The key issue is why Cohen conflates all pre-capitalist modes of production. His answer is brief: 'The "endless nuances" of pre-capitalist class history resist theorization as sets of production relations whose succession reflects a series of rises in the level of productive power. But the resulting damage to historical materialism, on our strongly technological construal of it, is smaller than at first might appear' (ibid: 200). He does not believe that his strategy damages historical materialism, for two reasons. First, the classification of four progressive economic structures provides substantial theses about the course of social development. These four structures are (1) pre-class society, (2) pre-capitalist class society, (3) capitalist society, and (4) post-capitalist society.[11] These four societies are classified by their levels of productive development — that is, (1) no surplus, (2) some surplus but less than moderately high surplus, (3) moderately high surplus but less than massive surplus, and (4) massive surplus. He contends that 'It is, for example, no small claim to say of each pre-capitalist class society that it was one because the surplus possible at the given time was limited, and that capitalism arose when and because the surplus became moderately high' (ibid).

This line of reasoning is amazing. The substantive thesis Cohen rescues from his reconstruction of historical materialism manages to be simultaneously banal, functionalist, and open to immediate empirical falsification even if it can be expressed in empirical non-functionalist language. The thesis is banal because historians, and especially Marxist historians, have surely wanted something more interesting to test than this hypothesis when

---

11 Cohen does not make clear whether specimens of this fourth society already exist (for instance, in the USSR, Eastern Europe, China, South East Asia, Africa or in Central America) or whether it has yet to come into existence.

investigating pre-capitalist class societies. It is functionalist, as Cohen explicitly defends it, because it assumes that some system-need for higher surplus (somehow) generated capitalism. And finally, it is likely to be false even if it can be made testable because one can justly argue that the aggregate surplus, and perhaps even the relative surplus, in some pre-capitalist societies was higher than in those pre-capitalist societies where capitalism in fact emerged. The Asiatic empires of India and China had higher aggregate surpluses than Western European regimes, and possibly higher relative surpluses as well. Moreover, most Marxists have wanted to explain the transition from pre-capitalist society to capitalism in a far more detailed way than Cohen's contestable and functionalist 'explanation' permits. A reconstruction of historical materialism which conflates all pre-capitalist modes of production simply jettisons all the questions which Marxists and non-Marxists have (rightly) found intriguing. In particular it excludes the stimulating 'old question': were certain pre-capitalist societies incapable of developing capitalism, and if so why (Runciman, 1987)?

Cohen's second reason for defending his reconstruction of historical materialism, through the conflation of all pre-capitalist class societies into one category, seems to be that it solves the problem of explaining the relations between a given quantitative level of the productive forces and variations in the economic structure. But his 'solution' simply denies what is the core productivist historical materialist argument, namely that the transitions from pre-capitalist order to pre-capitalist order must be explained by the argument that a structure persists as long as it develops the productive forces and disappears when it can no longer raise their development any further. For Cohen to describe his solution as comparatively undamaging to historical materialism must seem strange to the profession of Marxist historians who have followed generally productivist tenets. The moral seems plain. If the most rigorous defence of productivist historical materialism so far constructed has to accept its methodological and heuristic uselessness in the comparative study of pre-capitalist societies, in explaining their variation, their forms and their prospects for evolving into capitalism, then so much the worse for productivist historical materialism.[12]

However, Cohen is ambivalent. He immediately qualifies his second reason with the remark that 'explanations of economic structures (i.e. structures of pre-capitalist class societies) in terms of the qualitative characteristics of productive forces are not therefore excluded' (ibid: 201). He gives what he presumably means to be an illuminating example: the irrigation needs of agricultural societies at similar quantitative levels of development of the productive forces explain the differences which they display in their

---

12 Cohen is not alone. Similar arguments are advanced by Maxime Rodinson (1974) who uses the general label 'pre-capitalist systems of exploitation' much as Cohen uses the category 'pre-capitalist class society'.

economic structures. Cohen's revisionism, if not so extensive as it at first appears, is none the less obscure. Pre-capitalist class societies are not worth differentiating by their *quantitative* levels of development of the productive forces, nor can their economic structures be explained by their *quantitative* levels of development. However, the *quality* of productive forces may somehow explain the economic structure of pre-capitalist class societies![13] Moreover, the example Cohen gives, that different irrigation techniques may explain comparative economic structures, is precisely the same as that made famous by Wittfogel in *Oriental Despotism* (which we explore in detail in the next chapter). The AMP seems to be non-Freudian. It resists repression. All Marxists who reject the AMP seem to find themselves reinventing it.

It needs to be recalled, though, that Cohen's strategy is not unusual, it is representative (although its clarity and vigour are distinctly personal). In the Soviet Union critics of the AMP have followed similar lines of argument. The history of these arguments is instructive. The *Aziatchiki*, notably S. I. Kovalev, a prominent classicist, argued that the attempt to subsume the Asiatic under the feudal mode of production was too limited. 'In order to be consistent, the opponents of the Asiatic mode of production must liquidate the differences between all pre-capitalist social orders and unite them into a single formation' (cited in Dunn, 1982: 22). The *Aziatchiki* thought that this argument represented a *reductio ad absurdum* which established the case for the Marxist credentials of the AMP. It is therefore all the more intriguing to see a range of Soviet and Western Marxists, like Cohen, following the logic of Kovalev's intended rebuttal of anti-*Aziatchiki*, and liquidating the differences between all pre-capitalist social orders.[14] The AMP plainly poses insuperable problems for the conceptual and theoretical clarity of productivist historical materialism. Its empirical implausibility will be analysed in subsequent chapters.

STRUCTURALIST HISTORICAL MATERIALISM AND THE ASIATIC MODE OF PRODUCTION

Structuralist historical materialism also has general epistemological and methodological difficulties which are brought into sharp relief by the AMP.[15]

13 These manipulations of the words quantity and quality are reminiscent of the 'dialectical materialism' which Analytical Marxists are generally wont to disparage.

14 By contrast, Samir Amin, whom we discussed above (pp. 197–200) conflates two modes of production intermediate between primitive communism and capitalism (namely the Asiatic and feudal) into one mode of production, the tributary mode.

15 Althusser and Balibar inspired the structuralist reading of historical materialism. Their work influenced a range of British and French academics working on pre-capitalist societies, notably E. Terray, P.P. Rey, M. Godelier, B. Hindess, P.Q. Hirst and J. Taylor, to name the most prominent Althusser-inspired authors to have discussed the AMP.

The structuralist reconstruction of historical materialism faces similar problems to those which affect productivist and Hegelian historical materialist, despite being directed against both. However, it also faces some distinct difficulties. First, the structuralist rendering of the concept 'mode of production' is problematic, partly because the relationships between Marxist structuralist concepts and the real world are decidedly unclear. Second, the mechanisms through which transitions between modes of production occur are obscure in structuralist accounts. Finally, the best known structuralist critical analysis of pre-capitalist modes of production and the AMP self-aborted (Hindess and Hirst, 1977).

The central objective of structuralist Marxist explorations of pre-capitalist modes of production is to deduce a finite number of theoretical economic systems from historical materialist axioms, without recourse to what they disparagingly refer to as 'empiricist' and 'sub-theoretical' 'knowledge' of history. As Balibar puts it, modes of production must be specific 'states of variation' of certain 'invariant elements' (Balibar, 1970: 211). These elements are three:

the labourer, or direct producer;
the means of production (that is, the instruments of production and the object of labour − the raw material); and
the non-labourer who appropriates the social surplus.

These elements in turn must be combined, or (as Althusserians prefer to put it) 'articulated', by two relations:

the property connexion (relations of ownership and non-ownership); and
the materialist-appropriation connexion − a concept which is very obscurely defined and discussed by Balibar, but seems to mean something like the technical circumstances of production, or the (property-neutral) labour process.

The first relation, the property connexion which articulates the critical elements, is what defines the structuralists' mode of production. For structuralist Marxists, *contra* traditional understandings of historical materialism, it is relations of production rather than productive forces that are primary in defining modes of production.

Balibar also argues, or asserts, that these economic relations and elements always determine − albeit in the fabled 'last instance' − other levels or instances in a society. However, this determination takes the very indirect form of determining the hierarchical ranking of the non-economic levels in society and their articulation. Thus, for example, the economic relations of production may determine that ideological relations are *prima facie* dominant in lineage-based social formations. This style of argument/assertion seems to be merely a verbal manoeuvre to permit the economic mode of production

to determine the social formation, without the embarrassments which productivist historical materialists encounter. Objections to the effect that
non-economic practices seem to be paramount in explaining the workings
of any given social formation can be put to one side by the suggestion that
this 'appearance' is determined by the economic level. Apparently even if
things do not appear this way — for example, in Asiatic societies — we
know that the determination is working in this way to give this (false)
appearance!

The relationships between mode of production and social formation are
(obscurely) elaborated by Althusser. A mode of production is not a Hegelian
essence which determines the workings of a social formation. A social
formation is not centred by a mode of production; therefore it is unenlight-
eningly said to be 'decentred'. However, the absence of centres and essences
notwithstanding, a social formation is said to be composed of a distinct
hierarchy of practices (economic, political, ideological and scientific), each
of which is distinct and has its own 'specific effectivity'. None the less, the
economic level somehow determines things in the last instance — which
effectively squares the circle after having tried to establish the apparent
requirements for a non-essentialist, non-historicist and non-teleological
historical materialism.

These conceptions of a mode of production, its internal causal relations,
and its relations with its social formation — which are governed by a
mysterious 'structural causality'[16] — are exceedingly problematic. It is
unclear whether both mode of production and social formation are conceptual abstractions or whether only the former is a conceptual abstraction
while the latter refers to concrete societies. If the former, then the posited
relations between the two concepts are simply true by definition, and are
part of an Althusserian language-game. But if the latter, then apparently
fundamental Althusserian epistemological positions are implicitly being
denied. The determination of reality by a concept suggests three Althusserian
thought-crimes: historicism, essentialism and idealism.

However, rather than fall into the Althusserian epistemological vortex
which has been thoroughly explored by others (Benton, 1984; Callinicos,
1976; and Thompson, 1978), I will confine myself to the interaction
between the AMP and issues central to structuralist historical materialism.
Balibar's definition of the requirements for a mode of production, at least
at first glance, cannot exclude the AMP *a priori* as a legitimate mode of
production. Provided that the three elements (labourer, means of production

---

16 An idea derived from Spinoza's philosophy, as Althusser explicitly declares: 'the structure
is immanent in its effects, a cause immanent in its effects in the Spinozist sense of the term,
that the whole existence of the structure consists of its effects' (Althusser and Balibar, 1970:
188–9).

and non-labourer) and the two relations (property and materialist-appropriation) can be defined in a way which distinguishes an Asiatic from other modes of production, there seems to be no problem of legitimacy. A structuralist or 'Balibarian' AMP must have three elements:

the direct producers must be villagers engaged in a stable natural economy in which production is for consumption;
the means of production must consist of agricultural activities and limited manufacturing processes; and
the non-labourer must consist of state officials who extract a surplus from the direct producers in a combined tax/rent.

The last element sharply separates the AMP from the feudal mode of production, whereas the first element distinguishes it from the slave mode of production. A structuralist AMP must also be defined by two relations with the following characteristics:

the property relation must be defined by state ownership of the soil and the hereditary possession of the land by the direct producers; and
the materialist-appropriation relation must be defined by state intervention to organize the labour process and the reproduction of the three elements of the mode of production.[17]

The key problem with such a structuralist AMP, though, is simple: it is too good a structure! It defines a mode of production which is incapable of transformation — unlike other modes of production, notably the capitalist. Without theoretical innovation by structuralist Marxists this AMP seems to be devoid of structural contradictions which might generate transformative crises. In brief, as it stands a structuralist AMP has no 'laws of motion'. One might expect that structuralist Marxists would be happy with such a mode of production, since they wish to be free of the charge that the Marxist theory of history is a historicism or a teleology — and what could be less teleological or historicist than an account of a social structure which is essentially stable, just as in the accounts of primitive societies offered by anthropological functionalists, or the accounts of agrarian empires offered by structural-functionalist sociologists in the 1960s? However, most structuralist Marxists did in fact want to have a general theory of transition from one mode of production to another based on a theory of systemic contradictions, and at the same time to avoid a theory which suggests that modes of production have built-in contradictions which generate their own self-transcendence. They wanted to have the impossible (Hindess and Hirst, 1977).

There is an exceptional structuralist Marxist happy to argue that the

---

17 My construction of what a structuralist AMP must be like is very similar to that elaborated by John Taylor (1979, chapter 9).

AMP contains its own laws of structuralist transformation (Godelier, 1970 and 1978). Godelier argued first that the AMP develops as a result of contradictions in primitive societies, and second that the AMP can be transformed as a result of its own internal contradiction into either a slaveholding or a feudal mode of production. The source of this latter contradiction is that between the unity of communal structures (the primitive communities) and class structures (the state). The trouble with this position is that the defining elements of the mode of production are also the sources of its transformation and therefore Godelier's AMP becomes, like so much pre-structuralist Marxism, a conceptual teleology. Godelier's position is partly similar to that of classical Marxism, although it obviously radically revises the thesis that the AMP was stagnant, in order to make the concept consistent with the Marxist theory of historical dynamics. However, it seems to do so at the expense of structuralist consistency.

Unhappiness with this and similar reproductions of the 'Hegelian problematic' in the analysis of pre-capitalist modes of production prompted two English structuralist Marxists to try to exorcise the AMP and to rectify the problems historical materialists faced in 'theorizing transitions'. They defined a mode of production as 'an articulated combination of relations and forces of production structured by the dominance of the relations of production' (Hindess and Hirst, 1975: 9). Their definitions, both of relations of production and (especially) of productive forces, were idiosyncratic when compared with the productivist historical materialist tradition (and with Marx's own writings). However, they did remain within the Althusserian 'problematic'. Relations of production, according to Hindess and Hirst, refer to a specific mode of appropriation of surplus labour and the specific form of social distribution of the means of production corresponding to that mode of production. The forces of production by contrast refer to the mode of appropriation of nature; that is, the labour process transforming raw materials into goods, and the mode of organization of labour (ibid: 10). This definition of productive forces switched the emphasis away from technology – as in productivist historical materialism – and towards managerial organization. By defining the productive forces in this way, they sought to make more plausible their emphasis upon the causal primacy of the relations of production. Intuitively, at least, the organization of the labour process is more likely to be determined by relations of production than is technology.[18]

For our purposes what is significant is their attempted demolition of the AMP. They argued that: 'the question of the existence or non-existence of the Asiatic mode of production (AMP) cannot be settled by reference to

18 According to their critics, Hindess and Hirst's revisionism, was confounded by inconsistent application of their definitions (Asad and Wolpe, 1976: 470–506). Asad and Wolpe hoist

concrete social formations, it is a strictly theoretical question ... If its concept can be formed, then the AMP is a possible mode of production: whether forms of this mode have existed or not does not affect its validity as a concept' (Hindess and Hirst: 180). They defined the core elements of the AMP to be: state control of the extraction of the surplus product; the absence of private property in land; and the prevalence of non-commodity production. They then contended that the AMP is a self-contradictory concept, or as they put it 'non-formable', because on their definitions the possible relations of production of the AMP correspond with two sets of productive forces. The two sets of productive forces are independent peasant cultivation and communal village production. The relations of production are constituted by the state's control of the extraction of the surplus product (through the coincidence of rent and tax). They argue that since there is no strict articulation (correspondence) between relations of production and productive forces, the AMP is not a coherent Marxist mode of production. That one set of production relations can be compatible with two sets of productive forces is apparently not *kosher* historical materialism.

This 'refutation' is amongst the strangest of Marxist attempts at 'concepticide' amongst the many attempted assassinations of the AMP. The 'refutation' depends entirely upon their own construction of historical materialism, upon an eccentric definition of productive forces, and upon a novel and equally eccentric requirement that one set of production relations map exclusively in a one-to-one relationship with one set of productive forces.[19] However, I believe that their objection to the AMP can be demonstrated to be foolish through a *reductio ad absurdum*, which takes as given their own eccentric definitions and textual exegesis of Marx and Engels. Consistency should have demanded that Hindess and Hirst apply the very same 'refutation' to every other mode of production (slave, feudal and capitalist) which they analysed. Slave, feudal and capitalist relations of production, in Hindess and Hirst's own writings, 'corresponded' to more than one way of

Hindess and Hirst by their own petards. The critics seek to show that the revisionists' work rested upon a confused conception of empiricism, and that they habitually confounded theoretical necessity with empirical contingency – especially ironic given their 'anti-empiricist' fervour. More importantly they are charged with continually shifting their general definition of a mode of production to accommodate the ones they approve of and get rid of ones they dislike (notably the AMP). They also stand accused of failing to maintain their distinction between a mode of production and its conditions of existence (which they acknowledged – Hindess and Hirst, 1977); failing to consider the possibility that social formations might consist of articulations of modes of production; and coming to grief in analysing transitions between modes of production – another point they acknowledged in their auto-critique (Hindess and Hirst, 1977).

19 Consequently no orthodox Marxist defences of the AMP are jeopardized by Hindess and Hirst's arguments. And conversely no orthodox Marxism is saved by my refutation of their argument.

carrying out production. Slave relations of production in Marxist writings correspond both to gangs of slaves working on *latifundia* and to slaves engaged in works of construction in urban centres. Feudal relations of production are regularly said to encompass both serfs working for lords and indentured artisans working for guild-masters. Capitalist relations of production have been said to 'correspond' to large-scale mass manufacturing of products in authoritarian factories and to egalitarian professional communities delivering specifically designed services.[20] Therefore I submit that on Hindess and Hirst's own definitions these other modes of production should have been placed upon the same conceptual scrapheap where they wished to place the Asiatic. Perhaps it was unsurprising that both authors rapidly repudiated their book, the concepts modes of production and social formation, and their Marxism within two years of their critical attack on the AMP (Hindess and Hirst, 1977).

It is true and to their credit that Hindess and Hirst recognized many of the objections to the compatibility between the AMP and historical materialism, discussed in chapter 4 – particularly the criticism that forms of production characterized by classlessness can, on Marxist grounds, have no functional necessity for a state. They none the less placed their greatest emphasis upon their 'novel' argument that since the 'tax–rent couple' was compatible with two sets of productive forces it could not form the production relations of a 'formable' mode of production.[21] Moreover, there is also an argument against the structural coherence of the AMP which they failed to spot – and which would have been both in keeping with the spirit of their theoretical enterprise and more devastating in its impact. The presence of state ownership of the land, a defining trait of Asiatic production relations, is in contradiction to the presupposition of self-sufficient village communities which own the land in common.

However, Hindess and Hirst's attempted structuralist reconstruction of historical materialism, even if it self-aborted, did serve one useful if unintended purpose. Their work prompted other structuralist Marxists to develop the idea of 'articulated' or systematically combined modes of production. Marxists realized, only in the 1970s, that they had a simple way of adjusting their conceptual tools to theorize social formations which did not match any of the canonical modes of production. Such social formations could be understood either as a number of modes of production organized

20 It is ironic that these rigorous Althusserians placed such great emphasis upon *Capital* as the *fons et origo* of historical materialism. In chapter 15 of *Capital*, Volume I, Marx freely discusses the 'distinctions between modes of production based on different means of production, but also the connection between the social relations of production and those modes of production' (Marx, 1976a: 503).
21 Hindess and Hirst (1977) did note, correctly, in their auto-critique that some of their objections to the inconsistencies between the Marxist theory of the state and the AMP remained valid. However, they only had the instrumentalist model of the state in mind.

under the dominance of one mode of production, or more radically as symbiotic combinations of two or more modes of production. This idea of 'articulated modes of production' has found considerable favour amongst post-Althusserian Marxists (Wolpe, 1980). Neo-Marxist world-system theorists, notably Immanuel Wallerstein in *The Modern World System*, have also implicitly embraced the idea of articulated modes of production (Wallerstein, 1974). They argue not only that the coexistence of several modes of production from slavery to capitalism is possible, but also that capitalism requires pre-capitalist modes of production in order to survive − just as Rosa Luxemburg argued in *The Accumulation of Capital*.

There were many precedents for such thinking in Marxist work. Varga, Madi'iar and Riazanov, East European and Soviet proponents of the AMP in the 1920s, had analysed China as an articulation of the Asiatic and capitalist modes of production long before the Althusserian Marxists invented such terminology. Madi'iar and Varga made their criticisms in the light of the dominant orthodoxy in the CPSU, which asserted that contemporary China was largely capitalist albeit with very important 'feudal survivals'. The idea of articulated modes of production opens up historical materialism from the constraints imposed by five-stage or six-stage unilineal models of history. A judicious chemical composition of the elements of various modes of production promises to make historical materialism more capable of coping with historical, and contemporary, complexity. However, the question remains open of whether the AMP can be successfully articulated with this neo-structuralist Marxism. After all, to date the most orthodox idea of 'articulation' requires one mode of production to be dominant in any given articulation of modes of production (Althusser and Balibar, 1970). But any articulation in which the AMP was dominant would still pose, albeit in a diluted form, all the dilemmas, contradictions and problems with which we are now familiar − the nature of the Asiatic state, the nature and causes of its stagnant character, the nature of its class and exploitation relations, and the meaning of 'Asiatic' in the AMP. The fact that these anomalies would be merged with (perhaps) more comprehensible and defensible elements of other Marxist modes of production would not diminish their difficulties for historical materialism.

HEGELIAN HISTORICAL MATERIALISM AND THE ASIATIC MODE OF PRODUCTION

Hegelian historical materialism is the least empirical version of Marx's theory of history. Yet in the hands of Semenov, Hegelian historical materialism is intended to be a theory which is both realist in the sense that the concept of a mode of production is an essence which operates in the real world, and empirical in the sense that it is supposed to explain the acknowledged facts of history (Semenov, 1980).

Semenov presents a lucid and ingenious reconstruction, of unilinealism in which the AMP is rehabilitated as the first class-divided socio-economic formation.[22] Its ingenuity consists in its preservation of unilinealism for 'world history' as a whole, while rejecting the thesis that every territory in the world must go through the ordained programme of modes of production. There are, however, difficulties with Semenov's Hegelian reconstruction of historical materialism (Gellner, 1980: 70–82). First, while Semenov's reformulation of unilinealism means that not every society is expected to pass through the required stages, it cannot, if it is to retain its Marxist pedigree, mean that every society can develop as it pleases. It is clear that societies can avoid the traditional five-stage sequence if they are dragged into the orbit of a world centre of a higher mode of production. But what if they are insulated from the leading 'world centre'? Gellner suggests that to maintain unilineal consistency either such societies must autonomously go through the required five-stage sequence, *or* else they must remain stagnant. This consistency requirement is designed to create empirical embarrassment for Semenov. Awkward historical examples of insulated formations which go through cycles or retrogressions would point against Semenov's thesis. Slavery in the Caribbean and the southern states of the USA are Gellner's chosen examples. Here slavery developed *despite* the existence of a capitalist world centre. This counter-example might in term be countered by an *ad hoc* defence, such as the following: slavery in the Caribbean and the USA was in fact a transitional by-product of capitalist penetration of Africa, which had been a centre of traffic in slaves. However, this phase of slavery, in the time scale of history, was brief and its demise, with the full maturation of capitalism in the nineteenth century was rapid.[23] A stronger counter-example to Semenov's theory is perhaps provided by the evidence of the centrifugal and centripetal cycles which characterized most agrarian empires in Eurasia and pre-Columbian America (Weber, 1978). There is every reason to ask Marxists whether Max Weber's description of a patrimonial-feudal cycle in agrarian empires is, *mutatis mutandis*, a cycle in which the AMP alternates with the feudal mode of production.[24] These sequences are an embarrassment if, as Gellner suggests, Semenov must be committed to the thesis that either the traditional sequence or stagnation must occur

22 See earlier discussion on pp. 164–72.

23 Braudel cites the exemplary awkward case for historical materialists of the case of colonial Venezuela, which resembled a two-layered model of a 'feudal' and a 'slave-owning' society; in which slavery had developed first (Braudel, 1984: 63).

24 In Godelier's and Melotti's versions of historical materialism such cycles are no embarrassment because they have abandoned unilinealism (Godelier, 1970 and 1978; and Melotti, 1977). They accept that this cycle may have occurred in China, India and (perhaps) Japan.

in the zones isolated from the world centre carrying the torch of historical progress. Finally, there is also the very important case of Japanese development. The acknowledged existence of Japanese feudalism is anomalous. The absence of an antecedent slaveholding society (Gellner, 1980: 75–6) is one problem; and another is that the societies which did influence Japanese feudal development are regarded by *Aziatchiki* as examples of the AMP.

However, Gellner's requirements of Semenov's theory seem too strong. If one reads Semenov's theory as truly Hegelian, then unilinealism and the five-stage model need apply only to the social formations involved in the development of human history. The rest are 'meaningless', outside of history, or bereft of Spirit, as Hegel might have put it. On this truly Hegelian interpretation, Semenov's theory becomes immune to the consistency requirement and counter-examples which Gellner and I tried to impose on it in the previous paragraph. Moreover, even if Semenov's theory is read as a secular evolutionary reconstruction of unilineal historical materialism, rather than as a brazen rehabilitation of Hegelian Eurocentricity, it can still be immunized from the consistency requirements which critics demand. After all, at least in principle, the theory of evolution in biology does not require that a given mutation from X_1 to X_2 in an organism must be repeated in all subsequent mutations of X_1. Mutations are random and those which survive are simply those which are better adapted to their environments. Nor presumably does the theory of evolution, at least in principle, prevent the new organism X_2 from mutating back to X_1 – especially if survival is more likely in a new environment as a result of this 'retrogression'. Therefore, by analogy, an evolutionary account of historical materialism – the secular version of Hegelian historical materialism – can cope with mutations and retrogressions which do not figure in the ordained sequence of stages for the 'world-as-a-whole'.[25]

There are, however, other problems with Semenov's account of unilinealism. His model of historical development makes the following assumptions:

historical development is necessary – that is, it is destined to occur; and transition to a higher stage must take place on the periphery.

The first assumption makes the theory axiomatic, not capable of falsification, and therefore unempirical. However, the credibility of the neccessity axiom is reduced by the fact that the slave stage, though necessary for human progress on Semenov's own account, occurred only once, in the ancient Greece of classical European antiquity.[26] Therefore, while we have many

25 I owe these arguments to a discussion with my colleague Ernest Thorp.
26 The recent and controversial theses of Bernal, which suggest that Greek civilization developed on the periphery of Egyptian civilization, provide some empirical warrant for Semenov's assumption that Greek civilization did develop on the periphery of an Asiatic social formation. See Bernal (1987).

potential examples of the transition from primitive communism to the AMP, because of the uniqueness of the slave stage we have only one example of the transition from an Asiatic to a slaveholding society, one of a slaveholding to feudal society, and one of the transition from feudalism to capitalism. Necessity seems less credible when it is no more empirically plausible than contingency.

The second assumption, that transition takes place on the periphery, is also open to doubt. Consider the various transitions in turn. The first transition, from primitive communism to the AMP, could not take place on the periphery because there was *no* periphery! The second transition, from the AMP to slavery, occurred only once, and the peripheral status of Greece is problematic. To what centre was it peripheral — Egypt, Persia or ancient Crete? Moreover, why was Greece the sole peripheral zone of an Asiatic social formation to be the site of this transition? Surely not because it was the periphery of three centres? The third transition, from slavery to feudalism, took place on a much less contestable periphery — the Gallic, German and Anglo-Saxon hinterlands of the collapsed Roman Empire — although there is much scholarly controversy over how, when and whether feudalism replaced slavery. However, the fourth transition, from feudalism to capitalism, is more problematic, because it was a 'centre-preserving transition' (Gellner, 1980). Even if one accepts that Holland and England were peripheral feudalisms their development reinvigorated and eventually transformed the centre to which they were peripheral (the states of West and Central Europe).

The second assumption, like the first, can be secured against empirical counter-examples only by making it an unfalsifiable, but implausible, axiom. In short, Hegelian historical materialism, while compatible with the AMP — if we leave aside the central problems of stagnation and a state without a class rationale — cannot save any Marxist theory of history which claims to be scientific; that is, open to empirical verification or falsification.

THE FATE OF MARXIST HISTORIANS WITHOUT THE ASIATIC MODE OF PRODUCTION

The problems of Marxist historians, as opposed to Marxist philosophers of history, are well known. However, the difficulties Marxist historians of pre-capitalist social formations encounter with, or without, the AMP are less familiar. Discussions, evaluations and usages of the AMP by Marxist historians have shown great variety in standards of research and intellectual rigour. Most authors who have wished to employ the concept to describe a particular social formation have emphasized the evidence for the existence of certain traits highlighted by Marx. They have rarely considered systematically the evidence which does not conform with any elements of the

AMP. The partisan enthusiasts, or *Aziatchiki*, attempt to confirm the AMP in various social formations but neglect any evidence of *prima facie* falsification.[27] Moreover, few Marxist historians have as yet made use of the notion of 'articulated modes of production' to investigate social formations in which the AMP has been considered a minor or dominant component of the articulation of pre-capitalist modes of production. In any case, it might reasonably be objected, as I have attempted to demonstrate, that it is decidedly unclear how the AMP could ever be rigorously operationalized to permit scientific historical research.

However, the key purpose of the following discussion is to show how two Marxist historians, Perry Anderson and Geoffery de Ste Croix, both of whom are noted for their scholarship and respect for empirical evidence, come to grief in their attempts to jettison the AMP. It has a simple moral: historical materialists cannot get rid of the AMP even if they wish to do so.

Perry Anderson's magisterial surveys, *Passages from Antiquity to Feudalism* and *Lineages of the Absolutist State*, are widely praised by both Marxist and non-Marxist scholars, despite being subjected to some vigorous criticisms (Fulbrook and Skocpol, 1977; Gourevitch, 1978; Hirst, 1975; and Runciman, 1980). The monumental second volume terminates with a detailed appendix which discusses the 'AMP', which Anderson deliberately enclosed within quotation marks. He argues that the theoretical function of the concept of the AMP was to explain the failure of non-European civilizations, especially the major Asiatic land-empires, to develop capitalism as Western Europe had done. However, he contends that the AMP is not worthy to discharge this function.

Anderson musters a range of theoretical and empirical objections against the coherence of the AMP, and suggests its burial. First, he complains that a conceptual slippage, rooted in Marx and Engels's writings, makes the AMP imprecise. The early suggestion that the AMP was based upon a despotic state with a centralized bureaucracy, whose existence was explained by its functional role in promoting public irrigation works, differs sharply from Marx's account of the AMP developed in the *Grundrisse*, where self-sufficient and egalitarian villages serve to explain the state of the AMP. This conceptual slippage, never tidied up by Marx and Engels, continues to mar the work of latter-day *Aziatchiki*. On the one hand the concept's range is extended backwards so as to include the ancient empires of the Near

---

27 One historiographical essay on Byzantium and the AMP provides an example, rare in the French Marxist tradition, of the careful sifting of evidence for and against the proposition that the Byzantine Empire was dominated by the AMP (Antoniadas-Bibicou, 1977). However, the author fails to make clear which of the features she looks for are necessary or sufficient to confirm of falsify the existence of the Asiatic mode of production. Moreover, her eventual designation of Byzantium as 'pre-feudal' is symptomatic of the general difficulties Marxist historians have in designating pre-capitalist societies with classical Marxist categories.

East, Middle East and Mediterranean, all of which are traditionally held to have had powerful centralized states, hydraulic agriculture and corvée labour.[28] But on the other hand the concept's geographical range is enlarged to encompass the first state organizations of tribal or semi-tribal social formations and include all the peripheral societies of world history: Polynesian islands, African chieftainries and Amerindian settlements.[29] This conceptual extension produces an absurd conflation and reductionism: 'The consequent supra-historical melange defies all scientific principles of classification' (P. Anderson, 1974b: 486).[30] The understandable rejection of the theory of universal feudalism which Stalinist historiography had imposed upon Marxist intellectuals should not be compensated for by rehabilitating the AMP: 'A ubiquitous "Asiaticism" represents no improvement on a universal "feudalism": in fact it is even less rigorous as a term' (ibid). A ubiquitous AMP leads to a similar *reductio ad absurdum* produced by an indefinite extension of feudalism. If so many different socio-economic formations, 'of such contrasting levels of civilization' (ibid: 487), are all contracted to one mode of production, then the fundamental divisions and changes of history must derive from another source altogether, one that has nothing to do with the Marxist conception of modes of production.

Anderson also advances biting empirical objections to the AMP. He does not spare Marx and Engels's scholarship, believing that they inherited uncritically, virtually *en bloc*, a traditional European discourse on Asia (the theory of oriental despotism).[31] Moreover, their two main innovations – the notions of self-sustaining, egalitarian village communities and the despotic hydraulic state – were both scientifically and empirically unsound. Thus, as for Marx's portrait of the self-sustaining village of India and its putative system of communal property 'there is no historical evidence that communal property ever existed in either Mughal or post-Mughal India' (ibid: 488 – citing Thorner, 1966: 57). Marx's English sources were colonialist and erroneous. Indian villages were not egalitarian with residues of primitive communism. They were profoundly inegalitarian, based upon

---

28 Anderson cites Parain's work on Megalithic, Crypto-Mycenean and Etruscan social formations as the best example of this tendency amongst modern Marxists (Parain in CÉRM, 1969). Similar work has been done by Soviet archaeologists and ancient historians (Dunn, 1982).

29 Anderson rightly cites Godelier's work as an example of this trait (P. Anderson, 1974b: 485).

30 This objection is also advanced by Amin (1980). However, Anderson leaves us no wiser as to what exactly are scientific principles of classification.

31 Anderson even suggests Marx and Engels's knowledge of the Orient constituted an intellectual regression when contrasted with their sources (P. Anderson, 1975b: 492). Jones was more aware of political variations within Orient, Hegel perceived the role of caste in Indian history more clearly and Montesquieu demonstrated more acute interest in the religious and legal systems of the Orient.

intense caste differentiation. The villages were not detached from the state. How could they be when they were systematically exploited and administratively subordinated in Mughal India? These structural facets of Mughal India are wildly at variance with the portrait of India in the *Grundrisse*, although they help explain the great peasant *jacqueries* against Mughal domination and exploitation.

Anderson also notes, suggestively, that there is a fundamental problem with classifying the Muslim empires of Asia and North Africa under the same heading as the Chinese empires. The 'two phenomena singled out by Marx and Engels as the key-notes of Asian history paradoxically represented not so much cojoint as alternative principles of development' (P. Anderson, 1974: 491). The land-empires of Turkey, Persia and India – where monarchical ownership of the land prevailed – never possessed public irrigation works of any importance. Yet, by contrast, the Chinese empires – which did possess major public irrigation facilities – were marked by extensive private property in land. To drive home these sharp differences between the Chinese and Islamic empires, in an extended discussion Anderson provides an illuminating set of contrasts between the morphologies of each imperial system (ibid: 496–546), which I have summarized in table 5.1. These contrasts

merely resume some of the grossest indices of divergence between Islamic and Chinese civilizations (make-shift terminological objects which themselves need redefinition and retranslation for any scientific analysis), which preclude any attempt to assimilate them as simple examples of a common 'Asiatic' mode of production. Let this last notion be given the decent burial it deserves. (ibid: 548)

Finally, Anderson has explicitly theoretical objections to the use of the AMP by historical materialists. First, the presence of a powerful, centralized state presupposes the development of classes, but the prevalence of communal village property in the *Grundrisse* model implies a pre-class or classless society, a phenomenon at odds with 'the most elementary canons of historical materialism' (ibid: 490). Second, he suggests that a simple contradiction exists between the two versions of the AMP developed by Marx and Engels. The emphasis upon the hydraulic or functional foundations of state power in the AMP is incompatible with the later emphasis upon the autonomy and self-sufficiency of the village communities.

Anderson's assault upon the AMP is undoubtedly the most forceful made by a Western Marxist, combining historical knowledge with some theoretical rigour. It is all the more intriguing, therefore, that there are obvious objections to his arguments, as well as the presence of interesting inconsistencies. First, Anderson's objection to the 'ubiquity' of the AMP in some modern Marxist writings ignores one fundamental consideration. The ubiquity of the AMP, and the exceptionality of the slave and feudal

Table 5.1 Anderson's contrasts between Islamic and Chinese Empires

	Islamic empires	Chinese empires
Imperial apparatus	Military slave guards, praetorian guard	Civilian, scholar-gentry mandarinate
Ideology	Religiously saturated system	Secular morality and philosophy
Kinship	Kinship eclipsed or relegated	Clan organizations remained
Merchants	High–medium prestige	Medium–low prestige
Towns	Tangled, aleatory labyrinths	Bureaucratic, segmented grids
Monarchy and land system	Monarchical land ownership, little intensive agriculture	Private land ownership, intensive agriculture and irrigation role for state
Population	Stable – cyclical	Growing
Science	Little science by comparison with medieval Europe	Many more technical inventions than medieval Europe
Geopolitics	Contiguous with West and absorbed by it	Isolated from West

modes of production, provide the Marxist explanation of occidental uniqueness – just the theoretical function that, according to Anderson, Marx wanted the AMP to serve. As Anderson is concerned with precisely the same question, namely explaining occidental uniqueness, he cannot object *per se* to the ubiquity (minus Western Europe) of the AMP in pre-capitalist societies. Anderson's fundamental objection to the Stalinist notion of 'universal feudalism' was that it failed to provide a Marxist explanation of occidental uniqueness. As the AMP's ubiquity, with the solitary exception of Western Europe, does not have this flaw it is a better, not worse, Marxist explanatory tool than universal feudalism.

Second, Anderson never makes clear what is the methodologically correct basis for a scientific classification of particular social formations under the heading of dominance by a particular mode of production. He disarmingly leaves it to others to classify the exact status of the social formations of the Orient. However, if we rely on Anderson's own declared theoretical commitments, surely a Marxist classification of a mode of production must depend centrally upon the productive forces and production relations in a given social formation? If so, it is curious that Anderson's erudite display of the morphological contrasts between the Chinese and Islamic empires does not explicitly centre upon a comparison of these empires' productive forces and production relations. Anderson's morphological contrasts closely resemble those made by Max Weber in *Economy and Society* (Weber, 1978) – as Anderson's discussion of imperial apparatuses, urban structures, kinship and religious and legal systems, outlined in table 5.1, manifestly suggests.

Third, Anderson fails to recognize a fundamental inconsistency in his reasoning. The fact that there have been variations in feudal systems, notably in Western and Eastern European feudalism, indeed that there have been two divergent rather than cojoint principles of feudal development in Europe, did not lead him to recommend a 'decent burial' for the feudal mode of production. Yet that is one of the most important, and certainly the lengthiest, of his empirical bases for rejecting the AMP. The irony is that Anderson's work is fundamentally centred on a story about how differences in the genesis of different feudalisms explain why Western feudalism proved to be uniquely historically dynamic. But we must surely ask: if fundamental variations in the genesis, morphology and development of feudal systems, or in his words, '"the grossest indices of divergence" between civilizations', do not tell against the concept of the feudal mode of production, why should such objections tell against the AMP? The attempt to kill the AMP on these grounds must also lead to the execution of the feudal mode of production.

Fourth, a similar riposte can be made to Anderson's complaint about the tendency amongst the authors of the CÉRM collection to include under the Asiatic classification social formations with 'very different levels of civilization', such as the archaeological empires of the Near East, Manchu China and Mughal India. In *Lineages of the Absolutist State*, Anderson has no objection to describing both the absolutist regimes of late eighteenth-century Europe and the principalities of the eighth and ninth centuries as exemplars of the feudal mode of production. Yet on certain quantitative indices – for example, levels of literacy, population, urbanization and bureaucratization – we must conclude that (to use Anderson's own unrigorous and, as he puts it, 'make-shift' terms) the differences in levels of civilization between these exemplars of feudalism were as great as those between any alleged exemplars of the AMP.

Finally, it is an intriguing aspect of Anderson's first volume of his history, *Passages from Antiquity to Feudalism*, that his description of the Hellenistic kingdoms of antiquity presupposes a theory of oriental society which looks remarkably like our old friend the AMP. Anderson comments on the failure of Greek slaveholding to spread with the Macedonian conquests:

the anterior Near Eastern social formations – with their very different economic and political traditions – imperviously resisted Greek patterns in the countryside.

Thus slave-labour failed to spread to the rural interior of the Hellenistic East ... Agrarian relations of production were consequently left relatively unaffected by Greek rule. The traditional agricultural systems of the great riverine cultures of the Near East had combined landlords, dependent tenants and peasant proprietors with ultimate or immediate royal property of the soil ... Regal claims to a monopoly of land were centuries old ... If the towns were Greek in model, while the countryside remained Oriental in pattern, the structure of the states which integrated the two was inevitably syncretic, a mixture of Hellenic and Asian forms in which the secular legacy of the latter was unmistakably predominant. The Hellenistic rulers inherited the overwhelmingly autocratic traditions of the riverine civilizations of the Near East ... The divinization of monarchs soom became a general ideological norm throughout the Hellenistic world. The typical administrative mould of the new royal States revealed a similar development – a fundamentally Oriental structure refined by Greek improvements ... But in all these States, the existence of centralized royal bureaucracies was accompanied by the absence of any developed legal systems to stabilize or universalize their functions. No impersonal law could develop where the arbitrary will of the ruler was the source of all public functions. (P. Anderson, 1974a: 48–50)

This account of the Hellenistic kingdoms is a remarkable reproduction of conventional orientalist classicism by a Marxist historian opposed to the myths of oriental despotism and the AMP. The elements of stagnation, imperviousness to transformation by a (more advanced?) slaveholding society, centralization, arbitrary despotic rule, royal ownership of the soil, dependent but not slave-like direct producers, and 'riverine' foundations, are all faithfully reproduced by the man who calls for the burial of the AMP. It seems that, like a spectre, the AMP haunts Marxist historians, even those dedicated to its excommunication from the discourse of those who have heard the good news.

Geoffrey de Ste Croix is famous as a historian of classical antiquity, and his *The Class Struggle in the Ancient Greek World* is one of the most important pieces of recent Marxist history, based upon a breadth of scholarship which is truly impressive (de Ste Croix, 1981). De Ste Croix is also resolutely opposed to the AMP, and in fact expresses warm support for the position taken by Anderson (ibid: 262–2). First, he argues from authority, and cites Anderson's and Thorner's work (Thorner, 1966) as decisive rebuttals of the AMP. These essays are sufficient to condemn this 'outmoded notion' (ibid: 155). The AMP was based on defective knowledge of the Oriental world, even if it was based on the best sources available in Marx's day. The conclusion de Ste Croix draws from this summary, however, is uncharacteristically obscure: 'pre-classical modes of production' should be understood in a strictly·chronological sense, and need to be characterized 'quite differently and quite specifically'.

Second, de Ste Croix produces a supposed *reductio ad absurdum*. He tries to reject the views of the Marxist scholars Briant and Kreissig (Briant,

1975; and Kreissig, 1977). The former advanced the proposition that the Hellenistic kingdoms of antiquity were dominated by the AMP. Kreissig, reviewing forms of land tenure in the Hellenistic world, argued that dependent labour in the form of serfdom was predominant, and that the Orient in Hellenistic times was profoundly oriental rather than Greek. 'Hellenism' was confined to elements of the superstructure. (Indeed apart from their explicit use of the AMP, and their greater in-depth knowledge, Kreissig's and Briant's analyses are indistinguishable from the description which Anderson gives of the Hellenistic world – see pp. 231–2).[32] These arguments for the AMP, in de Ste Croix's view, lead to a 'patently ridiculous conclusion'. Since Kreissig and Briant reason that evidence of serfdom for temples or states is indicative of Asiatic relations of production, de Ste Croix ripostes that one must therefore conclude, on pain of inconsistency, that since such serfdom reappeared in the later Roman Empire it too was dominated by Asiatic production relations. He considers that since such a conclusion is self-evidently absurd the arguments of Kreissig and Briant have been refuted. Moreover, he contends that even 'if one were prepared to concede [the Asiatic mode of production's] existence in principle', a goodly part of the coastal areas of Asia Minor, its most fruitful and populated regions, would have to be removed from being classed under the oriental mode of production or AMP. In these areas chattel slavery was predominant. The evidence for serfdom in Hellenistic times is transitional: after Macedonian or Roman rule slavery was predominant. Rather dogmatically and equivocally he concludes that 'Outright slavery, as the mode of production most favoured by the Greek and Roman propertied class, must always have exercised a pervasive influence, even in areas where as yet it did not actually predominate' (de Ste Croix, 1981: 155–6).

There are several obvious problems with this hostility to the AMP despite the vigorous confidence with which it is articulated. First, in his arguments from authority de Ste Croix fails to recognize that the theoretical, as opposed to the empirical, foundations of Anderson's essay are insecure – as I have suggested above. Moreover, even if Marx was wholly wrong about India (and China) it does not mean that some version of the AMP cannot be appropriate for any other social formations in Asia, including the ancient Hellenistic kingdoms. Indeed since de Ste Croix does not engage in

---

32 Kreissig produced a book, *Geschichte des Hellenismus*, in 1982, the year after de Ste Croix's text was published. Moses Finley, the doyen of non-Marxist ancient historians, regards it as a major work (Finley, 1985: 21). Kreissig advances the argument that when the Hellenistic kingdoms of the East were absorbed into the Roman Empire the slave mode of production remained dominant only in the weak sense that the Roman ruling class drew its wealth directly from slave labour in Italy and Sicily. Over time, as the geographical base of the ruling class widened, so Asiatic exploitation of the provinces became predominant in the social formation.

clarifying the nature of 'pre-classical modes of production', his verbal gestures in the direction of the appropriate solutions which Marxists should seek can be ignored, as by themselves they constitute not an argument but rather give-away signs of difficulties with traditional Marxism.

Second, de Ste Croix's purported *reductio ad absurdum* can appeal only to those already converted to his position. To other Marxists, and non-Marxists, the description as 'Asiatic' of systems of exploitation based upon collective exploitation of villages through state or temple-based surplus-appropriation might seem 'patently' reasonable, whether such exploitation takes place in the later Roman Empire or upon Mars at some future juncture. Indeed since de Ste Croix is opposed to any unilineal schemata of historical development, it is difficult to see why it is even *prima facie* absurd for the slave mode of production to have been preceded and succeeded by the AMP within a given territory. An opponent of unilinealism cannot con-veniently use unilinealist arguments against a rival position – unless that position is explicitly committed to unilinealism. A stance like de Ste Croix's also implicitly rules out the possibility that social formations can be composed of several modes of production in which the salience of one mode of production might wax and wane. Such a position is compatible with a refurbished historical materialism and, more importantly, with the unac-knowledged position taken by de Ste Croix throughout his monumental book. As I demostrated earlier (pp. 189–91), de Ste Croix's taxonomy of pre-capitalist forms of exploitation, of which he finds specimens throughout the ancient Greek world, is nothing more than a re-representation of our old friends, the Asiatic, slave and feudal modes of exploitation.

Finally, de Ste Croix's 'empirical' objections to Kreissig and Briant are insufficient to reject the theoretical utility of the AMP *in toto* and its applicability to the Hellenistic kingdoms in particular. His argument is insufficient because it concedes the existence in principle of the AMP, and simply suggests that in Asia Minor it was not as important as the slave mode of production. But it is also insufficient because he does not demon-strate that the slave mode of production was in fact more important than the AMP in Asia Minor, since in his 'refutation' he gives us no quantitative indicators of the comparative importance of the two modes of production in geographical extent, numbers of people encompassed, or the scale of exploitative surplus generated under the rival systems. The 'argument' that outright slavery 'must always have exercised a pervasive influence, even in areas where as yet it did not actually predominate' indicates the contortions into which intelligent Marxists are driven when seeking to black out the AMP.

The contradictions in Perry Anderson's and Geoffrey de Ste Croix's writings – present in the best-known texts of very high-quality English Marxist historians – suggests that Marxist historians cannot easily work without 'Asiatic' assumptions even when they are explicitly hostile to the AMP. The AMP is not just the bastard child of historical materialism: it seems to have the resilience of a ghost which can haunt over several generations.

CONCLUSION

This chapter, and the preceding one, have demonstrated that the AMP poses fundamental problems and insoluble dilemmas for historical materialism. This conclusion stands irrespective of the particular version of historical materialism considered. On the other hand, the chapter has shown the interpretive and empirical problems which historical materialists face when they choose to work without the AMP in the analysis of pre-capitalist societies. As I set out to show, historical materialism is damned if it retains the AMP, and it is damned if it does not.

This conclusion suggests that historical materialism is severely conceptually flawed. The phenomena which the AMP draw attention to are problematic, but not implausible. Relatively centralized and autonomous pre-industrial state structures, capable of considerable fiscal exploitation of administratively subordinated urban settlements and corporate agrarian village communities, were features of some pre-industrial socio-political landscapes. These features, separately or combined, were not predominant in Western European agrarian polities between the collapse of the Roman Empire and the rise of the absolutist state. Their significance in explaining the absence of the development of capitalism in the Orient and its development in the Occident have become recurrent themes, especially in comparative historical sociology. However, historical materialism is not capable of illuminating these issues.

6

Wittfogel and Oriental Despotism

Can one be surprised ... that a theory built upon water is soggy from the outset?
                Godes, cited in Sawer, *Marxism and the Question of the Asiatic Mode of Production*

Oriental society is clearly something more complex than a system of canals
                Lichtheim, *Oriental Despotism, The Concept of Ideology and Other Essays*

Hitler ... has scored a victory if a graduate of his concentration camps imbibed
enough of the 'master-race' philosophy to damn so widespread a social phenomena
as 'Oriental'.
                                                Kosambi, *The Basis of Despotism*

Karl Wittfogel's *Oriental Despotism* was published in 1957, and immediately
received both effusive critical acclaim and virulent condemnation. The
extent of the praise and the contempt was mostly a simple function of
where critics stood in the Communist/anti-Communist ideological spectrum.
However, knowledge of Wittfogel's subject matter did seem to be in
inverse proportion to 'critical' extremes of approval and disapproval. Liberal
democratic social scientists were (and remain) reluctant to query Wittfogel's
arguments or empirical evidence. Gushing praise came in an American
journal in which *Oriental Despotism* was described as 'a work of flawless
scholarship' and the reader informed that 'Had Wittfogel's book been
published a hundred years ago, Marxism could not have developed.' The
text in question was 'a "watershed book", a book of which people are likely
to speak in terms of "before" and "after"' (Niemeyer, 1958: 264–70).
The review in *Problems of Communism* was equally enthusiastic. Here,
Wittfogel ranked 'with those few universal scholars whose contributions
future historians and social scientists dare not ignore'. The prophecy was
made that 'In the long run, this analysis of Oriental despotism could
deprive the Soviets of their claim to be leaders of a 'progressive' movement'

(Walker, 1957: 48—9).[1] There were some exceptions to the anti-Communist consensus which rapidly formed around the book's stature. An English scholar at the School of Oriental and African Studies regretted that 'a hoary stereotype' had been given fresh life, complained that Wittfogel's determinism showed that he had not divested himself of his Marxist antecedents, and hoped that *Oriental Despotism* would be forgotten when international tensions declined (Pulleyblank, 1958). And Arnold Toynbee in the *American Political Science Review* condemned *Oriental Despotism* for resuscitating a Greek myth, stirring up tribal animosities, being apologetic towards the West's worst periods of history (namely slavery and Nazism) and being a 'menace' (Toynbee, 1958: 195—8). However, their voices were barely heard in the rush to confer upon *Oriental Despotism* the status of a contemporary liberal classic.[2]

On the other hand, amongst Marxists or leftist progressives the standard response was to dismiss Wittfogel's work as the outpourings of a renegade charlatan, mixed with snobbish disdain. Savage contempt for Wittfogel's scholarship and motives was exhibited by the Sinophile Joseph Needham who described *Oriental Despotism* as 'a political tract [and] politically oriented fact-defying dogma' (Needham, 1959: 58—65). Soviet reviewers responded in the same vein (Levada, 1981). Nearly two decades later Perry Anderson was still fulminating over *Oriental Despotism*: 'The most extreme confusionism is, of course, not the work of a Marxist, but of a more or less Spencerian survival: K. Wittfogel ... this vulgar charivari, devoid of any historical sense ...' (P. Anderson, 1974b: 487). Sober appraisal of Wittfogel's historical knowledge, whether of pre-industrial China or of the almost innumerable other pre-industrial polities which he claimed to have examined systematically, was slower in coming to intellectual attention. Wittfogel's methodological procedures, by comparison with dogmatic endorsement or rejection of the political implications of their outcomes, were not scrutinized in the first rushes of blood to the head.

This chapter surveys and demonstrates pivotal logical flaws in *Oriental Despotism*. I have already shown that Wittfogel's contentions that Marx and Engels committed sins against science are based on wild speculation rather than careful textual exegesis (see pp. 139—41). In the next chapter the

---

1 Despite three decades of historical criticism social scientists are still loath to remove *Oriental Despotism* from its hallowed status in conservative and liberal ideology. For example, the political scientist Giovanni Sartori thought he was obliged to qualify a marginal criticism of Wittfogel with the comment that: 'My caveat does not detract from the stature of this classic work' (1987: 210).

2 It must be said that *Oriental Despotism* did help the production of a classic in a different genre. The *Dune* sequence of science fiction written by Frank Herbert is indebted to the thesis of hydraulic despotism — as its author explicitly acknowledged. In the *Dune* novels it is control of life-enhancing spice which forms the functional basis of an empire stretching across multiple galaxies.

empirical inadequacy of Wittfogel's evidence from Indian history is demonstrated. Combined, these three assaults are intended to refute *Oriental Despotism's* status as a classic. Although these conclusions are not news to historians they are insufficiently appreciated in the fields of political science and political sociology.[3]

THE ARGUMENTS OF *ORIENTAL DESPOTISM*

The chapter in *Oriental Despotism* entitled 'The Rise and Fall of the Theory of the Asiatic Mode of Production', which argues that Marx, Engels and Lenin sinned, is detachable from the main body of the argument. Wittfogel himself claimed that his conclusions about *Oriental Despotism* are true irrespective of the ideological or Marxological context in which he had developed them. His model, in the positivist social science tradition, was available for empirical confirmation or falsification. The arguments of the other nine chapters of the book do indeed form a relatively coherent whole, whose merits and demerits stand or fall independently of Wittfogel's dubious account of the rise and fall of the AMP.

3 Wittfogel's *magnum opus* was the culmination of over thirty years' study of Chinese history. It was also — and self-consciously — the theoretical culmination of a political trajectory which had seen a young German Communist, who had met Lenin in the 1920s, metamorphose into a venerable member of the American anti-Communist professoriate. To the end of his long life, and with deliberate irony, Wittfogel proclaimed himself a better Marxist than Marx, Engels or Lenin. They, not he, had betrayed historical materialism. An extensive examination of Wittfogel's political and intellectual biography is not attempted here. There is an intellectual biography available of Wittfogel's life and work (Ulmen, 1978). He was born in Woltersdorf in 1896. As a young socialist, in 1918 he joined the Independent Socialist party and its successor the German Communist Party. His political activism and CP membership were unusual amongst the scholars of the Intitüt für Sozialforschung — the basis of the Frankfurt School. However, Wittfogel was peripheral amongst the Frankfurt Marxist intelligentsia in the 1920s. His Sinological work did not arouse great interest and he was driven to the expedient of reviewing his own books under the pseudonym of Karl Peterson (Jay, 1973: 15). Wittfogel's first major work, *Economy and Society* (1931), a study of China, was published under the Institüt's auspices. In 1933 he was incarcerated in a concentration camp because of his Communist activities, but was released later in the year after international pressure was effective. His CP membership lapsed. He went on to do field research in China between 1935 and 1938, sponsored partly by the Institüt. By 1940, domiciled in America, Wittfogel had shifted his politics dramatically, partly under the influence of his third wife Esther Goldfrank. In the 1940s he established Sinological research at Washington and Columbia. In 1951 he testified before the McCarran Committee, the Internal Security Subcommittee of the Senate Judiciary Committee. His testimony implicated, among others, Moses Finley, who in consequence left the USA for the UK. Wittfogel's testimony included the recognition that his academic contacts dried up when he became an avowed anti-Communist. He died in May 1988 — see obituaries by Gellner (1988), Hirst (1988) and O'Leary (1988). Here I follow the maxim that any social science text can, and must, be evaluated independently of its author's biography — even if biographical knowledge should not be entirely excised, as in those forms of hyper-structuralism which proclaim 'the death of the author'.

The Material Basis and Character of Agrarian Totalitarianism

Wittfogel argued that there were two types of irrigation in agrarian societies: *hydro-agriculture*, or small-scale irrigation farming, and *hydraulic agriculture*, or large-scale and state-directed farming (Wittfogel, 1981: 12). The latter created the opportunity for despotism to emerge. The appropriate milieu for its emergence was in arid or semi-arid regions – where rainfall farming was problematic. Arid and semi-arid regions were more likely to develop stratified and civilized but despotic and state-dominated societies. He was not very clear about the whys and wherefores of riverine developments in ancient civilizations, although he knew that the mere existence of a major river did not suffice to start a despotic civilization. The common geographical factor of the earliest riparian cultures was that the rivers concerned flowed through a desert, thereby making it easier for agriculture to develop without the obstacle of forests: 'The jungles of the Amazon cannot be cleared without modern heavy machinery, while the tremendous sod of the Mississippi prairies was first broken by heavy ploughs which were not sent to that region till the last century' (Kosambi, 1956a: 53). However, on the basis of his reasoning Wittfogel confidently asserted that the arid, semi-arid and humid regions of northern India became historically prominent before the excessively humid area of Bengal (Wittfogel, 1981: 21).

Wittfogel's reasoning is summarized in the following causal representation, which also illustrates why his geographical productivist materialism is rightly compared to the theories of Montesquieu and Plekhanov:

Arid or semi-arid region	$\longrightarrow$	large-scale irrigation
Large-scale irrigation	$\longrightarrow$	hydraulic organization
Hydraulic organization	$\longrightarrow$	agro-hydraulic despotism

Wittfogel claimed that what is here shown by the arrows did not represent necessary causation – or better, sufficient conditions for despotism – since large enterprises for water control did not always create a hydraulic order. Rather the relationships represented dispositions, tendencies and opportunities. In this way he sought to avoid the potential embarrassments created by such possible counter-examples to his argument as the northern Italian, Venetian and Dutch water management systems – none of which had been associated with despotic states. These fortunate societies avoided the hydraulic despotic fate only because they were situated in a wider non-hydraulic nexus (ibid: 12).

Wittfogel contended that water has specific properties which made certain organizational formats inevitable for task-management: 'the bulkiness of all except the smallest sources of water supply creates a technical task which is solved either by mass labour or not at all' (ibid: 15). He even suggested, in a manner reminiscent of the early social contract theorists, that 'mankind' deliberated over the establishment of hydraulic agriculture, and that some peoples eventually chose the hydraulic route because of its recognized productive benefits. By contrast, the tribal peoples who failed to emulate them did so because they understood the consequences of political and economic subjection in a hydraulic regime.[4] They preferred the liberty of the forests to the despotism of hydraulic civilization.

Hydraulic agriculture was the agrarian analogue of the socialist command economy of the modern world, a claim made plain in the title of the second chapter of Wittfogel's book: 'Hydraulic Economy – A Managerial and Genuinely Political Economy'. The operation of heavy waterworks in agrarian society was compared to contemporary heavy industry (ibid: 27). Hydraulic agriculture was characterized by an extensive division of labour and state management of the economy. Making fields cultivable and protecting them against the dangers of flooding necessitated corvée labour, and therefore, Wittfogel contended, a centralized despotism. The hydraulic regime had managerial and construction functions – notably calendar making and astronomy – essential for agrarian planning, as well as the building of aqueducts, reservoirs and navigation canals (ibid: 28–34). The technologies of hydraulic society produced, as by-products, all of the major construction achievements of agrarian empires. The huge defence structures, like the Great Wall of China; the great roads, like those built under various Indian regimes;[5] and the major palaces, capital cities, tombs, monuments and temples, like those of the Delhi sultanate and the Mughal dynasty; all were evidence of the engineering and architectural knowledge available in these societies.

These artefacts were explained 'in the last instance' as functional responses to and by-products of hydraulic engineering. Hydraulic works (aqueducts, reservoirs, sluices, dikes, drainage and navigation canals) provided the necessary conditions for the development of great non-hydraulic works: 'the huge administrative cities and colossal palaces, temples and tombs of Asia, Egypt and ancient America express the organizational coordination and the mobilization potential of hydraulic economy and statecraft' (ibid: 45). Finally, this agrarian society was associated with massive state intervention in the non-hydraulic economy. State management of most major extractive and manufacturing industries existed. The despotic state enjoyed power over its labour force far greater than that exercised by capitalists. Wittfogel quoted an Indian authority for the extraordinary view that the

4 A Soviet critic of Wittfogel commented that 'the attempt to pretend that primitive tribes were able to evaluate the social consequences of irrigation cannot be judged other than completely absurd' (Levada, 1981 – cited in Bailey and Llobera, 1981: 84).

5 He mentions the roads built by the Mauryans and the Mughals (Wittfogel, 1981: 27). He also claimed, falsely, that the Roman road network was the fruit of 'a fateful transformation that made the Roman Empire a Hellenistically (Orientally) despotic state' (ibid: 38).

Mughal emperor Akbar 'by his *firman* (order) could collect any number of men he liked. There was no limit to his massing of labourers, save the number of people in his Empire' (ibid: 48 – citing Pant, 1930: 70), and commented, *Mutatis mutandis*, this statement is valid for all hydraulic civilizations' (ibid). The hydraulic regime differed from its socialist successor in that it was based on agriculture and operated in only part of the agrarian economy. But it nevertheless marked a social system distinct from all other agrarian societies.

Wittfogel's theoretical and ideological project became plainer in the third chapter, 'A State Stronger than Society', where he sought to develop a theory of pre-industrial totalitarianism.[6] Hydraulic regimes were portrayed as the ideal typical antonyms of pluralist agrarian regimes. In this way he extended the contrast between pluralist and monist regimes, developed for industrialized societies, back into agrarian society. Table 6.1. reconstructs and makes explicit Wittfogel's typology. It encodes the conventional wisdom of pluralist political theorists (who classified regimes by the degree of state fragmentation) and post-war elite theorists (who classified regimes by whether the ruling elite was cohesive or fragmented). This codification was popular and influential in the late 1950s and early 1960s – when the first Cold War was still in existence.[7]

Wittfogel argued that hydraulic states prevented non-state actors (kinship groups, religious organizations, tribal bands and independent property owners) from acquiring sufficient autonomy to act as countervailing powers. The sheer organizational power of the hydraulic state apparatus, which manifested itself in the state's census-making and record-keeping capacities,[8] was reinforced by its hydraulic management capabilities, its organization of roads and its surveillance resources. The last were buttressed by the placement of administrators and officers in all major settlements, which acquired the traits of garrison towns. The military dimension of the power of the hydraulic state was incomparably greater than that of European feudal lords. Hydraulic rulers did not share military authority with their nobles, enjoyed a monopoly of authority, and possessed the military theory and logistical capacity systematically to plan warfare and mobilize huge 'hosts' onto the field of battle. (ibid: 59–67). The fiscal acquisitive power of the hydraulic state was equally awesome. The state siphoned off the social surplus through two principal mechanisms: corvée labour on state fields and the extraction of a land tax. The latter predominated over the

6 The title of the chapter was taken from a famous book about Czarist Russia by Paul Milukow, and broadcast Wittfogel's desire to associate pre-revolutionary Russian history with oriental despotism.

7 See Dunleavy and O'Leary (1987: chapters 2 and 4).

8 Wittfogel cited the *Arthashastra*, Megasthenes and Islamic sources for the interest which Indian rulers took in counting their subjects and their revenues (Wittfogel, 1981: 51).

Table 6.1 Wittfogel's typology of regimes

		Regime	
		Pluralist	Monist
Economy	Agrarian	Greek and Roman slaveholding Medieval European feudalism	Oriental despotism Hydraulic regime
	Industrial	Liberal capitalism Liberal democratic capitalism	State socialism National socialism

former in hydraulic states (ibid: 69).[9] However, the hydraulic state was also capable of and disposed towards straightforward confiscation and embezzlement of its subjects' capital. Wittfogel doubted the 'declared reasons' (ibid: 73) for such confiscations — namely, accusations of political and administrative disloyalty — and preferred to suggest that they were an intrinsic feature of the workings of the state-managed economic system.

The organizational power of the hydraulic state was mirrored by the weak property rights of its subjects (ibid: 78–86). These weaknesses were attributed primarily to the laws of inheritance in hydraulic societies which required periodic and equal redistribution of the land. This alleged common feature — which he scarcely attempted to establish as *necessarily* connected to hydraulic society — in turn prevented the formation of a powerful independent landowning nobility which could act as a check on the monarch. Wittfogel argued, without providing supporting historical evidence, that hydraulic rulers deliberately reinforced such laws of inheritance as one strategy to maintain their power (ibid: 85).[10]

The hydraulic state's power was also buttressed ideologically, since 'Nowhere in hydraulic society did the dominant religion place itself outside the authority of the state as a nationally (or internationally) integrated autonomous church' (Wittfogel, 1981: 87). The majority of all hydraulic civilizations had large and influential priesthoods — although as a rule

9 He provided no systematic data to support this assertion. The table which he presented comparing the sources of the rural revenues of 'representative hydraulic governments' (Wittfogel, 1981: 70) was worthless because he did not say why it was a representative sample. Wittfogel also remarked that 'traces of public fields are reported for certain regions of India. Whether they reflect primitive tribal institutions, possibly of Dravidian or pre-Dravidian origin, is an open question.' He cited his authorities as Baden-Powell (1892) and Hewitt (1887).

10 It was a self-refuting argument since, in so far as it was true, the absence of primogeniture also weakened the durability and strength of dynasties: 'The absence of a strict rule of primogeniture was the cause of dynastic disputes, and ... undoubtedly led to the weakening of empires' (Basham, 1967: 92).

hydraulic governments were administered by 'professional officials'[11] who, though educated by priests, were not trained to be priests (ibid: 88–9). However, many hydraulic societies were theocratic. Secular and religious authority was fused. The emperor was a god, a demigod or the chief priest, or performed some permutation of these three roles.[12] The central point of his excursions on religion and religious organizations was to reinforce his ideal typical contrast between hydraulic and non-hydraulic societies and to bolster his explanation of the sources of Western pluralism. The organizational autonomy of the Roman Catholic Church, by contrast with the religions of hydraulic civilizations, contributed 'to the growth of the balanced late feudal order, which eventually gave rise to modern Western society' (ibid: 92).

Wittfogel's discussion of Indian religious history indicated considerable uncertainty about how to handle its divergence from the model of a state-religion. He argued that Hindu government had 'significant quasihierocratic [sic] features', and that

the relation between secular and religious authority underwent considerable transformation, but certain basic features persisted throughout and even after the close of the Hindu period. Available evidence suggests that in the early days of Hindu history the government depended less on priestly participation than it has since the latter half of the first millennium B.C. But whatever changes have occurred in this respect, secular and religious authority remained closely integrated. (ibid: 97)

This vacillating paragraph opened a page of confused remarks upon religion in Indian history.[13] The historical precedence of kingly over religious authority in Indian history was an embarrassment for the theory of oriental despotism. So for that matter were the constraints which the brahmins placed upon both Hindu and Muslim rulers. However, facts were not allowed to get in the way of the development of a neat typology. Hydraulic regimes fused religious, military and state authority, by contrast with the non-hydraulic regimes of Western Europe in which these three functions were politically and organizationally differentiated.

This fusion of functions was the source of the despotic power of the hydraulic regime, which was 'total and not benevolent'. Hydraulic regimes lacked effective constitutional restrictions on the ruler's power. Law codes were promulgated by the ruler from above and therefore did not circumscribe

---

11 By 'professional' he meant no more than somebody engaged in full-time employment in a given role (see Wittfogel, 1981: 239–43).

12 Wittfogel did confess difficulty in classifying Achaemenian Persia, Byzantium and Islamic regimes under such descriptions. These were at best 'marginally theocratic' (1981: 95–6).

13 See also chapter 7, pp. 303–5.

the ruler's own freedom (ibid: 101−2).[14] Hydraulic regimes lacked not only legal but also social pluralism. There were no independent intermediary powers. Furthermore, such regimes lacked lawful means for resisting the government. Wittfogel dismissed the 'so-called right of rebellion' − present in Hindu, Muslim and Chinese traditions − as unimportant constraints on the despot.[15] Even mechanisms and events like the election of the despot, the assassination of rulers, or violence within the ruling elite, did not temper the impact of oriental despotism. The absolutist regime was monocratic in spirit and practice.[16] Not even the occurrence of informal shifts of decision-making to the ruler's apparatus removed this absolutist trait. Despotic states existed because there was no institution with the power to balance or block the hydraulic institutions of the state. These facts were extrapolated into a sociological law: the 'cumulative tendency of unchecked power' (ibid: 106). The despotic ruler was checked by the laws of nature but 'his power over his subjects [was] no less total because it [was] limited by factors that mold human life in every type of society' (ibid: 108).

Some managerial realism entered Wittfogel's model of oriental despotism. The state's capacity to penetrate its population in a hydraulic despotism was limited by 'the law of diminishing administrative returns' (ibid: 109). Hydraulic despotisms were powerful enough to prevent the growth of rival organizations (distinguishing them from the ancient and medieval regimes of the West) but they lacked the ubiquitous authority of the USSR. The agrarian hydraulic regime neither nationalized agriculture nor pulverized *all* non-governmental human relations (ibid: 112). It left some freedom to individuals and secondary organizations. The workings of the family, guilds, village, village government, agriculture (apart from corvée labour), religious organizations and ideas were relatively autonomous from the state, though they were not as autonomous as was sometimes suggested (ibid: 113−24). These freedoms were in any case politically irrelevant, at best the institutions of a 'beggar's democracy' (ibid: 125−6).

14 Wittfogel cited an Indian authority for the view that in Hindu India the king was constitutionally in a position to accept or repudiate the laws accepted by his predecessor (Rangaswami, 1935). The significance of this point is debatable. Modern British governments are in a position to accept or repudiate the laws accepted by their predecessors. Pluralism is therefore feasible without a codified constitution which checks state power. In any case, the *Arthashastra* (upon which Rangaswami relies) is unusual amongst ancient Indian texts in suggesting that the king had innovative legislative functions. The traditions of Indian kingship suggested that the king was merely the interpreter of sacred law − *dharmashastra*.

15 Wittfogel's lack of jurisprudence and political theory manifested itself here. There is no right of resistance against laws in constitutional states. Civil disobedience may be habitual, it may be morally correct, but it is never legal. The right of opposition against a government in a liberal democracy is the right to try to change law(s), policy or government, not a 'right of rebellion'.

16 Wittfogel remarks in a footnote that there are a 'few temporary exceptions, like early India' (1981: 106). He was presumably referring obliquely to the embarrassing 'republics' of Buddhist India.

Wittfogel was equally concerned to argue that hydraulic despotisms were not benevolent. The unintended consequences of the operation of hydraulic institutions could not be construed as benevolent. Benevolence for him had to be intentional: 'The hydraulic state is a managerial state, and certain of its operations do indeed benefit the people. But since the rulers depend on these operations for their own maintenance and prosperity, their policies can hardly be seen as benevolent' (ibid: 126).[17] The despotic ruler maximized his personal consumption subject only to the constraint of meeting the functional requirements of hydraulic agriculture. Wittfogel refused to concede that such regimes were both functional *and* exploitative. To do so would be the agrarian equivalent of apologizing for Stalinism. To accept the 'functionality' of hydraulic regimes was to be fooled by their legitimation formulae and the myths they used to demobilize potential opposition. The despotic state engaged in a zero-sum game with its population.

Not content to leave the parallels with modern totalitarianism to such traits, Wittfogel contended that hydraulic regimes also practised 'total terror', producing 'total submission' and 'total loneliness' (ibid: chapter 5). Terror was legitimized in a rhetoric which justified punishment. The Hindu 'Laws of Manu' exemplified the ideology of hydraulic punishment. In addition, the despotic ruler had the physical implements essential for organized terror: 'unchecked control over the army, the police, the intelligence service; and he [had] at his disposal jailers, torturers, executioners, and all the tools necessary to catch, incapacitate, and destroy a suspect' (ibid: 141). The language and imagery of the whip represented the nature of hydraulic despotism. Wittfogel's concern to portray hydraulic despotism as the pre-industrial analogue of totalitarianism also led him to apply other central elements of totalitarian theory to agrarian societies. Hydraulic populations were atomized and socialized through education into complete submission to authority. Deference, exemplified and reinforced by prostration before the despot, was also evident in the absence of a participatory civic culture and the pervasiveness of resigned attitudes towards politics amongst hydraulic subjects.[18]

This portrait of unpredictable and capricious use of force by the despot, executed in a milieu of perpetually suspicious court politics, and implemented through terror in fiscal collection and judicial torture of peasant subjects, was sharply contrasted with occidental forms of rule. Occidental state terrorism was by contrast more limited and temporary (ibid: 145−7). This

---

17 This argument rests upon the fallacy that benevolence must be altruistic to count as benevolence.
18 These assertions were palpably anachronistic. All agrarian societies, East and West, were built around communal, caste and kinship relations. Atomization is only feasible in a social order in which such relations have been smashed. Such a feat of political engineering was beyond the pre-industrial despot.

dubious argument, intended to anticipate objections, was typical of, and essential to, Wittfogel's ideological enterprise. Whenever there was historical evidence which could not be discounted that an undesirable feature of hydraulic despotism had also existed in occidental regimes, he moved to choose one of four lines of rejoinder. First, he would contend that the appearance of equivalence was deceptive. Second, when this option was implausible, he would suggest that while the trait was systemic in the Orient, it was not an intrinsic feature of the Occident. Third, when these two strategies were insufficient he would contend that the Occident had experienced the trait in question in a 'weaker', more 'benign' or 'balanced' form. Through these stratagems, embarrassments in the history of occidental civilization (such as slavery, trial by ordeal and Nazi Germany) could be explained away. Finally, the existence of despotic traits in the Occident could, 'in the last instance', be attributed to the diffusion of the political technologies constructed in the first place by hydraulic despots. The Orient remained the font of original sin. The contrast between the angelic Occident and the devilish Orient, between the non-hydraulic and the hydraulic, was thus made more immune to falsification.

The Diffusion and Variation of Hydraulic Regimes

Having outlined his theses Wittfogel paused to deal with obvious objections. He conceded that hydraulic political institutions, namely monarchical absolutism, had existed in non-hydraulic geographical, technological and economic environments. His solution was to appeal to the importance of cultural diffusion and develop a typology of core, marginal and sub-marginal hydraulic societies (ibid: chapter 6). The hydraulic institutional order had indeed originated in the core area in the appropriate natural setting, but under certain cultural conditions it could diffuse to marginal and sub-marginal hydraulic zones.

The hydraulic core developed a continuous system of irrigation and flood control, in a landscape with one major accessible source of humidity (ibid: 162). Major examples could be found in ancient Peru, the Nile valley and, in India, Sindh in the Indus valley. Two indices defined the core: hydraulically cultivated land and flood control works erected by the state. The degree of 'core-ness' varied, in descending order, from:

where the hydraulically cultivated land comprised more than half of all cultivable land; through
where the hydraulically cultivated land yielded more than all other arable land; to
where the hydraulically cultivated land was small in relation to non-hydraulically cultivated land, but nevertheless sufficient to produce the despotic state and corvée labour.

The degree of 'core-ness' also varied according to the salience of flood control (ibid: 162−4). Bureaucratic density varied in its turn according to the degree of 'core-ness' of a regime. On the basis of these dimensions Wittfogel classified core areas into 'compact' and 'loose' hydraulic societies. The great empires of India were classed as loose hydraulic societies, built by the territorial expansion of one city state which had developed in a core region (ibid: 166−7). The great northern plain of India was the main area of hydraulic agriculture and 'the logical place for the political metropolis' (ibid: 170).

The hydraulic margin, by contrast, developed bureaucratic density not as a result of hydraulic management but as a by-product of non-hydraulic construction tasks. The margin had a despotic state with a service rather than a feudal nobility. Examples of the hydraulic margin were the Byzantine, Czarist, Liao and Mayan empires (although the last two specimens were on the border between loose core and marginal hydraulic societies). '[A]ll variants of the marginal type utilize the organizational and acquisitive methods of despotic statecraft. Thus, however, marginal they may be hydraulically, their methods of social control place all of them definitely in the 'Oriental' world' (ibid: 188). The diffusion of hydraulic despotic methods was attributed to the nomadic conquering tribes of central Asia.

The sub-margin of hydraulic society contained civilizations which 'exhibit[ed] stray features of hydraulic statecraft' (ibid: 195). Specimens of this type included the protohistorical Greek regimes (the Minoan and Mycenean civilizations), the Etruscans and early Romans, Japanese regimes, and pre-Mongol Russia. The stray features of hydraulic statecraft in these regimes resulted either from the previous incorporation of their territories in a wider hydraulic order, or through the voluntary adoption and imitation of oriental practices (ibid: 203). The sub-margin was obviously a residual category for regimes and civilizations which did not contribute towards occidental freedoms, but could not plausibly have the hydraulic label attached to them.

Wittfogel's typological excursion and extended discussion of historical empires confirmed that the original formation of hydraulic despotism depended upon the 'natural setting'. Thereafter its techniques of power were capable of cultural diffusion without the support of a natural setting. However, the key point remained: whether core, marginal or sub-marginal, hydraulic societies were institutionally incapable of emerging into multi-centred societies of the Western type (ibid: 227).[19]

19 However, Wittfogel devoted many pages to civilizations which 'crossed the institutional divide' between marginal and sub-marginal hydraulic orders (that is, either crossed over from one type to the other over time − and back again − or were difficult to classify as one or the other). Nomadic pastoral warriors with emergent state structures, and the 'societal transmutations of Greece, Rome, Spain, and Russia' were all examples of this kind (ibid: 204−25). Evidently marginal and sub-marginal hydraulic despotisms were capable of change and transformation − unlike core hydraulic despotisms − but Wittfogel did not elaborate the significance of this concession.

He also developed a further typology of hydraulic societies based on 'patterns of proprietary complexity in hydraulic society' (chapter 7). Hydraulic despotisms were distinguished by their simple, semi-complex or complex patterns of property rights in both mobile and immobile property (ibid: 228–300). In the simple form, independent private property existed as a minor and wholly subordinate component of both mobile and immobile property. In the semi-complex form, by contrast, there was considerable private property development in industry and commerce, but not in agriculture. Finally, in the complex form, relatively private property is well developed in all economic spheres.

India was described as a specimen of an hydraulic order with semi-complex proprietary rights[20] – 'almost from the dawn of written history to the 19th century' (ibid: 260). The development of a merchant class was recognized in various stages of Indian history, especially its earliest manifestations in the Vedic age and in Buddhist India (ibid: 264–7). However, although these merchants possessed private capital they had relatively little political influence or autonomy. He drew upon a few selected items from historians and Sanskritists to substantiate his judgement that Indian merchants had never developed autonomous guilds, and to question whether merchants had ever been politically prominent in Indian regimes (ibid: 266). He did not reject Weber's assumption that autonomous commercial communities had flourished in Buddhist India, but emphasized that the evidence never demonstrated that such flourishing was translated into political influence (ibid: 270). This concern to emphasize the fact that merchants never ruled in hydraulic societies, whether simple, semi-complex or complex, was peculiar. Merchants rarely ruled, directly or indirectly, in occidental regimes – with the notable exceptions of Venice and Amsterdam. Therefore Wittfogel's assertions about mercantile political weakness in hydraulic orders, whether or not they were historically accurate, served no theoretical purpose in contrasting the Orient and the Occident, since mercantile political weakness – on his definition of weakness – was a universal phenomenon in agrarian societies.

The land systems in the majority of hydraulic despotisms, of whatever type, kept private landownership in a quantitatively subordinated position to state-managed, state-regulated and state-assigned land (Wittfogel, 1981: 271ff). State-managed, imperial or crown land, used for the purposes of the imperial army and household, was never more than a minor part of all state-controlled land. The key agrarian sector in hydraulic society was state-regulated land; that is, land which the holder could not freely alienate. And under this category came both village communities regulated by the state and individual peasant possessors.[21] State regulation and the lack of the right to alienate prevented incipient agrarian landlordism from emerging,

20 Wittfogel (1981: 256–7, 260, 264–7, 270, 281, 286 and 297).
21 Wittfogel argued that the evidence of numerous inscriptions confirmed for 'the last

notably in both Hindu and Muslim India. State-assigned land, granted to favourites, functionaries, and religious organizations, was also important in hydraulic orders — although land assigned to religious orders was less salient in Hindu India, since the brahmins did not live on large and permanently granted temple lands.[22]

The 'value added' to Wittfogel's theory of oriental despotism by his excursus on property rights in an immense range of pre-industrial societies was the demonstration that hydraulic orders had 'beggar's property' institutions, which were analogous to and reinforced the political impotence of the 'beggar's democracy'. State regulation and control over property militated against the development of private capitalism and a multi-centred society. The hydraulic order was economically fragmented and politically atomized — conditions entirely propitious for despotism.

Wittfogel completed his theoretical argument with a lengthy discourse on classes in hydraulic society (ibid: 300–68). Sociological theory had been too much influenced by the class history of the Occident, and consequently was blind to the importance of state power as 'a predominant determinant of class structure, both in our time and in the past' (ibid: 302). In hydraulic societies relationship to the state apparatus determined class position. The state controlled 'big water' and 'big land', which weakened the salience of private-property-based class formation. The ruling class of the hydraulic apparatus was recognized as such by the ruled, and not mistaken as the instrument of a private-property-owning class. It was composed of the ruler's courtiers, 'ranking officials' and their underlings at the centre. Each of these three segments at the centre had family connections entrenched with them, and a bureaucratic gentry was attached to the 'ranking' officialdom. Horizontally the ruling class was made up of agents, such as the Persian satraps or subordinate princes like the rajas of Muslim India (ibid: 309). Hydraulic despotisms varied in the degree to which the despot's representatives in the periphery were politically subordinated. Satraps were extremely subordinated, whereas rajas were much more autonomous, but, Wittfogel insisted, they were never as autonomous as Western nobles serving an overlord in a feudal system. The ruling class

southern phase of Hindu India what was already certain for the Buddhist and post-Buddhist periods, namely that 'most villages' were occupied by ryotwari — that is, by peasants who were under the direct control of the state' (ibid.: 281). He presumably had in mind the Hindu Empire of Vijayanagara. Wittfogel's sources were Jolly (1896) and Appadorai (1936). However, Appadorai's work on the south Indian state, which is largely responsible for the portrait of Vijayanagara as a bureaucratic despotism, has recently been forcefully criticized by south Indian historians — see Stein (1975) and my discussion of Wittfogel's derivative errors in this respect on pp. 285–7.

22 An argument which was especially dubious, because in certain regions of India brahmins did do just that. My colleague Tom Nossiter, an authority on Kerala, points out that brahmins there lived on large temple-administered lands which had been granted by kings.

also included at its margins those attached to the apparatus by 'semi-, quasi- or pre-official status [sic]' (ibid: 317ff). Under this heading commercial agents, tax farmers, religious functionaries and students studying for bureaucratic places were all counted as members of the hydraulic ruling class.

The ruled consisted of those who did not participate in the state apparatus, namely peasants, artisans and some merchants. However, there were few slaves amongst their numbers. Slaves in the hydraulic societies of India, China and the Islamic world were largely domestic. They were not employed to any significant extent in agricultural labour or manufacturing. The prohibitive supervisory costs involved in the construction of public works in hydraulic society, and the lack of incentives facing slaves in irrigation farming, explained the absence of slavery in production (ibid: 322). The 'total power' of the state apparatus also explained the absence of class struggle in hydraulic society. 'The history of hydraulic society suggests that class struggle, far from being a chronic disease of all mankind, is the luxury of multicentred and open societies' (ibid: 329). While there were antagonisms in hydraulic societies, they were small scale, lacking in class consciousness, and did not resemble the class struggles of the medieval Occident. Conflicts within the ruling class centred on bureaucratic position and family and dynastic manoeuvre. Bureaucratic competition between hydraulic state apparatuses reinforced the power of the despot and did not create the authentic decentralization and competition found in feudal aristocracies.[23] In any case, in conquest societies (where a nomadic tribe had conquered the hydraulic society) ruling-class cohesion and loyalty to the despot were comparatively easy to maintain. Elsewhere (or in addition) the political mechanisms of the hydraulic despots (the apparatuses of eunuchs, slaves, semi-slaves or Mamelukes) served only to centralize the power of the despot and to prevent the fragmentation of the ruling class.

The historical moral Wittfogel drew from this portrait of the class structure of agrarian despotism was simple. The hydraulic bureaucracy had enjoyed a monopoly of class power which was far more unified, cohesive

---

23 Wittfogel argued, with a straight face, that there are three distinct types of social competition: the feudal, the economic and the bureaucratic. 'The medieval knight who makes a crucial mistake while competing with his fellows (on the battle field) may forfeit his life, but his property and honour usually remain untouched. The modern businessman who makes a crucial mistake while competing with his fellows (on the market) may lose his property, but his honour is rarely besmirched, and he certainly will not forfeit his life. The official of an agrarian despotism who makes a crucial mistake while competing with his fellows (in a bureaucratic or court intrigue) is likely to lose his honour, his property and his life. Where power is fragmented and balanced, punishment for a crucial mistake is limited. Under conditions of total power, it is total [sic!]' (Wittfogel, 1981: 337). This conception of the contrasting fates of the property and honour of feudal knights and occidental courtiers who made 'crucial mistakes' is testament to the triumph of theory over evidence.

and unchallenged than that which existed under monopoly capitalism (the term coined by the theorists of the Comintern for the multi-centred, competitive political regimes of the West), and was exceeded only by the power of the new ruling class in the USSR. He had no hesitation in drawing prescriptive and analytical conclusions for political development from these comparative researches into hydraulic societies. There were four basic types of pre-industrial society: stratified pastoral societies; slave, helotage and/or free peasant non-feudal societies; feudal societies; and hydraulic societies. The last was the most prevalent in the pre-industrial world, surpassing all other stratified agrarian societies in duration, extent and numbers governed, and was the outstanding case of societal stagnation. The hydraulic type was incapable of transformation except under the impact of external forces.

Here the lineage of the AMP in Wittfogel's thinking was most apparent. It was humanity's good fortune that historical development had been multi-linear: otherwise we would have remained forever imprisoned in the hydraulic condition. Indeed so deeply entrenched were the culture and institutions of hydraulic society that even Western imperialists in Asia had barely dented its structures. India, and especially Indonesia, remained fundamentally hydraulic societies. Wittfogel did not argue explicitly that Communist triumphs in the USSR and China represented an 'Asiatic restoration'; that is, the restoration of the old hydraulic order.[24] He was not, he claimed, a determinist. Communist totalitarianism was something novel in its ideological aspirations and organizational capacity to transform society. However, its path to victory was eased where the political and cultural benefits of multi-centred societies were not present – in hydraulic conditions. Consequently, Asian socialists were counselled against their statist dispositions, interventions against landed private property, and public-sector primacy in development projects. These hangovers from the old hydraulic psychology made them easy prey to Communist ideological penetration. An 'Asiatic restoration' was not on the cards, but Communism was, and promised the 'spectacular manifestation of a retrogressive societal development' (ibid: 406).

A CRITICAL APPRAISAL OF *ORIENTAL DESPOTISM*

Wittfogel's treatise is the most extensive reconstruction of the AMP written in the spirit of productivist historical materialism; and because of both its historiographical range and its ideological import it remains widely admired

24 It is Eastern European dissidents like Bahro (1981) and Shaferevich (1980) who have made this argument explicit.

in liberal circles and amongst dissidents living under Marxist regimes. However, the theoretical defects of this ideologically motivated reconstruction are still not sufficiently appreciated.

The 'Natural Setting' of Hydraulic Society

Consider first Wittfogel's starting point, the building block on which his treatise rests, namely the thesis of 'the natural setting for hydraulic society'. It is fundamentally unsound, factually and logically. The key factual problem is that although the 'natural setting' for the first major agrarian civilizations did involve peoples who employed irrigation techniques, they did not employ 'hydraulic' irrigation, but rather natural or riverine irrigation, or in Wittfogel's own terminology 'hydro-agriculture'. The mechanism for pristine irrigation in the ancient riverine civilizations was simple. The river carried mud and silt which, when in flood, deposited fertile alluvium on the land surrounding its banks. This process allowed crop yields to be higher than those produced under plain rain-watered land. However, the employment of this 'natural' irrigation mechanism required no hydraulic infrastructure whether of construction works or of centralized and bureaucratized state power. The major Indian candidate for inclusion under the description of a primordial hydraulic regime, the Harappan civilization of the Indus valley, seems to have been based upon just such 'spontaneous' hydro-agriculture.[25]

Second, contrary to what the reader of *Oriental Despotism* might expect, the journey from irrigation agriculture to urbanization was neither necessary nor rapid. Archaeologists and historians have discovered many relics of ancient irrigation systems without material evidence pointing to a high degree of social complexity – that is, indicators of urban or state development. One surveyor of the literature on archaeological civilizations points out that in Mesopotamia it took almost 2000 years for the settled population to 'advance' from irrigation to urbanization (Mann, 1986: 79). Such a long and variable lag puts grave strain upon the alleged relations between cause and effect suggested by Wittfogel; and since early irrigation was not organized by a centralized imperial state, arguments about the salience of the 'natural setting' are not convincing. A much better argument is to suggest that river-based irrigation agriculture tied certain peoples to particular environments and thus made them easier prey to conquest by a logistically and militarily organized apparatus (Mann, 1984 and 1986).[26] But this combination of an ecological argument with a theory of the role of force in history suggests a causality completely different from that posited by Wittfogel – and, for that matter, Marx and Engels. Centralization, the

25 See chapter 7, pp. 276–86.
26 See appendix 7.1.

concentration of coercion into states, was possible because of 'spontaneous' irrigation agriculture — because of 'hydro-agriculture' rather than 'hydraulic agriculture'. Such imperial states' origins were indeed exploitative, opportunistic and parasitic rather than functional. The peasants' sunk costs in hydro-agriculture obliged them on a cost-benefit calculus to resign themselves to military despotisms.

Third, there is a battery of subsidiary objections to Wittfogel's thesis. The 'natural setting' was spurned in historical conjunctures where one might have expected it to be exploited, and despotism existed in places where there was no natural (or diffused) hydraulic impetus. Investigations of pre-industrial empires and federations have shown that their 'despotic' structures are attributable neither to hydraulic agriculture nor to the diffused impact of a hydraulic neighbour: rather they are all seen as species of aristocratic empires (Kautsky, 1982). The idea that major artificial irrigation works and a centralized despotic state must coexist was also undermined by investigations of the ancient economy of Dahomey (Polanyi, 1966). The Quéme valley in Dahomey was a 'natural setting', in many respects similar to that of the Nile valley, for the evolution of a hydraulic despotism (Parain, 1966). The failure of such a system to emerge refutes any strong thesis about the causal relations between the natural setting and despotism — even when we make due allowance for Wittfogel's disclaimers about the 'non-deterministic' nature of his argument. The causal nexus between artificial irrigation and oriental despotism posited by Wittfogel seems, at best, to have been a spurious correlation based on faulty use of historical data; at worst, the product of the selective use of these data.

Perhaps most telling against Wittfogel's theses about the causal relations in the 'natural setting' is that complex and artificial irrigation systems seem to have survived in functioning order within societies which experienced cycles of centralization and feudalization. For example, the history of pre-industrial Ceylon is not only one of the persistence of irrigation, despite the periodic breakdown of the 'central state', but also one of decentralized organization of the irrigation systems (Leach, 1959). Much the same is true of the societies of medieval south India (Stein, 1975, 1980 and 1985). The Sinhalese case demonstrates, according to Leach, that hydro-agriculture and hydraulic agriculture were equally compatible with a social system which resembled that prevalent in Western European feudalism.

Wittfogel's use of historical evidence on hydraulic agriculture, as well as the logical structure of his arguments, has also been severely appraised. Wittfogel was by profession a Sinologist, but even his Sinological 'hydrology' has been challenged (Eberhard, 1958 and 1965; and Elvin, 1973). This challenge is of great significance because the development of the theses of *Oriental Despotism* occurred through extrapolation from China, through a theoretical reconstruction of the AMP, to much of the rest of the world of agrarian empires. However, throughout China and Chinese history, the political forms of water-control systems varied, as did their organizational formats. These facts are not highlighted in *Oriental Despotism*, even though Wittfogel's earlier work indicated his knowledge of such evidence. Many schemes for water regulation were small, and based locally or on villages. The role of the imperial state in China was greatest in large-scale, entire river-valley schemes, canal networks, and flood-control systems. However, works of the first type, the most reasonable specimens of hydraulic agriculture, were the least centralized and most dependent upon local implementation. Furthermore, *all* the major large-scale water-control systems in Chinese history emerged long after the formation of the imperial-despotic state; that is, Chinese state formation was causally independent of any alleged hydraulic functionalist imperative.

Similar objections apply to the history of the regimes which are *prima facie* uncontroversial confirmations of Wittfogel's hydraulic theses. Ancient Egyptian regimes, apparently the earliest proofs of Wittfogel's theses, are no longer universally regarded as having had their social foundations in hydraulic irrigation. The Nile after all was unstoppable; it could not be agro-despotically 'managed' from some strategic GOSPLAN in the Egyptian capital. The task was not feasible given current technological capacities. Local control and management of flooding and natural irrigation were all that were feasible, and all that were required to establish civilization and a demographic explosion. The new conventional wisdom is that no centralized irrigation bureaucracy existed in Egypt (Butzer, 1976; and Mann, 1986). The Nile was of importance for the emergence of the Egyptian state, but hydraulic irrigation agriculture *à la* Wittfogel was not. Similarly, in Mesopotamia an urban civilization and literacy existed before large-scale irrigation developed. The organization of irrigation was also localized and the despotic state was not found in its early history. Finally, evidence from later regimes in history – ones which should have been favourable sites for the confirmations of Wittfogel's arguments – also runs against him. For example, it has been argued both that it is possible to run even the very complex irrigation system of southern Iraq by means of decentralized tribal leadership, and that the decentralized management of irrigation was more efficient than the centralized controls which have superseded them in modern times (Fernea, 1970). In Iraq, at least, the consequences of state organization of irrigation were dysfunctional for society. This evidence is wholly antithetical to Wittfogel's functionalist premise. The 'natural setting' for hydraulic despotism was based in his imagination.

The 'Hydraulic Economy'

Consider next Wittfogel's description of certain agrarian societies as having had the pre-industrial equivalents of planned or managed economies. The remarkable feature of *Oriental Despotism* is that the reader is nowhere treated to a systematic account, based on primary or secondary sources, of the managerial operations of a centralized, bureaucratically administered hydraulic irrigation system – not even for China. The reader is simply given the impression that such systems existed in abundance in the pre-industrial world. This silence speaks volumes.

Aside from this gaping hole there are four key difficulties, neglected by Wittfogel's admirers, with the thesis of a 'genuine political economy', all of which are compounded by the imprecise jargon, 'reminiscent of Lewis Carroll's Jabberwocky' (Kosambi, 1957a: 1417), in which his arguments are framed. First, agrarian regimes tried, at most, to manage the extraction of a surplus – that is, the collection of some consistent fraction of the agrarian produce, or some consistent taxation of their subjects. To suggest that they tried any societal planning more ambitious than this is anachronistic. There was at most only a limited form of negative planning: the storage of stocks in case of famine – a theme echoed in writings as diverse as the Old Testament and the *Arthashastra* – but even such planning was (inevitably) locally based. Second, as Wittfogel himself admits, the scale of direct state ownership of land in hydraulic regimes was generally a very small fraction of the overall economy. The 'socialized' sector in agrarian civilizations was miniscule by the standards of a contemporary mixed economy.[27] Third, Wittfogel's argument that the technologies of hydraulic society produced, as by-products, all of the major construction achievements of agrarian empires is deficient in archaeological and historical support, as well as being logically questionable. There were many societies, as he admits, which developed major construction technologies outside of core hydraulic areas: the Roman Empire was merely the most conspicuous example. Finally, he provided no logical, engineering, or empirical underpinning for the idea that hydraulic innovations were necessary for the development of the design and constructions of roads, palaces, tombs and fortifications. Not only is the hydraulic economy not presented as the logical consequence of its natural setting, but also the relations between the hydraulic core and all its other alleged institutional consequences are asserted without elaboration or demonstration of the causal mechanisms at work.

A State Stronger than Society?

The notion of 'a state stronger than society', a phrase Wittfogel took from Russian historiography, is also problematic. In the first place there is a conceptual problem. Since Wittfogel understood oriental despotism as the agrarian analogue of totalitarianism, it is difficult to see how he could distinguish 'state' and 'society' in the Orient. A truly despotic state is one

27 By Wittfogel's standards all advanced liberal democracies are specimens of socialism.

in which the rule of law is absent; and where the state owns all the means of production the idea of an autonomous social sphere, 'society', is simply redundant. The state is society and vice versa. The conceptual and empirical separation of state and society is widely regarded as an exclusively occidental idea: at the very least Wittfogel's Orientalist ideology is deviant.

There is also a problem of operationalization. Even if we grant that we can separate state and society in non-occidental agrarian civilizations, and that Wittfogel's theses do imply such a separation, the problem is how to weight the power and resources of an agrarian society as against the despotic state. The mutual interpenetration of persons in both spheres – suggested by Wittfogel's own descriptions – and the incommensurability of many of the variables which necessarily enter into calculations of the powers of state or societal actors obviously make this task extremely difficult. The durability of dynasties, the longevity of monarchs and the frequency of successful revolts against the regime would all have to be systematically compared across feudal and despotic systems.

Since Wittfogel buttressed his assertions by examples and comparisons between multi-centred and despotic societies, it might seem possible to evaluate some of their strictly empirical components. An agrarian civilization in which the state is stronger than society should surely have had at least the following five measurable features:

stability and continuity in its leading dynasties and personnel;
the despot having the lion's share (over 50 per cent) of land ownership;[28]
the consumption of over half the surplus product by the despot's apparatus;
relatively stable territorial boundaries; and
artefacts which display the conspicuous subordination of all to the despot.

However, Wittfogel nowhere systematically organized his data to show how states which were allegedly stronger than their societies could be shown by such operational indicators both to have had such features, and to have had them to an extent consistently greater than did West European feudal systems and Graeco-Roman slave systems – specimens of multi-centred societies where the state apparently was weaker than society. Had Wittfogel performed at least this task there would have been an argument to evaluate; but since he simply presented selected potted narratives of a vast number of countries his 'evidence' is devoid of social scientific merit. And these tasks Wittfogel did not undertake would mark only the beginnings of a serious inquiry; preoccupied with scoring ideological points, he was not concerned with problems of a genuinely comparative and historically in-formed social science. He was content merely to assert that the state is stronger than society in oriental despotisms.

28 This is by analogy with Hayek's argument in *The Road to Serfdom* that freedom ends when the state owns more than half the national means of production (Hayek, 1944).

Momentary reflection and acquaintance with historical evidence in any case lead to the recognition that Wittfogel's portrait of a unitary, centralized and effective imperial regime in agrarian societies is largely mythical. The despotic power of the ancient despot was largely confined to the sphere of his own court, and his capacity to muster an army of greater power than any other potential contestants for his territory (Mann, 1984). Otherwise, his despotic aspirations were effectively constrained by a series of obvious administrative and infrastructural limits. Military logistics provided clear limits to the outer ambits of the implementation capability of a ruler. Agrarian despots could not easily and effectively marshal their resources and wield them to their full extent. In fact, agrarian empires were almost inherently 'dual polities'.[29] The centre, where it existed, contented itself with the management of 'high politics' − the management of extra-imperial relations, the army and the farming out of tribute collection − whereas the local polities were left in charge of 'low politics' − the implementation of tax-collection, law and order, cultural and religious administration and, if and where it existed, hydraulic agriculture! This dual polity structure, with restricted but none the less autonomous urban and/or village administrations at the base of every empire, explains why, upon the collapse of imperial infrastructures, cultural and productive stability was relatively easily achieved in agrarian societies. The 'secret' of Marx's allegation of Asiatic unchangeableness, in so far as it has any truth, is found in these dual political structures, rather than in the absence of private property in land or the alleged 'unity of manufacture and agriculture'.

Total, Malevolent and Terrorist Power?

The foregoing considerations have already cast doubt upon the alleged total power of the despot. It is possible to go much further. Agrarian emperors were disposed to proclaim divine lineages to legitimize a claim to absolute rule − but only wishful thinkers like Wittfogel have believed that these claims were both fully implemented and also widely accepted. Mere consideration of the contextual logic in which agrarian emperors found themselves is sufficient to raise scepticism about the extent of their despotic power. First, their technological capacity to penetrate their societies was weak, and further attenuated by the fact that their principal agent of implementation was generally an aristocracy. The development of a 'modern' bureaucracy as the ruler's obedient apparatus was never fully realized in

---

29 This expression, employed to describe the development of the UK territorial system of administration (Bulpitt, 1983), is a judicious way to understand the organization of all major pre-industrial empires.

agrarian empires.[30] Wittfogel was describing and attacking contemporary Communism rather than ancient despotic states. Few ancient emperors knew the wealth of their subjects, and they could rarely extract it without striking bargains — pre-industrial censuses and royal surveillance capacities notwithstanding. The fiscal and census–keeping capacities of Indian and even Chinese empires were not comparable to modern inland revenue agencies.

Second, the ideological power of the despots of agrarian civilizations has been exaggerated. The great 'world religions' of India — for example Hinduism, Jainism, Buddhism — spread and diffused with and without the support of despots. Despots adapted to or tolerated local religions where it was judicious to do so; likewise they generally reinforced the pre-existing penetration and advance of the 'world religion'; only rarely and incautiously did they attempt to compel their subjects to share their beliefs. The religious proclamations of self-styled despots did not resemble in any serious sense the Communist striving to create a 'new man'. Wittfogel also displayed remarkable selectivity in his selection of edicts, texts and religious documents for confirming religious accommodation with despotism in the Orient and the converse in the Occident. As an astute critic pointed out, Wittfogel did not discuss the one indisputably oriental book which praised despots 'provided they did not follow the wrong cult, and which gained tremendous authority as well as circulation in the West — the Old Testament' (Kosambi, 1957a; 1419). Christianity has had a long history of accommodation with despotism — in Byzantium, in Muscovy, in the late Roman Empire — not to mention some contemporary parallels. The association between Catholicism and liberal or pluralist freedoms in chequered to say the least. The association of Protestantism and such freedoms also has pluses and minuses. The partiality of Wittfogel's 'comparative inquiry' into total power is nowhere more apparent than in his sociology of religion.

Third, Wittfogel's suggestions about the sources of the despot's total power have been shown to be false. Hydraulic agriculture was not the source of despotic authority. None the less, even some of his most cogent critics have felt obliged to concede that there are merits to his arguments: 'The sociological mechanism of power usurpation is elegant and plausible' (Mann, 1986: 94). This praise concedes too much to Wittfogel. There is nothing 'elegant' about Wittfogel's theory of 'power usurpation'. He operated with a zero-sum conception of power: whatever power the despot had society lacked to the same degree. The despot's power was also invariably malevolent rather than benevolent. Yet any theory of power usurpation

---

30 The absolutist pretensions of much official Muslim political theory seem to provide some support to Wittfogel. However, Islamic rulers were generally total in aspiration rather than in fact. The scope of their power was limited by the combination of what Gellner describes as 'the divine legislature and ... tribal autonomy' (Gellner 1981: 82–3).

which is 'plausible and elegant' requires a non-zero-sum conception of power. The idea should have been that the despot may have been exploitative but that his society benefited to some degree from his domination − albeit to a lesser extent than the despot. In short, even if Wittfogel's premises had been borne out by the historical data, his theory of power usurpation was not coherently articulated. A more elegant theory of Asiatic despotisms would have stressed an alternative account of power and exploitation: emperors enjoyed some legitimacy until they raised the degree of exploitation to levels beyond which, for certain strategically placed groups, the costs of despotism exceeded the benefits. Beyond this point their regimes were wide open to civil strife and/or invasion from the nomadic peripheries.

Finally, Wittfogel's application of elements of the concept of totalitarianism to agrarian civilizations was wildly misplaced. Despots were not enthused by a single chiliastic ideology and did not often have the capacity to pulverize all local beliefs − and where they did it was against their interests. They presided not over a monopolistic political party suffused with convictions about transforming society, but rather over nobles and/or proto-bureaucrats interested in a share of fiscal rewards. Whatever terror they practised was generally in external warfare, within their own family, within the imperial apparatus and against peasants who resisted taxes. But these people were constant targets of all the rulers of all agrarian civilizations − including feudal monarchs. Despots' pretensions to monopolize the media were everywhere challenged by religious doctrines; and in any case there were no modern mass communications technologies with which to bewitch the masses. The despot's monopoly of weapons was constantly challenged by military and provincial revolts − usually fostered by the ambitions of members of his/her family. There was no centrally planned economy; often there was not even a centrally planned and coordinated fiscal apparatus. Finally, in many cases, the despotic regime was no longer territorially expansionist or in complete control of the judicial systems within its ambit. The absence of these features in so-called oriental despotisms makes the totalitarian analogy multiply inappropriate, because these are the features required in the most famous definition of totalitarianism (Friedrich and Brzezinski, 1965). Despite Wittfogel's success in persuading other post-Marxists of the presence of totalitarian elements in pre-industrial societies, notably Barrington Moore (1958b: 30−88), his contentions were anachronistic and depended upon the very selective use of historical materials.

Core, Marginal and Sub-marginal Manoeuvres

Consider next the limits and rationale of the typology of hydraulic societies. Wittfogel's natural-setting argument only ever applied plausibly to the four great river-valley civilizations of Egypt, Mesopotamia, China and the Indus valley. The extension of his hydraulic model to all large-scale empires in the ancient world, through the *ad hoc* acceptance of diffusion and the elaboration of a typology of hydraulic societies, considerably weakens his empirical persuasiveness.

First, Wittfogel's notion of diffusion, as he states it, undermines the strong version of the natural-setting argument. The admission that despotic forms need not have a hydraulic base in agrarian societies opens up the possibility that the relationship between hydraulic agriculture and despotism is a spurious correlation. If despotism could be diffused from hydraulic centres to non-hydraulic centres, what prevented it from diffusing from non-hydraulic centres to non-hydraulic centres, or, more damagingly, from non-hydraulic centres to hydraulic centres? Indeed Wittfogel's diffusionist arguments became almost comic: we learn that the Domesday Book of Norman England was a by-product of oriental influence — diffused through the Norman regime in Sicily which had been infected with the hydraulic bacillus passed from the Arabs and Byzantines. There are also considerable difficulties in operationalizing the differences between core, sub-core and marginal hydraulic societies. There were many ancient empires with so much internal regional variation within their frontiers that they could be classified under each of the three headings. Difficult questions must arise in operationalizing Wittfogel's typology, such as whether the Roman Empire became hydraulic when it was extended to Egypt. Finally, the 'sub-marginal' hydraulic societies are very obviously a residual category to sweep up regimes which were neither oriental despotisms nor occidental feudalisms. Their residual status is clearly ideological: since these non-core hydraulic regimes did not, in Wittfogel's estimation, contribute to occidental liberties it was important to tar them with the hydraulic brush. In this way the hydraulic mechanism could more plausibly be presented as the major obstacle to historical progress. This *ad hoc* classification of all regimes which did not contribute to the 'occidental miracle' as attenuated specimens of hydraulic despotisms is a clear example of what philosophers of science describe as an effort to 'save the phenomenon'.

Proprietary and Class Complexity in Hydraulic Society

Wittfogel's discussion of proprietary complexity is also unsuccessful on several counts. First, the scale of monarchical ownership of the land, as opposed to the taxation rights derived from doctrines equivalent to those derived under the power of 'eminent domain', was not as dramatic, even on Wittfogel's own evidence, as his rhetoric suggests. Therefore the difference between occidental monarchies and oriental despotisms, on this criterion, was at most one of degree rather than of kind. Second, Wittfogel's distinction between 'strong' and 'weak' property rights is almost entirely arbitrary, save on one criterion: regimes are classified under one heading or another to fit the requirements of the thesis that oriental despotisms were stagnant and occidental regimes dynamic. Third, Wittfogel paid no serious attention to the bewilderingly complex patterns of dependence in all agrarian civilizations, a fact which is especially serious in the case of Indian history, as it led him to subsume the phenomena of caste as sub-sets of classes − much as Marxists mistakenly have been inclined to do.

Wittfogel's theory of the class structure of oriental despotism was also remarkably inconsistent. He was not wrong to argue that the notion of a state officialdom indistinguishable from the corporately organized exploiter class caused an embarrassment to Marxists. However, he did not consistently follow through his own theoretical breakthrough, and thereby produced the ideological argument that class struggle was the luxury of the Occident. Wittfogel's inconsistency in this respect has not been noticed before. If state officials are to constitute a class in a theory of stratification or exploitation then it follows that those they dominate/exploit through fiscal appropriations must also be classifiable as subordinated/exploited classes. Amongst other strata, the exploited peasantry of the AMP must be regarded as an exploited class − irrespective of their class consciousness. It must therefore follow axiomatically, on the basis of Wittfogel's own sociology, that conflicts over fiscal extractions are class struggles, especially in 'hydraulic' societies. Conflicts over taxation must be considered as symptomatic of a fused class/state cleavage. Fiscal conflicts, especially between imperial officials and the peasantry, were in fact endemic in agrarian empires − in occidental despotic empires like the Roman (de Ste Croix, 1981), in oriental empires like the Chinese (Eberhard, 1965) and in the Mughal empire (Habib, 1963; and W. Smith, 1946). Therefore, Wittfogel's contention that class conflict was the privilege of the Occident was inconsistent with his own class theory. It was empirically inconsistent because state-defined classes in fact struggled over the scale and nature of taxation in pre-industrial empires; and it was theoretically inconsistent because the *ad hoc* ideological idea that class struggle exists only in societies in which there is private property destroys Wittfogel's key assumption that hydraulic societies were state-class structured societies. Since he ignored the implications of his own analysis of the social structure of oriental despotisms, it was inconsistent of him to accuse Marxists of neglecting class-domination and class-struggle in state-centred societies.

CONCLUSION

There are therefore fundamental theoretical flaws in the core arguments of *Oriental Despotism*. Its natural setting is neither logical nor supported by historical evidence. The argument that some pre-industrial societies had planned economies is equally flawed. The idea of a 'state which is stronger than society' is more difficult than Wittfogel's slogan suggests. Moreover, his portrait of the powers of agrarian despots, and the sources of their powers, was constructed in an anachronistic and one-sided manner, and depended upon a simplistic zero-sum conception of power. The typology of hydraulic regimes was entirely prompted by the urge to save his central arguments about the causes of occidental uniqueness. It also classified under the same heading regimes which differed in their degree of development of the productive forces – an assumption which was *prima facie* at odds with the thesis of oriental stagnation. Finally, his sketch of an alternative sociology of agrarian civilizations was inconsistent in its treatment of class, and too gross in its appreciation of the complex patterns of dependence which existed in these societies. These defects are brought into even sharper relief by my inspection in the next chapter of Wittfogel's arguments about India, a country which he thought – as Marx had done – exemplified the fateful consequences of the Asiatic mode of production. The empirical deficiencies of Wittfogel's Indian historical knowledge should remove any remaining doubts about the social scientific merits of *Oriental Despotism*. Conceived as a treatise against Marxism, its weaknesses only succeed, unintentionally, in demonstrating the considerable logical and empirical deficiencies in the idea of the AMP – at least as that concept is understood within the framework of productivist historical materialism. As for *Oriental Despotism's* ideological content, one succinct summary has not been bettered: 'If one wants to write about Communism and Stalin, the best way to do it is not necessarily through writing about Oriental despotism. Neither Oriental despotism nor modern Communism get their due in this way' (Eisenstadt, 1957–8; 446). *Oriental Despotism* was the consequence of hydrophobia and hydrocephalus in a Cold War warrior.

7

The Asiatic Mode of Production and Indian History

Historical research over the last hundred years or so, including the recent work of Marxist scholars, has shown that Marx's basic notions regarding Indian society were essentially incorrect.

B. Chandra, 'Karl Marx, his Theories of Asian Societies and Colonial Rule'

[T]he concept of the Asiatic mode, as [with] many of Marx's formulations, is based upon a profound perception which ought not to be lost, or consigned to the dustbin of historiography.

Stein, 'Politics, Peasants and the Deconstruction of Feudalism in Medieval India'

This chapter has two main purposes: first, to examine the merits of Marx's theory of Indian history, by the standards of the sources available to him in his day, and second, to evaluate the merits of Marx's theory of the AMP, and Wittfogel's theory of oriental despotism, by the standards of contemporary Indian historiography. The arguments advanced in this chapter are supported in three appendices. An alternative mode of understanding Hindu despotisms is sketched (appendix 7.1). The treatment of the AMP by Indian and Soviet Marxist historians of India is surveyed (appendix 7.2). Finally, the question of whether feudalism existed in Indian history is addressed (appendix 7.3).

JUDGING MARX'S THEORY OF INDIAN HISTORY BY HIS CONTEMPORARY SOURCES

Some of the major defects of Marx's analysis of Asian societies have already been highlighted. In the Indian context, discussion typically centres on the normative and analytical adequacy of Marx's view of imperialism as a progressive force, rather than upon the validity of Marx's understanding of pre-colonial India. The former issue is a subject of major debate in Indian history (Charlesworth, 1982). When the latter issue is discussed it is primarily in the light of the former debate.

It is customary to attribute Marx's errors in his study of India to such factors as his preoccupation with capitalist rather than pre-capitalist societies; the Eurocentric prejudices of his sources; his own unconscious Eurocentrism; and the exigencies of journalism (Purohit, 1979).[1] However, thanks to the critical exposés of some Indian Marxist historians, the empirical defects of Marx's writings on India, *even* given his own source materials, are now better known (Gunawardana, 1976; Habib, 1983; and S. Naqvi, 1973). These facts cast serious doubts upon Marx's scholarly integrity, although his Indian Marxist critics are reluctant to draw this conclusion.

The main sources of Marx's interpretation of India (and therefore of the AMP) in the early 1850s were travellers' tales (notably those of Bernier), official British parliamentary reports (especially the famous *Fifth Report* of 1812) and the historical works of British administrators (like Wilks and Campbell). Later, in the 1870s, Marx read the historical works of Elphinstone and Sewell. His use of these sources was demonstrably selective and lacking in judgement, suggesting that he shamelessly shaped materials to fit his preconceived ideas. Take first Marx's reliance on travellers' tales, especially Bernier's account of the social relations of the Mughal empire. He cited Bernier in support of the thesis that the Great Mughal had owned all the land in the empire. However, careful inspection of Bernier's text suggests that any reader drilled in the critical skills of the Enlightenment would have been sceptical of the French doctor's generalization (S. Naqvi, 1973: 48–57). First, the text was replete with allusions to the many rajas who existed within the empire and outside its borders. They are referred to as autonomous owners of land and as independent possessors of military capacity. The Great Mughal by no means enjoyed a monopoly of the means of legitimate violence, a strange 'strategic position' for an oriental despot. The presence of these tributary and quasi-feudal rajas seriously disturbs Bernier's interpretation of the empire's exploitative ruling class as composed entirely of a service nobility, the *mansabdars*. On Bernier's own evidence, beneath the imperial house and its alleged prototypical bureaucracy of *mansabdars* there was evidently a secondary stratum of hereditary local exploiters and landowners.[2] Second, the internal evidence of Bernier's text

1 Purohit's curious paper is a good example of an ultra-nationalist reaction to the idea of the AMP. He contends that Indian feudalism was immensely more advanced than that of England, that it was Europe's very backwardness which propelled it towards capitalism, and that Asia and India had experienced far more historical change than Europe: 'The historical furrow has been ploughed deep in India and Asia, it has merely scratched the surface of Europe' (Purohit, 1979: 9).

2 Moreover, Bernier's account was inevitably coloured by his residence in Delhi, the capital of the empire in which he spent the bulk of his time. Here he must have been primarily exposed to sources which expressed the aspirations of the regime, namely its officials at the centre. As Subrahmanyam remarks generally of the historiography of Indian states: 'It is worth remarking that when the sources used are administrative manuals, official diaries and manuals, the historiography is dominated by images of a powerful state, while when the sources used are inscriptions, and are generated by local institutions, the image is of diffused control' (Subrahmanyam, 1986: 360).

refutes the doctor's graphic suggestion that the monarch invariably appropriated the property of all those who died in his service. Not only does he give no example of this occurrence, but also the solitary story he cites that is relevant to the question suggests that Islamic law, as practised at the court, did not permit the emperor arbitrarily to interfere with the inheritance rights of his subjects.

The evidence of Bernier's text is also at odds with Marx's and Wittfogel's idea that the alleged centralized despotism of the Mughals was caused by (or associated with) the imperatives of hydraulic agriculture in arid regions. Bernier's travelogue described the Indian monsoons, the humid fertility of Bengal, the lack of agriculture in arid regions and entirely locally organized methods of irrigation (ditches and channels). Marx's sources for his belief that the state played a key role in hydraulic agriculture in India thus remain obscure, and from wherever they were derived they directly contradicted Bernier's eyewitness account, which at least in this respect was free of contradiction. There is also nothing in Bernier about village communities.[3]

Consider another element of the AMP: its sketch of parasitic administrative cities, or mobile armies on the march, entirely dependent upon the revenues appropriated by the despot. Here Marx drew uncritically upon Bernier but also upon Richard Jones – who was in turn indebted to Bernier. Once more, careful inspection of Bernier's text raises multiple doubts (S. Naqvi, 1973: 52–7). Bernier's descriptions of Delhi and Agra suggested that these populous and prosperous cities were immense and physically stable entities, and his estimates of the size of the imperial army are simply incompatible with the notion that the Indian city was just 'the army plus retainers'. Significantly, he did not suggest that the movement of the capital of the empire from Agra to Delhi had any serious repercussions upon the prosperity of the former. Furthermore, the evidence of other European travellers' tales, which Marx also consulted, painted portraits of Asiatic cities which suggested that in their heyday they were sites of a serious commercial capitalism, complete with a developed international trade network and financial system based on banking, money-lending and bills of exchange. In Mughal Hindustan, travellers reported that many cities produced cotton cloth in large quantities and at low prices.[4] Marx ignored the evidence, available in his time, which suggested that India's numerous and large ports and cities were prized as centres on long-distance maritime and

---

3 This fact supports the contrast developed in chapter 2: the idea of oriental despotism focused on relations between the monarchy and the aristocracy, whereas the idea of the AMP focuses on relations between villages and the imperial apparatus.

4 '[T]here is no means of finding out how cities like Dacca, which, as Marx himself noted later, had been a large centre of textile production before its decline began under the pressure of competition from English textiles, fit into his scheme of "parasitic cities"' (Gunawardana, 1976: 380).

land-based trade routes. Indeed the best current survey of the ancient and medieval economic history of the Indian Ocean describes Indian and Chinese cities as both commercial and administrative sites, and testifies to 'the strength of commercial capitalism in Asia' (Chaudhuri, 1985: 228).

Marx's use of his British administrative sources also demonstrated selective and uncritical abuses in induction, and suggest that he relied upon secondary stereotypes rather than careful consideration of the originals.[5] The parliamentary Fifth Report of 1812 contained many other collectors' notes which sketched Indian village life in a way which was incompatible with the interpretation of the village as either a species of primitive communism or an integral element of the AMP.[6] Some reports, notably that of the Principal Collector of Canara (31 May 1800) on the large Vijayanagar Empire, spoke freely of the unrestricted sale of land, hereditary property rights and the renting of land. Moreover, although Marx correctly cited Campbell for the contrast between democratic and despotic villages, he failed to note key passages in Campbell's text at odds with Marx's theses about communal ownership of the land and autarkic village communities, engaged in production for use and exchange in kind. Campbell described village headmen as 'landowners', noted the existence of hired agricultural labourers, and discussed monetary relations within the village. These perspectives are, to say the least, at odds with the idea of 'the unity of crafts and agriculture'.[7] In this instance, Marx's concern to attack Carey's enthusi-

5 Naqvi points out that Marx never directly quotes the passage from the *Fifth Report*, and seems to have derived it second-hand from Wilks and Campbell (S. Naqvi, 1973: 57–8). Marx does quote the pertinent passage in his letter to Engels of 14 June 1853 (Marx and Engels, 1959: 313–15) but does not indicate whether he read the report directly. However, Naqvi is right that the report is not cited in the bibliographical notes in *Capital*, Volume I, which does suggest that Marx read it second-hand. It was, and is, available in the British Museum.

6 Much later Marx was to read, in Kovalevsky's studies of *Communal Landholding*, more inconsistent evidence – accounts of private property *within* the village. The fact that the evidence was available to him earlier further confirms that Kovalevsky's book was not, as suggested by Nikiforov (1975), the 'turning point' in Marx's idea of the AMP.

7 Campbell also described landed property as existing during the disintegration of the Mughal empire. Elphinstone's *History of India*, published in 1841, suggested the existence of submerged property rights, though collectively held, but his story was drowned out by the popularity of Mill's *History of India* (Gunawardana, 1976: 369–70). However, Marx may not have read Elphinstone until the 1870s. Gunawardana omits to note that Elphinstone was sceptical of the thesis that the king was the absolute owner of all the land: 'the conclusive argument is, that the king's share being limited . . . to one-sixth, or at most one-fourth, there must have been another proprietor for the remaining five-sixths or three-fourths, who must obviously have had the greatest interest of the two in the whole property shared' (Elphinstone, 1889: 23). Moreover, although Elphinstone did faithfully reproduce the stereotypes of Indian village life (ibid.: 68–9) – quoting extensively from Sir Charles Metcalfe's *Report of the Select Committee of the House of Commons* (1832, iii: 331) – he also presented evidence of private property rights in various regions of India (Elphinstone, 1889: 71). My evidence is based on the seventh edition of Elphinstone's book but the relevant sections were not revised from the editions available in Marx's lifetime.

asm for the unity of crafts and agriculture seems to have been behind his selective and partial use of his sources.[8]

Marx's later writings and readings produced similar empirical inconsistencies, especially for any interpretation of pre-colonial India as a specimen of the AMP. For example, Marx's sources for his journalism of the mid-1850s alerted him to the existence of a class of *zamindars* intermediate between the villagers and the imperial apparatus (Marx and Engels, 1959: 191–4). However, these observations, which were entirely correct, were ignored in his discussion of the tributary state in *Capital*, Volume III. At the very least the class of *zamindars* suggested partial feudalization within the Mughal regime. Much the same empirical inconsistency can be suggested in relation to Marx's recognition that Islamic conquest might have had something to do with alleged state property in land (that is, with the attempted imposition of a centralized land-tax). He failed to integrate this important fact with his subsequent suggestion that Indian history had displayed no change. There are also many inconsistencies in his writings over the existence and scale of monetary exchange in pre-colonial India. It is not clear whether he thought monetary exchanges were confined to relations between the monarchs and merchants and/or between villagers and tax officials, or whether he thought they were present in the village itself. All these perspectives are suggested at various places and at various times, but no attempt to make them contextually specific can make Marx immune to the suggestion of inconsistency. Furthermore, throughout the gamut of Marx's writings on India and Asia he cites second-hand evidence of different forms of land tenure in Asia: communal property or survivals of primitive communism; private agrarian property (south of the Krishna river in areas not under Muslim rule); feudal property (in areas like Oudh); and developed feudal property (in Japan). This variation seems some way away from Marx's axiom that royal property in the soil is 'the key to the whole of the East' (Gunawardana, 1976: 376–7).

Therefore one can only judge harshly Marx's interpretation of Indian

---

8 Naqvi's careful destruction of Marx's interpretation of his sources is inadequate in only one respect. He is too generous to Marx: 'That Marx and Engels could not come to a correct view of Indian social history was perhaps unavoidable, in the circumstances under which they lived and functioned, specially due to the stresses and pressures on their time and energy' (S. Naqvi, 1973: 66). However, the thrust of his analysis of Marx's sources suggests that, at best, Marx was an incompetent and uncritical reader of primary evidence on India and, at worst, that he deliberately selected that which he wanted and ignored any inconvenient evidence. Gunawardana is equally over-generous: 'To reduce his views to a rigid formulation more like an echo of the popular refrain from Kipling's "Ballad of the East and West" would be to do Marx an injustice and to ignore the significant contribution he made to deepen the understanding of Asian society' (Gunawardana, 1976: 388). Kindness to Marx takes the form of giving Marx credit when he reports accurate statements and evidence, letting him off lightly when he is wrong and misleading, and discounting the importance of his use of evidence to build the stereotype of the AMP.

historiography, especially in his 1853 journalism and in the *Grundrisse*. His errors went beyond the forgivable offences of simplification and summarization required in social scientific model-building. His use of his sources was selective; he ignored contrary evidence in his source materials; and his use of Indian social features as illustrations of key themes showed little sensitivity to the historical context (which is less surprising if he was operating with the Hegelian premise that India had no history). Finally, throughout his writings he cited with approval, or without comment, historical interpretations of India and Asia which were mutually inconsistent.[9] These charges are not the conventional historian's complaints about the uniqueness of every *explanandum* and the rejection of causal in favour of idiographic explanations. They are more damaging. They call into question Marx's integrity as a social scientist.

JUDGING THE ASIATIC MODE OF PRODUCTION BY CONTEMPORARY HISTORIOGRAPHY

It is integral to scientific method that any concept is independent from its architect or the mode of its genesis. Just because Marx's historical knowledge was poor does not, by itself, establish the inappropriateness of the idea of the AMP to some region or time in Indian history. The empirical merits of the AMP can only be judged on the basis of critical scholarly standards better than those Marx displayed. However, before I proceed with this task, it is important to note some of the limitations faced by the reader of Indian history.

Key Ideological and Empirical Problems in Indian History

Since its inception the study of Indian history has been pervaded by two dominant ideological prejudices: Orientalism (or cultural imperialism), and its obverse, Indian nationalism (Habib, 1966; and Thapar, 1968 and 1982). European Orientalists and Indologists began the study of ancient Indian history in the late eighteenth century, largely through linguistic and philological research. Some of the best known did not even visit India, and not surprisingly their work displayed predictable symptoms: uncritical reproduction of brahmin sources and biases,[10] and eulogies for India's allegedly harmonious villages. The early Orientalists' study of Vedic India was also

9 Here I have deliberately neglected the *Ethnological Notebooks*, as their partial and unfinished character cannot fairly be used to evaluate Marx's considered views.

10 Elphinstone, whom Marx read in the 1870s, exemplifies this particular failing. He took *Manu*, an ancient-Indian lawbook, to be a literal description of Hindu society (Elphinstone, 1889: chapter 1).

driven by the search for a common Indo-European past, which frequently took the form of projecting back into the past the picture of some historical Eden. By contrast, the British historiographical tradition, exemplified by Vincent Smith, regularly contrasted ancient India with classical Greece, and tended to assume that whatever was glorious in India could be traced back to the diffusion of Greek culture. British administrative historiography was Orientalist in the ideological sense of that term, and took the form of dynastic histories which concentrated upon the great emperors — Ashoka, Chandragupta II and Akbar — mainly because these figures could be understood as the predecessors of the British Raj. The Orientalist assumptions in Hegel's and Marx's work, and those of imperialist administrators, have already been appraised in previous discussion (pp. 24–7, 69–71 and 262–7). But Hegel and Marx were typical rather than perverse amongst Europeans of the late and post-Enlightenment period. What they shared, apart from a trusting faith in generalizations from travellers' tales, was a failure to appreciate that the India portrayed in the translations of key texts, such as the *Dharmashastras, Manu* and the *Arthashastra*, might have differed dramatically from the historical India. The ideological sketches of India portrayed in the writings of the brahmins and royal counsellors often represented nothing more than aspirations of priestly or warrior elites, rather than realities.

Orientalist assumptions of a stagnant, unchanging and invariably despotic East still enter historical writing on India.[11] However, such biases are now less prominent than their converse — the biases of Indian nationalist history. Nationalists are primarily preoccupied with demonstrating the existence of a primordial golden age of Indian civilization, and secondarily concerned to show that the Muslims (and/or the British) destroyed some of the best features of this superior civilization (Sharma, 1966a; and Thapar, 1968 and 1982). Nationalist historians like Jayaswal, Mookerji and Raichaudhuri writing in the 1920s rejected the relevance of the theory of oriental despotism to India, but replaced it with inventions of their own. Their concern to glorify the Indian past was expressed in admiration of Indian spiritualism as against occidental materialism; a misplaced stress on the antiquity of the political unity of the subcontinent; a propensity to understand the rise of the Mauryan empire as confirmation of the birth of an all-Indian consciousness; exaggerated attacks on the theory of Greek cultural diffusion; support for the idea of the distinctiveness and separateness of Indian civilization; praise for the Hindu period of Indian history (by

---

11 See pp. 24–7. Even Fernand Braudel falls victim to this trait: 'In the thousand years or so before the fifteenth century, Far Eastern history is simply a monotonous repetition of the same events; one port would rise to prominence on the shore of the Red Sea, only to be replaced in time by one of its identical neighbours' (Braudel, 1984: 485).

contrast with the Muslim period); and (perhaps the most misleading) generalizations from evidence about the history of the Gangetic region to the whole of India. The reader of Indian history must carefully avoid the resulting inventions and weaknesses: in particular the nationalists' portraits of India's pristine village 'communities' and the medieval states of south India.

There is a third, and more tragically deep-rooted, ideological growth which affects Indian historiography: 'communalism', which glorifies or denigrates either Hindu or Muslim civilization (Thapar, 1975). The sources of these prejudices lie in the religious and nationalist conflicts which preceded and succeeded the bloody partition of the subcontinent. Each side attributes the perceived failures in Indian development to the flaws in the other side's culture. Indian Marxists have generally escaped these three ideological obstacles to the study of Indian history: Orientalism, nationalism and communalism. In this respect at least their contributions to the study of Indian history will be enduring.

There are also more objective and permanent obstacles to scientific research in Indian history. First, the primary source materials for pre-Muslim Indian history are profoundly limited. The writing of history – at least as developed by the Greeks – was not part of Vedic culture, and historians of pre-Muslim India have great difficulty in establishing reliable chronologies from the mixture of religious myths, law books, chronicles and epigraphic sources with which they are obliged to work. Second, although chronology and basic historical data improve considerably in the Muslim period, they are limited by the courtly concerns of the Islamic chroniclers, who paid little attention to village and Hindu India. The reconstruction of Muslim agrarian and revenue systems has involved immense labour. Third, the early European sources show predictable biases: they reflect the concerns of the big companies and imperial administrators. Finally, the educational bias of the early European Orientalists, primarily linguists and students of literature and the arts rather than social or economic historians, hindered the development of modern historical research.

However, this picture has been changed in the twentieth century. The quality and quantity of research by Indian historians in the subcontinent's mutliple languages, past and present, have gone a considerable way towards surmounting some of the objective and subjective obstacles to understanding the main contours of Indian history. Indian Marxists, notably D.D. Kosambi, I. Habib and R.S. Sharma, have made notable contributions in this area. There have been several major studies of the Mughal empire, medieval India and other regimes in pre-colonial India. The study of the subcontinent on a regional basis is also well established. There is now so much good material that it is impossible for one person to survey it adequately in a work of this kind. However, despite these improvements, it remains the case that given the limitations of the primary sources, especially in the Hindu era, Indian history will always remain more shrouded in uncertainty than that of China or Western Europe.

These constraints must be borne in mind when considering the validity of the AMP, or oriental despotism, as applied to Indian history. My method will be to follow three forms of presentation – each dependent upon secondary sources. First, I evaluate the merits of Wittfogel's command of Indian history (pp. 270–5). Second, I run through the major social formations which have been considered as specimens of the AMP by Marxists (and Wittfogel). I use materials from historians of India to highlight the key difficulties with these categorizations (pp. 275–99). In each case the best arguments are examined for classifying a regime as a social formation dominated by the AMP – whether put forward by Marxists or by Wittfogel. Contrary arguments and evidence are then considered. Third, the validity of three key features of the AMP, namely the village community (pp. 299–302), the despotic state apparatus (pp. 303–5), and limited urban and commercial development (pp. 305–6), are separately treated against the evidence of Indian history.

Was India a Natural Setting for a Hydraulic Society and were Indian Empires Natural Hydraulic Despotisms?

Wittfogel could claim no specialized knowledge about India comparable to his Sinological expertise. However, regular passages, asides and illustrations from Indian history are present in *Oriental Despotism*. They are dramatically ill-informed and serve only to undermine any remaining confidence one might have in Wittfogel's historical investigations. The shakiness of Wittfogel's hydraulic materialism is confirmed by his arguments that Indian empires were specimens of hydraulic despotisms.[12]

He described the great northern plain as the principal centre of hydraulic agriculture in India (Wittfogel, 1981: 170). The facts are otherwise (Habib, 1962: 57–9).[13] Hydraulic agriculture was never the dominant form of agricultural cultivation in any region of India. The eastern flank of the northern plains – parts of Bengal and Bihar – was irrigated chiefly through rainfall or inundations. In the central zones – Uttar Pradesh and

---

12 The poverty of his basic data collection to support the thesis of the 'natural setting' was very evident in his treatment of Indian physical and historical geography. For example, he asserted that the annual inundations in Egypt and India, amongst other countries, were caused by the summer sun melting part of the accumulated snow in the remote mountains (Wittfogel, 1981: 24), a betrayal of ignorance of school-level geography. He hardly considered the monsoon worth mentioning as a salient feature of Indian agrarian production.
13 I rely on Habib's stringent and impressive critique at several junctures below.

Eastern Punjab — rainfall was supplemented mostly by individually constructed wells and naturally formed 'tanks', rather than by artificially constructed tanks, although some of these existed in Eastern Punjab. In the Indus basin — the western flank of the 'great northern plain' — ground irrigation did indeed replace rainfall, but before the nineteenth century this irrigation was overwhelmingly natural and not artificial, 'hydro-agricultural' rather than 'hydraulic agriculture'. Wittfogel was oblivious to his own distinction in the Indian context, and casually classified Sindh as a specimen of hydraulic agriculture although the predominant form of agriculture in Sindh was *bosi*; that is, spring crops raised on land naturally flooded by the seasonal rise of the Indus. Irrigation agriculture in India, where it was important in Indian history, was natural rather than artificial, and was almost wholly administratively decentralized. There was no demand for the despotic mobilization of corvée labour for hydraulic task-management on the scale required by Wittfogel's theses. The 'hydraulic state' in India was, if it ever existed, an imperialist invention of the British in India.

It is possible to be kinder to Wittfogel than he was to the facts of Indian history. Thus, for example, one might point out that major canal constructions were built in Mughal India in the northern plains. However, the percentage of land area irrigated by these canals cannot warrant the description of the region as a hydraulic core. Moreover, he neglected the existence of hydraulic constructions elsewhere in India — in central India, the Deccan and southern India — where archaeological and epigraphic materials prove the relative importance of such enterprises. However, these regions, especially in peninsular India, are an embarrassment for Wittfogel's theses precisely because they cannot be portrayed as having had sustained centralized and despotic political histories. Their political histories, in so far as they can be reconstructed, are overwhelming tales of internecine feudal and segmental tribal conflicts (Antonova, Bongard-Levin and Kotovsky, 1979, 1: 184—201; V. Smith, 1981: 213—19; and Thapar, 1966: 167—220 and 241—65). Moreover, irrigation in south India was locally managed at the level of the *nadu* (Stein, 1980):

> In most parts of south India . . . 'mastery of the means and processes of production' was vested in local peasant communities under whose chiefs there was sustained and successful development of irrigation potentials in the southern peninsula . . . both major and minor works and the provision for their maintenance were set up long before [the British], and not by centralized states, but by local communities of peasants. (Stein, 1985: 85)

Wittfogel's operationalization of a hydraulic agriculture region required either that the hydraulically controlled land be greater than 50 per cent of all arable land, or that the produce of hydraulically cultivated land exceed that of all other arable land.[14] However, Wittfogel was not disturbed by any serious problems of statistical operationalization. Had he been he might have revised his portrait of India: 'For India even criteria ten times less strict would still have failed to reveal any 'core' of hydraulic land. For all practical purposes hydraulic enterprises were as significant in the economy of pre-British India as they were in ... Ancient Greece and Rome' (Habib, 1962: 59).

The deficiencies in Wittfogel's physical geography and his failure to apply his own criteria of operationalization were matched by serious flaws in his historical geography. His theory required that state power should arise in arid and semi-arid areas. To support this thesis he claimed that the arid, semi-arid and humid regions of the north became historically prominent before 'the excessively humid area of Bengal' (1981: 21). This assertion betrays an *ad hoc* and unconvincing expansion of the core hypothesis. A humid region was dragged into the arid and semi-arid category because of the contiguous existence of an excessively humid region! The same reasoning presumably must allow an excessively humid region into the category of 'arid' if there exists a contiguous hypertropical permanent rain forest. Second, even if one accepted the premise that the first Indian civilization, the Harappan-Mohenjo-darro civilization of the Indus valley, did arise in the semi-arid region, Wittfogel's causal explanation of this 'fact' was false. The arid and semi-arid regions were sites for the development of alluvial agriculture because, at least before the iron age, forestation made the humid regions unsuitable for extensive agriculture. Moreover, these riverine areas were settled without major artefacts of hydraulic enterprise. The archaeological excavations of the Harappan civilization have not unearthed evidence that hydraulic, as opposed to hydro-agricultural, enterprise was important in the Indus valley (Allchin and Allchin, 1968: 129−44 and 274−95, and Piggott, 1950: 153). The most cautious verdict is that 'it is not certain that irrigation was known, although this is possible' (Basham, 1967: 18). Harappan civilization was remarkable for its urban sewerage system, but though drains may be the foundations of civilization, this was surely not what Wittfogel had in mind as hydraulic technology.

Wittfogel described, without qualifications, *all* of the great Indian empires established between the Aryan conquests and migrations and the British conquest of India as specimens of 'hydraulic' regimes − notably the Magadhan-Mauryan empires, but also the empires of the Guptas, the Delhi sultans and the Mughals. His arguments were erroneous in several

---

14 This criterion, to be reasonable, must measure aggregate outputs rather than comparative productivity in the two sectors. Moreover, as it stands, the former criterion is very loose, since the greater the number of methods of agrarian production the easier it is for hydraulic production to achieve the winning plurality share.

respects (pp. 275–99), but one of the assertions used to support this contention was doubly fallacious (Habib, 1962: 61). He contended that the capitals of the Hindu and Muslim empires were all situated in the hydraulic northern plain. Yet hydraulic agriculture was not in fact more prevalent in the great northern plain than elsewhere, and the capital of both the Mauryan and Guptan empires was Pataliputra (Patna), situated in the region of heavy rainfall!

Wittfogel especially emphasized that the Mauryan empire had a 'grandiose hydraulic economy' (1981: 170). In fact he simply stressed those features of the Mauryan empire which made it an empire – a central administration, a developed communications network and a massive military apparatus. His sole evidence for its hydraulic character relied upon a contentious interpretation of the *Arthashastra* (the most famous, indeed notorious, ancient Indian text on politics and administration). In fact 'Kautilya's'[15] *Arthashastra* listed the types of irrigated land in the empire, but canal-irrigated land and hydraulic technology were not mentioned. The solitary public irrigation function which the monarch is advised to provide in the *Arthashastra* is *setubandha*; that is, the construction of a reservoir made by damming a stream (Kautilya, 1923: 50–1, 278 and 362). Indeed the central economic function encouraged in the *Arthashastra* has nothing to do with hydraulic agriculture: it is the extension of cultivation to wasteland. To promote this project the monarch was advised to allow the use of slave-labour and to grant taxation concessions (ibid: 55, 138ff). Finally, one must distinguish between the rhetorical aspirations of the *Arthashastra* and the actual organizational capacities of the Mauryan Empire. The materials for classifying the Mauryan Empire as a hydraulic despotism existed largely in Wittfogel's imagination.[16] Primary and epigraphic sources suggest that Wittfogel was wrong about the Mauryan Empire. The edicts and inscriptions which Ashoka posted throughout his subcontinental empire boast of the establishment of wells on the roads and 'watering places' – that is, tanks – rather than canals.[17]

Wittfogel's reasoning on the Mauryan Empire was representative of the hydraulic evidence he mustered for other Indian regimes – it was selective and unconvincing. The inadequacies of his portrait of Indian empires as

15 The quotation marks indicate that there is an unresolved debate over the dating and authorship of the *Arthashastra*. I am not competent to evaluate this much discussed question of ancient Indian history – and nothing in this book hinges upon this controversy. Here and throughout this paragraph I am relying upon Habib (1962).

16 The only supporting secondary evidence comes from the Greek geographer Strabo, who presumably relied upon the Seleucid ambassador to the Mauryan Empire, Megasthenes. Strabo made reference to officers who inspected closed canals from which the water was distributed into conduits (Majumdar, 1960: 268). Habib argues that this reference is probably based on a confusion between canals and dammed-up streams. (1962: 62).

17 Evidence about irrigation in northern India in the period after the Mauryan Empire

centralized agro-despotic bureaucracies are further accentuated through any careful examination of the literature on major Indian social formations. Contrary to the impression generated by *Oriental Despotism*, Indian history has not, generally speaking, been a tale of large-scale centralized empires. In fact, before the British conquest there were only six regimes of any duration which might plausibly be described as large-scale and centralized. Five were based largely in northern and western India. The first was that of the prehistoric and pre-Aryan Harappan state, which existed in what is now Pakistan. The second was that of the Magadhan-Mauryan Empire (fifth to third centuries BC), centred in northern and eastern India, but which under Chandragupta Maurya, Bindusara and Ashoka incorporated modern Afghanistan, the Deccan and most of peninsular India.[18] The third, the Gupta monarchy (fourth to fifth centuries AD), was centred in the Ganges, and is accorded the description of the 'golden age' of India — by Indian nationalists and romantics. The fourth and fifth were the empires established by Islamic conquerors, the Delhi Sultanate (thirteenth to fifteenth centuries AD), centred in northern and western India, and the Mughal Empire (sixteenth to eighteenth centuries AD), which at its peak incorporated almost the entire subcontinent and extended into Afghanistan. Finally, in the south of India only the Hindu Empire of Vijayanagara can plausibly, albeit controversially, fit the description of a large-scale and centralized empire, and even then only in its last phase of development.

Therefore *at best* Wittfogel's categorization fits certain regimes in Indian history, and some regions of India rather than others. Wittfogel conveniently ignored all the interludes between these allegedly hydraulic despotisms, and all the regions in which the 'natural setting' arguments did not apply. He skirted over the problems created by the 'republican' communities of Buddhist India of the fifth century BC, which flourished in the places he alleged to be the hydraulic heartlands of Indian civilization. He also wholly

---

confirms this impression. Irrigation, although evident and important in some areas, was a local rather than a state function and the chief hope of the peasants lay in the inundation of their land by the flooded rivers during the rainy season. The evidence in the *Arthashastra* of state intervention in irrigation cess is also weakened by the following observation: '[it] was not considered so important as to warrant the provision of a separate superintendant for it; this work was done by the *sitadhyaksa* or the superintendent of agriculture' (Sharma, 1966a: 99). Sharma's essay, a review of primary, epigraphic and archaeological evidence on irrigation, avoids a summary of the importance of irrigation in agriculture which would enable the reader to have his unambiguous verdict on Wittfogel's assertions on the Mauryan Empire. In conversation at LSE in 1987 Professor Sharma told me that the primary evidence is too flimsy to permit a clear evaluation of the role of irrigation — but he is sceptical of Wittfogel's arguments.

18 I neglect the Saka-Kusana period (first century BC to second century AD), when Scythians and Kusanans established large empires in northern India, because so little is known about them — apart from the importance of Buddhism in the Kusanan Empire. I also neglect the 'empire' of Harsha Vardhana (seventh century AD) because no historian, to my knowledge, has suggested it was either centralized or bureaucratic, let alone hydraulic.

ignored the period between the fall of the Guptas and the Turkish and Muslim conquests, which is the period in which many scholars believe feudalism prevailed in much of the subcontinent (see *inter alia* the debate in Byres and Mukhia, 1985; Kosambi 1956: 275–372; Mazumdar, 1960; and Sharma, 1958, 1965 and 1966). Moreover, had Wittfogel compared India and China, a country he knew about, he would have found instructive dissimilarities:

The early history of India contrasts strikingly with that of China, where, from the third century BC, a single empire was the rule, and division the exception. In India the Mauryas succeeded in creating a unified empire for a century, and in the heydays of the Guptas much of North India was under one hand, but with these exceptions numerous factors prevented the unification of the recognized cultural unit of *Bharatavarsa*, which so many monarchs desired. (Basham, 1967: 125)

Finding the reasons for these differences would constitute a major project in comparative history, and would have to include two facts which Wittfogel neglected: no Hindu monarch, *pace* the impression rendered by 'Kautilya's' *Arthashastra*, developed anything resembling a genuine bureaucracy capable of functioning when the monarch was ineffective, and no Indian regime seems to have achieved a monopoly of the means of violence in its quasi-feudal territories.

Finally, Wittfogel's Indian specimens of 'states stronger than their societies' are by no means convincing examples of strong centralized states. Even small-scale exploration of Indian history suggests that the facts are almost the converse of Wittfogel's assertion: for much of Indian history, as Basham (1954: 88) has put it, society was stronger than state, including those periods in which centralized empires existed.

Major Indian Social Formations and the Asiatic Mode of Production

Six major Indian social formations have been considered as potential specimens of the AMP, either by Marxists or by non-Marxists like Wittfogel. They are:

the Harappan civilization,
the Mauryan Empire,
the Empire of the Guptas,
the Vijayanagar Empire,
the Delhi Sultanate, and
the Mughal Empire.

These represent specimens of the antique, Hindu and Islamic civilizations in Indian history, and therefore provide something resembling a representative sample of kingdoms from the entire history of the subcontinent. I shall consider each of these social formations in turn.

Harappan, Indus Valley or Mohenjo-Darro Civilization   Only one Marxist scholar has argued at length that the earliest civilization in India, the Harappan or Indus valley society, was a specimen of a social formation dominated by the AMP (Chakraborty, 1983). Chakraborty's reconstruction of the Indus social formation is derived from the works of scholars who dealt with the subject (that is, the archaeological evidence) from a materialist standpoint (Childe, 1926, 1942 and 1954; Kosambi, 1956 and 1965; Mallick, 1968; Piggott, 1950; Sharma, 1966; and Wheeler, 1953). From these sources he attempts to reconstruct the productive forces, exchange relations and relations of production which characterized Indus society.

He asserts that the level of development of the productive forces of Indus civilization can be deduced from its cities, which were centres of large-scale manufacturing of consumer goods, as well as means of production and exchange. The productive forces must therefore have been at a higher level of development than that which obtained in the early Aryan period. The remains suggest that manufacturing industry ran on a mass scale with the help of organized labour.[19] Large numbers of producers were engaged in industrial activities – brick making, timber cutting, metal casting, pottery and clothing. The specialization of skills was centrally controlled (the evidence for this inference being the argument that things must have been produced *en masse* because of the lack of variation in the design and dimensions of the available artefacts).[20] The general impression, conveyed by the ordered street plans, is of a planned and disciplined urban life. The ruins of big, well-constructed houses also suggest that some Indus inhabitants enjoyed a luxurious life style. This urban life and the privileged stratum in the cities were dependent upon a rural surplus, testified to by the importance of big granaries in the urban infrastructure. Fertile and productive agriculture made this surplus possible, based as it was upon a system of natural flood irrigation through the damming of rivers. However, the productive forces reached a lower level of development than that achieved in Mesopotamia or Egypt. The latter civilizations employed shaft-hole axes, spears, swords, ploughs, clay tablets for records and (sometimes) canal irrigation, whereas the Indus producers remained satisfied with harrows, dam irrigation and very flimsy types of weapon. The archaeological evidence also suggests that the Indus valley was technologically stagnant, a bronze-age civilization devoid of any significant improvement in the productive forces over several hundred years. The evidence about

19 Chakraborty's unpaginated quotation from Kosambi does not in fact support this inference (Chakraborty, 1983: 2137).

20 A strange inference, especially given the fact that the authorities he cites discuss the (post-Harappan) 'painted grey ware' culture, the remains of which are certainly homogeneous in character although nobody suggests that the culture was centrally coordinated.

exchange relations implies some long-distance trade with Mesopotamia – copper, textiles, and pottery were exported, and gold and silver imported. The external trade was, however, non-productive. It led simply to the accumulation of treasure rather than to productive investment. The existence of weights and measures prove that some internal trade existed, but it apparently took place without coinage.

There is also 'archaeological evidence' about the production relations in Indus society. Chakraborty reports broad agreement that it was a class-divided society, in which the urban and rural direct producers were very poor, judging by the evidence of the material remains of their dwellings. Production was apparently organized by a central authority – both volume and quality were under its jurisdiction. His sources suggest that Indus society was governed by a dominant priest class (a conjecture derived entirely from comparison with similar citadel buildings in Mesopotamia); that the direct producers included temple slaves; and that the planned construction and organization of the cities points to the centralized co-ordination and control of labour. Chakraborty surmises that merchants engaged in long-distance trade were politically subordinated, and paid tribute, to the temple; but argues that it was improbable that the artisans were slaves of the temple. He asserts (with no supporting evidence) that the direct producers were 'subjected to extreme degrees of explojtation by the temple which reduced them to bare subsistence' (ibid: 2133). Indus society knew five classes: priests, traders, temple slaves, craftsmen and metal workers, and village cultivators.[21] The rural social structure was classless. The suggestion that it was composed of village communities is backed by the 'positive' evidence of hamlets in surrounding areas and by 'negative' evidence – no traces of *latifundia* or slave-operated estates.[22] Chakraborty confidently infers that the Indus valley civilization was a specimen of the AMP rather than of slavery: 'The exploiting class did not consist of private owners of the means of production or their representatives. It derived its power from its collective ownership of all the means of production' (ibid: 2134). He conjectures that all agricultural land was owned by the central authority. The temple slaves were not comparable to helots, as they were not primarily held down by force of arms. The evidence of a weak military apparatus even suggests that temple slaves were ideologically rather than militarily subordinated (ibid, citing Kosambi, 1956: 58–9). He argues that the Indus valley society displayed no imperialist or expansionist dynamic precisely because it was not a slave-based society. Furthermore, the adverse

21 The last two classes Chakraborty explicitly adds to those his sources were prepared to infer.

22 We are left none the wiser as to what sort of material remains might prove the existence of such estates.

geographical environment (the desert which surrounded the Indus valley) created incentives for the maintenance of social cohesion, as did the functional requirements of irrigation.

This case can be reduced to five assertions. First, the central temple authority enjoyed a monopoly over the entire surplus of the economy. Second, it extracted a surplus, mainly in the form of tribute from agrarian producers but also from the surplus labour of temple slaves. Third, the centrally planned and coordinated cities were centres of specialized crafts and external trade, under the dominance of the temple. There were also centrally organized public works, including irrigation. Fourth, the civilization was technologically and territorially stagnant. Finally, the class structure exhibited the traits of an order transitional between a classless and a class-divided society. The state appeared not as a military oppressor but as a religiously sanctified benefactor. In brief, the AMP was dominant in the Harappan formation (as witnessed by village communities paying tribute to a central authority), but other modes of exploitation were also present, notably temple-based exploitation and semi-independent producers engaged in exploiting the proceeds of unequal exchange.

This confidence, if it could be accepted, would boost unilineal historical materialism considerably. If the Harappan civilization was a specimen of an Asiatic social formation it would be easier to suggest that India went through the required canonical sequence of stages – Asiatic, slave and feudal – because the first stage would be established. However, this reconstruction of the archaeological evidence is open to numerous objections. Two are decisive.

First, Chakraborty's use of his secondary sources is selective. He relies upon them when they tell the story he wants, ignores them when they tell others, and also omits secondary sources which are at odds with his reconstruction. Since we are dealing here with archaeological induction this selectivity is questionable. To cite one instance among several which might have been chosen: Kosambi, upon whom Chakraborty relies heavily, clearly regarded Harappan civilization as close to a slave-based formation, although he was too cautious and careful a historian to commit himself (Kosambi, 1956: 55).

Second, Chakraborty's reconstruction is in the last analysis dependent upon archaeology, a treacherous bed of shifting sand. One of his own sources on Indian prehistory commented (when writing on European pre-history) that it may seem

hard doctrine to some people [but] the observational data of prehistory seem to me in almost every way to be more ambiguous, and more capable of varied interpretations, than the normal run of material available to historians. What we have ... is the accidentally surviving durable remnants of material culture, which we interpret as best we may, and inevitably the peculiar quality of this evidence dictates the ...

information we can obtain ... Furthermore, we interpret the evidence in terms of our own intellectual make-up, conditioned as it is by the period and culture within which we were brought up, our current assumptions and presuppositions, and our age and status. (Piggott, 1965: 4–5 cited in Finley, 1986b: 88)

This hard doctrine' seems especially apposite to Chakraborty's inferences.[23] The central thrust of his arguments, admittedly present in some of his sources, is entirely vulnerable to the core weakness of archaeology, well described by a leading historian of classical antiquity: 'there is sufficient evidence that identical artifacts and arrangements of artifacts can result from different socio-economic arrangements of procurement, manufacture or distribution ... *on all available evidence, it is impossible to infer social arrangements or institutions, attitudes or beliefs from material objects alone*' (Finley, 1986: 90 and 93 – my italics).

Interestingly, in the case we are examining, the same artefacts have been used to argue for the existence both of slavery and a caste structure in Mohenjo-daro (Allchin and Allchin, 1968: 137). Such inferences are part and parcel of counterfeit history – the professional vice of some archaeologists. In the case of the Harappan civilization, devoid as we are of epigraphic and written information, it is not possible to have any scientific confidence in assertions such as those of Chakraborty. Consider only one of the most obvious difficulties with his reasoning. The alleged joint presence of a weak military apparatus[24] with slavery is exceptionally hard to accept on the basis of rational social theory. The emergence of slaves is not attributed to the conquest of peripheral tribes – there were none in the desert. Instead the slaves are alleged to have been ideologically produced and dominated into submission, rather than coerced, all of which suggests a success in and scale of brain-washing not known elsewhere in human history.

The fairest verdict available on the Mohenjo–darro civilization is simply that we do not know whether it was a republic, a city state, an empire, a slaveholding society or a specimen of the AMP. It is less surprising therefore that Marxist-Leninist scholars are clearly divided between those like Struve, of the USSR, and Ruben, of the DDR, who regard Harappan civilization as a slave-society, and others who evidently assimilate it to the AMP (Antonova, Bongard-Levin and Kotovsky: 1979, 1: 23). There is general agreement that it was technologically stagnant in its 500–600 years of

23 The most strong cultural assumption evident in Chakraborty's argument is that uniformity in the cultural artefacts of Harappan implies the existence of strong centralized authority, a conviction he shares with Basham (1967: 15). One does not need to be an anarchist to believe that in principle uniformity can be the outcome of voluntary cooperation, tradition and exchange, as opposed to state control.

24 Kosambi (1956: 59) puts it thus: 'the tools of violence were curiously weak, though nothing is directly known of their social mechanism for wielding force, which we call state.'

existence,[25] but that cannot count as proof of the existence of the AMP since such stagnation has characterized other non-Asiatic social formations for lengthy periods of their existence. There is also no persuasive evidence that the Harappan civilization was either hydraulic or despotic in Wittfogel's sense of these terms. The best we can say about the political structures of the Harappan civilization is that we have nothing to rely upon other than the speculative, frequently contradictory and disputed extrapolations of archaeologists from material remains.[26]

The Mauryan Empire (321—184 BC) The empire established by Chandragupta Maurya after his seizure of the Nanda-built state of Magadha in 321 BC has also been hailed as a social formation dominated by the AMP. We are better informed about the Magadhan state when it evolved into a peninsular empire under its Mauryan kings, Chandragupta, Bindusara and Ashoka, than we are about Harappan civilization. From its core in the Ganges river basin the empire eventually expanded over most of the subcontinent. The pillars of Ashoka are found throughout India, with the exception of the deep south. Wittfogel regarded it as the Hindu paradigm of hydraulic despotism, and more recently an Indian Marxist, Dipankar Gupta, has described it as the 'nadir of Asiatic society' (Gupta, 1980).

Judging on the evidence of the *Arthashastra* this regime had many of the alleged features of an oriental despotism: a centralized military, administrative and fiscal apparatus, state mercantilist monopolies in trade in luxuries and manufactures, and subordinated village settlements, evidence which unites the arguments of Wittfogel and the French-speaking Marxist Dambuyant (1974). For the moment I leave to one side the question of whether the portrait of the *Arthashastra* is an accurate one, since unfortunately for Wittfogel's theses the functional base of this state rested not upon hydraulic irrigation but upon a monopoly of iron which allowed the empire to play the leading role in the colonization of new land. The empire was a colonial rather than a hydraulic despotism, far more directed towards maximizing settlement and production on the land than exploiting any alleged hydraulic expertise. Moreover, while evidence 'of family and communal construction of irrigation works is not lacking . . . there is nothing to

25 However, even this consensus is breaking down: 'Recent excavations have shed new light on the Harappan civilization that need now no longer be regarded as inflexible and stagnant' (Antonova et al., 1979: 27).

26 A stream of publications in the early and mid-1980s has contended that Harappan civilization, far from being centralized, was in fact made up of several independent states. Whether this contention is better founded than the previous conventional wisdom is a moot-point. As Edmund Leach's astringent review of Joseph Tainter's book *The Collapse of Complex Societies* points out, Harappan civilization is regularly used for unconvincing 'reconstructed history' (Leach, 1988: 16).

show that a large bureaucracy developed in Mauryan times in response to the needs of irrigation' (Sharma, 1981: 57). The empire's duration was also brief as it rapidly disintegrated into separate fiefdoms after, *inter alia*, the levels of ability generated through the dynasty's genes displayed a marked decline. It therefore had none of the ironclad stability associated with hydraulic despotisms, leaving to one side the issue of whether it had any hydraulic functions to perform. Even royal ownership of land was confined to new colonies planted in waste land (Sharma, 1981: 58).

A far more narrowly defined notion of the AMP is Gupta's starting point. He claims the *Grundrisse* as his textual authority, and follows the ideas of Godelier. For him a powerful centralized state built on hydraulic technology, and an undifferentiated peasant mass, are not necessary conditions for the existence of the AMP. He argues that the *general* exploitation of the people directly by the superior community or the state is the crucial feature of the AMP. Indeed stratification and differentiation amongst the exploited are integral features of the AMP. Gupta then seeks to identify the era in which this (revised and reconstructed) AMP was dominant in Indian history. In the Rig-Vedic age (1500–600 BC) of the Aryan conquests and the diffusion of Aryan culture through the subcontinent, a stateless society was differentiating into distinct castes, based on the *varna* categories. Following an established orthodoxy Gupta presumes a causal relationship between *varna*, understood to mean colour, and the ethnic differences between the conquering Aryans and the subjugated *dasas*. This nomadic conquest society was demonstrably differentiating into separate classes, with peasants gradually being subjected to a grain-tithe by the superior castes.[27] However, it remained largely tribal until state formations began to crystallize towards the end of the Vedic age. The cause of the emergence of states he finds in the development of the productive forces, notably the discovery and manufacture of iron. Beginning with tribal confederations, or republican oligarchies, these pristine state formations found their final expression in Chandragupta's empire. But although the empire was associated with development in the productive forces it did not lead to qualitative change in the production relations. Rather, the state engaged in

27 There is an extended discussion of the complex relations between the *dasas* and the formation of slavery and the *sudra* caste in the work of Sharma (1980). He argues that 'it would appear ... the name *dasa* in the sense of slave was derived not from the non-Aryan inhabitants of India but from a people allied to the Indo-Aryans ... later ... the term ... may have been employed indiscriminately not only to cover the survivors of the original Indo-European *dasas* but also pre-Aryan peoples such as *Dasyus* and *Raksasas* and also such sections of the Aryans as were impoverished or reduced to subjection on account of internal conflict within their ranks' (ibid: 27). Sharma also argues that the caste of *sudras* arose out of an Aryan tribe of the same name (ibid: 35).

general exploitation of peasants and artisans in a stratification system based on the *varna* order.[28]

Contrary to received interpretations of the AMP, Gupta also argues that within the Mauryan Empire there were internal contradictions which facilitated the transition to feudalism. The simple class structure of the monarch and his salaried officials (*pauri janapada*) dominating the peasant mass disintegrated under the combined impact of the emergence of private property and artisan differentiation, and as a consequence of the state's own policy of the forcible settlement of *sudras* in new villages. The feudalization of the state apparatus was matched by the development of a localized system of exploitation based on the *jati* caste system, which had established itself within the self-sufficient village economies, and by the emergence of untouchability. This new pattern of localized exploitation marked the transformation of the Asiatic into the feudal mode of production.[29]

What are we to make of this classification of the Mauryan Empire as a specimen of a social formation dominated by the AMP? First, it is at best a stripped-down version of the AMP which is alleged to have existed – one devoid of stagnation, of villages displaying primitive communist traits *and* of hydraulic irrigation. Second, the 'laws of motion' which explain the self-transcendence of the AMP into the feudal mode of production are not adequately sketched. Third, the stripped-down model creates the obvious difficulty that it becomes difficult to distinguish the AMP from the feudal mode of production, at least on Marxist criteria. Gupta's own demarcation criterion, the distinction between generalized *varna* and particularized *jati* exploitation, is both vague and problematic. What makes exploitation general rather than particular? After all, the presence of an 'external authority' which 'generally' exploits a village community is compatible with the existence of either the state of the AMP or the feudal lord. Conversely, if particular exploitation refers to the *jati* caste system, then it is a big logical leap to conclude that this mode of exploitation is identical with feudal production relations. Serfdom has traditionally been regarded as central to the feudal labour process, so the question arises of why serfdom and the *jati* system are equivalents. It would have been better for Gupta to argue that the AMP is characterized by tax-exploitation whereas feudalism is characterized by rent-exploitation, because such an argument would clearly

28 This argument is based on a rather generous interpretation of the 'Formen' passages in the *Grundrisse*. Gupta argues that around 1858 Marx 'undertook a more intensive study of Indian history' (Gupta, 1980: 251), leading him to revise the image of India he had conveyed in his 1853 journalism. However, as I argued in chapter 3, not only is the clarity of the *Grundrisse* in doubt but also there are many examples of the later Marx repeating his 1853 themes after 1858.

29 It is often suggested, by contrast, that untouchables were the unmentioned and denied fifth category in the *varna* scheme, an interpretation at odds with Gupta's schema – see *inter alia* Dumont (1970a: 32).

have differentiated distinct modes of exploitation. But making this distinction fit Mauryan and post-Mauryan times would have required the production of better empirical evidence than is available.[30]

Fourth, Gupta, like many historians, takes as axiomatic the degree of centralized political power attributed to the Mauryans in 'Kautilya's' *Arthashastra*. However, there are multiple challenges to this conventional wisdom, perhaps expressed best by the Dutch scholar Heesterman:

> we should dismiss the deceptive appearances of a centralized setup held together by a bureaucracy reaching from the king down to the grass roots. This [is] the ideal presented in the *Arthashastra*, but its reticence of chains [of] command and reporting would suggest otherwise. Instead we find almost pathetic stress on the necessity of official's trustworthiness, and a concomitatant all-pervading spy-system, which can only block administrative action and in the end reduce it to chaos ... [T]he realization of a centralized bureaucratic setup would require objective conditions, such as [a] high degree of [monetization] ... which would make it possible to separate the functions of government from rights in the soil. (Heesterman, 1970: 2 – see also Heesterman, 1971)

This textual analysis of the *Arthashastra* persuasively suggests the implausibility of the notion that an extensive centralized bureaucratic state existed in the Mauryan Empire, and is a salutary reminder of the anachronistic danger of attributing modern features to pre-modern regimes.

Finally, we must recognize the severe limitations of the historiography of the Mauryan Empire. These gaps are nowhere more salient than when one tries to establish what were the relations of production in Mauryan times. In fact deciding what mode of production the Mauryan Empire was dominated by is extremely problematic: the primary literature is very limited, and the interpretation of the *Arthashastra* is a minefield.[31] While numismatic evidence suggests the existence of an empire which attempted standardization and the organization of a taxation system, we must be wary of reliance on the *Arthashastra* portrait, which may represent aspiration more than reality. Mere consideration of communications difficulties outside of the Ganges river basin casts doubt on whether the empire was genuinely centralized, and makes more plausible the suggestion that it had a centralized core but

30 Gupta also bypasses the controversial evidence from the *Arthashastra* that on crown lands the fields were tilled by slaves and hired agricultural labourers, evidence which has led other scholars to infer that the Mauryan Empire was based on the slave mode of production (see note 31 below).

31 For example, Chanana builds a case for the idea that the Mauryan Empire was based on slavery by reference to the *Arthashastra* (Chanana, 1960). But, as he himself notes, maltranslations in the best-known English translation exaggerated the impression of discussion of slavery in the text. Soviet Marxist orthodoxy is that the regime was based on slavery (see appendix 7.2). There is in fact no consensus on the scale and importance of slavery in the production of the surplus product in the Mauryan Empire. (There is also no consensus on how prevalent slavery must be before one can describe the dominant mode of production as slaveholding.)

a large tribute-paying periphery of client regimes, which in some cases might have been little more than ritually subordinated to the centre.[32] The fact that the Mauryan Empire collapsed so quickly suggests that its efforts to build a bureaucracy and a sound fiscal system were much less successful than those of Mesopotamian or Chinese emperors. Moreover, its chequered association with Buddhism suggests a failure to establish a state religion – surely a key element in any model of an oriental despotism or the ideological state apparatus of the AMP. Once more we must conclude that the evidence for the AMP in a key period of Indian history is at best partial and also compatible with alternative interpretations.[33] Perhaps the Mauryan Empire is best considered as a prototype of the segmentary political system established much later in the history of the subcontinent, notably in the Vijayanagar Empire of the south.

The Empire of the Guptas   The Gupta Empire, created four or five centuries later by another Chandra Gupta, was also based in the Ganges. By all historians' accounts it never acquired the scale of centralized and despotic features nor the territorial range sometimes associated with its antecedent. The ability of the Guptan kings to penetrate the lives and resources of 'their' villages was limited and the regime, and its successors, displayed all the centrifugal symptoms associated with feudal (and/or) segmentary political structures. Sharma's arguments that the Gupta period was in fact feudal, based upon detailed evaluation of primary, epigraphic, and archaeological data, are very persuasive (Sharma, 1965, 1966 and 1986; and see appendix 7.3). He has recently strengthened these contentions by a convincing demonstration, through the use of archaeological and epigraphic evidence, of urban and economic decay, or the re-ruralization of the life of dominant elites, in Guptan times (Sharma, 1987).[34] Because of all this evidence, no author has regarded the empire of the Guptas as a specimen of the AMP – except of course Wittfogel. However, since he drew upon discredited nationalist history and supplied no 'hydraulic' evidence for his contentions

---

32 I owe this point to discussion with Professor R.S. Sharma. The vulnerability of the population in the river-basin core of the empire is explicable less by Wittfogelian considerations than by the caging of the population created by natural (rather than hydraulic) irrigation – which made military conquest easier (see appendix 7.1).

33 Professor Sharma pointed out in discussion that there are good reasons to question, especially on his orthodox Marxist definition of feudalism, whether feudalism plausibly can be attributed to the Mauryan Empire. None of the inscriptions of Ashoka mention land grants – unlike the evidence of the Gupta and post-Gupta periods – which leaves us without any of the material evidence associated with feudal production relations in later phases of Indian history. He remains judiciously agnostic as to the categorization of the Mauryan regime.

34 A shocking thesis for Indian nationalists, who regard the Guptan era as the 'golden age' of ancient India, but an important component of Sharma's account of the origins of Indian feudalism.

we can safely dismiss the suitability of any version of the AMP to explain the workings of the Gupta Empire.

The Vijayanagar Empire However, Wittfogel was not eccentric in interpreting the Vijayanagar Empire as the exemplary south Indian example of oriental despotism. In this instance he was merely following received opinion. South Indian historians, such as K.A. Nilakanta Sastri (1955) T.V. Mahalingam (1967), A. Appadorai (1936) and A. Krishnaswami (1964), had and have established this notion as historical orthodoxy. However, recent work has cast considerable doubt on this conventional wisdom (Stein, 1975, 1980, 1982 and 1985). New historical evidence and more plausible interpretations of both the state and the economy of south India are incompatible with the theses of the AMP − especially if a centralized state and hydraulic bureaucracy are regarded as fundamental features of the AMP.

The states which preceded the Vijayanagar Empire in south India are no longer portrayed as unquestionably centralized, bureaucratized monarchies. As Stein points out, the evidence of the earliest historians who thought otherwise is refuted by their own descriptions of local political and 'administrative' organization in south India in the period of the Cholas. The brahmin village assemblies (*sabha*), local assemblies (*nadu*), castes and guilds are described as involved in such governmental functions as the control and regulation of land, management of (localized, and small-scale) irrigation works, temples, tax-collection, charities and justice, and record-keeping. Such descriptions are incompatible with the notion that there were salient functions to be performed by a centralized and bureaucratized state. Inscriptions are also more compatible with the idea that south Indian monarchies were based on loose 'ritual sovereignty' rather than upon centralized apparatuses capable of penetrating south Indian villages and imposing cultural or political uniformity. The Chola kings were little more than predatory, warring, tribal warrior-rulers irregularly extracting tribute from autonomous villages − which varied considerably, according to ecological conditions, in both their social structures and political institutions, even if they had invariably been touched by brahmin culture. Moreover, these kings never enjoyed anything resembling a monopoly of the means of violence. Rather, medieval south Indian 'states' were, in Stein's words, 'custodial, tributary, locally based and oriented to rural networks' (1975: 76). They were custodial in the sense that they did not try to monopolize the coercive powers held by other collectives in their surrounding societies. The king was an 'overlord, not a manager', and 'no South Indian state, including Vijayanagar, had a department of irrigation' (ibid: 77). The king's role, apart from protecting the social order, was the organization of war: the south Indian king was not a legislator. 'Laws' were an integral part of the caste system, which was close to self-regulating, and the king's role as an adjudicator was severely limited.

Moreover, the Chola and Vijayanagar kings depended upon tribute, exacted through intermittent displays of force, rather than upon a settled system of taxation. The taxation which existed was local — extracted locally for local purposes — something true also of the centre of the kingdoms. Such forms of exploitation as existed (notably dominant castes holding communal possession of village land and forcing untouchables to work for them) were insufficient to produce a surplus to sustain a managerial state or a bureaucracy. The king's control was confined to his immediate environment. The rest of the 'state' (if this term is at all appropriate) was linked through networks of ideology and culture rather than bureaucratic channels. The key mediators of culture were the brahmins, the mobile priests who linked the custodial state with the caste-divided villages, but while they diffused a shared culture they did not serve as instruments of royal control. The 'society beneath' the 'state' was mostly segmented into separate caste-divided villages. The 'state' was mainly an irrelevance. As possibly with the Mauryan Empire and other Hindu regimes in India, the south Indian monarchy should not be mistakenly assumed to have matched the statist aspirations articulated in texts like the *Arthashastra*. The custodial, segmentary confederation was neither hydraulic nor the prototype of the modern bureaucratic state.

The significance of this revisionist critique of the nature of the south Indian state is simple. '[P]erhaps the greatest Hindu system of dynastic power was ... centred in Vijayanagar' (Frykenberg, 1968: 107–25). If this picture is true of the last and most powerful of Hindu regimes before the Muslim conquest, it is also suggestive of the nature of the Hindu regimes which preceded it elsewhere on the subcontinent. The most reasonable interpretation of the Vijayanagar Empire (despite extensive 'territorial' sovereignty, the establishment of major trade linkages in the Indian Ocean and the effective colonization of south-east Asia) is that this state did not develop a bureaucracy (Heitzman, 1987; Subrahmanyam, 1986). Stein is entirely consistent to describe the early south Indian state as segmentary, rather than centralized, based upon ritual sovereignty rather than territorial and fiscally extractive sovereignty, upon collaboration between the chieftains of dominant peasant-caste groups capable of independent military action rather than upon a despotic ruler, and as unified, if at all, by the cultural mediation of the brahmins.[35] However the great military capacity of

---

35 Stein has also drawn attention to the strength of local, corporate institutions in south Indian village life — a picture which refutes Wittfogel's idea of the weakness of Indian guilds and corporations. Wittfogel was badly misled by his 'urbanist' assumptions (Stein, 1985: 58–9).

Vijayanagar also makes reasonable the suggestion that the later period of the regime displayed feudal features too. But if Stein's wholesale transfer of the African-derived category of segmentary states to south India seems overdone,[36] this minor criticism is of little comfort to enthusiasts for the idea of oriental despotism.

Irrigation was far more important in agrarian production in pre-nineteenth-century south India than it was in the north, but it never took forms which required hydraulic bureaucratic management. Most agrarian production in the south was organized in what Stein calls 'dry ecotypes' dependent upon the monsoon or in mixed ecotypes involving wet and dry agriculture based upon local tanks, wells and small-scale riverine channels and ditches. Equally, south India was not settled in enormously dense demographic clusters surrounding centres of hydraulic agriculture or centres of extensive industrial production. Therefore the preconditions of the successful formation of a centralized state apparatus – a population thoroughly caged by ecological and economic interest and vulnerable to conquest, exploitation and penetration – were not present on the required scale. The implications of Stein's analysis are therefore devastating for any notion of the AMP incorporating a hydraulic order and a centralized state.

Only a radically reconstructed AMP, based upon the notion of stratified villages, divided internally by class and caste, and upon a loose ritual superstructure, is compatible with the south Indian evidence. Stein himself shows some inclination to believe that the reconstruction of the AMP along these lines is worth considering, although as yet he has not spelled out the details (Stein, 1985: 84–6). However, the editor of the journal in which Stein's piece occurs rightly comments that 'Stein's version [of the AMP] is so far removed from anything that Marx said; and so manifestly not a serious attempt to define a mode of production in a Marxist sense (stressing, merely the 'importance' or irrigation in south India), as hardly to constitute a serious effort at rehabilitation' (Byres, 1985: 12). Indeed, so far Stein's own work has contributed to the rejection of most conventional understandings of the AMP and oriental despotism to south Indian history. The evidence he surveys fits far better either with his own segmentary model, or with a model of feudalism, as the best means of understanding south Indian social formations.

The Delhi Sultanate   The Delhi Sultanate (1206 AD–early fifteenth century) was the first major Islamic state established in India.[37] It has not, to my

36 As Professor Sharma complained to me in conversation.
37 My picture of the Delhi Sultanate relies on Thapar (1966: 266–320); Antonova et al. (1979, I: 202–29); Raychaudhuri and Habib (1982: 45–101), Majumdar (1951-, VI) and Kosambi (1956: 326–72).

knowledge, been upheld by any Indian Marxist as a specimen of the AMP, although it has a well-established place in the annals of oriental despotism, if only by virtue of its famous first rulers, the slave dynasts. The sultanate was established by conquest, its creation being greatly aided by its superior military organization and the fragmented, tribal or 'quasi-feudal' opposition it faced from Hindu chieftains. However, after some perfunctory missionary efforts the conquerors made little serious attempt to convert their subjects to Islam.

The Delhi Sultanate undeniably marked a decisive, if fragile, change in the extractive capacity of Indian state formations. The sultans created a coercive administrative organization which, in aspiration at least, resembled a linear hierarchy running down through various authorities to the villages which it endeavoured to keep under firm control. This fiscal and military apparatus was designed to enable the sultanate simultaneously to stimulate production and confiscate a considerable fraction of the surplus output from the countryside. However, the expectation that these Islamic rulers taxed villages and merchants to the point of revolt, as might be expected from the image of oriental despotism, has only partial elements of truth. There was a measure of (self-interested) enlightenment amongst the despots, who attempted to encourage further production and new settlements. Some sultans built improved roads, developed transport networks and engaged in the building of canals and even works of irrigation. The scale of their irrigation activities does not, however, lend any credence to Wittfogel's hypotheses because their overall importance in agrarian production remained small,[38] and in this case the despotism demonstrably *preceded* the establishment of irrigation works. Moreover, under the sultanate the central Asian trade routes flourished once more; coinage revived; there was growth in (Muslim) urban civilization; and all of these processes were directly and indirectly linked to the partial success of the sultans in extracting revenue in money rather than in kind.

The regime was partly stabilized by the deals which the sultans made with their conquered Hindu subjects. It is under the sultanate that the *zamindars* first emerge, holding their own land without paying revenue or sharing in the proceeds of the imperial revenue. However, the enduring image of the sultanate is its very instability; the constant waxing and waning of its territorial ambit; and the relative ease with which the Islamic mechanism of monarchical control, the *iqta*-holder, became an instrument for the independence of the nobility. Moreover, the sultanate's history is one of uninterrupted aggressive campaigns of conquest, or the beating off of

---

38 One informed estimate suggests that in later (Mughal) times public irrigation works probably did not cover more than 5 per cent of the cultivated land of India (Maddison, 1971: 23).

external conquerors from central Asia, creating the impression of a regime built on booty which had only a superficial impact upon the Hindu society over which it precariously presided.

Much more is known about the sultanate's political and dynastic conflicts that about the production relations and level of development of the productive forces, which are critical to a historical materialist classification.[39] Given these historiographical limitations I shall, for ease of exposition and brevity, assess the nature of the sultanate's social structure in the light of the regime which succeeded it, that of the Mughal empire. This second Islamic empire built upon the institutional achievements of the sultanate and had much in common with it.

The Mughal Empire The Mughal Empire (1526–1757), whose collapse began before and was completed during the European conquest of India, is the pre-colonial social formation about which there is the greatest primary historical evidence. Moreover, since Marx many Marxists (including Indian Marxists) have regarded it as the classical example of the AMP. Marx evidently thought of it as such when he wrote his Indian journalism of the 1850s, and strongly rejected Kovalevsky's classification of the Mughal Empire as feudal in the late 1870s. Marx was followed in these judgements notably by the Soviet Indologist I.M. Reisner (discussed in appendix 7.2), by the Indian Marxist K.S. Shelvankar (1943) and of course by Wittfogel.

More, recently the Indian neo-Marxist Anupam Sen has restated this contention (1982: 15–46).[40] Sen's argument, that the Mughal Empire exhibited all the classical Asiatic features, forms part of a wider thesis that the distinct pattern of India's development is to be explained by the dramatic autonomy of its state apparatus from social classes in the pre-colonial, colonial and post-colonial periods. The presence of the AMP precluded capitalist development in India in the pre-colonial era (ibid: 16–19). The unity of agriculture and industry in the villages and the absence of a landed aristocracy with legal rights of ownership made it impossible for a potential bourgeoisie to separate peasants from the means of production: '[t]hus in the Asiatic mode of production in India, the *jagirdars*, *zamindars*, etc., i.e. the nobility, could not emerge as an independent class outside of the state as the feudal lords in Europe did'

---

39 Habib in his contribution to the *Cambridge Economic History of India* describes the condition of the direct producers in the villages as that of 'semi-serfs' (Habib, 1982: 54), which is perplexing in the light of his reluctance to use the concept of feudalism to explain the workings of medieval Indian social formations.

40 Two papers by D. Banerjee, one published, the other unpublished, also defend Marx's interpretation of Mughal India (1986 and 1987). (I am grateful to Professors Sharma and Banerjee for the references.) However, I find Banerjee's defence of Marx not as clear as Sen's, so I confine my attention to the latter.

(ibid: 17). Consequently the development of wage-labour, a necessary condition of capitalism, was hindered. Just as importantly the centralized, despotic and non-feudal state apparatus made the political position of the bourgeoisie more precarious than that of their counterparts in Western Europe. Merchant capital was therefore less capable of dissolving the anterior mode of production. These features of the AMP, its most salient morphological differences with occidental feudalism, explained the failure of capitalism to develop in India in the pre-British period.

Sen's argument that the Mughal Empire was an example of the AMP relies on two main sources. First, he takes as unquestioned facts the propositions advanced by Marx in his 1850s journalism, and does not question the veracity of Marx's sources, or the validity of Marx's deductions from his sources (ibid: 20−1, 24−32 and 227). Such faith, as I have shown (pp. 262−7), is not warranted; if it was ever excusable, it is no longer. Thus Sen cites Bernier, Maine and the famous *Fifth Report* from the Select Committee on the Affairs of the East India Company of 1812, with no hint that these accounts of pre-colonial India are in any way controversial (ibid: 21, 33 and 229). He also repeats Marx's analysis of the Indian city and cites the *Grundrisse* as his authority for the evidence that Indian towns were a source of weakness for the Indian bourgeoisie (ibid: 32−3). Second, with less fideistic citation, Sen relies upon evidence from the work of twentieth-century historians, notably Moreland (1929) and the Marxists Irfan Habib (1963) and D.D. Kosambi (1956). He uses the latter sources to emphasize the degree of centralization in the empire and the relative weakness of the prebendal Mughal nobility.

There are two reasons why Sen's sources undermine confidence in his general thesis. First, the two Marxists upon whom Sen relies *never* accepted that the Mughal social formation was an example of the AMP, and one of them, Irfan Habib, has persistently denied the utility of the AMP in the analysis of Indian history (Habib, 1962, 1969, 1973, 1975 and 1983).[41] Second, Sen nowhere acknowledges that these secondary sources interpreted the Mughal evidence in a strikingly different way to him. Moreover, arguments against the idea that the Mughal social formation was Asiatic in the relevant senses are not only advanced by Habib, Sen's main source, but are also highly persuasive.

The best way to appraise the merits of Sen's case is to evaluate the evidence and arguments of historical scholars on the Mughal social formation against the key elements of the definition of the AMP I advanced earlier (pp. 16−18). First, the level of development of the productive forces in

---

41 It is a remarkable fact that the exponents of the 'Aligarh' school's view of Mughal India − that is, those who believe that the Mughals had an enormously powerful and penetrative bureaucratic apparatus − are very hostile to the identification of this regime with the AMP.

Mughal society was greater than that of the primitive communist mode of production but less than that of advanced capitalism. In this respect it meets a necessary condition for the existence of the AMP. However, this condition is certainly not sufficient. Throughout its history Mughal society was characterized by technological developments superior to many past and contemporaneous slaveholding and feudal societies, facts which put its 'Asiatic' status in doubt, at least for unilineal productivist historical materialists. One possible index of its level of development of the productive forces was its large population.[42] The population of India was huge when compared with any or all of the Europen countries of the seventeenth century — somewhere between 115 million and 155 million people (Cassen, 1978: 3—4). The 'average European' may have been richer than the 'average Indian' — on some notional comparison of real income — but comparisons of distributions of income do not directly enter Marxist analyses of the level of development of the productive forces.[43] More dramatically, the level of urban real wages in north India in Akbar's time was probably very similar to that prevailing in north India at the turn of the twentieth century (Chandra, 1982: 465). If Mughal India was a specimen of the AMP then twentieth-century India has taken a very long time to go past the fabled retardation of the earlier mode of production — at least on this index. Moreover, the level of development of the productive forces must have been considerable, for one simple reason. The social formation sustained a scale of surplus extraction which made the Mughal nobility a byword for luxurious and ostentatious living amongst sixteenth- and seventeenth-century Europeans. In part, of course, the scale of the surplus was related to the scale of exploitation, but the scale of surplus is also one other historical materialist indicator of the development of the productive forces.

Second, agrarian production was the major economic activity in the Mughal social formation, thus meeting another necessary condition for the existence of the AMP. However, this fact is also compatible with the presence or dominance of other modes of production. Moreover, there was extensive urban growth in Mughal society. The largest cities were sites of manufacturing, marketing, banking and other entrepreneurial activities. They were also built on a scale which captured the imaginations of European travellers (Hambly, 1982: 434—52). The Muslim artisans of the cities were less constrained by caste stratification than their Hindu counterparts in the villages. The pioneering research of Naqvi (H.K. Naqvi, 1968) has pointed to the existence of four types of urban centre in Mughal India: primarily

---

42 See my discussion in chapter 5, pp. 208 and 210.
43 There is a useful discussion of the standard of living in Mughal India by Chandra, in the *Cambridge Economic History of India* (S. Chandra, 1982: 458—71).

administrative centres, primarily commercial or manufacturing cities, primarily pilgrimage centres and single-product trade centres. This typology is suggestive of a degree of autonomous urban growth and differentiation incompatible with the dominance of the AMP. Moreover, the scale of village autarky in Mughal India has been much exaggerated, being no more dramatic than that which prevailed in feudal Western Europe. For a start the villagers' surplus was converted into cash for payment of the state's revenue demands, whereas Marx's sketches of the AMP suggest that tributary payments in kind were definitive of this mode of production (Habib, 1963 and 1982: 235–49). Such monetization suggests systemic interdependencies between town and country rather than the relations of 'an indifferent unity', as suggested by Marx in the *Grundrisse*.

Third, the scale, range and penetration of exchange relations in urban and rural Mughal India were so extensive that they violate certain necessary conditions of the AMP. External and internal trade networks were considerable (Chaudhuri, 1982: 382–407, and 1985; Dasgupta, 1982: 407–33; and Raychaudhuri 1982: 325–59). Internally 'exchange of goods, found at virtually every level and sphere of economic life, was impressive in its magnitude and complexity. The dominance of subsistence-oriented production was modified by surpluses and deficits necessitating multi-tiered and multi-faceted commercial activity' (Raychaudhuri, 1982: 325). Inter-village trade, with pedlars intermediating between villages, coexisted with extensive intra-local trade between towns and cities. It is true that flows were predominantly from the rural to the urban sectors, and that the villages, seen through modern eyes, were to a great extent self-sufficient. None the less, the picture was far more nuanced than any theory of the AMP can absorb. There was nothing more remarkably autarkic about the Indian by comparison with the European village. There was production for exchange as well as for consumption, and the division of labour was by no means entirely static – the *jajmani* system was capable of facilitating gradual changes in production techniques and services. Moreover, class differentiation within the villages of Mughal India was creating an effective demand for goods and services from outside of the village, especially by dominant caste groups. Similar demands and economic stimuli were produced in the urban environment by the cosiderable expenditures of the nobility, which had luxury-goods' multiplier effects: 'Moreland [was right:] "spending not hoarding" was the dominant characteristic of the pattern of life of the nobles' (S. Chandra, 1982: 468).

Fourth, the technology of agrarian production in Mughal society was not 'hydraulic' in any important sense (Habib, 1962; and Maddison, 1971: 23). The canals constructed by the Delhi sultans were not lost, but it remained the case that nearly all irrigation projects were small-scale and locally organized, and were only under the loosest form of government regulation – encouraged rather than managed.

Fifth, the relations of production in the Mughal empire certainly give the appearance of being associated with 'Asiatic' exploitation, especially as the evidence of the Aligarh school of historians suggests the apparently over-whelming presence of the imperial state apparatus in surplus appropriation. But even here caution is required in assuming the presence of the AMP. This surplus was, wherever possible, monetized; creating according to Habib (1982b: 360—81), an economy in which some 250 million rupees circulated. Furthermore, the class relations of the Mughal Empire were more complicated than the AMP model in which there exist at most two primary classes enmeshed in exploitation relations (state officials and vil-lagers). First of all the emperor theoretically claimed to be the sole person entitled to receive the land revenue within the imperial domains. *Contra* the impression given by Bernier, Marx and others, the Mughal emperor did not claim to own the land:

The claim that the king was the owner of the soil is not made by any Indian authority before the eighteenth century, whereas it was the usual statement on the lips of European observers from the sixteenth century onwards. It was clearly the land-tax, often termed by them 'rent', which suggested to them the existence of an all-embracing royal property in land. (Habib, 1983: 104 — see also Habib, 1963: 112—13)[44]

To the direct producers this difference may have seemed academic. But it is important to note that the surplus appropriated by the empire was neither a rent, in the feudal sense, nor a tax on the land; rather it was a claim to a share of the actual crop (Habib, 1982: 235). In practice this claim was modified, as administering a tax on the crop was extremely difficult to implement (ibid: 236—40). None the less, beneath the complex methods of implementation, the aspiration of the Mughal administration was obvious: to secure the bulk of the peasants' surplus. However, this goal was not pursued entirely through short-sighted maximization of revenues. Assessments were modified to take account of crop failures and to en-courage the development of waste land. Loans were also advanced, called *taqavi* (literally 'strength-giving'), to enable peasants to buy seed and cultivate land.

The administration of exploitation was largely carried out through inter-mediaries (*zamindars, ta'allugadars/* and *muqaddams/patels*) rather than through direct extraction from individual producers (*asami*). This fact, the

---

44 One influential discussant of these questions puts the state ownership thesis of European travellers down to 'gross ignorance of the workings of the *jagir* system', and points out that the emperor was merely the proprietor of the jungles and unclaimed land. He had no absolute proprietary rights over cultivable lands already in hereditary possession; and even the Mughal administrators of Akbar's time, judging by the evidence of the *A'in-i Akbari*, claimed the tax revenue as a tax on the property of their subjects (Grover, 1963: 2). (The *A'in-i Akbari* is the third part of the *Akbar Nama*, written by Abul Fazl, and provides the most important contemporary description of the administration of Akbar's empire — I. Hasan, 1980: 7—10.)

emperor's dependence upon a fundamentally aristocratic apparatus, which 'contracted out' its tax-farming, created the fundamental tensions in the Mughal economy and polity. The intermediaries, also interested in revenue maximization, had different interests to the emperor, which led them to over-exploit the peasantry. The Mughal fiscal economy, at least in the agrarian sector, discouraged economic growth in so far as it subverted the motives for improving cultivation, but at the same time it also fostered dramatic class-differentiation.

The Mughal ruling class, the *jagirdars* or *mansabdars*, did in some ways resemble what might be expected of the dominant class in a social formation dominated by the AMP. They were a small elite, numbering 8000 at most, initially largely composed of ethnic Turks, Iranians and Afghans. They were in theory a service nobility: the *mansab* (rank) was not inheritable; the noble's tenure of his *jagir* (land) was temporary and judicial powers belonged to the *qazi*, the emperor's representative (Habib, 1963 and 1982: 241−4; and Spear, 1970). However, over time, what had started as a conquest nobility began to acquire *de facto* rights of inheritance and to develop some of the traits of feudal lords. Moreover, beneath the *mansabdars*, debatably prototypes of a bureaucratic ruling class,[45] there existed an important stratum of intermediary exploiters and landowners, the *zamindars* (from the Persian, meaning the the keeper or holder of the *zamin* − land). Some *zamindars* were evidently chieftains, descended from pre-conquest tribal elders, or original Hindu aristocrats, while others were appointed to their positions through the patronage of *jagirdars*. However, the majority of *zamindars*, to whom Nural Hasan (1963) gives the title 'primary *zamindars*', claimed to be *maliks* or landowners. Even though the correctness of this designation is sometime disputed there is no doubt that the rights of *zamindars* were heritable, alienable and saleable. Their land, *khud-kashta*, was either rented out or cultivated by servants and/or hired labourers. Moreover, as a class *zamindars* extracted for themselves at least a tenth of the agricultural surplus.[46] Their claims to the land were further extended as the Mughal empire collapsed, and they had largely succeeded in constituting themselves as a feudal nobility in north India by the time of the British conquest. The existence of this stratum of landowning exploiters beneath the imperial apparatus of the *mansabdars*, together with the presence of autonomous *rajas* inside the imperial frontiers, complicates the picture of the Mughal class structure, and spoils any neat affinities with the class structure of the AMP.[47] There was a dual class structure, made of dis-

45 They resemble the prefects or provincial governors of other pre-industrial empires more than they do modern 'bureaucrats'.
46 Habib (1963: 162−7) estimated 10 per cent in his earlier work, but now puts this figure as a minimum (1982: 242).
47 *Mansabdars* did intersect with *zamindars*: it was possible to ascend from the latter to the former, and be demoted from the former to the latter.

tinguishable sets of exploiters, superimposed upon the direct producers in the villages.

Similar complications arise with the village structure of the Mughal Empire, especially as constructed from Mughal sources by Habib. Far from the undifferentiated, communal village, the real village structure of Mughal India was marked by extreme caste and class differentiation: 'caste was used to create the class of hired labourers despite the plentiful availability of land. The lower castes were forbidden to cultivate land on their own' (B. Chandra, 1981: 57). Cultivation was carried out by a variety of groups stratified by caste and class: individual owner-cultivators belonging to locally dominant peasant castes from whom the *zamindars* were often drawn, tenants with rights of occupancy, tenants-at-will, share-croppers and wage-labourers. The communal ownership of land was very rare, and found only in the most peripheral and inaccessible villages. The village 'community' was in practice the community of the dominant landowners and caste-members, who organized the payment of the revenue through the village headman. Finally, far from this 'village community' being an historical survival from a previous primitive communist period, there is good reason to believe that the Mughal 'village community' was initially created (or, at the very least, reconstructed) coterminously with the revenue collection system, as a deliberate artefact of imperial regulation (Habib, 1982: 248).[48] The *mansabdars*, the officials of the imperial state apparatus, the intermediary *zamindars* and the peasantry − internally differentiated by class and caste − together had certain rights in the share of the produce of the land, rather than explicit property rights. This structure conflicts with the simplistic expectations suggested by the AMP. Neither kings nor peasants owned the land in the ways required. Indeed talk of watertight demarcations of property rights is anachronistic in the context of many pre-capitalist societies.

Acquaintance with the historical literature on the Mughal agrarian system must disabuse one of the empirical validity of the AMP. The use of the category blinds the analyst to key features of the social formation. In particular, there is evidence of severe class antagonisms in the Mughal Empire − contrary to Wittfogel's suggestions about India in *Oriental Despotism*. At the very least, if the Mughal social formation was dominated by the AMP the thesis that the Orient experienced weaker forms of class struggle must be revised. There were two levels of inter-class struggle in Mughal India: between the royal authorities and the *zamindars*, and between the *zamindars* and the peasants − themselves internally differentiated with

48 Habib has changed his mind on this interpretation of the village community. Earlier he embraced the idea that the primordial village community had gradually disintegrated from within (1963: 128−9). Now he is persuaded that the Indian village community was an imperial creation, an idea first mooted by Baden-Powell (1892, 1: 137).

respect to property, production and appropriation rights. Then there were at least two levels of intra-class struggle, within the Mughal nobility and within the village. Unlike the absolutist monarchs of Western Europe, whom they resembled in some respects, the Mughals made the strategic error of failing to strengthen the peasantry and the merchant class against the aristocracy. Instead their revenue-maximization system encouraged the *jagirdars* to seek short-run returns, a propensity that by the mid-seventeenth century had prompted revolts further down the line, revolts which were endemic by the early eighteenth century. *Zamindars* often led the peasants in great rural insurrections. The peasants also frequently quitted their plots in preference to facing extortionate exactions from imperial officials and/or *zamindars*. The Mughal Empire finally collapsed as much due to its internal fiscal-class contradictions as to other causes (W. Smith, 1946: 21–40).[49]

The final element in investigating for the presence of the AMP requires an examination of the imperial superstructure. The argument is widespread that the Mughals created a highly centralized administration, a prototype of a modern bureaucracy. The thesis, common currency amongst the Aligarh school, has been advanced most notably by the English historian Percival Spear (1970: 1–16). Therefore another necessary condition of the AMP, namely the presence of a highly centralized despotic apparatus used to exploit peasants, seems to be met. In Spear's view the *mansabdars* were the administrative class of the Mughal Empire.[50] Yet the dependence of

---

49 M. Athar Ali (1975: 385–96) argues that there are five traditional explanations of the decline of the Mughal Empire. First, personal deterioration in the quality of the kings and nobles is held responsible. Second, the consequences of Hindu–Muslim conflicts, especially the Hindu reaction to Aurangzeb's religious policy, are emphasized. Third, the failure to maintain the *mansab* and *jagir* systems is invoked (as suggested by S. Chandra, 1959). Fourth, the converse is also argued, especially by Indian Marxists; namely that the collapse of the empire was an effect of the workings of these very systems, and the *jagir* transfers and consequent exploitation produced rebellions by both *zamindars* and peasants. Finally, some Soviet Marxists and American historians emphasize the 'rise of nationalities'. Ali chides all these explanations for being too insular. The simultaneous collapse in the early eighteenth century of other Islamic empires – the Safavid Empire and the Uzbek Khanate – and the visible decline of the Ottoman Empire are neglected. Ali poses the question: was the West subverting the Islamic polities and societies of the East even before military conquest? Ali argues that the rise of Europe as the centre of world commerce had an impact upon Islamic trade centres, raised the costs of luxuries and forced the Mughals to raise the rate of exploitation and thereby increase the dangers of rebellion. (As an argument this is replete with speculation but it is an interesting hypothesis.) He also points to a relative decline in Indian urban development. Whereas in 1600 Lahore and Agra dwarfed European cities, by 1700 European cities like Paris and London outranked Indian cities: 'One need not be a follower of Marx's theory of the unchangeableness of traditional Indian society to accept the fact that there was no conscious spirit of technological innovation (and scientific enquiry) here and in the Islamic East to match the spirit already motivating a large part of European society in the seventeenth century ... The failure of the Mughal Empire would seem to derive essentially from a cultural failure, shared with the entire Islamic world' (Athar Ali, 1975: 389–90). For another idiosyncratic theory of the collapse of the Mughal Empire see Leonard (1979).

50 However, he also points out that 'They illustrate the fact that the Mughal Empire was

the Mughal monarchs upon the aristocratic elite from which they came themselves was always obvious. Moreover, the *mansabdari* system did not emerge fully blown with the Mughal conquests. Even Spear points out that the first of the Mughals, Babur, was enmeshed in feudal-like relations with his Turkish *begs*, while his son Homayun was at best the head of a confederation of jealous aristocrats — of Turkish, Afghan and local origin. It was Akbar who made a deal with the *rajputs* and allegedly created a bureaucracy which involved 'working to rule and by decree, and operated by a salaried and graded officer corps' (ibid). Akbar took a central Asian idea for organizing the furnishing of troops and extended it. Rank was indicated by numbers commanded, and a graded distinction was established between this and the obligation to furnish troops. [51] Nominally at least, the *mansabdars* were entirely dependent upon the government for their maintenance. Akbar paid them in cash from land revenues collected through a separate administrative system of *karoris*, but his successors quickly substituted a system of land assignments. Under Akbar, in fact as well as in theory, the officer given an assignment of the land revenue of a given area was not in charge of a landed estate or a permanently established property. Not only was he dismissable, but also the assignment was returned to the emperor upon death, and a strict system of imperial audit and accounting was mounted. There was even something resembling a pension for the *mansabdar's* family — the *altamgha*.[52] At the apex of this administrative class was a corps of about 500 high officers, 'comparable to the higher ranks of the later British I.C.S, which really ran the Empire' (Spear, 1970: 8).

Spear's portrait of the *mansabdars* as a proto-bureaucracy resembles Max Weber's discussion of patrimonial bureaucracies (Weber, 1978: 1006–1109). The differences from a modern bureaucracy are, none the less, so considerable as to call in question the merits of seeing the *mansabdars* as even proto-bureaucrats. Even the editors of the collection in which Spear's

not what used to be called an Asiatic despotism, or, in other words, an irresponsible and all-powerful autocracy. Not many Oriental monarchies have been wholly irresponsible and few have been all-powerful. The distinction between Asiatic and other despotisms should in fact be relegated to the limbo of historical jargon' (Spear, 1970: 2).

51 Abu'l Fazl's description of the system in *A'in-i Akbari* places its origins in the decimal classification of the numbers of horsemen commanded by a noble: 10,000 for a *khan*, 1000 for a *malik* and 100 for an *amir*.

52 The system was accepted by the nobility for four reasons, according to Spear (1970). First, it established the possibility of a career open to talents, since no office was barred on grounds of birth up to provincial governorships and chief ministries. Second, class solidarity was established at the expense of particularism — for instance, the *rajputs* derived more satisfaction as officers of an all-Indian empire than they could have as autonomous chieftains. Third, loyalty to a series of remarkable emperors, from Babur to Bahadur Shah, was relatively easy to maintain. Finally, the Persian culture of the court acted as a magnet of attraction for the aristocratic elites of the subcontinent.

chapter appeared introduced his arguments with scepticism: 'His arguments imply that, at least in embryo, the *mansabdari* came close to being a bureaucracy in the Weberian sense, a view which surely stretches this ideal concept some way beyond its normal limits' (Leach and Mukherjee, 1970: xi). The verdict of Maddison is convincing: the Mughal Empire 'was a regime of warlords and not a bureaucracy' (1971: 12). The *mansabdars* were primarily soldiers, recruited from tribal and aristocratic warrior elites. Their recruitment was nominally in the hands of the king, and their evaluation was based on their military rather than their administrative capacities. Honour in war rather than bureaucratic skills was the route to promotion. Moreover, crises in assignments after Akbar's time were a regular occurrence, and many emperors experienced difficulties in enforcing transfers. The 'bureaucracy', if such it was, rapidly dissolved into a confederation of personal fief-holders − in this respect paralleling the evolution of the early Turkish sultanate. The Mughal Empire was, in short, inadequately centralized from the perspective of its rulers − rebellious *jagirdars*, rajas and *zamindars* were all-pervasive − and the rulers never established the crushing controls obtained by their contemporaries, the new and emergent absolutist monarchs of Western Europe.[53]

Even if we are charitably lax and concede that the empire resembled the AMP during its most centralized phases, there is still the problem for historical materialists of a historical cycle of modes of production. The periods preceding both the rise and dissolution of the Mughal Empire had most of the trappings of feudal vassalage and parcellized sovereignty, suggesting that even if the AMP was ever dominant it was both preceded and succeeded by feudalism, and that the social formations in which the AMP was dominant displayed a cyclical pattern of state formation and state degeneration, suspiciously like Weber's account of patrimonial-feudal cycles (Weber, 1978). The Mughal social formation therefore poses serious difficulties for traditional historical materialists.

Having briefly cast many doubts on the utility of the AMP in highlighting salient features of Indian social formations, I must explore some issues in greater depth to be convincing. Three core components of the AMP − the 'village community' (pp. 299−302), the despotic state's capacities, proprietary and taxation powers and rights (pp. 303−5) and the underdevelopment of trade and commerce (pp. 305−6) − must be retained if the concept is to make any sense once it is stripped of its hydraulic traits, and to serve the theoretical purpose of helping to explain why some societies

53 Dipankar Gupta, whom I discussed earlier as an advocate of the thesis that the Mauryan Empire was dominated by the AMP, also rejects the idea that the Mughal Empire can be classified as a non-feudal social formation (Gupta, 1980: 263−4). He argues that although the Mughals regenerated a powerful royal bureaucracy they did not dismantle the feudal economic substructure they had inherited from previous regimes.

developed capitalism before others. However, as I shall show, each of these three elements — at least in India — has little to commend it as a way of understanding pre-capitalist development before the spread of European imperialism.

Indian Villages

The choice of 'villages' in this subheading rather than 'village' is deliberate. The singular noun creates the misleading image of an unchanging unit which had identical features throughout the huge subcontinent. The historians' bias for particularity is in this instance much better judged than that of the range of ideologists who, in common with Marx, have spoken of 'the village community'. Matters are still more complicated, because even the ideological rendering of 'village community' has altered over time. A seminal essay has helpfully distinguished three meanings of the Indian 'village community', each of which has predominated in successive historical phases (Dumont, 1970a). First, it has been seen as a political society; second, it was seen as a body of co-owners of the soil; and third, it became the emblem of Indian tradition in the ideology of Indian nationalism. Whichever meaning has prevailed Dumont rightly complains that caste has been ignored or underplayed in these images, which in one way or another portray the village as egalitarian.

As for the first meaning, it is evident that the idealization of the Indian 'village republic' in the early British administrative literature glossed over the limits of the village's sovereignty implied by the imperial or *zamindari* share in the agrarian surplus, as well as the political inequality within the village. The false image of 'India [as] a worm whose segments are the villages' (Dumont, 1970b: 203) needs to be revised. With regard to the second meaning, the earliest descriptions of the village community made it clear that the collective rights of a body of co-sharers in the land were not independent of political relations outside the village, and that the rights of these co-sharers were superior rights, as opposed to the inferior rights of others in the village, and to those who had no rights (such as domestic slaves). Dumont comments acidly: 'from what we know ... it seems that the competent observers, as well as the British administrators who generalized from their own and their colleagues' observations, never lost sight of those two points and that those who did were second-hand writers who had an axe to grind, such as Maine, and to a lesser extent, Marx' (1970a: 122). The impression of selectivity and derivation from defective sources in Marx's idea of the village community is considerably reinforced by Dumont's analysis. Subsequently, Indian Marxists have subjected the third meaning of the village community, that associated with Indian nationalism, to the kind of materialist class criticism one might have expected, but it is a curious fact that Indian Marxists have generally been as blind to the reality and importance of caste as have the nationalists.

At least from the Middle Ages the Indian village was open to the outside world; being subject to some imperial control and engaged in some market interactions. In periods of relative centralization state officials managed to extract its surpluses and monetize its economy. (India had been partly monetized long before the Mughals and before the Delhi Sultanate). In Mughal times village society had three elements: first, the *khud-kashta*, who were also called *malik-i-zamin* or owners of land in official documents, and who claimed to be the original proprietors of the land; second, the *pahi* or *uphari*, outsiders from other villages who did not have the rights of the first group; and third, the *muzari-an* or share-croppers who rented land from the *khud-kashta* peasants or the *zamindars* (S. Chandra, 1982: 458–9). There was also a small class of landless peasants. The mistake of Marx, and some of his sources, was to treat the rural population as an undifferentiated mass – especially curious given their sometimes explicit recognition of the presence of the caste order in the Indian village.

The extent to which the villages were administratively controlled from outside is, however, a matter of continuing debate, especially in different regions and at different times. Were they simply administrative units, as they appear to have been under the Mughals? The objective of the Islamic imperial authorities and tax-collectors was certainly to treat the villages as administrative units. Or were the villages independent proprietary units – whether collectively possessed by dominant castes, or owned by brahmins to whom the land had formally been alienated by monarchs (as may have been the case, in certain places and times, especially under Hindu regimes)? Were they both administrative and proprietary units, or first one and then the other? The very fact that these questions are open to a range of plausible possible responses, depending upon the region and time under discussion, indicates how crude and unhelpful was Marx's categorization of village India.[54]

The villages, it seems, were controlled from both within and without by their own caste hierarchy and the caste system.[55] The brahmins created an

54 The surprising thing is the relative rarity with which discussion has taken place in Indian history over the relations between land rights and the caste system, and between the political system and the caste system. Dumont writes 'As far as the "communities" go, to the extent that they existed they represented joint possession by the dominant caste or lineage. To look for 'ownership' of the land is a false problem, since everything shows a complementarity between different rights bearing on the same object, for example those of the "community" and those of the king' (1970b: 201).

55 Caste has been neglected by some of the major historians of Mughal India: Moreland barely touches upon it, and the same complaint has also been levelled at Habib (B. Moore, 1966: 317–8). The explanations for this must lie in the neglect of caste by the Islamic sources upon whom the historians have relied, and in their concentration upon relations between villages and the state rather than relations within the village.

effective cultural unity across India, one which transcended particular kingdoms and localities. Their knowledge of agriculture, ability to integrate tribes into the caste system and control of ritual created a unified civilization which could persist despite the absence of a centralized political authority. The villages were certainly not culturally autarchic given this subcontinental penetration of the village by the hierarchically dominant organized caste. Yet this feat of cultural uniformity was achieved without the state and without a recognizable Church. However, the geographic variety in the caste system and its many historical vicissitudes, emphasized by modern anthropologists and historians, must never be forgotten. One might almost say that each village had its own castes. At least in this sense the compartmentalization and segmentation of villages stressed in Marx's 1850s journalism were apposite. However, what was fundamentally inadequate in Marx's writings was his failure to appreciate that caste represented a brute denial of 'community'. The caste system, built upon a distinction between the pure and the impure, upon an ideological emphasis on hierarchical difference and interdependence and upon material differences in rights in the agrarian surplus, is antithetical to a unified community based upon people who are tied to one another by kinship and primordial lineages. The villagers shared a cultural 'unity' which emphasized the starkest imaginable differences between the castes – making the notion of 'community' singularly inept.

The members of dominant castes were invariably the pre-eminent holders of land rights. In Mughal times the 'village headman' was always from the dominant caste(s), who always represented the village 'community'. In exchange for the individual ownership of the fields that the dominant castes farmed themselves – with the aid and labour of subordinate castes – they were collectively responsible to the state (or the local overlord) for the payment of taxes on behalf of the whole village. They also received a share of the money collected. The dominant castes plainly enjoyed 'state' and 'class' powers within the village: they had the major rights over the land and powers to grant land, employ other castes and administer judicial conflicts, and they were often related to royal castes (Dumont, 1970b: 207). Village artisans were much more restricted in their access to social resources, wedded to their trades by caste. They shared in the communal harvest, in some cases receiving a plot of land to cultivate and in other cases earning wages. But the life of the rest of the direct producers was scarcely that of 'community' members. The status of the subordinate peasant-castes, while usually removed from slavery, and 'not unfree . . . was definitely . . . dependent' (Chandra, 1976: 84).

Faced with these difficulties some Indian Marxists have tried to defend Marx's portrait of the Indian village by suggesting that he recognized explicitly that the class-divided village was part of a mode of production distinct from that of the primordial communist village. Banerjee has argued that there were not one but two village communities in Marx's writings on India (D. Banerjee, 1983).[56] The first was the original form, and the second the developed form which evolved from the first. The developed form was not a transitional stage from pre-class to class society, but a class society, characterized by slavery and serfdom. The evidence for this interpretation is based on Marx's letters of Zasulich. Banerjee's argument is that the alleged unchangeableness of the Indian village (a confusion Banerjee concedes was caused by Marx) was only a 'relative' unchangeableness, a contrast with Europe.

However, the validity of Marx's conception of the Indian village has not gone unchallenged amongst other Indian Marxists, less concerned to rejig the master to make his views possess greater sense. Menon (1983) has recently argued, in a spirit of evident generosity, that Marx's model of the Indian village was valid for north India, but had little relevance south of the Krishna. She notes that Marx recognized this important fact, and sets out to vindicate this insight by reinforcing the key features which make the south Indian village 'community' incompatible with the AMP. Primary and epigraphic eighteenth-century sources show that elements of private property were widespread in south Indian villages, and that landownership was relatively concentrated amongst the superior right holders – the dominant peasant-castes. There was also greater class stratification within the south Indian village than Marx's stereotype of the Indian village suggested. There was even much greater economic interdependence between villages, and between villages, merchants and the state, than Marx's model allowed. Finally, there were far greater commodity and money relations within the village than Marx had envisaged.

Menon's arguments confine the importance of the AMP village to certain regions of India, and exclude the south from its ambit. But, as I have shown, we can go much further. Much the same objections can be made to understanding the north Indian 'village' in the way suggested by Marx. Indian villages, in brief, cannot play the role assigned to them in the theory of the AMP. In too many spheres the connections between villages and the external political and economic world are too extensive. Their internal divisions are also too considerable to make acceptable the idea of a 'community'. Indeed the focus on 'community' of whatever kind, original or secondary, distracts attention from the salience of caste in explaining India's political and economic structures.

---

56 I am grateful to Professor Sharma for enabling me to trace this paper.

Indian 'Despotic States'

Two fundamental questions arise in evaluating the historiography of the Indian state in the light of the AMP: first, were Indian kings the ruthless and cruel rulers of oriental despotic fame? And second, what is the best analytical way of appreciating the nature of pre-industrial Indian regimes?

I shall answer the first question through a further assault on Wittfogel's *Oriental Despotism*. Throughout this text Wittfogel displayed great selectivity in his choice of exploitative, malign and cruel despots, choosing simply to ignore the (doubtless highly questionable) tales of benevolent and just rule in Indian history. However, by so doing he failed to treat in a balanced manner the available evidence. It did not occur to him that an Indian ruler, far from being a wholly capricious and wild political animal, might have played a crucial role in the administration of caste justice, a system which is repulsive for contemporary Western culture, but nevertheless a system of justice, and by no means entirely arbitrary.

The old texts written on ancient Indian statecraft emphasized that the king's primary role was protection. Indeed early Vedic legends suggest that the origins of kingship lay in military leadership of the tribe: the king's role was that of leader and protector rather than one of malevolent imposition. A genuine Indian version of social contract theory is present in Buddhist legends, notably in the story of the *Mahasammata*, where the origins of state are explained as the outcome of the quest for order after social decay from a previous harmonious existence. The theme of monarchy as a solution to anarchy was widespread in Indian political reflection. For example, the period between Mauryans and Guptas generated a fear of lawlessness and anarchy amongst Indian sages, a fear of what they called *mātsyanyāya* (literally 'the way of the fishes') where the strong eat the weak (Basham, 1967: 85). Consequently they recommended monarchy as a solution to the problem of order. Wittfogel relied too much on the *Arthashastra* which was atypical in classical Indian literature in suggesting that the king could override all other sources of law. He never paused to consider whether the more blood-curdling recommendations of *Manu* or the *Arthashastra* were rhetorical and prescriptive rather than descriptive. Generally, the king's function was seen primarily as that of protection rather than legislation: protection from invasion and protection of the order of society — that is, the right way of life, the *varnasrama-dharma*, as laid down in the sacred texts. If the king failed to carry out either protection function (by failure in war or infringement of sacred custom) he risked the hostility of the brahmins and possibly of the lower castes too. The *Mahabharata* sanctioned revolts against a king who was oppressive or failed in his function of protection, declaring that such a ruler was no king at all and was worthy of being killed like a mad dog. Aside from these ideological checks on the king, provided by the sacred law and the power of the brahmins, many Indian kings were also institutionally checked by tribal assemblies, their own hereditary counsellors and the multitude of caste and guild organizations at the level of the village and the town. These facts, available to any scrupulous reader of Indian history, were simply bypassed by Wittfogel.

On a less systematic level one might simply trade anecdotes with Wittfogel on the issue of the egoism or altruism of Indian monarchs. One of his Indian Marxist critics summarized the flaws in his normative appraisal of Indian monarchies and regimes in this excellent riposte: 'In a study of "Oriental despotism" why is it essential to omit periods when the rule struck all observers as being singularly kindly and unoppressive, not only in form but also in fact?' (Kosambi, 1957: 1417). The benign rule of Ashoka, the greatest of the Mauryans, is part of the stock-in-trade of the English Indophile historian and of the hagiography of nationalist Indian historians – but it does not even receive a dismissal in *Oriental Despotism*. Similarly Wittfogel ignored the primary evidence provided by the accounts of Chinese travellers in India during the era of the Guptas (the fourth and fifth centuries AD) and the time of Harsha (in the early seventh century AD). These travellers suggested that penal legislation was mild by comparison with what they were used to, and (remarkably in the eyes of the Chinese observers) there was no judicial torture.[57] It is interesting to note that Basham, an acknowledged Indophile but a genuine scholar, remarked, on the basis of more extensive study than Wittfogel's, that despite some despicable features in early Indian civilization 'our overall impression is that in no other part of the ancient world were the relations of man and man, and of man and the state, so fair and humane. In no other early civilization were slaves so few in number, and in no other ancient lawbook are their rights so well protected as in the *Arthashastra*' (Basham, 1967: 8–9). He considered the Indian less cruel and oppressive than other early cultures: 'To us the most striking feature on ancient Indian civilization is its humanity' (ibid.: 9).

The second issue which arises in evaluating Indian states in the light of the AMP, the analytical classification of pre-modern regimes, is complicated by the fact that there is an enduring temptation on the part of all political scientists, political sociologists and historians to read back into history the presence of many core features of the modern state – sovereignty, centralization, territoriality and bureaucratization. My discussion of Indian regime has highlighted these difficulties. The salutary judgement that limited historical evidence makes models of early state formation difficult to apply must be accepted (Thapar, 1984). However, following recent analyses and my own survey, it seems that pre-modern Indian regimes are best classified

---

57 There was judicial torture in India – but its scale and character was similar to that in medieval Europe (Basham, 1967: chapter 4).

as specimens of three basic types: custodial (or segmentary state) regimes, conquest empires and feudal polities. (The last two types are also arguably phases of the same system). How do these classifications fit with the concept of the AMP?

The custodial regime is only compatible with a reconstructed model of the AMP which accepts the presence of class- and caste-stratified villages and a very wide dispersion of coercive authority beyond the royal authority; and which also excludes the presence of a centralized hydraulic bureaucracy. However, even such a reconstructed model cannot cope with the absolute autonomy of ideology required to make it fit the reality of Hindu polities. As I have suggested, it was the brahmins, independently of state apparatuses, who created whatever civilization and normative pacification existed in pre-Muslim India. Moreover, such a reconstructed model of the AMP could not have been dominant in social formations like the Mughal Empire, and therefore could play no important role in explaining India's failure to evolve capitalism before the British conquest. Making an AMP with a custodial superstructure even roughly compatible with key features of Indian history deprives historical materialists of its use in explaining the occidental origins of capitalism.

By contrast, the problem with the conquest and feudal superstructures is that they are very difficult to portray as functional for the development of the productive forces. This problem makes it difficult to understand them as the states of any Marxist modes of production, let alone of the AMP. Conquest empires and feudal polities in India were also neither hydraulic, in Wittfogel's sense, nor free of intermediate exploiters (between the regime and the class- and caste-divided villages). Even if we accept the idea of a patrimonial-feudal cycle in Indian history, in their feudal phases such regimes were the superstructures of a different mode of production. And in their 'conquest' phases they were associated with economic bases considerably more productive and populous than those associated with European feudal polities.

The analysis of pre-industrial regimes is generally problematic for historical materialists: Indian history is not uniquely so. Marxists are handicapped by an image of the state – centralized, coercive, bureaucratic and politically and ideologically functional for the economy – constructed from the history of the capitalist and industrialized West, but inappropriate for most agrarian societies. The problems encountered with the AMP and Indian regimes are merely aspects of this wider difficulty.

Indian Trade and Commerce

At several junctures the fragmented and partial character of Indian historiography has been stressed. Nowhere is this more obvious than in Indian economic history. However, there is now sufficient scholarship to challenge van Leuer's (1955) well-known stereotype of south Asian traders as mere pedlars travelling with small quantities of luxury goods. As Braudel has put it:

Everywhere, from Egypt to Japan, we ... find genuine capitalists, wholesalers, the rentiers of trade, and their thousands of auxilliaries – the commission agents, brokers, money-changers and bankers. As for the techniques, possibilities or guarantees of exchange, any of these groups of merchants would stand comparison with its western equivalents. Both inside and outside India, Tamil, Bengali and Gujerati merchants formed close-knit partnerships business and contracts passing in turn from one group to another, just as they might in Europe from the Florentines to the Lucchese, the Genoese, the South Germans or the English. (Braudel, 1984: 486)

The networks of sea-based trade ranked in volume and diversity with the Mediterranean and north Atlantic, and were considerable long before the arrival of the Europeans (Chaudhuri, 1985). The British conquerors made use of local merchants and bankers everywhere in India, and it was only when British rule was firmly established in Bengal that the native capitalists of Calcutta were excluded from the most profitable sectors – banking and foreign trade – and confined to land, usury and tax-collecting.

Evidence from Mughal urban history (Hambly, 1982; and H.K. Naqvi, 1968), which I have already discussed (see p. 291), suggests that Indian urban development is not merely reducible to administrative parasiticism. Combined, this evidence of extensive trade and urban growth suggests that even if we conceded that the AMP had existed in some Indian social formations its operations did not manage to restrain some nascent capitalist traits from emerging. In fact it may be, paradoxically, that the Mughals were insufficiently bureaucratic, despotic and centralized to permit a full flowering of capitalism. It was after all the bureaucratic, absolutist and centralized states of Western Europe which were able to create the rule of law and the space for autonomous capitalist development. There were regular conflicts between traders, *rajas*, and Mughal officials over the local taxation of merchandise and merchants' caravans – despite imperial *firmans* outlawing such practices (H.K. Naqvi, 1968: 227, 272 and 282) – which suggest that the regime was not sufficiently centralized to restrain localized predatory behaviour. Had the Mughal state been centralized enough to organize a strategy of looking after the geese that laid the golden eggs, perhaps things might have been different. However, this speculation also suggests that the relative absence of such thinking may be just as important in explaining India's failure to develop capitalism. Nowhere in Mughal India was there anything resembling what became liberal political economy, beyond administrative injunctions not to tax subjects too harshly. It seems reasonable to conclude that the Indian 'failure' to develop capitalism must be sought elsewhere than in the dysfunctional constraints of the AMP.

CONCLUSION

This examination of the historiography of major Indian social formations has posed insuperable difficulties for the proposition that the AMP existed throughout pre-colonial India. In the first place difficulties arise from the sheer paucity of reliable data and inferences about production relations and productive forces. In the case of four social formations (that of the Indus valley, the Mauryan Empire, the Vijayanagar Empire and the Delhi Sultanate) the problem is acute, and compels a verdict of ignorance about the Indus social formation.

Second, for the two Hindu social formations, the Mauryan and the Vijayanagar empires, there is sufficient evidence and reasonable inference to refute the idea that two elements of the AMP were dominant for any considerable time or in any considerable region of the empires – namely, centralized hydraulic agriculture and a centralized, bureaucratic state apparatus. These regimes had superstructures which are better described through Stein's category: custodial segmentary states. If one wants to argue that the AMP was present in these societies then a thoroughly radical revision of its superstructural elements is required.

Third, in so far as there is reliable evidence about Indian villages, it suggests that caste- and class-divisions were extreme. Indian villages were not survivals of primitive communism, in transition from classless to class society. Provided we abandon the occidental notion that the definition of class requires the clear delineation of property rights in the means of production, it is also clear that there were class divisions in these villages – reflected in differential rights in the division of the output.[58] Moreover, the explanation of Indian stagnation, as far as it is true, is better sought in the presence and workings of the caste system within the village, rather than in Marx's emphasis upon the autarkic village community.

Finally, quite separate difficulties arise with accepting the applicability of the AMP in the case of the two major Islamic formations. Although the sultanate and the Mughal polities established something resembling administrative and bureaucratic centralization, they seem best comprehended as conquest empires, rather than as regimes whose superstructures are explained as functionally supportive of the economic structure. In both instances centralized hydraulic agriculture was insignificant. Moreover, monetization of the surplus was extensive, and both long-distance trade and inter-village trade were by no means negligible. Urban growth was not

58 Schematically one might argue that the bias of Marxist class analysis is always on the side of inputs into the prodution process. For Marxists the key questions are: who owns the means of production, labour power, spaces and premises? This schema seems appropriate for capitalist societies. However, in pre-capitalist formations, such as those which existed in India, it is better to analyse the *output* side of the production process. The key questions are: to whom do the differential benefits from the distribution of the product flow? And who shares in the division of the spoils?

based only on parasitic militarism, and technological developments by no means confirm the story Marx and others told of millennial stagnation. The villages were not autarkic. Most tellingly, there was a complex structure of rights and classes in the Muslim regimes: classes which do not fit neatly into any model of the AMP and which engaged in what can only be described as class struggle over the fiscal exactions of the imperial officialdom and the *zamindars*.

The foregoing set of stylized facts extracted from the best Indian historiography fits equally ill with Wittfogel's portrait of India as a home of 'hydraulic despotisms'. At best the Mauryan and Muslim empires pass the first hurdle of acceptability: the presence of something resembling a centralized state apparatus (although this interpretation of these Indian states is being increasingly challenged). Not only was hydraulic agriculture insignificant in all these regimes in comparison with spontaneous irrigation and monsoon-fed irrigation, but also they lacked the durability and degree of centralization which Wittfogel's model suggested. The application of the stereotype of oriental despotism, which is found in the European imperial administrative historiography and upon which Wittfogel uncritically relied, was especially inappropriate since 'authority for routine functions was rarely concentrated at the centre in the Indian political systems. The unique feature of Indian society – the caste system – integrated as it was to both politics and professional activity, localized many of the functions which would normally be associated with a truly "oriental despotism"' (Thapar, 1966: 19).

The stereotype of oriental despotism *à la* Wittfogel, and the concept of the AMP *à la* Marx, are inappropriately applied to Indian history for four key reasons. First, genuine empires were infrequent and had short durations in the history of the subcontinent. Second, the concepts clash with the many references in Indian history to private property in land. In the *Dharmashastras* and even in the *Arthashastra* there are discussions of laws on the sale and inheritance of land, and furthermore there is multiple evidence from inscriptions of royal transfers of land which confirms the existence of different categories of landownership, including private ownership. Third, these stereotypical concepts are anachronistic because they read back the glorification of centralized British administration into the Indian past, despite the fact that the available evidence shows that most governmental functions were performed locally in pre-colonial times.

Finally, the emphasis placed on the power and divinity of Indian kings as confirmation of the salience of oriental despotism in Indian history betrays insensitivity to cultural context, and considerable ignorance. Vedic India attributed divinity to virtually everything which moved, and to many things which did not. 'Divinity was cheap in ancient India. Every Brahman was in a sense a god, as were ascetics with a reputation for sanctity ... Moreover the gods were fallible and capable of sin' (Basham, 1967: 86). The

Mauryans — the monarchs most universally recognized as coming close to the 'despotic' image — were the patrons of sects which denied the existence of any god (Thapar, 1961)! Both Buddhists and Jains explicitly denied royal divinity and were never prosecuted for this transgression. Wittfogel's oriental despotism and Marx's AMP obfuscate the real significance of religion in the workings of the Hindu polity. The fact is that the brahmins managed to monopolize the sacred religious sphere, the sphere of *dharma*, whereas the kings were left with the sphere of force, the domain of interest and advantage, *artha*. Kings required their brahminical chaplain, the *purohit*, to preside over their sacrifices. The brahmins renounced politics and firmly secularized the political sphere. This division between the temporal and the spiritual was far more dramatically declared and implemented in Hinduism than in other world religions: 'comparatively . . . in India the king lost his religious prerogatives' (Dumont, 1970a: 68). Therefore Wittfogel's attempt to incorporate Indian kings with Mesopotamian and Chinese emperors as examples of the fusion of religious and political power was misconceived. (Ashoka, who experimented with Buddhism, was exceptional in trying to fuse *dharma* and *artha*.)

There were features of Indian social formations which may have made them inhospitable to capitalist, industrialist and democratic developments, but these are not illuminated by Wittfogel's model of a 'hydraulic despotism', its antecedent idea of 'oriental despotism' or Marx's concept of an AMP. Too many important historical facts are hostile to key elements in these ideas. In particular, any reconstruction of the AMP to make it fit the facts of any major Indian social formation must jettison so many core elements of the original conception — hydraulic agricultural production, a centralized, bureaucratic and despotic state, surplus extracted in kind, minimal urban development, autarkic and communist village communities, and millennial stagnation — that it would cease to be a recognizable reworking of the original idea.

APPENDIX 7.1   RATIONAL CHOICE AND INDIAN DESPOTISM

Formal political analysis, under various synonyms such as collective, social, public, or rational choice, has been well received by contemporary political scientists (McLean, 1987; and Mueller, 1979). Its traits of methodological individualism and deductive rigour have won widespread admiration, because they do not depend upon functionalist 'leaps of faith' when attempting to explain political phenomena. However, the axiomatic foundations of rational choice theory in the free and consequentialist choices of individuals leaves it vulnerable to the charge that its models of political behaviour are ahistorical (MacPherson, 1973; and Toye, 1976). The rational choice approach is widely considered ideological because it *naturalizes* the maximizing individual, treating him or her as eternal, when in fact historical knowledge suggests that this individual is novel, the product of a bourgeois or capitalist society.[59]

None the less, the modelling of pre-industrial political systems should not be left to the duopoly of Marxists and structural-functional sociologists. Rational choice methodology, *pace* its critics, can provide illuminating insights into the workings of non-individualistic social systems, because it provides compelling answers to one of the key questions of political analysis: why do people put up with the regimes which govern them? Rational choice explanations are compelling because they do not rely heavily on problematic theories such as 'socialization' or the power of 'dominant ideologies', which pay little respect to the fundamental feature of human beings: their capacity for rational deliberation upon whatever situation they find themselves in and their ability to formulate alternatives.

However, rational choice modelling, to win social scientific respectability, must pay more than lip-service to the knowledge generated by historical research (and the work of some sociologists and Marxists when it is empirically productive), and it must generate fresh insights which these other approaches have precluded. I believe that the rational choice understanding of the legitimacy of despotism, pioneered by Rogowski (1974), with some important modifications, aids the synthesis of existing knowledge of Hindu political systems, and provides insights denied to other approaches.

Consider first the following key questions about Hindu political systems in the pre-colonial period,[60] many of which raise issues that have emerged in discussions of the relevance of the AMP to India, and none of which have received satisfactory answers from Marxists:

Why did the Hindu social system, apparently without the presence of slave-labour in production or of widespread serfdom, coexist with apparently despotic political institutions?
What were the relations between the caste and the political systems?
Why was despotism legitimate in India — if it was ligitimate?
Why were Hindu political regimes relatively fragile, subject to systematic failure to expand their territories and to periodic collapses?
What best explains the apparent unchangeableness of Indian villages?

The first question has received answers from Marxists and Western sociologists which are essentially functionalist. The consequences of the state's emergence are regarded as sufficient to explain its emergence. For example, the despotic state's alleged functional role in hydraulic irrigation

---

59 I shall leave to one side the interesting question of whether peasant, aristocratic and 'Communist' behaviours are amenable to rational choice explanation.

60 Indian historians generally use this phrase to cover the four centuries before the British conquest. I am using it broadly to cover the entire period from the Rig-Vedic age to the British conquest.

has been a popular explanation of the emergence of despotic empires in India. This explanation, popularized by Wittfogel's *Oriental Despotism* is, as we have seen, at odds with the evidence of Indian history. Moreover, the evidence of early Indian history suggests that the first political systems were not despotic, but rather republican. In other words we have to explain the emergence and existence of despotic states which did not have functionally beneficial consequences, at least in the sphere of irrigation.

The best general sociological explanation which might reconcile these facts is the conquest theory of Michael Mann, which stresses the autonomous importance of military organization in the history of social power. Mann argues, developing the ideas of the Chicago historian W. H. McNeill and Carneiro's (1970) theory of environmental circumscription, that the first 'empires of domination' emerged from the development of military organization in particular ecological niches. Where alluvial agriculture developed in the early river valley civilizations, a rapid population explosion was the natural consequence. The populations in such areas were effectively 'caged' into their working environments because they could not migrate elsewhere without losing all their investments in agriculture. Such populations were open to military conquest by 'marcher lords' who developed the logistical and military capacity to concentrate coercion at potential points of dissent. When developments in military technology led to the supersession of 'democratic' or 'republican' military organization, the emergence of despotism was more or less inevitable: 'The gigantic protection racket of political history began: Accept my power, for I will protect you from worse violence — of which I can give you a sample, if you don't believe me' (Mann, 1986: 100).

This 'protection-racket' conception of the despotic state would happily be accepted by rational choice theorists, despite Mann's professed sympathy for 'sociological' reasoning. However, Mann modifies its implications, and suggests that the despotic state produced five beneficial consequences, which he argues were 'functions' of this state: military pacification; a military multiplier — or the agrarian analogue of Keynesianism; the authoritative stabilization of economic exchanges; the intensification of labour through coercion; and the coerced diffusion of the literate culture of the imperial core. Thus the despotic state was both exploitative and functional. The state emerged and was acceptable where Leviathans could compel individuals to make cost-benefit calculations which meant that the benefits of rebellion, discounted by the probability that their rebellion would make a difference, would rarely exceed the costs of rebellion — although Mann would not put the argument in this language. The merit of this approach is that it succeeds in spelling out why certain environments rather than others made the first extended Leviathans possible.

However, Mann's theory, illuminating though it may be for the early

Mesopotamian and Egyptian civilizations, is insufficiently finely grained to be capable of wholesale transplantation to Indian civilizations. A military – ecological nexus compelling rational individuals to accept despotism, while not entirely absent, did not exist to the same extent. Until the advent of Muslim conquerors with military capabilities superior to those of their Hindu predecessors, extensive military and organizational penetration by rulers was relatively rare in Indian history. Indian despotisms in the pre-Muslim era were fragile by comparison with their Egyptian, Mesopotamian, Chinese and Roman counterparts. Their periods of duration and their grip on their territories were much weaker, as far we can tell from primary, epigraphic and archaeological source materials. It is true that the wheat-growing and rice-cultivating populations of northern India were vulnerable to military conquest, and the ecology of the northern Indian plains facilitated any conqueror's ambitions – whether the conqueror was indigenous or at the head of a nomadic army from central Asia. 'The ancient and medieval history of Northern India is based principally on two geographical facts: the one that the north-western barrier is not complete, and the other that, when once an invader crosses the passes, he finds no physical barriers to check his advance' (I. Hasan, 1980: 32). But the model of an exploitative military-ecological nexus creating despotic opportunities does not account for two features of Hindu political systems which establish their distinc-tiveness in a comparative perspective. First, in India the diffusion of Aryan culture preceded the establishment of medium- or large-scale despotic states, and that religious culture was both distinctive and important in explaining the nature of political power in early India. Unlike Sumer or Egypt, religious and military power were never fused in Hindu India. Second, the subjects of Hindu regimes had much greater opportunities to flee the fiscal ambitions of exploitative despots. Much of India remained covered in forests and inaccessible to the 'inland revenue' services of emperors. These facts help to explain some of the comparative weaknesses of Indian despotisms.

The combination of Mann's military-ecological nexus and Rogowski's rational choice conception of despotism provides an elegant and historically informed way of understanding the key features of these Hindu political systems. Mann's model explains the ecological, military and logistical limits to the ambitions of despots before the Mughals. It illuminates the political environment, especially of northern India. Rogowski's model, by contrast, explains why monarchical regimes were legitimate, despite an environment which was not propitious for the establishment of strong despotisms, pre-cisely because it explains the limitations on Indian despots. Rogowski's neglected and startling innovation was to apply individualist reasoning to understanding the caste system. In his discussion of segmented societies – that is, societies in which ethnic or occupational strata are organized – he develops theses about the likely behaviour of such strata on the basis of individualist premises. The formation of a segment is more likely if the members share a common and unique stigma than if they do not; and the stronger the stigmata, the less severe will be the need for penalties for disloyalty to the group. He reasons that in a stratified society the potential influence of a group depends predominantly on the degree to which it can credibly claim to monopolize an essential social skill; that the formation of segments is likely to be a chain reaction in any highly stratified society (the formation of one will usually lead to the formation of many); and that conversely, the dismantling of segments is extremely difficult since all would have to be abandoned simultaneously if all were to avoid the loss of political influence. He also reasons that segments are likeliest in those strata with the fewest members; that is, in elites.[60] Moreover segments of fewer members can generally bear higher costs of coalition than can segments of many members, are less likely to need harsh punishments to maintain segmental cohesion, and are less likely to require common stigmata to maintain themselves. The nub of Rogowski's argument, crudely put, is that the theory of justice in a given society will roughly be 'to each group according to its threat advantage', which in turn is a function of its stigmata and its skill-monopolies or lack of them.

The Indian caste system, according to Rogowski, is an example of a stratified social system in which individuals share uniform perceptions about the power of different castes. The conviction is widespread that castes have unequal probabilities of coalition and therefore they will be thought to have by right an unequal influence, proportional to these relative probabilities. There will be 'proportional justice' based on an inequality of estates. Each caste depends upon the others but their chances of successfully withholding services from society are unequal. Therefore, rational individuals will accept blatantly unequal justice because of the absence of workable alternatives. Inter-caste conflict-regulation requires either direct negotiations between segmental leaders or adjudication by an arbiter who is not a member of either segment concerned − or most likely is a member of a 'higher' segment. The stability of such a system is likely to be undermined if there are weaknesses amongst the internal leaderships of the segments, if there is a high rate of economic or occupational change, and if there is disagreement on the 'neutral' arbiter. The arbiter will be weakest where perceptions of relative strengths of segments are nearly uniform − in highly stagnant agrarian economies − and strongest where rapid economic change creates doubts about the relative strengths of segments.

Such in stark outlines are the elements of Rogowski's argument. Consider its application to Hindu political systems. First, upon their arrival the Aryan

---

61 The validity of these derivative assumptions cannot be discussed here.

invaders of India already had a highly stratified society, subdivided into four castes (priests, warriors, farmers and artisans). In the conquest of India they reserved the first three occupations to themselves and imposed upon the original inhabitants, who at that stage were clearly physiologically different, the degrading and servile occupations. Obvious stigmata which differentiated the castes were gradually reinforced by prohibition on exogamous marriage and the development of a range of cultural demarcations, notably in diet. Eventually the myths of the Rig-Veda asserted the separate origin of each caste – albeit from different organs of the same god – based on distinctions of *varna* (a word etymologically related to 'colour'). In the *Bhagavadgita* (composed between the fifth and third centuries BC) Krishna asserts: 'The four orders of men arose from me, in justice to their natures and their works. Know that this work was mine, though I am beyond work, in Eternity' (Mascaró, 1962: 62). From this fourfold division (fivefold when unmentioned untouchables are included) the further segmentation of society into the minutely differentiated caste system of *jati* was a logical development. It terminated in a frozen division of labour based, at least in theory and very considerably in practice, upon a strictly hereditary basis. This précis of the origins of the caste system would not be too strongly dissented from by many theorists and historians of different theoretical dispositions (Basham, 1967; Chanana, 1960; Dutt, 1968; Senart, 1930; and Sharma, 1980: 9–45), but what is distinctive about Rogowski's version is that he tries to demonstrate the integral links between this story of caste society and Hindu political systems.

First, each caste (except the caste of 'outcastes') in a sense had its own government, almost from the inception of the system; its own caste laws, customs, 'village council' and the right to discipline its own members. Within each village-based caste, relations between members of the caste were egalitarian – at least for the males. Their writs of judgements on their members were accepted by the king. In this respect he was legitimate and not at all despotic. Intra-caste conflict was therefore largely internally regulated. Second, inter-caste conflicts were, as far as feasible, adjudicated by the relevant castes themselves, but where this proved insufficient the village headman, and finally the king, played the role of arbiter. Settlements of inter-caste conflicts normally closely followed the proportional weight of the respective castes in the society. Here the 'despot' enjoyed some discretion in arbitration, but was guided by the existing pattern of caste relations. In brief, in this political system, 'society' scarcely required the 'state', or the despot, save only to regulate inter-caste relations during economic change or turbulence of some other kind which upset the balance of power among the castes. The weighty authority of Basham makes the historically valid generalization that in the Hindu political system 'Society, the age-old divinely ordained way of Indian life, transcended the state and was independent of it' (1954: 88).

Indeed the nearly self-equilibriating character of the caste system helps explain two other striking features of the pre-Muslim Indian social system: its relative tolerance for non-Hindu monarchs who did not try to proselytize, and its tolerance for the deviant world religions of Buddhism and Jainism. The non-caste status of non-Hindu rulers facilitated the performance of the role of neutral arbiter in inter-caste conflicts, while the deviant religions were largely urban phenomena, and capable of being reabsorbed into the caste system. Village India was mostly untouched by these urban faiths because they scarcely affected the operation of the caste system where it mattered. The key political importance of caste is not just its hierarchical stratification system, to which nearly all attention has been given, but rather the fact that the caste structure performed functions that might otherwise have been organized by a state apparatus.

Thus once Indian territory was conquered the ruler had an easy task – simply to ensure that he sat astride the caste system (Karve, 1961). It was the relative stability of the caste system, rather than the village *per se*, which permitted what Marx described as the storm cloud of politics to pass overhead without affecting the social terrain. Hence, by combining elements of Mann's military and ecological model of vulnerability to conquest with Rogowski's theory of rational legitimacy in a segmented society, we have the key elements of a social scientific explanation of several salient features of the Hindu political system – its seeming unchangeableness, its apparently remote and easily conquered political superstructures, and the fragile and almost socially irrelevant character of its political despotisms. Only with the arrival of the Muslims was the capacity of states in India to penetrate society established by dint of transformed fire-power and by the arrival of a significant segment of people who operated outside the caste system.

The problematic of the AMP, at least in the Indian case, is thus better explained by methodologies and concepts foreign to the presuppositions of historical materialism. The Hindu social system, without the presence of slave-labour in production or of widespread serfdom, coexisted with super-ficially despotic political institutions but was in fact largely self-equilibriating. The monarch played the role of occasional steersman. The caste system determined the limited autonomy of the political system. Despots were legitimate in India in so far as they preserved the autonomously stratified social order and balanced proportionately the powers of the unequal seg-ments. They were relatively fragile, subject to systematic failure to expand their territories and periodic collapses, because they were largely superfluous to the maintenance of the social systems they nominally regulated and, at least in northern India, wide open to external conquest or destabilization from the steppes, since the population at large could afford to be indifferent to their fate. The apparent unchangeableness of Indian villages, as far as it is true, must be sought in the structural patterns of the caste system – albeit explained though individualist premises – and not in the flawed concept of the AMP. Indeed the general conclusion of this appendix is that the phenomena allegedly explained by the AMP, as far as they correspond at all with the historical evidence of the operations of the Hindu social system, are best explained by synthesizing Mann's ecological-military nexus theory with Rogowski's rational choice model of legitimacy in a segmented society.

APPENDIX 7.2   INDIAN AND SOVIET MARXISTS ON INDIA AND
THE ASIATIC MODE OF PRODUCTION

The writings of both Indian and Soviet Marxists on Indian history reveal much about the strengths and weaknesses of historical materialism. The strengths include the attention paid to questions of technology, agriculture, class and property relations – the features in which one would expect materialist historians to display their forte. Their weaknesses likewise highlight the key difficulties in Marxist sociology: the failure to comprehend ideologies and political formations whose influences and developments are autonomous from material structures, and are neither necessarily functional for the latter nor derived from them. This appendix briefly surveys the analysis of Indian history and the treatment of the AMP by Soviet and Indian scholars.

Soviet Marxism and Indian Historiography

We are fortunate to have an English translation of a review of early Soviet Indology by L.B. Alayev (1964: 59–66). The earliest Soviet study of Indian history had to begin almost from scratch. Traditional Russian Orientalism had no use for it, given its focus upon philology and religious studies. The growth of historical studies of India in the Russian language was indebted solely to Marxist historians working under the auspices of Soviet Indology (Kovalevsky's work on Indian landholding was ignored by Alayev). A small cadre of professional historians of India formed by the early 1930s. Between 1917 and 1934 they were chiefly preoccupied with assessing the work of foreigners without making original contributions. An article by A. Mishulin on 'Indian Antiquity' was typical – it comprised a short appraisal of English bourgeois literature in the field, a survey of sources and some attempt at a general definition of the social-economic system of early India.

Early Soviet historiography of India reflected the conflict with the 'unscientific and artificial' constructions of M.N. Roy, who was accused of exaggerating the progressive aspect of British policy in India. Alayev points out censoriously that 'The social-economic order of pre-colonial India, even in the works of the better equipped Indologists, was for some while described as *"a system of the Asian method of production"* [sic]' (ibid: 60 – my italics[62]). I.M. Reisner was apparently the major Soviet enthusiast for an 'Asiatic' interpretation of Indian history in the 1920s.[63] However, unlike Marx, Reisner did not regard the British destruction of the AMP as an unalloyed blessing. For in 1922, in line with Comintern perspectives on imperialism, he advanced the thesis that British domination had been a historically adverse influence in *all* periods of colonial exploitation. His work pushed Soviet historical research towards a preoccupation with demonstrating the havoc created in Indian handicrafts at the beginning of the nineteenth century, and with proving that the British had deliberately frustrated the development of native capitalist industry by systematically pumping a huge colonial tribute out of its Indian empire. Alayev obliquely informs us about Reisner's work:

Obscurity as to what kind of exploitation the Indian peasant suffered was a mark of many works in this period: for example, I.M. Reisner's *Land Ownership and Rent in India*, 1928. The rule (*formuliirovka*) on The Prevalance of Feudal Survivals in the agriculture of the countries of the east, including India, was recognized only with effect from the VIth Congress of the Comintern. (ibid: 62–3).

These remarks suggest that Reisner believed that Asiatic rather than feudal exploitation prevailed in India, and that he was obliged to alter his views as the party line shifted with the decrees of the Comintern.

Other sources inform us that I.M. Reisner addressed the Sociological Section of the Society of Marxist Historians in May 1929 (Sawer, 1977a). He believed that research on Mughal India demonstrated that the Asiatic rather than the feudal mode of production had dominated this social formation. In the conclusion to his paper he directly rebutted the charges of Orientalism and Eurocentricity attached to this concept: 'It is necessary for us to turn back directly to Marx. The charge against us "Aziatophiles" of Eastern chauvinism is quite groundless. Our task, despite the Indian nationalists who blanket Indian history with the fog of mysticism, consists in discovering in this history the laws of the class struggle' (Reisner – cited in Sawer, 1977a: 93).[64]

---

62 The translator of Alayev's article was presumably not familiar with Marxist terminology since the 'Asian method of production' is clearly the AMP. Alayev, along with another Soviet Indologist, K.A. Antonova, is described as having been in a minority in opposing the resurrection of the AMP in a seminar held in the Philosophy Institute of the USSR Academy of Sciences in December 1964 (Danilova, 1966: 6).

63 I have been unable to obtain copies of his works.

64 In 1930 two brief works were produced in the Soviet Union which presented Marx and Engels's writings on India: A.I. Shtusser's *Marx and Engels on India*, edited and with a foreword by L.A. Madi'iar and an article by P. Fox, *Letopisi marksizma*, 1930, III, 3–29 (Sawer, 1977a: 94). Paul Fox was a British Communist resident in Moscow, but I have been unable to find any details of his life.

Alayev also informs us that Reisner's *Essays on the Class Struggle in India*, published in 1932, covered the entire period of modern history and

were remarkable for the light they shed on the basic social-economic and political issues of the pre-colonial period. In a preface Reisner wrote how after some leanings towards the *'Asian method of production'* [sic] he had come around to the conviction that no genuine explanation of the economy and class contradictions of pre-colonial India could be arrived at except on the postulate of a FEUDAL system of production. He noted the salient features of Indian feudalism — features which in his opinion warranted one's terming it 'eastern'. He then *creatively applied* Karl Marx's announcements on Eastern society, demonstrating the extraordinary stagnation and conservatism of such a society, and posed the question of its development and expansion. Societies of the sort have, as he put it, 'already gone out of the communistic stage', bear the stigma of material and social inequality, and are altogether remote from that 'veritable democracy' which certain apologists of the 'golden age' of India have been wont to rhapsodize. Reisner's whole work was a denial of the anti-Marxist position commonly taken in bourgeois literature which pretends that the class struggle was not characteristic of India. (ibid: 61 — my italics)

We are not told what led Reisner to change his mind, but it is patently clear that his recantation and creative application of Marx's announcements on Eastern society amounted to little more than a re-labelling of the alleged Asiatic features of Indian society as feudal. What really happened to persuade Reisner to alter the tenor of his work on India after 1932 is unclear, but it seems reasonable to infer that the *Aziatchiki's* position had become officially unthinkable in Marxist-Leninist circles.[65]

Subsequently Soviet work on India went into the doldrums. As one authority puts it, 'any extensive bibliographical study reveals that India enjoys a predominant place in Soviet orientology', but 'Stalin's downgrading of the East necessarily led to a dark age in Soviet orientology lasting for the final twenty-five years of Stalin's rule' (Clarkson, 1979: 9). Clarkson's analysis is apposite as is his division of the Soviet study of India before the 1950s into three stages. First, the period of revolutionary enthusiasm, in which little analysis or empirical knowledge was evident, lasted from 1917 to 1920, and was characterized by a literature of propaganda and exhortation. Second, the period in which M.N. Roy's analysis of India held sway lasted throughout most of the 1920s: 1922–8.[66] The third period was that of

---

65 Alayev (1964: 65) tells us, rather obscurely, that 'Despite the difficulties and the mistakes that commonly beset an untrodden road, despite the baneful influence of the personality cult which began to make itself felt from the late '20s onwards, Indologists had the courage to take up the most important political questions and sought to elucidate them objectively from Party positions. For this, many of them were in the sequel injustly [sic] subjected to repression.' We are not told which Indologists were unjustly subjected to repression. My efforts to gain enlightenment on these matters through correspondence with Soviet scholars proved fruitless.

66 Roy's book, *India in Transition*, was hailed in the foreword to its Russian translation of

Stalinization, the 'dark ages' of Marxism. A fourth period which takes us up to the present has been characterized by intermittent and interrupted de-Stalinization, with more nuanced and scholarly work becoming increasingly evident in Soviet Indology.

However, since de-Stalinization 'official' Soviet historiography has continued to reject Marx's idea of a distinctive AMP in favour of Lenin's analysis of the Afro-Asian situation as a deviation from classical European feudalism. The arguments of R.A. Ulyanovsky and V.I. Pavlov (1975) express the orthodox Soviet position well. Indian development has been characterized by a deviant feudalism, and British colonial policy retarded India's development by creating a new pattern of feudal and semi-feudal relations. The Soviet analysts of contemporary India are completely supported by their colleagues with knowledge of pre-colonial India. *The* Soviet text on the history of India, which draws carefully and in a scholarly way upon non-Soviet sources as well as upon the Indology of Soviet scholars, none the less almost completely ignores the issue of the AMP and fits Indian history into the conventional Stalinist strait-jacket (Antonova, Bongard-Levin and Kotovsky, 1979). The authors argue that the Mauryan empire was a slaveholding society and that after the fall of the Mauryans (up until the collapse of the Mughal Empire) India was feudal.[67] One can only conclude that Soviet Marxist historians working on India have not been attracted by the AMP to anything like the degree of enthusiasm displayed by Soviet scholars of the ancient civilizations of the Near East.

However, there are asides in the text of the Soviet *History of India* which indicate that the authors are aware that the debate over the AMP has implications for Indian historiography. Thus we are told briefly of arguments over the status of the Harappan social formation:

A subject that remains very controversial is the nature of political power in the Harappan cities and that of the overall class structure in this civilization. Certain scholars (such as V.V. Struve from the USSR and W. Ruben from the GDR) put

---

1923 as the 'first Marxist research on India' (Clarkson, 1979: 21 and 279 – the Soviet reviewer either was unaware of Marx's Indian writings or did not regard them as research). Roy argued that India was already fully capitalist in the 1920s. Feudalism had disappeared in 1857. Despite British attempts to retard India's development, capitalist industrialization had occurred, especially rapidly in the decades before 1914. Roy had no time for the idea that India was still characterized by important pre-capitalist survivals in its social structure, and he was followed by most Soviet analysts in this respect until 1928. (I.M. Reisner was clearly an exception.) Roy's theses were condemned and his decolonization theory rejected at the Comintern Congress of 1928. The Hungarian Varga, an exponent of the AMP in later life, was influential in rejecting Roy's theses.

67 On slaveholding Antonova et al. cite G.F. Ilyin (Antonova et al., 1979: 91) as the Soviet exponent of the thesis that the Mauryan Empire was slaveholding, and Antonova explicitly states that 'Slavery was not the only form of exploitation, yet at the same time it was the most important one' (ibid: 93), although she does not provide any systematic argument to back this assertion.

forward the hypothesis that the Harappan civilization was based on patterns of slave-ownership. However, as yet the data and evidence in support of this theory are inadequate. Other scholars have compared its political organization with that of ancient Mesopotamia assuming that power in the Indus valley was wielded by priests, who were in possession of all the land. (Antonova et al., 1979: 23)

It is reasonable to infer from this passage that we are being told, albeit in coded language, of a debate over whether the Harappan civilization was a specimen of the AMP or the slave mode of production. Struve was the primary academic enemy of the AMP, and the keeper of the Stalinist 'conscience' from the late 1930s through until the early 1960s. It is also known that amongst Soviet scholars of the ancient Near East there has been most enthusiasm for the AMP (Dunn, 1982). Similarly for the Mauryan period we are told that 'The complex picture of social relations, and also the data in written sources with regard to the various types of landownership, explain why scholars have put forward various hypotheses with reference to the nature of landownership in India' (Antonova et al., 1979: 89). What is noteworthy about contemporary Soviet Indian historiography, as indicated by these two excerpts, is its increasingly dispassionate nature, and the emphasis given to evidence or to the difficulties in drawing inferences from evidence.[68] None the less, as far as I am aware the AMP has remained unexamined in recent Soviet Indology, unlike other areas of Soviet Orientalism.

Indian Marxists and the Asiatic Mode of Production

The history of Marxist movements in India, with the notable regional exceptions of Kerala, Tripura and West Bengal, is largely a tale of political defeat in apparently advantageous conditions. Marxism has not achieved salience let alone hegemony in Indian political culture, especially in its Hindi-speaking heartlands. Moreover, Indian Marxist intellectuals, whilst not lacking in numbers or ability, have sometimes displayed the characteristics of cultural dependency, showing, over several generations, a surprising degrees of deference towards the intellectuals, programmes and comrades of British, Soviet and Chinese Communist parties, and more lately a penchant for the products of Western Marxism. These propensities suggest a genuine degree of internationalism on the part of Indian Marxist intellectuals and freedom from the assumptions of their own cultural milieu, but these traits have probably been counter-productive from their own point of

---

68 Such scholarly caution is also the hallmark of an essay by G.M. Bongard-Levin (1978) on production relations in ancient India. He concludes that the Mauryan empire did mark the transition from a classless to a slaveholding society, but the manner in which he derives the conclusion is devoid of Stalinist dogmatism.

view. (This judgment, in case it needs emphasizing, stands independently of evaluations of the desirability of their success.)

Explanations of the weakness of Indian Marxism are various. Undoubtedly one factor has been the failure on the part of Indian Marxists, at least on the national level, to analyse coherently and plausibly the distinctive features of the Indian social formation and develop appropriate strategies and tactics for a Communist victory. The neglect or failure to analyse the phenomenon of caste in a convincing way from a theoretical perspective and the practical failure to mobilize successfully against its pervasive presence is another. Moreover, outside Kerala,[69] West Bengal and Tripura, Marxists have remained overwhelmingly oriented to the urban working class at the expense of developing a rural proletarian or peasant movement. Indian Marxists also underestimated the political significance and mobilization potential of nationalism, especially during World War II. Finally, until the 1960s and beyond, even the more imaginative of the two Indian Communist parties, the Communist Party of India – Marxist (CPI–M), remained within the intellectual strait-jacket of Stalinism (Wielenga, 1976). This general evaluation of the defects of Indian Marxism helps distinguish the history of Indian Marxism from that of the other major Asian civilizations in which Marxist movements have triumphed in this century.

The Communist Party of India more or less unwaveringly followed Soviet orthodoxy on everything until the 1960s. It followed Soviet Marxists in arguing that the ancient Mauryan Empire had been a slaveowning society with 'slightly' different forms from those of classical antiquity. Equally it argued that India had undergone the transition to feudalism, in the sense of serfdom, in the fourth century AD, in which condition it remained until the seventeenth century. Although once again it was conceded that some features of Indian feudalism differed from the European norm, the parallels both in stages and chronological order of stages between Europe and India were vigorously asserted. Humanity, including Indian humanity, was programmed to undergo the transition to slavery in the fifth century BC, to feudalism in the fourth century AD, and to capitalism in the sixteenth and seventeenth centuries. These perspectives were sharply and dogmatically enunciated by S.A. Dange, who became the dominant figure in the Communist Party of India and eventually its most servile Russophile. In his book, *India: From Primitive Communism to Slavery – A Marxist Study of Ancient History in Outline*, which achieved widespread sales amongst Indian cadres, Dange applied the Stalinist unilineal model in an uncompromising form. His primary goal was to establish that India had indeed experienced a slaveholding society.

69 For the critical discussion of Kerala's distinctiveness see Nossiter (1982).

Dange's arguments were rejected, and ridiculed, by independently minded Marxist intellectuals:

The adoption of Marx's thesis does not mean blind repetition of all his conclusions (and even less, those of the official, party-line Marxists) at all times. India had never a classical slave economy in the same sense as Greece or Rome ... [N]o single mode prevailed uniformly over the whole country at the same time ... India showed a series of parallel forms which cannot be put into the precise categories, for the mode based on slavery is absent, [and] feudalism greatly different from the European type with serfdom and the manorial economy. (Kosambi, 1956: 11, 14 and 15 – see also Kosambi, 1949)

However, Kosambi's efforts were in vain, and Dange's interpretation of history rapidly achieved the status of an Indian classic as Indian Communism underwent its own localized version of the cult of personality.

E.M.S. Namboodiripad, the man who was to become the leading figure in the Communist Party of India (Marxist), the more successful of the two Communist parties in Kerala and West Bengal, differed from Dange in that he at least recognized the AMP. He referred to it, albeit casually and without substantive elaboration, in *The National Question in Kerala*, published in 1952, but subsequently has not discussed it further at any great length.[70] The only interesting feature of Namboodiripad's discussion of the AMP is that it occurred at all – in the final phase of Stalin's rule over international Communists.

The historiographical survey in the body of this chapter (pp. 262–309) has shown that the neglect of the AMP by Indian Marxist activists has been remedied in the last two decades as leftist intellectuals have debated its merits as a way of understanding pre-colonial Indian history.[71] Moreover, the best arguers, and arguments, have been hostile to both the logical coherence and the empirical appropriateness of the AMP to Indian history.[72]

70 I have been unable to trace a paper by Namboodiripad published in Madras: E.M.S. Namboodiripad (1972), 'Marx, the Asiatic Mode of Production and the Study of Indian History', *The Radical Review*, 3: 2, April–June. It is presumably much the same as Namboodiripad's non-committal review of Eric Hobsbawm's *Pre-Capitalist Economic Formations*, which can be found in his selected writings (Namboodiripad, 1982).

71 In correspondence Professor Diptendra Banerjee of Burdwan University responded to my interest in researching the study of the AMP by Indian Marxists and historians thus: 'my ... reservation is that many of us here have actually not studied it, not with the seriousness it deserves. Our interest has been either casual or based upon certain received impressions; none of us have reconstructed the concept [sufficiently]' (letter of 10 November 1987). Banerjee's point is well taken but there has been considerable discussion of the AMP by Indian Marxists in the 1970s and 1980s, as my survey has shown, and in any case it is not possible to reconstruct the AMP without severe damage to historical materialism.

72 Those against the AMP include B. Chandra (1981), B. Wielenga (1976), S. Naqvi (1973), R.A.L.H. Gunawardana (1976), I. Habib (1983) and V. Purohit (1979). The best known and most respected Marxist historians of India, R.S. Sharma, D.D. Kosambi, R. Thapar and I. Habib, have either been silent about the AMP or contemptuous of its relevance for Indian history. Those in favour of the AMP include A. Chakraborty (1983), D. Gupta (1980), A. Guha (1975), A. Sen (1982) and D. Banerjee (1983, 1986 and 1987).

Therefore only one interesting question remains to be answered: would the AMP have made any difference to the political strategies of Indian Marxists? Here, the answer must be a speculative 'yes': speculative because the question is counterfactual, and because the gap between theory and practice in all political movements is extremely wide. However, the answer must be 'yes' because acceptance of the relevance of the AMP to understanding Indian history (even though it was empirically inappropriate and logically insupportable) would have dictated a different political strategy.

Acceptance of the AMP might, first, have led Indian Communists to question the credentials and strategic position of the Indian national bourgeoisie; and, second, it might have led them to embrace a political strategy based on winning support in the villages rather than the towns of India. Where Indian Marxists followed these premises in practice, in Kerala and West Bengal, they have achieved greater success, although of course this correlation might be spurious. The theory of the AMP suggests that only a weak, indigenous bourgeoisie is likely to emerge as a result of endogenous development, and a bourgeoisie dependent largely upon the state. Therefore Marxists who accept this idea are less likely to follow the theory that they should offer critical support to the progressive national bourgeoisie. But in fact exactly opposite thinking has predominated amongst Indian Communists, except during the period of World War II, when they took an internationalist line which differed dramatically from that of the nationalist intellectuals of the Indian Congress. Moreover, if the idea of the AMP, or something functionally equivalent to it, had been accepted by Indian Marxists, then the myth of primordial village communism could have been deployed for Communist purposes, to develop an agrarian mass-mobilization, much as such myths were used notably by Gandhi and others elsewhere in Asia. Thus I conclude on a note of speculative irony: had Indian Marxists embraced the wrong-headed idea of the AMP they might have been more politically successful.

APPENDIX 7.3   FEUDALISM IN INDIAN HISTORY?

Historical materialists have faced many problems in placing pre-modern India under general conceptual or theoretical categories. The evidence is both scanty and problematic for some favourite labels. Some Soviet Marxist-Leninists, as well as the former leader of the Communist Party of India, S.A. Dange, and the leader of the Communist Party of India (Marxist), E.M.S. Namboodiripad, have embraced the idea that India experienced a slaveholding order (Dange, 1949; Namboodiripad, 1952). But only the occasional Indian Marxist with a knowledge of Indian history has applied the category of 'slaveholding society' with confidence to any Indian social order (Chanana, 1960). It is now widely agreed to be an unacceptable definition of any Indian social order. Only household rather than agrarian slavery achieved prominence in Indian history. Therefore Marxists have been left with five fundamental choices in classifying the social formations of pre-colonial India.

First, they can accept that India has had a history in which the AMP has been prevalent throughout the sub-continent since the first formation of states (although subject to processes in which its clear institutional delineation has waxed and waned). This choice, as we have seen, is fraught with conceptual and empirical problems for the major regimes in Indian history. Second, they can accept that both the AMP and the feudal mode of production have been present at some stages in Indian history, but without the 'classical European' chronological order. This choice falls foul of historical materialism's programmatic philosophy of history. Third, they can conclude that Indian social formations have been *sui generis*, impossible to subsume coherently under either the Asiatic or the feudal label, or for that matter any other label derived from classical Marxism. This choice admits that Indian civilization escapes the analytical net of historical materialism altogether. It is an admission of defeat for Marxist historians, albeit one which several have made (P. Anderson, 1974b; Mukhia, 1981). Fourth, they can argue that Indian social formations have been characterized by the presence of plural modes of production organized under the domination of one of them. This idea abandons the programmatic philosophy of history associated with historical materialism, and pushes the approach closer to the idea that all 'agrarian societies' have more in common than they have that differentiates them. Finally, they can argue that feudalism has prevailed in much of Indian history. This option has generated by far the most useful debate in Indian Marxist historiography.

Serious debate on whether India experienced feudalism is now over two decades old. Daniel Thorner established the debate in his contribution to a collection of essays in comparative history by pointing out the paucity of good arguments for and conceptual rigour in the conventional application of the feudal label to certain regimes in Indian history (1965: 133−50). Thorner had little difficulty in arguing that Rajputana and certain Muslim polities in north India differed markedly from classical (that is, European) feudal systems. For him a feudal regime without castles, without serfs, without feudal contracts and without fiefs was not feudal.

Since then, however, both Indian and Soviet Marxists have argued that India did indeed experience feudalism. In several books and essays the Indian Marxist historian R.S. Sharma has persuasively advanced this idea (Sharma, 1958, 1965, 1966, 1983, 1985, 1986 and 1987; and Sharma and Jha, 1974), especially for the period following the collapse of the Mauryans and preceding the Delhi Sultanate (300−1200 AD).[73] He remains reticent

73 Sharma has achieved a certain notoriety amongst Indian nationalists and Hindu chauvinists

about classifying Indian polities before this period, arguing that the available data is so scanty and problematic as to preclude confident Marxist classification.[74] The thesis that much of the subcontinent did experience feudalism has been subjected to considerable criticism, notably in a collection of essays edited by D.C. Sircar (1966), and more recently in a major debate in the *Journal of Peasant Studies* (Byres and Mukhia, 1985).

None the less, despite these onslaughts, Sharma's case remains impressive, both empirically and conceptually. Moreover, several non-Marxist scholars have shared his assumptions. Basham, for example, discusses 'quasi-feudalism' (1967: 93−6), pointing out that some define feudalism to refer to the complex structure of contractual relations covering the whole of society from king to villein, while others use the term loosely to refer to any political system in which power is chiefly in the hands of those who own the land. He argues that

Something very like European feudalism did evolve among the Rajputs after the Muslim invasions ... Ancient India had, however, a system of overlordship, which was quasi-feudal, though never as fully developed as in Europe, and resting on a different basis ... After the fall of the Mauryas the typical large kingdom has a central core of directly administered territory, and a circle of vassal kingdoms subordinate in varying degrees to the emperor. (Basham, 1967: 94−6)

Similar arguments are also advanced by the non-Marxist historian Coulborn (1968), who defines feudalism as consisting of relations which are 'personal, honorific, moral ... arising among magnates in a transitional period between two cycles in the history of a civilized society'. He also points out that the functional equivalent of chivalry was present in India, as well as devotion to the lord, pride in bloodstock and noble rivalry. (So, *contra* Marx's arguments against Kovalevsky, India experienced the full ideological battery of traits associated with feudalism, at least in pre-Muslim times.)[75]

Sharma's theses rely upon a broad definition of feudalism: a social order in which the possessing class appropriated the surplus produce of the peasants by exercising superior rights over their land and persons (1965: 272). This definition fuses political and economic elements: the political order is based upon the decentralized distribution of coercion amongst a large number of agents, each enjoying a high local jurisdictional autonomy, and the economic order is based on predominantly peasant production, the

---

because of his ability to confound cherished myths with hard evidence, and his effective demonstration that the 'golden age' of the Guptas was in fact a period of economic decay − a notoriety which he evidently enjoys.

74 Personal conversation.

75 Moreover, contrary to Thorner's claim that there could have been no feudalism in India because of the lack of castles Max Weber accurately talked of the existence of castles in pre-modern India (Weber, 1978: 1223).

subordination of mercantile and industrial interests to landed interests, low urbanization and largely localized exploitation. He argues that after the collapse of the Mauryan Empire no subsequent regime enjoyed anything remotely like the same degree of centralized authority. North Indian kings also gradually abandoned the ambitions of establishing a subcontinental empire. Political decentralization become the norm throughout the subcontinent. Inscriptions, epigraphs and primary source materials testify to the loss of kingly authority. The impairing of royal power can be traced in the evidence of declarations of land grants (Sharma, 1966c: 78−88). To begin with grants were made to brahmins (and Buddhists) to colonize new land, in order to create tax revenues for the state apparatus. It is evident that even if monarchs had previously owned the land, then they were surrendering these rights to promote greater production − hardly what one would expect from kings of a social formation dominated by the AMP. Moreover, this process of decentralization of land rights was followed in pre-Guptan and Guptan times by the explicit transfer of state or administrative powers to elites who were obviously in possession of autonomous jurisdictions. Sharma points out that the inscriptions explicitly acknowledge that the king's coercive powers did not extend into the jurisdictions of those receiving the land grants, and that royal revenue-rights were explicitly waived. Thus we have the parcellization of sovereignty which Marxists and non-Marxists have generally seen as at some stage integral to a feudal social formation. Indeed by the era of the Gupta Empire the inscriptions suggest headlong feudalization. All the standard state functions were being surrendered by monarchs: revenues from taxation, the monopoly of coercion, the distribution of punishment and obligatory labour for certain purposes. The land grants were also increasingly being made to temples and to brahmins as religious functionaries rather than as warriors. Several centuries later, in the period immediately preceding the Muslim conquests, Sharma also detects evidence of vassalage, sub-infeudation and other social relations regarded as important components of feudalism (1966c, 1985 and 1987).

The objections to these arguments that feudalism prevailed in Hindu India, though numerous and fashionable, are fundamentally inadequate. Briefly, the objections rest upon one of three strategies. First, some single out one allegedly pivotal feature of feudalism, and suggest that its absence or weakness in India shatters Sharma's case (for example, Mukhia, 1981). Second, the anti-comparativists object that any differences between European feudalism and Indian social systems are sufficient to discount the idea that India experienced its own version of feudalism. This objection can safely be discounted because even non-Marxist scholars have been persuaded by Sharma's empirical evidence, if not his Marxist theoretical framework, that Indian feudalism indeed displayed some of the same cultural traits as European feudalism. The third objection suggests that

Sharma's case does not apply to certain regions of India.[76] This riposte can also be safely ignored as it implies no fundamental objection to Sharma's argument, merely a qualification on its scope.

The first strategic objection, not uncommon amongst Indian Marxists, is the most serious. The primary version of the argument is that one cannot talk of feudalism as a Marxist mode of production without the presence of serfdom. However, the weaknesses in this objection are noted, even by those of Sharma's critics who do not want the label feudalism to be applied to the later period of the Delhi Sultanate or the Mughal Empire. Irfan Habib has responded with a *reductio ad absurdum* (Habib, 1985). Since under both capitalism and socialism wage-labour remains the basic form of labour, it follows that the social form of labour cannot be the determining factor in classifying the mode of production. Analogously the presence of peasant production in which rent is paid by a small producer cannot determine the nature of a pre-capitalist mode of production.[77] However, Habib is certainly right that the presence or absence of serfdom is not sufficient to disprove the existence or otherwise of feudalism. Indeed Habib's case, which in effect lends weight to Sharma's argument, can be fortified. As one of Habib's critics has pointed out, he was implicitly making serfdom equivalent to 'labour services' and not, as Maurice Dobb had done, equivalent to the extraction of surplus from the peasantry through extra-economic coercion (Patnaik – cited in Baru, 1983: 2014). And no Indian Marxist disputes that such extraction of surplus labour was present in pre-Muslim times.

Sharma himself has effectively replied to all the objections to his theses (Sharma, 1985). He argues, with literary, epigraphic and archaeological evidence, that feudalism in India was characterized by a class of landlords and by a class of subject servile peasantry, the two living in a predominantly agrarian economy marked by a decline of trade and urbanism. He therefore has successfully established the relations of production and productive forces typically regarded as fundamental features of (at least early) feudalism. The evidence for the decline in trade and urbanism he has fully elaborated

76 Thus Stein complains that the fief as an explicit jurisdiction is largely absent in medieval south India, that the binding ties of allegiance – lord–vassal relations – were missing, that a moral order comparable to the Roman Catholic church was missing (since Hinduism did not penetrate the masses, who were still involved in non-Vedic folk religions) and that the growth of a distinctive warrior class or estate was a late development in Vijayanagar (Stein, 1975: 83–7). There are four replies to this argument. First, Sharma's case is built largely on north Indian materials, so Stein's objections are irrelevant to the general issue of whether any part of India experienced feudalism. Second, there is epigraphic evidence that land grants were made in south Indian states. Third, the presence of caste in south India, as Stein should know, is sufficient proof that Hinduism had established a moral order. Finally, the late development of a feudalism cannot stop it from being called feudal!

77 Habib was aware that these issues raise the same questions over the meaning of feudalism

in his most recent study of the decline of urban prosperity in Gupta and post-Gupta times (1987). He concedes that feudalism was not universal in the pre-capitalist world, recognizes that it exhibited enormous variation and that Indian feudalism differed from Western European feudalism, but none the less insists that India experienced feudalism. According to Sharma, the two minimal necessary and sufficient conditions for feudalism are a 'lord – serville-peasant relationship and the exploitation of the landed estate by its owner, controller, employer or beneficiary'; and these conditions were definitely characteristic of the early medieval Indian social structure. Since Indian peasants had rents extracted from them either in kind or in cash the issue of the presence or otherwise of serfdom is immaterial.

What is the significance of this continuing debate over whether or not India experienced feudalism? What is important for our purposes is that so far the best arguments, and best historical evidence, are in favour of a feudal rather than Asiatic social formation in the Hindu period immediately before the Muslim conquest. Therefore if the subsequent period of the sultans and the Mughals is to be regarded as dominated by the AMP, historical materialists face the embarrassment of the AMP post-dating

which emerged in the dialogue between Paul Sweezy and Maurice Dobb in the 1950s and which has continued ever since. Maurice Dobb defined feudalism as serfdom whereas Paul Sweezy's definition was much broader: production for use (Hilton, 1978).

None the less, Habib is hostile to Sharma's and Kosambi's idea that India experienced feudalism, and prefers to argue that a 'medieval Indian system' or 'medieval economic formation' existed in Muslim India, and underwent two phases: the Delhi Sultanate (thirteenth to fifteenth centuries), and the Mughal Empire (sixteenth to seventeenth centuries). Habib also suggests that there were hardly any forces internal to this formation which might have brought about its dissolution – which makes it seem similar to the AMP, at least on this criterion. This argument, however, left Habib vulnerable to the same objection which Marxists raised against Sweezy's definition of feudalism. Prabhat Patnaik objected that mode of production was an abstract analytical construct and not a descriptive category, and therefore if it was necessary to distinguish European feudalism and medieval India as separate social formations it was essential to identify their different laws of motion (Patnaik—cited in Baru, 1983: 2104). A mode of production without laws of motion of self-transcendence is not a Marxist mode of production, but it does look suspiciously like the AMP.

Habib's consistent goal has been to refuse the appropriateness of both the AMP and feudalism as a way of categorizing Mughal India. His argument, although he does not say so, is in effect an admission of defeat for historical materialism. He argues that Marx was correct to distinguish European feudalism from Indian historical development (by which he means Mughal India). In India, according to Marx, it was the village community rather than the individual peasant which was the object of subjugation by the exploiting class; the surplus extracted from the village was converted into commodities, which facilitated commodity circulation but kept the village community outside this sphere; and the state played an important role in irrigation. Habib argues that these points were correct ways of distinguishing India from European feudalism but that Marx was wrong to suggest that Indian society was 'unchangeable'. However, apart from the first point, the evidence of Habib's own work (1962, 1963 and 1982) counts against his own argument! The village was not autarkic and the state's role in irrigation was much exaggerated. Habib seems to have retreated from historical materialism into the historian's defence of the particularity and distinctiveness of each social formation.

feudalism. Second, as the Islamic regimes were established by conquest and superimposed upon the Hindu social system, it suggests that feudal social relations may have persisted intact at the base of these empires. The flourishing of feudal patterns following the collapse of the Mughal Empire provides some support for this speculation. This reasoning also suggests that the relevant elements of the AMP applicable to the Muslim regimes were superstructural only − the alleged presence of a strongly centralized bureaucracy. Not only are such superstructural criteria insufficient for Marxists to establish the domination of the AMP in any social formation, let alone particular Indian formations, they also make it more difficult to distinguish the absolutist regimes of the late (or post-) feudal period in Western Europe from the Islamic empires of India. These implications of the debate over Indian feudalism are devastating for 'Asiatic' readings of Indian history.[78]

78 The conclusion of this appendix (my support for Sharma's demonstration that India experienced feudalism) is compatible with the model of appendix 7.1. Sharma also portrays the Hindu political order (300−1200 AD) as remarkably weak, but as presiding over a highly stratified society sustained by the cultural domination of the brahmins.

8

Conclusion

The words of a dead man
Are modified in the guts of the living.

W.H. Auden, *In Memory of W.B. Yeats*

The Asiatic mode of production is the Loch Ness Monster of historical materialism, rarely sighted and much disbelieved. Unlike the Monster the AMP's existence is doubted in three senses. Whether the AMP existed in Marx's writings (at all, merely intermittently or continuously) has been constantly doubted. The AMP's existence as a coherent concept has also been challenged. Finally, its existence in the external as opposed to the textual or conceptual worlds has been doubted. The arguments of this book confirm that the AMP did have a textual existence, but have suggested that its conceptual and historical status is on a par with such fabled entities as Proteus, the Loch Ness Monster, chimaeras and unicorns.

The scholarly, ideological and political sources of the AMP's controversial status were identified in chapter 1. The analogy between the AMP and contemporary socialism was identified as the primary cause of controversy, despite the fact that there are some obvious weaknesses in the parables based on this idea. Moreover, no matter how negative is the social scientific verdict presented in books of this kind on the validity of the concept, the idea of the AMP will remain as a potential soure of heretical criticism or anti-Communist polemics as long as Marxism remains the official ideology of authoritarian regimes.

The AMP's intellectual antecedents, real and alleged, were examined in Chapter 2. The history of the idea of despotism suggests that Marx and Engels's writings on India and Asia, in so far as they contained a clear model of the AMP at all, were more indebted to the writings of utilitarian political economists on oriental society than to the tradition of political theorizing and typologizing inaugurated by Aristotle. The idea that the AMP was simply a renaming of the idea of oriental despotism is an example of the *post hoc ergo propter hoc* fallacy.

This conclusion was confirmed by our examination of the texts of Marx and Engels in chapter 3. Much polemical and ideological writing based on the theme that Marx and Engels's repressed the alleged political implications which oriental despotism had for the future of socialism has been both far-fetched and misplaced. Moreover, many other interpretations of these texts are erroneous and tendentious – the products of ideological or wishful reading. However, the textual evidence does confirm an immense lack of clarity and rigour in Marx and Engels's writings about the AMP and India. None the less, Marx and Engels definitely believed in the existence of a separate and in some respects distinctive Asiatic social order, mode of production or social formation. This conclusion is not inconsistent with evidence of inconsistency on the part of the founding fathers of Marxism. Marx and Engels's theoretical foci of attention on Asiatic societies wavered considerably. Towards the end of their intellectual careers Marx and Engels had become more inclined to regard the AMP, under various synonyms, as an archaic formation, as the oldest survival of either primitive communism or a formation transitional between primitive communism and class-divided societies. However, this shift was very tentative, and sometimes contradicted. Therefore Marxists' and Marxologists' competing claims that the AMP referred to primitive communism, a transitional form and an independent pre-capitalist order all enjoy some textual warrant.

The separate and most important question of whether the AMP makes any theoretical sense was investigated in chapters 4 and 5. In chapter 4 I argued that the AMP poses fundamental problems and insoluble dilemmas for historical materialism – damned if it retains the AMP, but damned if it does not. This conclusion stands irrespective of the particular version of historical materialism considered: productivist, structuralist or Hegelian, as I showed in chapter 5. The interpretive and empirical problems which historical materialists face when they choose to work without the AMP in the analysis of pre-capitalist societies also brings into sharp relief the conceptual problems posed by the AMP. These conclusions in turn suggest that it is historical materialism which is flawed, rather than the phenomena to which the AMP draws attention. Relatively autonomous pre-industrial state structures, capable of considerable fiscal exploitation of administratively subordinated urban settlements and corporate agrarian village communities, were key features in some pre-industrial socio-political landscapes – if not perhaps of India for much of its known history. Historical materialists cannot appreciate the importance of such phenomena without fundamental inconsistencies arising in their overarching methodological commitments.

In chapter 6 one famous reconstruction of the AMP was shown to be both theoretically and empirically defective. Wittfogel's *Oriental Despotism* is a political tract rather than a serious study in comparative political analysis. An anti-Communist treatise, its weaknesses confirm the logical and empirical deficiencies in the idea of the AMP — at least as that concept is understood within the framework of productivist historical materialism. The core 'hydraulic' hypothesis is logically flawed, and its association with an *ad hoc* diffusion hypothesis especially unconvincing. The assumptions Wittfogel made about the coercive, penetrative and ideological power of pre-industrial states are anachronistic and unsubstantiated. Moreover, as shown in chapter 7, Wittfogel's command of Indian history was lamentably inadequate. Like Marx's, his understanding of the subcontinent's history was selective. Limited materials and limited understanding were squeezed to fit predetermined ideas.

Several important empirical conclusions about the appropriateness of the AMP to Indian history were reached in chapter 7. Marx's interpretation of Indian historiography was shown to be seriously deficient. Moreover, whichever major Indian social formation is considered there are insuperable problems of evidence and plausibility in accepting the idea that the AMP was dominant. Core features of Indian social and economic history — the nature and development of 'the' Indian village community, pre-industrial states and Indian trade and commerce — neither fit the model of the AMP nor serve adequately to explain why India failed autonomously to develop a capitalist-dominated social formation. Moreover, in three appendices I argued that the problematic of the AMP (at least in the case of India before the Muslim conquests) is better explained by methodologies and concepts foreign to the presuppositions of historical materialism (appendix 7.1); I showed that the AMP has played little role in either Soviet or Indian Marxist historiography or political practice, but suggested, ironically, that this flawed idea might have helped revolutionaries arrive at a better political strategy (appendix 7.2); and finally I agreed with those who contend that the best arguments, and evidence, tell against the presence of the AMP in the Hindu period of Indian history, and who suggest, in contrast, that India experienced its own version of feudalism (appendix 7.3).

The AMP is theoretically and empirically deficient, and I believe it to be both incapable and unworthy of reconstruction. It remains only to consider briefly what lessons might be extracted from our analysis of the imbroglios associated with historical materialism's bastard child. This negative analysis does assist the clarification of some issues in the debate about the origins of capitalism. The AMP was intended to play a role as part of a theory of comparative historical analysis; it was meant to draw attention to the most salient contrasts between Western and Indian social structures, in order to explain why the former rather than the latter had developed capitalism first. The question of why capitalism first developed in the West seems reasonable, and important, and it is one that has been constantly asked ever since social theory began.[1] The argument of this book is that any approach

1 The question 'why did capitalism develop first in the West'? is different from the question

which contrasts the AMP and the feudal mode of production in order to arrive at an answer cannot give us a solution, because the concept of the AMP is deficient.

The conceptual debacle of the AMP also prompts us to ask whether the question is a good one. For some the right question is: why did the West experience industrialization (rather than capitalism) before India? Others suggest that research should centre not so much on the origins of capitalism or industrialism, but rather upon why some countries capitalize or industrialize more quickly than others – the problematic of political and economic development. It can be no part of this book to answer these questions. Moreover, we have now much greater cause to doubt whether Marxists (or anybody else) can answer them properly. Were it true that the pre-industrial world had very large numbers of social formations dominated by the AMP, and only one or two dominated by feudalism, then the requirements for a representative social scientific sample might have been met. Marx's theses might have been confirmed through the 'quasi-experiments' advocated in the disciplines of comparative politics, sociology and history, through the application of Mill's methods of comparison and difference. However, the facts are: the AMP cannot be confidently ascribed to large numbers of agrarian societies in the way required; we do not have a large number of civilizations which we can confidently classify as potentially capable of developing into industrialized societies; the interactions between agrarian civilizations, the diffusion of cultural, economic and political practices, and these societies' constant enmeshment in war with each other, make the analytical focus upon isolated units of civilization much more contestable than it might seem at first glance; and the impact of capitalist imperialism made the societies where it emerged first so economically and militarily powerful that they precluded non-European societies from the possibility of autonomously developing in the same way. The upshot of these four elementary historical considerations is that the empirical preconditions for the 'quasi-experiment' in comparative analysis cannot be met. We are reduced to speculation in deciding what account for the origins of capitalist development in the West. It may even be that there is no causal explanation; rather a series of inexplicable and unconnected contingencies 'explain' Western uniqueness.

'why did capitalism develop?' The first question implies that mankind had a rendezvous with capitalism. It is asking: why did the Western European (and its North-American cousin) runner beat the Eastern European, Asian, African and (pre-Columban) American contestants? (Others, more ethnically inclined, ask: why did capitalism develop first in northern Italy (or Holland, or England)?) The second question implies that the development of capitalism was altogether more contingent: there was no race, merely a series of miraculous accidents, which allowed it to emerge (Gellner, 1979: 285ff).

There is one by-product, rather than lesson, which emerges from my discussion of the AMP and oriental despotism and their inapplicability to Indian history. This by-product for the moment must remain entirely speculative. What may best explain the success of capitalist development in the West by comparison with India is the coexistence of three inter-related traits not usually associated with capitalism sufficiently emphatically, namely, a rule-governed bureaucracy, a predictable universal legal order, and the social equality associated with the absence or weakness of caste-based stratification.[2] The connection between this speculative argument and the AMP is this: the notions of the coexistence of a centralized, predatory despotism and autonomous, autarkic villages are used to explain how the AMP impeded economic development of a capitalist (or feudal) kind. However, as we have seen, India did not experience bureaucratized centralization in the modern sense, although it certainly experienced predatory behaviour by elites. Such predatory behaviour was easier in an environment in which the functional equivalent of a universal and predictable legal order, such as English common law or Roman law, was missing. The ideological, political and economic importance of the consequences of caste-stratification are neglected in discussions of the AMP, which usually emphasize village autarky in seeking to explain the failure of autonomous capitalist development to occur in Oriental societies. Given that village autarky in India was not dramatically different to that which prevailed in feudal and medieval Europe reflection on the AMP pushes us back towards emphasizing the distinctive feature of Indian civilization: caste. Therefore, in so far as comparative analysis is feasible, these reflections suggest that modern bureaucracy, a universal legal order, and the norms associated with social equality are the critical features of occidental uniqueness, since these traits of the Occident most starkly contrast with those of Indian history. In so far as comparative analysis is defensible these conclusions suggest that modern bureaucracy and the norms associated with social equality may be the critical features of occidental uniqueness, since these traits of the Occident most starkly contrast with those of Indian history. This reasoning is heretical for both Marxist and bourgeois social theories, because it is generally assumed that the entrenched absolutist bureaucracy of the late feudal era was an obstacle to capitalist modernization and bourgeois democracy. The orthodoxy in both materialist neo-Marxist and neo-Weberian cultural accounts is that the capitalist mode of production, or the market, is functionally and causally responsible for Weberian bureaucracy. The converse may be more accurate. Weberian, rational-legal bureaucracy may be functionally and causally responsible for capitalism.

---

2 Discussion and correspondence with Dr Hans Blomkvist of Uppsala University clarified these issues.

Perhaps research into the origins of capitalism and occidental distinctiveness should not seek to explain the origins of the spirit of capitalism (which like original sin has always been with at least some of us), nor, *pace* Marx, the separation of direct producers from the means of production, nor, *pace* modern political development theorists, the absence of centralized bureaucratic obstacles to development. Indeed given that modern capitalist development primarily 'took-off' in Holland and England, perhaps it is even more important to explain the development of a predictable legal order which left capitalism alone: why did some occidental rulers allow the development of autonomous and stable legal systems which in turn facilitated the emergence of modern capitalism?

There are various answers to these questions. Some seek the secret in the political logic of the European states-system, others in the cultural logic of medieval theological reflections on the passions and the interests (Hirschman, 1977), and others in even more exotic and remote causes. By contrast agnostics like Hayek and Gellner see the questions as unanswerable. For them the uniqueness of occidental development is simply a miracle, albeit a secular miracle. We can describe how the European miracle occurred without knowing why it occurred. However that may be, these questions and issues are not ones to which the AMP, or historical materialism, however reconstructed, are ever likely to furnish compelling answers. The AMP thoroughly deserves its place in the intellectual graveyard to which so many have consigned it, but I have no illusions that its powerful ideological resonance will diminish in the face of the multiple contradictions, dilemmas and empirical deficiencies which I have documented. And in defence of the AMP it must be said that its periodic exhumation and interrogation prompts important questions about the nature of agrarian societies, and therefore teaches us something about the distinctiveness of our world.

Bibliography

This bibliography lists all the items consulted or quoted in the construction of this book, as well as all the items noted in the main body of the text. All items in English and French were directly consulted. Relevant items in other languages which were cited or summarized by other authors are also included. Marx and Engels's sources on the AMP are listed separately in the appendix to chapter 3, and are only repeated here if used directly in the main text.

Abdel-Malek, A. (1981a) *Civilizations and Social Theory: Social Dialectics Vol. 1*, Macmillan, London.

Abdel-Malek, A. (1981b) *Nations and Nationalism: Social Dialectics Vol. 2*, Macmillan, London.

Abrahamian, E. (1975) European Feudalism and Middle Eastern Despotisms, *Science and Society*, XXXIX, 2: 129–56.

Acton, H.B. (1955) *The Illusion of the Epoch*, Cohen and West, London.

Acton, H.B. (1967) *What Marx Really Said*, MacDonald, London.

Adhikari, G., ed. (1971–) *Documents of the History of the Communist Party of India*, vols I–III, People's Publishing House, New Delhi.

Adhya, G.L. (1966) *Early Indian Economics*, Bombay Publishing House, Bombay.

Adler, M. (1978) Selections on 'The Theory and Method of Marxism', in T. Bottomore and P. Goode, eds, *Austro-Marxism*, Oxford University Press, Oxford, 57–84.

Alavi, H.	(1965)	Peasants and Revolution, *The Socialist Register 1965*, eds R. Miliband and J. Saville, Merlin Press, London.
Alavi, H.	(1972)	The State in Post-Colonial Societies: Pakistan and Bangladesh, *New Left Review*, 59–81.
Alavi, H.	(1975)	India and the Colonial Mode of Production, *The Socialist Register 1975*, eds R. Miliband and J. Saville, Merlin Press, London.
Alavi, H.	(1980)	The Transition from Feudalism to Colonial Capitalism, *Journal of Contemporary Asia*, 10, 4: 359–99.
Alayev, L.B.	(1964)	Soviet Studies of the History of India 1917–34, *Central Asian Review*, xii, 1: 59–66.
Alayev, L.B.	(1968)	Soviet Historians on Indian Feudalism (Proceedings of the Seminar on Problems of Social and Economic History, Aligarh Muslim University). Mimeograph.
Allchin, B. and Allchin, R.	(1968)	*The Birth of Indian Civilization, India and Pakistan before 500 B.C.*, Penguin, Harmondsworth.
Allchin, B. and Allchin, R.	(1982)	*The Rise of Civilization in India and Pakistan*, Oxford University Press, Oxford.
Althusser, L.	(1969)	*For Marx*, Penguin, Harmondsworth.
Althusser, L.	(1982)	Montesquieu: Politics and History, in Althusser, *Montesquieu, Rousseau, Marx*, Verso, London 31–109.
Althusser, L. and Balibar, E.	(1970)	*Reading Capital* (trans. B. Brewster), New Left Books, London.
Amin, S.	(1974)	*Accumulation on a World Scale*, vols I and II, Monthly Review Press, New York.
Amin, S.	(1976)	*Unequal Development*, Monthly Review Press, New York.
Amin, S.	(1980)	*Class and Nation: Historically and in the Current Crisis*, Heinemann, London.
Anderson, B.O'G.	(1981)	Review of L. Tichelman 'The Social Evolution of Indonesia. The Asiatic

		Mode of Production and its Legacy' *Pacific Affairs*, 54: 562−4.
Anderson, P.	(1974a)	*Passages from Antiquity to Feudalism*, Verso, London.
Anderson, P.	(1974b)	*Lineages of the Absolutist State*, New Left Books, Verso, London.
Anderson, P.	(1976)	*Considerations on Western Marxism*, Verso, London.
Anderson, P.	(1984)	*In the Tracks of Historical Materialism*, Verso, London.
Andreski, S.	(1964)	Oriental Despotism or Agrarian Bureaucracy in Andreski, *Elements of Comparative Sociology*, Weidenfeld and Nicolson, London, 163−77.
Andreski, S., ed.	(1983)	*Max Weber: Capitalism, Bureaucracy and Religion*, George Allen and Unwin, London.
Anquetil-Duperron, A.H.	(1778)	*Législation Orientale*, Amsterdam.
Anquetil-Duperron, A.H.	(1786)	*Recherches historiques et géographiques sur l'Inde*, Berlin.
Anstey, V.	(1952)	*The Economic Development of India*, Longmans, Green & Co., London.
Antoniadis-Bibicou H.	(1977)	Byzantium and the Asiatic Mode of Production, *Economy and Society*, 6, 4: 348−76.
Antonova, K., Bongard-Levin, G. and Kotovsky, G.	(1979)	*A History of India*, vols 1 and 2, Progress Publishers, Moscow.
Appadorai, A.	(1936)	*Economic Conditions in Southern India (1,000 A.D.−1,500 A.D.)*, 2 vols, Madras University Historical Series, Madras.
Aristotle	(1962)	*The Politics* trans. T.A. Sinclair Penguin, Harmondsworth.
Aron, R.	(1968)	*Main Currents in Sociological Thought* Pelican, London.
Asad, T., ed.	(1973)	*Anthropology and the Colonial Encounter*, Ithaca Press, London.
Asad, T. and Wolpe, H.	(1976)	Concepts of Modes of Production, *Economy and Society*, 5.4: 470−506.
Athar Ali, M.	(1975)	The Passing of Empire: The Mughal Case, *Modern Asian Studies*, ix: 385−96.

Avineri, S.	(1969a)	Marx and Modernization, *Review of Politics*, 31, 2: 172–88.
Avineri, S., ed.	(1969b)	*Karl Marx on Colonialism and Modernization: His Dispatches and Other Writings on China, India, Mexico, the Middle East and North Africa*, Double Day, Anchor, Garden City, New York.
Avineri, S., ed.	(1974)	*Varieties of Marxism*, Martinus Nijhoff, The Hague.
Babar	(1921)	*Babar-nama* (trans. A.S. Beveridge) Luzac, London.
Baden-Powell, B.H.	(1892)	*The Land Systems of British India*, three vols, Clarendon Press Oxford, London and New York.
Baden-Powell, B.H.	(1896)	*The Indian Village Community*, Clarendon Press Oxford, London.
Baechler, J.	(1975)	*The Origins of Capitalism*, Basil Blackwell, Oxford.
Bahro, R.	(1981)	*The Alternative in Eastern Europe* (trans. D. Fernbach), NLB & Verso, London.
Bailey, A.M.	(1974)	On the Specificity of the Asiatic Mode of Production: The Genealogy of a Concept. M. Phil. Thesis, University of London.
Bailey, A.M.	(1981)	The Renewed Discussions on the Concept of the Asiatic Mode of Production, in J. Kahn and J.P. Llobera, *The Anthropology of Pre-Capitalist Societies*, Macmillan, London.
Bailey, A.M. and Llobera, J.P.	(1974–5)	The Asiatic Mode of Production: An Annotated Bibliography, Parts I and II, *Critique of Anthropology*, 3: 95–103, and 4–5: 165–76.
Bailey, A.M. and Llobera, J.P.	(1979)	Karl. A. Wittfogel and the Asiatic Mode of Production: A Reappraisal, *Sociological Review*, 27, 3: 541–59.
Bailey, A.M. and Llobera, J.P., eds.	(1981)	*The Asiatic Mode of Production: Science and Politics*, Routledge and Kegan Paul, London.
Balazs, E.	(1964)	*Chinese Civilization and Bureaucracy:*

		Variations on a Theme, Yale University Press, New Haven, Connecticut.
Balibar, E.	(1970)	On the Basic Concepts of Historical Materialism, in L. Althusser and E. Balibar, *Reading Capital*, New Left Books, London, 119–308.
Banaji, J.	(1976)	The Peasantry in the Feudal Mode of Production: Towards an Economic Model, *Journal of Peasant Studies*, 3: 299–328.
Banerjee, D.	(1975)	The Asiatic Mode of Production and the Marxian World View. Mimeograph.
Banerjee, D.	(1983)	Marx and the 'Original Form' of Pre-Colonial India's Village Community. Paper presented to The Marx Centenary Seminar, organized by the Editorial Board of *Social Scientist*, New Delhi, 6–8 October 1983.
Banerjee, D.	(1986)	Marx, Kovalevsky and Precolonial India, *Social Science Probings*, September, 3, 3: 321–79.
Banerjee, D.	(1987)	Marx, the Asiatic Mode of Production and India. Paper presented to the Marx – Weber Seminar, Max Mueller Bhavan in collaboration with India International Seminar, New Delhi, October 1987.
Banerjee, N.C.B.	(1925)	*Economic Life and Progress in Ancient India, being the Outline of an Economic History of Ancient India*, Hare Press, Calcutta.
Banu, I.	(1967a)	La formation sociale 'asiatique' dans la perspective de la philosophie orientale antique, *La Pensée*, 132: 53–70.
Banu, I.	(1967b)	La formation sociale 'tributaire', *Recherche Internationales a La Lumière du Marxisme*, 57–8: 251–53.
Banu, S.	(1983)	Marx's Centenary: Karl Marx and Analysis of Indian Society, *Economic and Political Weekly*, XVIII, 50 (10 December), 2102–8.

Barker, E.	(1946)	*The Politics of Aristotle* (trans. with intro, notes and appendices) Oxford University Press, Oxford.
Barnes, H., ed.	(1948)	*An Introduction to the History of Sociology*, University of Chicago Press, Chicago.
Baron, S.H.	(1958)	Plekhanov's Russia: The Impact of the West upon an Oriental Society, *Journal of the History of Ideas* 19, 3: 388–404.
Baron, S.H.	(1963)	*Plekhanov: The Father of Russian Marxism*, Stanford University Press, Stanford.
Baron, S.H.	(1974)	Plekhanov, Trotsky and the Development of Soviet Historiography, *Soviet Studies* 26, 3: 380–95.
Baron, S.H.	(1975)	Marx's 'Grundrisse' and the Asiatic Mode of Production, *Survey*, 21, 1/2: 128–47.
Barry, B.	(1978)	*Economics, Sociologists and Democracy*, Chicago University Press, Chicago.
Bartra, R., ed	(1969)	*El modo producción asiático*, Ediciones Era, Mexico.
Basham, A.L.	(1954)	*The Wonder that was India: A Survey of the Indian Sub-Continent before the coming of the Muslims*, Sidgwick and Jackson, London.
Basham, A.L.	(1958)	A New Interpretation of Indian History, *Journal of the Economic and Social History of the Orient*, I, Part 3: 333–47.
Basham, A.L.	(1967)	*The Wonder That Was India*, Sidgwick and Jackson, London, third edition.
Baudin, L.	(1961)	*A Socialist Empire: The Incas of Peru*, van Norstrand, Princeton, NJ.
Bayle, P.	(1966)	Réponse aux Questions d'un Provincial, in Bayle, *Ouvres Diverses* Vol. 3, George Olms, Hildesheim.
Beloff, M.	(1958)	Review of Oriental Despotism, *Pacific Affairs*, 31, 2: 186–7.
Benton, T.	(1984)	*The Rise and Fall of Structural Marxism: Althusser and His Influence*, Macmillan, London.

342   *Bibliography*

Bernal, M.   (1987)   *Black Athena: The Afro Asiatic Roots
                                  of Classical Civilization, Vol. 1. The
                                  Fabrication of Ancient Greece, 1785—
                                  1985*, Rutgers University Press,
                                  New Brunswick, NJ.
Bernier, F.   (1914)   *Travels in the Moghul Empire,
                                  A.D. 1656—1668* (trans. A. Con-
                                  stable) Milford, Oxford, second
                                  edition.
Bhaskar, R.   (1978)   *A Realist Theory of Science*, Harvester,
                                  Brighton.
Bloch, M.   (1937)   Feudalism, *European Encyclopaedia of
                                  the Social Sciences*, vol. V: 203—10.
Bloch, M.   (1962)   *Feudal Society*, vols 1 and 2, Routledge
                                  and Kegan Paul, London.
Bloch, M.   (1983)   *Marxism and Anthropology*, Oxford
                                  University Press, Oxford.
Bloch, M., ed.   (1984)   *Marxist Analyses and Social Anthro-
                                  pology*, Tavistock Publications,
                                  London.
Blomkvist, H.   (1988)   *The Soft State: Housing Reform
                                  and State Capacity in Urban India*,
                                  Department of Government, Uppsala
                                  University PhD thesis, Uppsala.
Bodin, J.   (1955)   *Six Books of the Commonwealth*
                                  (abridged and trans. M.J. Tooley),
                                  Basil Blackwell, Oxford.
Boersner, D.   (1957)   *The Bolsheviks and the National
                                  and Colonial Question (1917—28)*,
                                  Librarie E. Doz, Geneva.
Bongard-Levin, G.M.   (1974—5) On the Problem of Land Owner-
                                  ship in Ancient India, *Soviet Anthro-
                                  pology and Archeology*, XIII, 3: 41—81.
Bongard-Levin, G.M.   (1978)   Some Problems of the Social
                                  Structure of Ancient India, in
                                  D. Chattopadhyaya, ed., *History and
                                  Society, Essays in Honour of Professor
                                  Niharranjan Ray*, K.P. Bagchi &
                                  Co., Calcutta, 197—227.
Boorstein, D.J.   (1983)   *The Discoveries: A History of Man's
                                  Search to Know His World and
                                  Himself*, Penguin, Harmondsworth.

Bose, N.K.	(1953)	The Hindu Method of Tribal Absorption, in Bose, *Cultural Anthropology and Other Essays*, Indian Assoc. Publishing Co., Calcutta.
Bradby, B.	(1975)	The Destruction of Natural Economy, *Economy and Society*, 4, 2.
Braudel, F.	(1984)	*Civilization and Capitalism, 15th–18th Century. Volume III, The Perspective of the World* (trans. Sian Reynolds), Fontana Press, London.
Brenner, R.	(1977)	The Origins of Capitalism, *New Left Review*, July–August, 105: 25–82.
Brewer, A.	(1980)	*Marxist Theories of Imperialism: A Critical Survey*, Routledge and Kegan Paul, London.
Briant, P.	(1975)	Villages et communautes villageoises d'Asie acheminide et hellenestique, *Journal of the Economic and Social History of the Orient*, 18: 165–88.
Buckley, R.B.	(1893)	*Irrigation Works in India and Egypt*, E. and F.N. Spon, London and New York.
Bukharin, N.	(1926)	*Historical Materialism: A System of Sociology*, Allen and Unwin, London.
Bulpitt, J.	(1983)	*Territory and Power in the United Kingdom*, Manchester University Press, Manchester.
Burn, R., ed.	(1937)	*Cambridge History of India*, vol. 4, Cambridge University Press, Cambridge.
Butzer, K.	(1976)	*Early Hydraulic Civilization in Egypt*, Chicago University Press, Chicago.
Byers, T.J.	(1985)	Modes of Production and Non-European Pre-Colonial Societies: The Nature and Significance of the Debate, in T.J. Byers and H. Mukhia, eds. Feudalism and Non-European Societies, *Journal of Peasant Studies*, 12, 2–3: 1–18.
Byres, T.J. and Mukhia, H. eds	(1985)	Feudalism and Non-European Societies, *Journal of Peasant Studies*, 12, 2–3.

344   *Bibliography*

Caldwell, M.   (1977)   Foreword to Melotti, U., *Marx and
                                   the Third World*, Macmillan, London.
Callinicos, A.   (1976)   *Althusser's Marxism*, Pluto Press,
                                   London.
Callinicos, A.   (1982)   *Is There a Future for Marxism?*,
                                   Macmillan, London.
Calvez, J.-Y.   (1956)   *La Pensée de Karl Marx*, Collections
                                   Esprits, Éditions de Seuil, Paris.
Cameron, K.N.   (1980)   The Fallacy of the Superstructure,
                                   Monthly Review, 31, 8: 27–36.
Campbell, G.   (1852)   *Modern India: A Sketch of the System
                                   of Civil Government*, John Murray,
                                   London.
Carneiro, R.L.   (1970)   A Theory of the Origins of the
                                   State, *Science*, 169: 733–8.
Carrasco, P.   (1981)   On the Inapplicability of Oriental
                                   Despotism and the Asiatic Mode of
                                   Production to the Aztecs of Texcoco,
                                   American Antiquity.
Carrère d'Encausse, H.   (1969)   *Marxism and Asia, 1853–1964*,
  and Schram, S., eds   Penguin, Harmondsworth.
Cassen, R.H.   (1978)   *India: Population, Economy, Society*,
                                   Macmillan, London.
CÉRM   (1969)   *Sur le 'mode de production asiatique'*,
                                   Préface de Roger Garaudy, Editions
                                   Sociales, Paris.
CÉRM   (1970)   *Sur les Sociétés Précapitalistes, Textes
                                   choisis de Marx, Engels, Lénine*,
                                   Éditions Sociales, Paris.
CÉRM   (1974)   *Sur le 'mode de production asiatique'*,
                                   second edition ed. J. Suret-Canale,
                                   Éditions Sociales, Paris.
Chakraborty, A.   (1983)   The Social Formation of the Indus
                                   Society, *Economic and Political
                                   Weekly*, 10 December, 2132–6.
Chanana, D.R.   (1960)   *Slavery in Ancient India: As Depicted
                                   in Pali and Sanskrit Texts*, People's
                                   Publishing House, Delhi.
Chandra, B.   (1979)   *Nationalism and Colonialism in
                                   Modern India*, Delhi, Orient
                                   Longman.
Chandra, B.   (1981)   Karl Marx, his Theories of Asian
                                   Societies and Colonial Rule, *Review*,
                                   V: 1.

Chandra, S.	(1959)	*Parties and Politics at the Mughal Court*, 1717–40, Aligarh University, Aligarh.
Chandra, S.	(1966)	Some Aspects of the Growth of a Money Economy in India During the Seventeenth Century, *Indian Economic and Social History Review*, III, 4: 321–31.
Chandra, S.	(1976)	Some Institutional Factors in Providing Capital Inputs for the Improvement and Expansion of Cultivation in Medieval India, *Indian Historical Review*.
Chandra, S.	(1982)	'Standard of Living' in Mughal India, in, *Cambridge Economic History of India*, vol. 1, Cambridge University Press, Cambridge, T. Raychaudhuri and I. Habib, eds 458–71.
Charlesworth, N.	(1982)	*British Rule and the Indian Economy 1800–1914*, Macmillan, London.
Chattopadyaya, D.	(1959)	*Lokayata: A Study in Ancient Indian Materialism*, People's Publishing House, New Delhi.
Chattopadyaya, D.	(1969)	*Indian Atheism: A Marxist Analysis*, Manisha, Calcutta.
Chattopadyaya, D., ed.	(1978)	*History and Society, Essays in Honour of Professor Niharranjan Ray*, K.P. Bagchi & Co., Calcutta.
Chaudhuri, K.N.	(1979)	*Economy and Society: Essays in Indian Social and Economic History*, Oxford University Press, Oxford.
Chaudhuri, K.N.	(1982)	European Trade with India, in T. Raychaudhuri and I. Habib, eds, *Cambridge Economic History of India*, vol. 1, Cambridge University Press, Cambridge, 382–407.
Chaudhuri, K.N.	(1985)	*Trade and Civilization in the Indian Ocean, An Economic History from the Rise of Islam to 1750*, Cambridge University Press, Cambridge.
Chesneaux, J.	(1964)	Le mode de production asiatique: une nouvelle étape de la discussion, *Eirenc*, III: 131–46.

Chicherov, A.I.   (1971)   *India: Economic Development in the Sixteenth – Seventeenth Centuries*, Nauka Publishing House, Moscow.

Childe, G.   (1926)   *The Aryans, A Study of Indo-European Origins*, Routledge and Kegan Paul, London.

Childe, G.   (1936)   *Man Makes Himself*, Watts, London.
Childe, G.   (1942)   *What Happened in History*, Penguin, Harmondsworth.

Childe, G.   (1951)   *Social Evolution*, Watts, London.
Childe, G.   (1954)   *New Light on Most Ancient East*, Routledge and Kegan Paul, London.

Churchill, A.   (1732)   *Churchill's Collection of Voyages*, vol. 1. (collected and ed. Awnsham and John Churchill, including sections based on an original manuscript of Sir Thomas Roe), London.

Claessen, H.J.M. and   (1978)   *The Early State*, Mouton, The
  Skalnik, P., eds   Hague.
Clarkson, S.   (1974)   Non-Impact of Soviet Writing on Indian Thinking and Policy, *Survey*, 20, 1: 1–23.

Clarkson, S.   (1979)   *The Soviet Theory of Development: India and the Third World in Marxist-Leninist Scholarship*, Macmillan London.

Clastres, P.   (1977)   *Society against the State*, Basil Blackwell, Oxford.

Cohen, G.A.   (1979)   *Karl Marx's Theory of History: A Defence*, Oxford University Press, Oxford.

Cohen, G.A.   (1982)   Reply to Elster, 'Marxism, Functionalism and Game Theory', *Theory and Society*, 11: 483–96.

Cohen, G.A.   (1983)   Reconsidering Historical Materialism, *Nomos*, XXVI: 226–51.

Cohen, J.   (1982)   Review of Karl Marx's Theory of History: A Defence, *The Journal of Philosophy*, 79: 253–73.

Colletti, L.   (1975)   Introduction to *Karl Marx, Early Writings* (trans. R. Livingstone and G. Benton), Penguin/New Left Review, Harmondsworth, 7–56.

Cook, S. (1977) Beyond the Formen: Towards a Revised Marxist Theory of Pre-Capitalist Formations, *Journal of Peasant Studies*, 4: 360–9.

Cooper, S. and McFarlane, B. (1966) Asiatic Mode of Production – Economic Pheonix, *The Australian Quarterly*, XXXVIII: 2.

Cornforth, M. (1952–4) *Dialectical Materialism*, three vol., Lawrence and Wishart, London.

Coulborn, R., ed. (1956) *Feudalism in History*, Princeton University Press, Princeton, NJ.

Coulborn, R. (1968) Feudalism, Brahmanism and the Intrusion of Islam upon Indian History, *Comparative Studies in Society and History*, X: 3.

Cox, O.C. (1948) *Caste, Class and Race*, Monthly Review Press, New York.

Critchley, J. (1978) *Feudalism*, Allen and Unwin, London.

Currie, K. (1978) Review of U. Melotti, 'Marx and the Third World', *Journal of Peasant Studies*, 5,4: 518–23.

Currie, K. (1980) Problematic Modes and the Mughal Social Formation, *The Insurgent Sociologist*, 9, 4.

Currie, K. (1984) The Asiatic Mode of Production: Problems of Conceptualising State and Economy, *Dialectical Anthropology*, 8: 251–68.

Currie, K. (1985) Marx, Lubasz, and the Asiatic Mode of Production: A Comment, *Economy and Society*, 14, 3: 399–403.

Cutler, A., Hindess, B., Hirst, P. and Hussain, A. (1977) *Marx's Capital and Capitalism Today*, two vols, Routledge and Kegan Paul, London.

Dambuyant, M. (1974) Un État à 'Haut Commandement Économique': L'Inde de Kautilya, J. Suret-Canale, ed., *Le Mode de Production Asiatique*, Editions Sociales, Paris.

Damodaran, K. (1960) Special Features of Feudalism in India, *New Age*, IX, 5: 1–8.

Dange, S.A. (1949) *India: From Primitive Communism to Slavery-A Marxist Study of Ancient*

History in Outline, People's Publishing House, New Delhi.

Dange, S.A. (1954) Some Problems of Indian History, *New Age*, September.

Danilova, L.P. (1966) A Discussion of an Important Problem, *Soviet Studies in History*, IV, 4: 3–12.

Danilova, L.P. (1971) Controversial Problems in the Theory of Pre-capitalist Societies, *Soviet Anthropology and Archeology*, 9, 4: 269–328.

Dasgupta, A.S. (1982) Indian Merchants and the Trade in the Indian Ocean, in T. Raychaudhuri and I. Habib, eds, *Cambridge Economic History of India*, vol. 1, Cambridge University Press, Cambridge, 407–33.

Davey, B. (1975a) Modes of Production and Socio-Economic Formations, *South Asia Marxist Review*, 1, 2.

Davey, B. (1975b) *The Economic Development of India*, Spokesman, Nottingham.

Day, W.M. (1949) Relative Permanence of Former Boundaries in India, *Scottish Geographical Magazine*, 65: 113–22.

Degras, J., ed. (1956–60) *The Communist International, 1919–43. Documents*, Oxford University Press, Oxford.

Degas, J., ed. (1967) *The Impact of the Bolshevik Revolution, 1917–67. The Influence of Bolshevism on the World outside Russia*, Royal Institute of International Affairs, London.

della Volpe, G. (1980) *Logic as a Positive Science*, New Left Books, London.

de Ste Croix, G.E.M. (1981) *The Class Struggle in the Ancient Greek World*, Duckworth, London.

Deutscher, I. (1966a) *Ironies of History. Essays on Contemporary Communism*, Oxford University Press, Oxford.

Deutscher, I. (1966b) *The Unfinished Revolution*, Oxford University Press, Oxford.

Dhoquois, G.	(1966)	Le mode de production asiatique, *Cahiers Internationaux de Sociologie*, xxli: 83–92.
Dhoquois, G.	(1971)	*Pour l'Histoire*, Paris, Editions Anthropos.
Dickinson, J.	(1853)	*India: Its Government Under a Bureaucracy*, London, Saunders and Stanford.
Diviçioglu, S.	(1967)	Essai de Modeles Economiques A Partir du M.P.A., *Recherches Internationales à la lumière du Marxisme*, 57–8: 277–93.
Dobb, M.	(1963)	*Studies in the Development of Capitalism*, Lawrence and Wishart, London, second edition.
Donaldson, R.H.	(1974)	*Soviet Policy Towards India. Ideology and Strategy*, Cambridge, Mass., Harvard University Press.
Draper, H.	(1977)	*Karl Marx's Theory of Revolution. Volume 1: State and Bureaucracy*, Monthly Review Press, New York.
Drekmaier, C.	(1962)	*Kingship and Community in Early India*, Stanford University Press, Stanford.
Druhe, D.N.	(1960)	*Soviet Russia and Indian Communism: 1917–47*, Bookman Associates, New York.
Dumont, L.	(1966)	The 'Village Community' from Munroe to Maine, *Contributions to Indian Sociology*, IX, December, 67–89 – reprinted in Dumont, *Religion, Politics and History in India: Collected Papers in Indian Sociology*, Mouton and Co., Paris The Hague, 112–32.
Dumont, L.	(1970a)	*Homo Hierarchicus*, Paladin, London.
Dumont, L.	(1970b)	The Conception of Kingship in Ancient India, in Dumont *Religion, Politics and History in India: Collected Papers in Indian Sociology*, Mouton & Co., Paris/The Hague, 62–88 – first published in *Contributions to Indian Sociology* 1962, VI.

Duncan, G.   (1973)   *Marx and Mill*, Cambridge University Press, Cambridge.

Dunleavy, P.   (1982)   Is there a Radical Public Administration? *Public Administration*, 60, 2: 215–33.

Dunleavy, P. and O'Leary, B.   (1987)   *Theories of the State: The Politics of Liberal Democracy*, Macmillan, London.

Dunn, S.   (1982)   *The Fall and Rise of the Asiatic Mode of Production*, Routledge and Kegan Paul, London.

Dunn, S. and Dunn, E.   (1974)   *Introduction to Soviet Ethnography*, Berkeley.

Dutt, N.K.   (1968)   *Origin and Growth of Castes in India*, Mukhopadhyay, Calcutta.

Eagleton, T.   (1976)   *Marxism and Literary Criticism*, Methuen, London.

Eberhard, W.   (1958)   A Review of 'Oriental Depotism' by K.A. Wittfogel, *American Sociological Review*, 23, 4: 446–8.

Eberhard, W.   (1965)   *Conquerors and Rulers*, Brill, Leiden.

Ehrenburg, V.   (1938)   *Alexander and the Greeks*, Basil Blackwell, Oxford.

Eisenstadt, S.N.   (1957–8)   The Study of Oriental Despotisms as Systems of Total Power, *Journal of Asian Studies*, xviii, 3: 435–6.

Eisenstadt, S.N.   (1963)   *The Political System of Empires*, Free Press, Glencoe, Illinois.

Elphinstone, M.   (1889)   *The History of India: The Hindu and Mahometan Periods*, John Murray, London, seventh edition.

Elster, J.   (1980)   Cohen on Marx's Theory of History, *Political Studies*, XXVIII, I: 121–8.

Elster, J.   (1982)   Marxism, Functionalism and Game Theory, *Theory and Society*, 11: 453–82; and Reply to comments, *Theory and Society*, 12: 111–20.

Elster, J.   (1983)   *Explaining Technical Change*, Cambridge University Press, Cambridge.

Elster, J.   (1985)   *Making Sense of Marx*, Cambridge University Press, Cambridge.

Elster, J.   (1986a)   *Karl Marx: A Reader*, Cambridge University Press, Cambridge.

Elster, J. (1986b) The Theory of Combined and Uneven Development, in J. Roemer, ed., *Analytical Marxism*, Cambridge University Press, Cambridge, 54–63.

Elster, J. (1986c) *Karl Marx: An Introduction*, Cambridge University Press, Cambridge.

Elvin, M. (1973) *The Pattern of the Chinese Past*, Stanford University Press, Stanford.

Engels, F. (1964) *Dialectics of Nature*, Progress Publishers, London.

Engels, F. (1969–70a) Afterword to Social Relations in Russia, in Marx and Engels, *Selected Works*, vol. 2, Progress Publishers, Moscow.

Engels, F. (1969–70b) On Social Relations in Russia, in Marx and Engels *Selected Works*, vol. 2, Progress Publishers, Moscow.

Engels, F. (1976) *Anti-Dühring*, Foreign Languages Press, Peking.

Engels, F. (1978) *The Origin of the Family, Private Property and the State*, Foreign Languages Press, Peking.

Fehér, F., Heller, A. and Márkus, G. (1983) *Dictatorship over Needs, An Analysis of Soviet Societies*, Basil Blackwell, Oxford.

Ferguson, A. (1966) *An Essay on the History of Civil Society* (ed. Intro. D. Forbes), Edinburgh University Press, Edinburgh.

Fernbach, D. (1973) Introduction to *Surveys From Exile. Political Writings*, vol. 2, Penguin/ New Left Review, Harmondsworth.

Fernea, R. (1970) *Sheikh and Effendi*, Harvard University Press, Harvard.

Feyerabend, P. (1975) *Against Method*, New Left Books, London.

Finley, M. (1985) Ancient Society, in *A Dictionary of Marxist Thought*, T. Bottomore L. Harris, V.G. Kiernan, and R. Miliband, eds, Basil Blackwell, Oxford, 19–22.

Fifth Report (1812)	(1969)	*Fifth Report from the Select Committee on the Affairs of the East India Company, 1812*, photo offset edition, Irish University Press Series of British Parliamentary Papers, Colonies: East India: 3, 1969, Irish University Press, Dublin.
Finley, M.	(1973)	*The Ancient Economy*, Chatto and Windus, London.
Finley, M.	(1986a)	Archaeology and History, in Finley, *The Uses and Abuses of History*, Chatto and Windus, London, 87–101.
Finley, M.	(1986b)	*The Uses and Abuses of History*, Chatto and Windus, London.
Friedrich, C. and Brzezinski, Z.	(1965)	*Totalitarian Dictatorship and Autocracy*, Harvard University Press, Mass. Cambridge, second edition.
Frykenberg, R.	(1968)	Traditional Processes of Power in South India, in R. Bendix, ed., *State and Society*, Little, Brown, Boston, 107–25.
Fulbrook, M. and Skocpol, T.	(1977)	Review of Perry Anderson's 'Lineages of the Absolutist State', *The Journal of Development Studies*, 13, 3: 290–5.
Fustel de Coulanges, N.D.	(1956)	*The Ancient City: A Study of the Religion, Laws, and Institutions of Greece and Rome*, Doubleday, Garden City New York.
Gafurov, B.G. and Grankovskii, Yu. V.	(1967)	*Fifty Years of Soviet Oriental Studies* (Brief Reviews, 1917–67), Nauka, Moscow.
Gamayunov, L.S. and Ulyanovsky, R.A.	(1960)	Marx on Kovalevsky, *New Age*, ix, 11, 44–54.
Gardezi, H.N.	(1979)	South Asia and the Asiatic Mode of Production – Some Conceptual and Empirical Problems, *Bulletin of Concerned Asian Scholars*, 11, 4: 40–4.
Gellner, E.	(1964)	*Thought and Change*, Weidenfeld and Nicolson.
Gellner, E.	(1974)	The Soviet and the Savage, *Times Literary Supplement*, 3789, 18 October, 1166–8.

Gellner, E.　　　　　(1979)　*Spectacles and Predicaments: Essays in Social Theory*, Cambridge University Press, Cambridge.

Gellner, E.　　　　　(1980)　A Russian Marxist Philosophy of History, in E. Gellner, ed., *Soviet and Western Anthropology*, Duckworth, London, 59–84.

Gellner, E.　　　　　(1981)　*Muslim Society*, Cambridge University Press, Cambridge.

Gellner, E.　　　　　(1983)　Stagnation without Salvation, *Times Literary Supplement*, 4163, 14 January, 27–8.

Gellner, E.　　　　　(1986)　Soviets against Wittfogel: or, the Anthropological Preconditions of Mature Marxism, in J. Hall, ed., *States in History*, Basil Blackwell, Oxford, 78–108.

Gellner, E.　　　　　(1988)　Obituary, Karl Wittfogel, *The Times*, 18 June.

Geras, N.　　　　　(1972)　Althusser's Marxism: An Account and Assessment, *New Left Review*, 65, 71: 57–86.

Ghosh, S.K.　　　　(1984)　Marx on India, *Monthly Review*, January, 39–53.

Gibbon, E.　　　　　(1980)　*The Decline and Fall of the Roman Empire* (one vol. abridgement D.A. Saunders), Penguin, Harmondsworth.

Giddens, A.　　　　(1981)　*A Contemporary Critique of Historical Materialism*, Macmillan, London.

Godelier, M.　　　　(1964)　Les écrits de Marx et d'Engels sur le mode de production asiatique, *La Pensée*, 117: 17–23.

Godelier, M.　　　　(1965a)　The Concept of the Asian Mode of Production and the Marxist Model of Social Development, *Soviet Anthropology and Archeology*, IV, 2: 39–41.

Godelier, M.　　　　(1965b)　La notion de 'mode de production asiatique', *Temps Modernes*, 20, 2: 2003–27.

Godelier, M.　　　　(1965c)　The Notion of 'Asiatic Mode of Production' and the Marxist Scheme of the Evolution of Societies, *Enquiry*, New Series 2: 76–102.

Godelier, M.	(1969)	La notion de 'mode de production asiatique' et les schemas Marxistes d'évolution des sociétes, in CÉRM, *Sur le 'Mode de Production Asiatique'*, Editions Sociales, Paris.
Godelier, M.	(1970a)	La Pensée de Marx et d'Engels Aujourd'hui et les Recherches de Demain—preface to *Sur les sociétés précapitalistes*, Editions Sociales, Paris.
Godelier, M.	(1970b)	Préface to *Sur Les Sociétés Précapitalistes, Textes choisis de Marx, Engels, Lénine*, ed. CÉRM, Éditions Sociales, Paris, 1–142.
Godelier, M.	(1972)	Structure and Contradiction in Capital, in R. Blackburn, ed., *Ideology and Social Science*, Fontana, London, 334–68.
Godelier, M.	(1978a)	Infrastructures, Societies and History, *New Left Review*, 112, November–December, 84–96.
Godelier, M.	(1978b)	The Concept of the 'Asiatic Mode of Production' and Marxist Models of Social Evolution, in D. Seddon, ed., *Relations of Production, Marxist Approaches to Economic Anthropology*, Cass, London, 209–57.
Godelier, M.	(1980)	The Emergence of Marxism in Anthropology in France, in E. Gellner, ed., *Soviet and Western Anthropology*, Duckworth, London, 3–18.
Godes, M. Ia.	(1981)	The Reaffirmation of Unilinealism, in A.M. Bailey and J.R. Llobera, eds, *The Asiatic Mode of Production Science and Politics*, Routledge and Kegan Paul, London (trans. R. Croskey from *Diskussia ob Aziatskom sposobe proizvodstva po dokladu M. Godesa [Results of the Discussion on the Asiatic Mode of Production]*, Moscow–Leningrad, 1931).

Gouldner, A.	(1980)	*The Two Marxisms, Contradictions and Anomalies in the Development of Theory*, Macmillan, London.
Gourevitch, P.	(1978)	The International System and Regime Formation: A Critical Review of Anderson and Wallerstein, *World Politics*, 10, 3: 419–38.
Gramsci, A.	(1971)	*Selections from the Prison Notebooks*, Lawrence and Wishart, London, eds. Q. Hoare and G. Nowell-Smith.
Grover, B.R.	(1963)	Nature of Land Rights in Mughal India, *Indian Economic and Social History Review*, I, 1, July–September, i, i: 1–23.
Guha, A.	(1975)	Marxist Approach to Indian History: A Framework, in K. Mathew Kurian, ed., *India – State and Society: A Marxist Approach*, Orient Longman, Bombay, 33–55.
Gunawardana, R.A.L.H.	(1976)	The Analysis of Pre-Colonial Social Formations in Asia in the Writings of Karl Marx, *The Indian Historical Review*, II, 2: 365–88.
Gupta, D.	(1980)	From Varna to Jati: The Indian Caste System from the Asiatic to the Feudal Mode of Production, *Journal of Contemporary Asia*, 10, 3: 249–71.
Habermas, J.	(1974)	Between Philosophy and Science: Marxism as Critique, in Habermas, *Theory and Practice*, Heinemann, London, 195–222.
Habib, I.	(1962)	An Examination of Wittfogel's Theory of Oriental Despotism, *Enquiry*, 6: 57–9.
Habib, I.	(1963)	*The Agrarian System of Mughal India.* Asia Publishing House, Bombay.
Habib, I.	(1966)	India Looks at Herself, *Times Literary Supplement*, 28 July: 687–8.
Habib, I.	(1969)	Potentialities of Capitalistic Development in the Economy of Mughal India, *The Journal of Economic History*, XXIX, 1: 32–78.

Habib, I.   (1973)   Problems of Marxist Historical Analysis, in S.A. Shah, ed., *Towards National Liberation. Essays on the Political Economy of India*, Black Rose, Montreal 1–13.

Habib, I.   (1974)   The Social Distribution of Landed Property in Pre-British India, in R.S. Sharma, ed., *Indian Society: Historical Probings. In Memory of D.D. Kosambi*, People's Publishing House, New Delhi. 264–316.

Habib, I.   (1975)   Problems of Marxist Historical Analysis, in K. Mathew Kurian, ed., *India – State and Society: A Marxist Approach*, Orient Longman, Bombay, 20–32.

Habib, I.   (1982a)   Agrarian Relations and the Land Revenue: North India, in T. Raychaudhuri and I. Habib, eds, *Cambridge Economic History of India*, vol. 1, Cambridge University Press, Cambridge, 235–49.

Habib, I.   (1982b)   The Monetary System and Prices, in T. Raychaudhuri and I. Habib, eds, Cambridge Economic History of India, vol. 1, Cambridge University Press, Cambridge, 360–81.

Habib, I.   (1983)   Marx's Perception of India, *The Marxist*, 1, 1: 92–143.

Habib, I.   (1985)   Classifying Pre-Colonial India, *Journal of Peasant Studies*, 12, 2–3: 44–53.

Halliday, F.   (1970)   Marxism and Asia, *New Left Review*, 61: 93–6.

Hambly, G.R.G.   (1982)   Towns and Cities: Mughal India, in T. Raychaudhuri and I. Habib, eds, *Cambridge Economic History of India*, vol. 1, Cambridge University Press, Cambridge, 434–52.

Hasan, I.   (1980)   *The Central Structure of the Mughal Empire*, Munshiram Manoharlal Publishers Pvt. Ltd, New Delhi.

Hasan, N.	(1963)	The Position of the Zamindars in the Mughal Empire, *Indian Economic and Social History Review*, 1, 4: 107–19.
Hayek, F. von	(1944)	*The Road to Serfdom*, Routledge and Kegan Paul, London.
Heesterman, J.C.	(1970)	Power and Authority in Indian Civilization. Study Conference on Tradition in Indian Politics and Society, Centre of South Asian Studies, School of Oriental and African Studies, University of London, 1–3 July.
Heesterman, J.C.	(1971)	Kautilya and the Ancient Indian State, *Weiner Zeitschrift für die Kunde Südasiens*, 15: 5–22.
Hegel, G.W.F.	(1956)	*The Philosophy of History* (trans. J. Sibree), Dover, New York.
Hegel, G.W.F.	(1967)	*The Philosophy of Right* (trans. with notes T.M. Knox), Oxford University Press, New York.
Heichelheim, F.	(1958)	*An Ancient Economic History: From the Paleolithic Age to the Migrations of the Germanic, Slavic and Arabic Nations* (trans. J. Stevens), three vols, Leiden.
Heitzman, J.	(1987)	State Formation in South India, 850–1280, *Indian Economic and Social History Review*, 24: 35–61.
Hewitt, J.F.	(1887)	Village Communities in India, Especially Those in the Bengal Presidency, the Central Provinces and Bombay, *Journal of the Society of Arts*, XXXV: 613–25.
Hilton, R., ed.	(1978)	*The Transition from Feudalism to Capitalism*, Verso, London.
Hindess, B. and Hirst, P.	(1975)	*Pre-Capitalist Modes of Production*, Macmillan, London.
Hindess, B. and Hirst, P.	(1977)	*Mode of Production and Social Formation: An Autocritique*, Routledge and Kegan Paul, London.

358 *Bibliography*

Hirschman, A.   (1977)   *The Passions and the Interests: Political Arguments for Capitalism Before Its Triumph*, Princeton University Press, Princeton, NJ.

Hirst, P.   (1975)   The Uniqueness of the West, *Economy and Society*, 4, 4: 446–76.

Hirst, P.   (1988)   Obituary of Karl A. Wittfogel, *The Independent*, 14 June 1988.

Hobbes, T.   (1968)   *Leviathan* (ed. C. B. MacPherson), Penguin, Harmondsworth.

Hobsbawm, E., ed.   (1964)   *Pre-Capitalist Economic Formations*, Lawrence and Wishart, London.

Hodgson, G.   (1975)   *Trotsky and Fatalistic Marxism*, Spokesman Books, Nottingham.

Hoffman, E.   (1965)   Social Economic Formations and Historical Science, *Marxism Today*, 9, 9.

Honderich, T.   (1982)   Against Teleological Historical Materialism, *Inquiry*, 25: 451–69.

Hook, S.   (1933)   *Towards the Understanding of Karl Marx. A Revolutionary Interpretation*, John Day, New York.

Hume, D.   (1953)   That Politics May be Reduced to a Science, in Hume, *Political Essays* (ed. with intro. Charles W. Hended), Indianapolis, Bobbs-Merrill.

Hutton, J.J.   (1946)   *Caste in India. Its Nature, Functions and Origins*, Cambridge University Press, Cambridge.

Irvine, W., ed.   (1907)   *Moghul India* (translations of Storio de Mogor), four vols, Calcutta.

Islamoglu, H. and Keyder C.   (1977)   The Ottoman Social Formation, *Review*, 1, 1: 37–55.

Jardine, R.   (1961)   Stages of Social Development, *Marxism Today*, 5, 7: 223–4.

Jay, M.   (1973)   *The Dialectical Imagination, A History of the Frankfurt School and the Institute of Social Research, 1923–1950*, Heinemann, London.

Jolly, J.   (1896)   Recht und Sitte, in *Grundrisse der Indo-Arischen Philologie und Altertumskunde*, II, Fasc, 8, ed. G. Bühler, Strassburg.

Jones, E.   (1981)   *The European Miracle*, Cambridge University Press, Cambridge.

Jones, R.   (1831)   *An Essay on the Distribution of Wealth and the Sources of Taxation*, London.

Jones, R.   (1833)   *An Introductory Lecture on Political Economy, Delivered at King's College London*, London.

Jones, R.   (1852)   *Textbook of Lectures on the Political Economy of Nations*, Hertford.

Joshi, P.C.   (1959)   *Homage to Karl Marx*, Communist Party of India, People's Publishing House, Delhi.

Kachanovskii, Iu. A.   (1971)   *Rabovladenia, feodalizm ili aziatskii sposob proizvodstva?*, Nauka, Moscow.

Kahn, J.S. and Llobera, J.R.   (1981)   *The Anthropology of Pre-Capitalist Societies*, Macmillan, London.

Karve, I.   (1961)   *Hindu Society: An Interpretation*, Deccan College, Poona.

Kautilya   (1958)   *The Arthashastra* (ed. T. Ganapti Sastri, tr. R. Shamasastry), Mysore, First edition 1923.

Kautsky, J. H.   (1982)   *The Politics of Aristocratic Empires*, University of North Carolina Press, Chapel Hill.

Kedourie, E.   (1957)   Review of 'Oriental Despotism', *Spectator*, 27 September.

Keyder, C.   (1976)   The Dissolution of the Asiatic Mode of Production, *Economy and Society*, 5: 178–96.

Kiernan, V.   (1967)   Marx and India, *The Socialist Register 1967*, eds R. Miliband and J. Saville, Merlin Press, London.

Knei-Paz, B.   (1977)   *The Social and Political Thought of Leon Trotsky*, Oxford University Press, Oxford.

Koebner, R.   (1951)   Despot and Despotism: Vicissitudes of a Political Term, *Journal of the Warburg and Courtauld Institutes*, XIV, 3–4: 275–302.

Kokin, M.   (1981)   The Asiatic Bureaucracy as a Class, in A.M. Bailey and J.P. Llobera, eds, *The Asiatic Mode of Production: Science and Politics*, Routledge and Kegan Paul, London.

360 *Bibliography*

Kolakowski, L.   (1981)   *Main Currents of Marxism*, three vols, Oxford University Press, Oxford.

Konrad, G. and   (1979)   *The Intellectuals on the Road to Class*
Szelenyi, I.   *Power* (trans. A. Arato and R.E. Allen), Harvester, Brighton.

Kosambi, D.D.   (1949)   Marxism and Ancient Indian Culture (review of S.A. Dange), *Annals of the Bhandarkar Oriental Research Institute*, XXIX: 271–7.

Kosambi, D.D.   (1956a)   *An Introduction to the Study of Indian History*, Popular Prakasham, Bombay.

Kosambi, D.D.   (1956b)   On the Development of Feudalism in India, *Annals of the Bhandarkar Oriental Research Institute*, XXXVI, III–IV: 258–69.

Kosambi, D.D.   (1957a)   Book Review: The Basis of Despotism, *Economic Weekly*, ix, 44, 2 November: 1417–19.

Kosambi, D.D.   (1957b)   *Exasperating Essays: Exercises in the Dialectical Method*, People's Book House, Poona.

Kosambi, D.D.   (1958)   The Text of the Arthashastra, *Journal of the American Oriental Society*, XXVIII, 2: 169–73.

Kosambi, D.D.   (1959)   Primitive Communism, *New Age*, VIII, 2: 26–39.

Kosambi, D.D.   (1965)   *The Culture and Civilization of Ancient India in Historical Outline*, Routledge and Kegan Paul, London.

Krader, L.   (1972)   *The Ethnological Notebooks of Karl Marx*, Van Gorcum, Assen.

Krader, L.   (1975)   *The Asiatic Mode of Production, Sources, Development and Critique in the Writings of Karl Marx*, van Gorcum, Assen.

Krader, L.   (1976)   *Dialectic of Civil Society*, Van Gorcum, Assen.

Krader, L.   (1982)   Theory of Evolution, Revolution and the State: The Critical Relation of Marx to His Contemporaries Darwin, Carlyle, Morgan, Maine and Kovalevsky, in E. Hobsbawm, ed.,

		The History of Marxism. Volume One: Marxism in Marx's Day, Harvester Press, Brighton, 192–226.
Kreissig, H.	(1977)	Landed Property in the 'Hellenistic' Orient, *Eirene*, 15: 5–26.
Kreissig, H.	(1982)	*Geschichte des Hellenismus*, Akadamie Verlag, Berlin.
Krishnaswami, A.	(1964)	*The Tamil Country under Vijayanagar*, Annamalai University, Annamalai-nagar.
Lach, D.F.	(1965)	*Asia in the Making of Europe*, vol. 1, University of Chicago Press, Chicago.
Lach, D.F.	(1968)	*India in the Eyes of Europe. The Sixteenth Century*, Pheonix Books, Chicago.
Laclau, E.	(1977)	*Politics and Ideology in Marxist Theory*, New Left Books, London.
Laclau, E. and Mouffe, C.	(1985)	*Hegemony and Socialist Strategy: Towards a Radical Democratic Politics*, Verso, London.
Lacoste, Y.	(1984)	*Ibn Khaldun: The Birth of History and the Past of the Third World*, Verso, London.
Lambrick	(1937)	Early Canal Administration in Sind, *Journal of the Sind Historical Society*, III, Part i: 15–16.
Leach, E.	(1959)	Hydraulic Society in Ceylon, *Past and Present*, 15, April: 2–26.
Leach, E.	(1988)	Sudden Losses of Complexity, *London Review of Books*, 10 November 1988: 16.
Leach, E. and Mukherjee, S.	(1970)	*Elites in South Asia*, Cambridge University press, Cambridge, introduction.
Lefort, C.	(1978)	Marx: From One Vision of History to Another, *Social Research*, 45, 4: 615–66.
Lenin, V.I.	(1965)	*Collected Works*, vol. 10, Progress Publishers, Moscow.
Lentsman, Ia. A.	(1966)	A Contribution to the Discussion of the Asiatic Mode of Production, *Soviet Studies in History*, IV, 4: 22–30.

362   Bibliography

Leonard, K.   (1979)   The Great Firm Theory of the
                                 Decline of the Mughal Empire,
                                 Comparative Studies in Society and
                                 History, XXI: 151–67.

Levada, I.A.   (1981)   Wittfogel's 'Oriental Despotism': A
                                 Soviet Review, in A.M. Bailey and
                                 J.P. Llobera, eds, The Asiatic Mode
                                 of Production: Science and Politics,
                                 Routledge and Kegan Paul, London,
                                 trans. (from Sovetskoe kitaevednie,
                                 1958), 1, 3: 189–97)

Levine, N.   (1977)   The Myth of Asiatic Restoration,
                                 The Journal of Asian Studies, xxxvii,
                                 1: 73–85.

Levitt, C.   (1978)   L. Krader's Research on the Asiatic
                                 Mode of Production, Critique of
                                 Anthropology, 11: 39–56.

Lichtheim, G.   (1963)   Marx and the Asiatic Mode of
                                 Production, St Anthony's Papers
                                 No. 14, 86–112, Chatto and Windus,
                                 London (reprinted as, 'Oriental
                                 Despotism', in Lichtheim. (1967).
                                 The Concept of Ideology and Other
                                 Essays, Random House, New York.

Lichtheim, G.   (1967)   Oriental Despotism, The Concept of
                                 Ideology and Other Essays, Random
                                 House, New York.

Linguet, S.-N.-H.   (1767)   Théorie des lois civiles, ou Principes
                                 fondamentaux de la société, vol. 1,
                                 London.

Lowe, D.   (1966)   The Function of 'China' in Marx, Lenin,
                                 and Mao, University of California
                                 Press, Berkeley, Cal.

Löwith, K.   (1948)   Meaning in History, University of
                                 Chicago Press, Chicago.

Lubasz, H.   (1984)   Marx's Concept of the Asiatic
                                 Mode of Production: A Genetic
                                 Analysis, Economy and Society, 13, 4:
                                 456–83.

Lubasz, H.   (1985)   Reply to Kate Currie, Economy and
                                 Society, 14, 3: 404–06.

Lukács, G.   (1967)   History and Class Consciousness,
                                 Merlin, London.

Lukes, S.   (1983)   Is It Possible to Separate the Basis
                                      from the Superstructure?, in D.
                                      Miller and L. Seidentop, eds, *The
                                      Nature of Political Theory*, Oxford
                                      University Press, Oxford.

Machiavelli, N.   (1975)   *The Prince* (trans. with intro. George
                                      Bull), Penguin, Harmondsworth.

MacPherson, C.B.   (1973)   *Democratic Theory: Essays in Retrieval*,
                                      Oxford University Press, Oxford.

Madan, G.R.   (1979)   *Western Sociologists on Indian Society*,
                                      Routledge and Kegan Paul, London.

Maddison, A.   (1971)   *Economic Growth and Class Structure.
                                      India and Pakistan since the Moghuls*,
                                      Allen and Unwin, London.

Madi'iar, L.I.   (1981)   The Legitimacy of the AMP, in
                                      A.M. Bailey and J.P. Llobera, eds,
                                      *The Asiatic Mode of Production: Science
                                      and Politics*, Routledge and Kegan
                                      Paul, London, 76–94.

Mahalingam, T.V.   (1967)   *South Indian Polity*, University of
                                      Madras, Madras, revised edition.

Majumdar, R.C., ed.   (1951)   *The Vedic Age, The* Bharatiya Itihasa
                                      Samiti's *History and Culture of the
                                      Indian People*, vol. 1., eds. R.C.
                                      Majumdar and A.D. Pusalkar, Allen
                                      and Unwin, Bombay.

Majumdar, R.C., ed.   (1960)   *Classical Accounts of India* (trans-
                                      lations), Calcutta.

Majumdar, R.C. and   (1951)   *The* Bharatiya Itihasa Samiti's
Pusalkar, A.D., eds.   *History and Culture of the Indian
                                      People*, 11 vols, Allen and Unwin,
                                      Bombay.

Majumdar, R.C.,   (1946)   *An Advanced History of India*,
Roy Choudhary, W.C.   Macmillan, London.
and Dutta, K.K.

Mallick, S.C.   (1968)   *Indian Civilization: The Formative
                                      Period*, Indian Institute of Advanced
                                      Study, Simla.

Mandel, E.   (1971)   *The Formation of the Economic Thought
                                      of Karl Marx*, New Left Books,
                                      London.

Mandel, E.   (1979)   Why the Soviet Bureaucracy is Not
                                      a New Ruling Class, *Monthly Review*,
                                      31, 3: 63–76.

Mann, M.   (1980)   The Pre-Industrial State, *Political
                                      Studies*, XXVIII, 2: 297–304.
Mann, M.   (1984)   The Autonomous Power of the
                                      State, *Archives Europénnes de Socio-
                                      logie*, 25: 185–213.
Mann, M.   (1986)   *The Sources of Social Power*, vol. 1,
                                      Cambridge   University   Press,
                                      Cambridge.
Marsilius of Padua   (1980)   *Defensor Pacis* (1324) (trans. and
                                      Intro. Alan Gewirth), University of
                                      Toronto Press, Toronto.
Marx, K.   (1954)   *La Russie et l'Europe* (Revelations on
                                      the Diplomatic History of the
                                      Eighteenth Century, intro. B.P.
                                      Hepner), Galliamard, Paris.
Marx K.   (1956)   Introduction to the Critique of
                                      Hegel's Philosophy of Right, in
                                      Marx and Engels, *Werke*, ed. Instïtüt
                                      für Marxismus-Lenirismus beim
                                      ZK des SED, Berlin, 39 vols.
Marx, K.   (1959a)   Lord Canning's Proclamation and
                                      Land Tenure in India, *New York
                                      Daily Tribune*, 7 June 1858, in K.
                                      Marx and F. Engels, *On Colonialism*
                                      Progress   Publishers,   Moscow,
                                      191–4.
Marx, K.   (1959b)   *Notes on Indian History, 664–1858*,
                                      Foreign   Languages   Publishing
                                      House, Moscow.
Marx, K.   (1961)   *Capital*, vol. I, Progress Publishers,
                                      Moscow.
Marx, K.   (1964)   *Pre-Capitalist Economic Formations*
                                      (ed. and intro. E. Hobsbawm),
                                      Lawrence & Wishart, London.
Marx, K.   (1967a)   *Capital*, vol. I, International Pub-
                                      lishers, New York.
Marx, K.   (1967b)   *The Communist Manifesto*. (intro. A.J.P.
                                      Taylor), Penguin, Harmondsworth.
Marx, K.   (1969)   *Secret Diplomatic History of the
                                      Eighteenth Century and the Story of
                                      Lord Palmerston*, Lawrence &
                                      Wishart, London.

Marx, K.	(1970)	*A Contribution to the Critique of Political Economy* (trans. S.W. Ryazanskaya and intro. Maurice Dobb), Progress Publishers, Moscow.
Marx, K.	(1972)	The Secret Diplomatic History of the Eighteenth Century, in T. Payne, ed. *The Unknown Karl Marx*, London.
Marx, K.	(1973a)	Surveys From Exile. *Political Writings*, vol. 2, Penguin/New Left Review, Harmondsworth.
Marx, K.	(1973b)	The British Rule in India, in D. Fernbach, ed. *Surveys From Exile. Political Writings*, vol. 2, Penguin/New Left Review, Harmondsworth, 301–7.
Marx, K.	(1973c)	The Communist Manifesto, in D. Fernbach, ed. *The Revolutions of 1848*, Penguin/New Left Review, Harmondsworth, 62–98.
Marx, K.	(1973d)	The Eighteenth Brumaire of Louis Bonaparte, in D. Fernbach, ed. *Surveys From Exile. Political Writings*, vol. 2, Penguin/New Left Review, Harmondsworth, 143–249.
Marx, K.	(1973e)	*The Grundrisse* (ed. M. Nicolaus), Penguin/New Left Review, Harmondsworth.
Marx, K.	(1975)	*Early Writings*, tr. R. Livingstone and G. Benton, Sec. L. Conelli, Penguin/New Left Books, Harmondsworth
Marx, K.	(1976a)	*Capital*, vol. I, Penguin/New Left Books, London.
Marx, K.	(1976b)	Results of the Immediate Process of Production [Resultate], in *Capital*, vol. I, Penguin/New Left Review, Harmondsworth.
Marx, K.	(1977)	*Selected Writings* (ed. D. McLellan), Oxford University Press, Oxford.
Marx, K.	(1978)	*Theories of Surplus Value*, three vols (trans. E. Burns), Progress Publishers, Moscow.

Marx, K.	(1981)	*Capital*, vol. III, (trans. D. Fernbach and intro. E. Mandel.), Penguin/ New Left Review, Harmondsworth
Marx, K. and Engels, F.	(1934)	*Selected Correspondence, 1846–1895*, Martin Lawrence, London.
Marx, K. and Engels, F.	(1951)	*Selected Works*, two vols, Progress Publishers, Moscow.
Marx, K. and Engels, F.	(1952)	*The Russian Menace to Europe*, selected and edited by P.W. Blackstock and B.F. Hoselitz, Free Press, Glencoe, Illinois.
Marx, K. and Engels, F.	(1956)	*Werke*, 39 vols, ed. Institüt für Marxismus-Leninismus beim ZK der SED, Berlin.
Marx, K. and Engels, F.	(1959)	*On Colonialism*, Progress Publishers, Moscow.
Mark, K. and Engels, F	(1967)	*The Communist Manifesto*, intro. A.J.P. Taylor, Penguin, Harmondsworth.
Marx, K. and Engels, F.	(1969–70)	*Selected Works*, three vols, Progress Publishers, Moscow.
Marx, K. and Engels, F.	(1970)	*The German Ideology* (ed. C. Arthur), Lawrence & Wishart, London.
Marx, K. and Engels, F.	(1975)	The Holy Family, in *Collected Works*, vol. 4, Progress Publishers, Moscow.
Mascaró, J., trans.	(1962)	*The Bhagavad Gita*, Penguin, Harmondsworth.
Mazumdar, B.P.	(1960)	*The Socio-Economic History of Northern India (11th and 12th Centuries)*, Calcutta.
McIlwain, C.H.	(1932)	*The Growth of Political Thought in the West. From the Greeks to the End of the Middle Ages*, Macmillan, New York.
McLean, I.	(1987)	*An Introduction to Public Choice*, Basil Blackwell, Oxford.
McLellan, D.	(1973a)	*Karl Marx*, Macmillan, London.
McLellan, D	(1973b)	*Marx's Grundrisse*, Paladin, London.
McLellan, D.	(1976)	*Karl Marx, His Life and Thought*, Paladin, London.
Medvedev, E.	(1969)	La Régime Socio-Économique de l'Inde Ancienne, *Cahiers du CÉRM*, 71: 3–19.
Meek, R.	(1967)	*Economics, Ideology and Other Essays*, Chapman Hall Ltd London.

Meek, R.	(1971)	Smith, Turgot, and the 'Four Stages' Theory, *History of Political Economy*, 3, 1: 9–27.
Meillassoux, C.	(1973)	Are there Castes in India?, *Economy and Society*, 2: 89ff.
Melikishivili, G.A.	(1976–7)	The Character of the Socio-Economic Structure in the Ancient East (A Preliminary Classification of Class Societies by Age and Type), *Soviet Anthropology and Archeology*, 15, 2–3: 29–49.
Melotti, U.	(1977)	*Marx and the Third World*, Macmillan, London.
Menon, P.	(1983)	The South Indian Village Community and the Marxian Model Paper presented to The Marx Centenary Seminar, organized by the Editorial Board of *Social Scientiest*, New Delhi, 6–8 October 1983.
Merquior, J.G.	(1986)	*Western Marxism*, Paladin, London.
Mill, J.S.	(1848)	*Principles of Political Economy*, George Routledge and Sons, London and New York.
Mills, C.W.	(1962)	*The Marxists*, Dell, New York.
Milnar, M.	(1975)	*Marx, Engels et al Politique Internationale*, Gallimard, Paris.
Milnar, M. and Witzig, C.	(1974)	L'influence de la mentalité colonialiste britannique sur le concept asiatique de Marx, *Relations Internationales*, 2: 37–45.
Moore, B.	(1958b)	Totalitarian Elements in Pre-Industrial Societies, *in Moore, Political Power and Social Theory*, Harvard University Press, Cambridge, Mass., 30–88.
Moore, Barrington, Junr	(1958)	*Political Power and Social Theory*, Harvard University Press, Cambridge, Mass.
Moore, Barrington, Junr	(1966)	*The Social Origins of Dictatorship and Democracy: Lord and Peasant in the Modern World*, Penguin, Harmondsworth.

368 *Bibliography*

Moore, C.   (1974–5) The Prolet-Aryan Outlook of Marxism: Were Marx and Engels White Racists?, *Berkeley Journal of Sociology*, XIX: 125–56.

Moore, S.   (1980) Marx and Lenin as Historical Materialists, in M. Cohen, T. Nagel and T. Scanlon, eds, *Marx, Justice and History, A Philosophy and Public Affairs Reader*, Princeton University Press, Princeton, NJ.

Moreland, W.H.   (1929) *The Agrarian System of Moslem India*, Heffer, Cambridge.

Moreland, W.H.   (1972) *From Akbar to Aurangzeb*, Oriental Books Reprint Co., Delhi – original 1923.

Morgan, L.H.   (1877) *Ancient Society, or Researches in the Lines of Human Progress from Savagery, through Barbarism to Civilization*, Macmillan, London.

Mosher, M.A.   (1984) The Particulars of a Universal Politics: Hegel's Adaptation of Montesquieu's Typology, *American Political Science Review*, 78: 179–88.

Mueller, D.   (1979) *Public Choice*, Cambridge University Press, Cambridge.

Mukherjee, S.N.   (1971) The Idea of Village Community and British Administration, *Enquiry*, III, 3, Winter: 57–67.

Mukhia, H.   (1981) Was There Feudalism in Indian History?, *The Journal of Peasant Studies*, 8, 3: 273–310.

Murray, J.A.H., ed.   (1897) *A New English Dictionary on Historical Principles*, vol. III, Oxford, Clarendon Press.

Murvar, V.   (1966) Some Tentative Modifications of Weber's Typology: Occidental versus Oriental City, *Social Forces*, 381–89.

Namboodiripad, E.M.S. (1952) *The National Question in Kerala* Bombay.

Namboodiripad, E.M.S. (1972) Marx, the Asiatic Mode of Production and the Study of Indian History, *The Radical Review*, 3, 2, April–June.

Namboodiripad, E.M.S.   (1982)   Marx, the Asiatic Mode and the Study of Indian History, *Selected Writings*, vol. 1, National Book Agency, Calcutta.

Naqvi, H.K.   (1968)   *Urban Centres and Industries in Upper India, 1556–1803*, Asia Publishing House, Bombay.

Naqvi, S.   (1973)   Marx on Pre-British Indian Economy and Society, *Socialist Digest*, 7: 36–70.

Needham, J.   (1959)   Review of 'Oriental Despotism', *Science and Society*, 23: 58–65.

Neznanov, V.   (1978)   *The Logic of History: From Capitalism to Socialism: Basic Features of the Transition Period*, Novosti Press, Moscow.

Nicolaus, M.   (1973)   Introduction, in K. Marx, *The Grundrisse*, Penguin/New Left Review, Harmondsworth.

Niemeyer, G.   (1958)   The Structure of Total Power, *Review of Politics*, 20, 2: 264–70.

Nikiforov, V.   (1967)   Une discussion a l'institut des peuples d'Asie, *Recherches Internationales à la lumière du Marxisme*, 57–8: 240–53.

Nikiforov, V.   (1975)   *Vostok i vsemirnaia istoria*, Nauka, Moscow.

Nilakanta Sastri, K.A.   (1955)   *The Colas*, Madras University Press, Madras.

Nossiter, T.J.   (1982)   *Communism in Kerala*, Royal Institute of International Affairs, London.

Nozick, R.   (1974)   *Anarchy, State and Utopia*, Basil Blackwell, Oxford.

Oakeshott, M.   (1975)   *On Human Conduct*, Oxford University Press, Oxford.

Offe, C.   (1984)   *The Contradictions of the Welfare State*, Hutchinson, London.

O'Leary, B.   (1984)   Review of S.P. Dunn, 'The Fall and Rise of the Asiatic Mode of Production', *Communist Affairs: Documents and Analysis* 3, 2: 245–6.

O'Leary, B.   (1985)   Is there a Radical Public Administration?, *Public Administration*, 63, 3: 345–52.

O'Leary, B.	(1987)	The Odyssey of Jon Elster, *Government and Opposition*, 22, 4: 480–98.
O'Leary, B.	(1988)	Obituary: Karl Wittfogel: Hydrophobic Cold War Warrior, *The Guardian*, 20 June 1988.
O'Leary, B. and Dunleavy, P.	(1987)	*Theories of the State: The Politics of Liberal Democracy*, Macmillan, London.
Omvedt, G.	(1977)	Review of L. Krader, 'The Asiatic Mode of Production', *Contemporary Sociology*, 6, 4.
Overstreet, G.D. and Windmiller, M.	(1959)	*Communism in India*, University of California Press, Berkeley, Cal.
Pant, D.	(1930)	*The Commercial Policy of the Moguls*, D.P. Taraporevala Sons & Co. Bombay.
Parain, C.	(1966)	Protohistoire méditerranéénne et la MPA, *La Pensée*, 127: 24–43.
Parain, C.	(1969)	Proto-Histoire Mediterranéenne et Mode de Production Asiatique, in CÉRM, *Sur le 'Mode de Production Asiatique'*, Editions Sociales, Paris, 169–94.
Pavlov, V.	(1979)	*The Historical Premises for India's Transition to Capitalism*, Progress Publishers, Moscow.
Pavlovskaia, A.I.	(1966)	On the Discussion of the Asiatic Mode of Production in *La Pensée* and *Eirene*, *Soviet Studies in History*, IV, 4: 38–45.
Pecirka, J.	(1967)	Les discussions soviétiqes sur le mode de production asiatique et sur la formation esclavagiste, *Recherches internationales à la lumière du Marxisme*, 57–8: 59–78.
Piaget, J.	(1971)	*Structuralism*, Routledge and Kegan Paul, London.
Piggott, S.	(1950)	*Prehistoric India*, Penguin, Harmondsworth.
Piggott, S.	(1965)	*Ancient Europe from the Beginnings of Agriculture to Classical Antiquity*, Edinburgh University Press, Edinburgh.

Pigulevskaia, N.V.	(1966)	The Question of the Asiatic Mode of Production, *Soviet Studies in History*, IV, 4: 31–7.
Plamenatz, J.	(1954)	*German Marxism and Russian Communism*, Longman, London.
Plato	(1955)	*The Republic*, tr. with intro. H.D.P. Lee, Penguin Books, Harmondsworth.
Plekhanov, G.	(1961a)	'Our Differences', in Plekhanov, *Selected Philosophical Works*, vol. 1, & Wishart, London.
Plekhanov, G.	(1961b)	*Selected Philosophical Works*, vol. 1, Lawrence & Wishart, London.
Plekhanov, G.	(1969)	*Fundamental Problems of Marxism*, Lawrence & Wishart, London.
Plekhanov, G.	(1981)	Civilization and the Great Historical Rivers, in A.M. Bailey and J.P. Llobera, eds, *The Asiatic Mode of Production: Science and Politics*, Routledge and Kegan Paul, London, 58–70.
Polanyi, K.	(1966)	*Dahomey and the Slave Trade*, AES Monograph 42, University of Washington Press, Washington DC.
Popper, K.R.	(1957)	*The Poverty of Historicism*, Routledge and Kegan Paul, London.
Popper, K.R.	(1962)	*The Open Society and its Enemies, vol I and II*, Routledge and Kegan Paul, London.
Prasad, B.	(1928)	*The State in Ancient India*, The Indian Press, Allahabad.
Pryor, F.	(1977)	*The Origins of the Economy: A Comparative Study of Distribution in Primitive and Peasant Societies*, Academic Press, New York.
Pryor, F.	(1980)	The Asian Mode of Production as an Economic System, *Journal of Comparative Economics*, 4: 420–42.
Pulleyblank, E.G.	(1958)	Karl Wittfogel. Oriental Despotism, *Journal of the Economic and Social History of the Orient*, 1, Part 3: 351–3. Also *Bulletin of the School of Oriental and African Studies*, XX, 3: 657–60.

Purohit, V.	(1979)	The Asiatic Mode of Production and Feudalism in Indian History and Historiography. Paper presented at the 40th Session of Indian History Congress, Waltair, Andhra Pradesh, India, 27–9 December.
Rader, M.	(1979)	*Marx's Interpretation of History*, Oxford University Press, New York.
Rangaswami, A.K.V.	(1935)	*Considerations On Some Aspects of Ancient Indian Polity*, University of Madras Press, Madras.
Rapson, E.J., ed.	(1922)	*Cambridge History of India*, vol. 1, Cambridge University Press, Cambridge.
Rastrianikov, V.G. et al., eds	(1980)	*Gosudarstvo i agarnaia evolutsia* [Government and Agrarian Evolution], Nauka, Moscow.
Ray, B.	(1957)	Some Features of Pre-Capitalist India, *New Age*, VI, 5: 40–50.
Raychaudhuri, T.	(1965)	The Agrarian System of Mughal India, *Enquiry*, 2, 1: 92–121.
Raychaudhuri, T.	(1982)	Inland Trade, in T. Raychaudhuri and I. Habib, eds, *Cambridge Economic History of India*, vol. 1, 325–59.
Raychaudhuri, T. and Habib, I.	(1982)	*Cambridge Economic History of India. vol. 1, c.1200–1750 AD*, Cambridge University Press, Cambridge.
Reisman, D.	(1976)	*Adam Smith's Sociological Economics*, Croom Helm, London.
Reynolds, C.J. and Lysa, H.	(1983)	Marxism in Thai Historical Studies, *Journal of Asian Studies*, xliii, 1: 77–98.
Richter, M.	(1977)	*The Political Theory of Montesquieu*, Cambridge University Press, Cambridge.
Rodinson, M.	(1974)	*Islam and Capitalism*, Penguin, Harmondsworth.
Roemer, J.	(1982)	*A General Theory of Exploitation and Class*, Harvard University Press, Cambridge, Mass.
Roemer, J.	(1986a)	Should Marxists be interested in exploitation?, in J. Roemer, ed.,

		Analytical Marxism, Cambridge University Press, Cambridge, 260–82.
Roemer, J., ed	(1986b)	*Analytical Marxism*, Cambridge University Press, Cambridge.
Roemer, J.	(1988)	*Free to Lose: An Introduction to Marxist Economic Philosophy*, Radius, London.
Rogowski, R.	(1974)	*Rational Legitimacy, A Theory of Political Support*, Princeton University Press, Princeton, NJ.
Rosdolsky, R.	(1977)	*The Making of Marx's Capital*, Pluto Press, London.
Rosen, M.	(1986)	*Hegel's Dialectic and its Criticism*, Cambridge University Press, Cambridge.
Roxborough, I.	(1977)	Review. L. Krader, 1975, The Asiatic Mode of Production, *British Journal of Socioloy*, xxviii, 3: 410.
Roy, M.N.	(1922)	*India in Transition*, Geneva.
Rubel, M.	(1957)	Les cahiers de lecture de Karl Marx: 1840–1853, *International Review of Social History*, New Series, 2: 392–40.
Runciman, W.G.	(1980)	Comparative Sociology or Narrative History? A Note on the Methodology of Perry Anderson, *Archives Européenne de Sociologie*, 21: 162–78.
Runciman, W.G.	(1987)	The Old Question, *London Review of Books*, 9, 4: 7–8.
Rybakov, V.	(1984)	Family Politics, *Granta*, 14, Winter: 72–84.
Sachs, I.	(1967)	Une Nouvelle Phase de la Discussion Sur Les Formations, *Recherches internationales à la lumière du Marxisme*, 57–8: 294–307.
Safarov, G.	(1923)	*Predislovie to M.N. Roy, Novaya Indiya*, Moscow and Petrograd.
Sahai-Achuthan, N.	(1983)	Soviet Indologists and the Institute of Oriental Studies: Works on Contemporary India in the Soviet Union, *Journal of Asian Studies*, XLII, 2: 323–43.

Sahlins, M.	(1972)	*Stone Age Economics*, Chicago University Press, Chicago.
Said, E.	(1977)	*Orientalism*, Routledge and Kegan Paul, London.
Salvadori, M.	(1977)	*Karl Kautsky and the Socialist Revolution*, New Left Books, London.
Samuelson, P.A.	(1954)	The Pure Theory of Public Expenditures, *Review of Economics and Statistics*, 36: 387–9.
Sardesai, S.G.	(1960)	Interpretation of History, *New Age*, ix, 2: 1–22.
Sartori, G.	(1987)	*The Theory of Democracy Revisited, Part One*, Chatham House, Chatham, NJ.
Sawer, M.	(1975)	Note on Baron, *Survey*, 21, 4: 223–24.
Sawer, M.	(1977a)	*Marxism and the Question of the Asiatic Mode of Production*, Martinus Nijhoff, The Hague.
Sawer, M.	(1977b)	The Concept of the Asiatic Mode of Production and Contemporary Marxism, in S. Avineri, ed., *Varieties of Marxism*, Martinus Nijhoff, The Hague, 333–71.
Sawer, M.	(1978–9)	The Politics of Historiography: Russian Socialism and the Question of the Asiatic Mode of Production, *Critique*, 10–11: 15–35.
Sawer, M.	(1979)	The Soviet Discussion of the Asiatic Mode of Production, *Survey*, 24, 3: 108–27.
Seddon, D.	(1978)	*Relations of Production, Marxist Approaches to Economic Anthropology*, Cass, London.
Semenov, Iu.	(1967)	Le Régime Socio-Économique de l'Orient Ancien, *Recherches internationales à la lumière du Marxisme*, 57–8: 196–218.
Semenov, Iu.	(1980)	The Theory of Socio-economic Formations and World History (trans. E. Gellner), in E. Gellner, ed., *Soviet and Western Anthropology*, Duckworth, London, 29–58.

Sen, A.	(1982)	*The State, Industrialization and Class Formations in India: A Neo-Marxist Perspective on Colonialism, Underdevelopment and Development*, Routledge and Kegan Paul, London.
Sen, S.P., ed.	(1973)	*Historians and Historiography in Modern India*, Institute of Historical Studies, Calcutta.
Senart, E.C.M.	(1930)	*Caste in India: The Facts and the System*, Methuen, London.
Sen Gupta, B.	(1972)	*Communism in Indian Politics*, Columbia University Press, New York.
Shafarevich, I.	(1980)	*The Socialist Phenomenon*, Harper and Row, New York.
Shah, S.A., ed.	(1973)	*Towards National Liberation: Essays on the Political Economy of India*, Black Rose, Montreal.
Shanin, T., ed.	(1983)	*The Late Marx and the Russian Road, Marx and the 'Peripheries of Capitalism'*, Macmillan, London.
Shapiro, M.	(1962)	Stages of Social Development, *Marxism Today*, 6: 282–4.
Sharma, R.S.	(1958)	Origins of Feudalism in India (A.D. *c.*400–650) *Journal of the Economic and Social History of the Orient*, I, part iii, 297–328.
Sharma, R.S.	(1965)	*Indian Feudalism: c.300–1200 A.D.*, Calcutta University Press, Calcutta.
Sharma, R.S.	(1966a)	Historiography of the Ancient Indian Social Order, in Sharma, *Light on Early Indian Society and Economy*, Manaktala, Bombay, 1–18.
Sharma, R.S.	(1966b)	Irrigation in Northern India during the Post-Mauryan Period (*c.*200 B.C. – A.D. 200), in Sharma, *Light on Early Indian Society and Economy*, Manaktala, Bombay, 90–101.
Sharma, R.S.	(1966c)	*Light on Early Indian Society and Economy*, Manaktala, Bombay.
Sharma, R.S.	(1968)	*Aspects of Political Ideas and Institutions in Ancient India*, Motilal Banarsidas, Delhi, second edition.

Sharma, R.S. (1980) *Sudras in Ancient India, A Social History of the Lower Order Down to Circa A.D. 600*, Motilal Banarsidass, Delhi, second edition.

Sharma, R.S. (1981) The Socio-Economic Bases of 'Oriental Despotism' in Early India, in S.K. Bose, ed., *Essays in Honour of Dr. Gyanchand*, People's Publishing House, New Delhi, 55−65.

Sharma, R.S. (1983) *Material Culture and Social Formations*, Macmillan, Delhi.

Sharma, R.S. (1985) How Feudal was Indian Feudalism?, *Journal of Peasant Studies*, 12, 2−3: 19−43.

Sharma, R.S., ed. (1986a) *Survey of Research on Social and Economic History of India*, ICSSR, Ajanta Publications, Delhi.

Sharma, R.S. (1987) *Urban Decay, 300−1,000 A.D.*, Munshiram Manoharlal Publishers, New Delhi.

Sharma, R.S. and Jha, V., eds (1974) *Indian Society: Historical Probings in Memory of D.D. Kosambi*, People's Publishing House, New Delhi.

Shaw, W. (1975) Productive Forces and Relations of Production. University of London, PhD thesis, October.

Shaw, W. (1978) *Marx's Theory of History*, Hutchinson, Cambridge.

Shelvankar, K.S. (1943) *The Problem of India*, Penguin, Harmondsworth.

Shiowaza, K. (1966) Marx and the Asiatic Mode of Production, *Developing Economics*, IV, 3: 299−315.

Shtusser, A.I. (1930) Marx and Engels on India (ed. with foreward L.A. Mad'iar), Vzgliady Marksa i Engels'sa na aziatskii sposob proizvodstva i ikh istochniki, *Letopisi marksizma*, 1930, III: 3−29.

Simon, J. (1962) Stages in Social Development, *Marxism Today*, 8.

Sircar, D.C. (1966) *Land System and Feudalism in Ancient India*, Calcutta University Press, Calcutta.

Skalnik, P. and Pokora, T.	(1966)	Beginning of the Discussion of the Asiatic Mode of Production in the USSR and the People's Republic of China, *Eirene*, V: 179–87.
Smith, A.	(1976)	*The Wealth of Nations*, The University of Chicago Press, Chicago.
Smith, V.	(1981)	*The Oxford History of India*, revised and ed. P. Spear, fourth edition, Oxford University Press, New Delhi.
Smith, W.	(1944)	The Mughal Empire and the Middle Classes, *Islamic Culture*, xviii, October: 349–63.
Smith, W.	(1946)	Lower-class Uprisings in the Mughal Empire, *Islamic Culture*, January, XX, 1: 21–40.
Sofri, G., ed.	(1969)	*Il modo di produzione asiatico: Storia di una controversia marxista*, Einaudi, Turin.
Solzhenitsyn, A.	(1980)	Foreword to I. Shafarevich, *The Socialist Phenomenon*, Harper & Row, New York.
Spear, P.	(1965)	*A History of India*, vol. 2, Penguin, Harmondsworth.
Spear, P.	(1970)	The Mughal Mansabdari System, in E. Leach and S. Mukherjee, eds, *Elites in South Asia*, Cambridge University Press, Cambridge, 1–16.
Stalin, J.	(1938)	*Dialectical and Historical Materialism*, International Publishers, New York.
Stalin, J.	(1973)	*The Essential Stalin: Major Theoretical Writings 1905–1952*, ed. B. Franklin, Croom Helm, London.
Steedman, I.	(1977)	*Marx after Sraffa*, New Left Books, London.
Stein, B.	(1975)	The State and the Agrarian Order in Medieval South India: A Historiographical Critique, in B. Stein, ed., *Essays in South India*, University Press of Hawaii, Honolulu, 64–92.
Stein, B.	(1980)	*Peasant State and Society in Medieval South India*, Oxford University Press, Delhi.

Stein, B. (1982a) South India: Some General Considerations of the Region and Its Early History, in T. Raychaudhuri and I. Habib, eds, *Cambridge Economic History of India*, vol. 1, Cambridge University Press, Cambridge, 14–44.

Stein, B. (1982b) Vijayanagara *c.*1350–1564, in T. Raychaudhuri and I. Habib, eds, *Cambridge Economic History of India*, vol. 1, Cambridge University Press, Cambridge, 102–24.

Stein, B. (1982c) The South, in T. Raychaudhuri and I. Habib, eds, *Cambridge Economic History of India*, vol. 1, Cambridge University Press, Cambridge, 203–13.

Stein, B. (1982d) The Far South, in T. Raychaudhuri and I. Habib, eds, *Cambridge Economic History of India*, vol. 1, Cambridge University Press, Cambridge, 452–7.

Stein, B. (1985) Politics, Peasants and the Deconstruction of Feudalism in Medieval India, *Journal of Peasant Studies*, 12, 2–3: 54–86.

Stelling-Michaud, S. (1960–1) Le Mythe du Despotisme Oriental, *Schweizer Beitrage Zur Allgemeinen*,: 328–46.

Stokes, E. (1959) *The English Utilitarians and India*, Clarendon Press, Oxford.

Stoye, J. (1969) *Europe Unfolding 1648–1688*, Fontana, Glasgow.

Struve, V.V. (1940) Marksovo opredelenie ranneklassovogo obshchestva, *Sovetskaia etnografia*, 1: 5–27. See also 1967 Struve.

Struve, V.V. (1965) The Concept of the 'Asian Mode of Production', *Soviet Anthropology and Archeology*, IV, 2: 41–6.

Struve, V.V. (1966) Some Aspects of the Social Development of the Ancient Orient, *Soviet Studies in History*, IV, 4: 13–21.

Struve, V.V.	(1967)	Comment Marx definissait les premieres sociétes de classes, *Recherches internationales à la lumière del Marxisme*, 57–8. 79–97.
Stukevski, I. and Vasilev, L.	(1966)	Three Models for the Origin and Evolution of Pre-capitalist Societies, *Soviet Review*, 8, 3: 26–39.
Subrahmanyam, S.	(1986)	Aspects of State Formation in South India and Southeast Asia, 1500–1600, *Indian Economic and Social History Review*, 23: 357–77.
Suret-Canale, J.	(1965)	Transitional Societies in Tropical Africa and the Marxist Concept of the Asian Mode of Production, *Soviet Anthropology and Archeology*, IV, 2: 38–9.
Suret-Canale, J.	(1966)	Sur la notion Marxiste de 'mode de production asiatique', *Cahiers du Communisme*, mars, 3: 62–9.
Suret-Canale, J.	(1967)	Problemes theoriques de l'étude des premieres societes de classes, *Recherches internationales à la lumière du Marxisme*, 57–8: 5–16.
Sweezy, P.	(1980)	*Post-Revolutionary Society*, Monthly Review Press, New York.
Tainter, J.	(1988)	*The Collapse of Complex Societies*, Cambridge University Press, Cambridge.
Tavernier, J.-B.	(1976)	*Travels in India* (trans. from his *Les Six Voyages*, 1676), Macmillan, London.
Taylor, J.	(1975)	Review Article: Pre-Capitalist Modes of Production (Parts One and Two), *Critique of Anthropology* Part One, 4, Autumn: 127–55; and Part Two, 5/6, Spring: 56–9.
Taylor, J.	(1979)	*From Modernization to Modes of Production: A Critique of the Sociologies of Development and Underdevelopment*, Macmillan, London.
Thapar, R.	(1961)	*Ashoka and the Decline of the Mauryas*, Oxford University Press, Oxford.

380   *Bibliography*

Thapar, R.   (1966)   *A History of India, vol. 1*, Penguin, Harmondsworth.

Thapar, R.   (1968)   Interpretations of Ancient Indian History, *History and Theory*, VIII, 3: 318–35.

Thapar, R.   (1975)   *The Past and Prejudice*, National Book Trust, New Delhi.

Thapar, R.   (1978)   *Ancient Indian Social History*, Orient Longmans, New Delhi.

Thapar, R.   (1982)   Ideology and the Interpretation of Early Indian History, *Review*, V, 3: 389–411.

Thapar, R.   (1984)   *From Lineage to State: Social Formations in the Mid-First Millennium B.C. in the Ganga Valley*, Oxford University Press, Bombay.

Therborn, G.   (1976)   *Science, Class and Society*, Verso, London.

Thompson, E.P.   (1978)   *The Poverty of Theory and Other Essays*, Merlin, London.

Thorner, D.   (1965)   Feudalism in India, in R. Coulborn, ed., *Feudalism in History*, Archon Books, Hamden, Connecticut, 133–50.

Thorner, D.   (1966)   Marx, India and the Asiatic Mode of Production, *Contributions to Indian Sociology*, IX, December: 33–66.

Tichelman, F.   (1980)   *The Social Evolution of Indonesia: The Asiatic Mode of Production and Its Legacy*, Martinus Nijhoff, The Hague.

Tichelman, F.   (1983)   *Marx on Indonesia and India*, Schriften aus dem Karl Marx-Haus, Trier.

Timasheff, N.   (1948)   The Sociological Theories of Maksim M. Kovalevsky, in H.E. Barnes, ed., *An Introduction to the History of Sociology*, The University of Chicago Press, Chicago.

Tökei, F.   (1958)   Les conditions de la propriété foncière dans la Chine de l'époque Tchou, *Acta Antiqua Acad. Sci. Hung*, 6, 3–4: 245–99.

Tökei, F.	(1967)	Le M.P.A. en Chine, *Recherches internationales à la lumière du Marxisme*, 57–8: 165–87.
Tökei, F.	(1979)	*Essays on the Asiatic Mode of Production*, Akademiai, Budapest.
Tökei, F.	(1982)	Some Contentious Issues in the Interpretation of the Asiatic Mode of Production, *Journal of Contemporary Asia*, 12, 3: 294–303.
Tolstov, S.	(1950)	For Advanced Soviet Oriental Studies, in *Current Digest of the Soviet Press*, August 11: 33–4.
Toye, J.F.J.	(1976)	Economic Theories of Politics and Public Finance, *British Journal of Political Science*, 6: 433–47.
Toynbee, A.	(1958)	Karl Wittfogel. Oriental Despotism, *American Political Science Review*, 52: 195–8.
Trotsky, L.	(1932–3)	*History of the Russian Revolution*, Victor Gollancz, London.
Trostsky, L.	(1969)	*The Permanent Revolution*, Pathfinder Press, New York.
Tucker, R.C.	(1961)	*Philosophy and Myth in Karl Marx*, Cambridge University Press, Cambridge.
Turner, B.	(1974)	The Concept of Social Stationariness: Utilitarianism and Marxism, *Science and Society*, XXXVIII, 1: 3–18.
Turner, B.	(1978)	*Marx and the End of Orientalism*, Allen & Unwin, London.
Turner, B.	(1981)	*For Weber: Essays in the Sociology of Fate*, Routledge and Kegan Paul London.
Ulmen, G.L.	(1978)	*The Science of Society: Towards an Understanding of the Life and Work of Karl August Wittfogel*, Mouton, The Hague.
Ulyanovsky, R.A. and Pavlov, V.	(1975)	Afterword to V. Pavlov et al., *India: Social and Economic Development (18th–20th Centuries)*, Progress Publishers, Moscow.
Varga, Y.	(1968)	*Politico-Economic Problems of Capitalism*, Progress Publishers, Moscow.

van Leur, J.C.	(1955)	*Indonesian Trade and Society*,
Veblen, T.	(1915)	*Imperial Germany and the Industrial Revolution* Macmillan, London.
Venturi, F.	(1963)	Oriental Despotism, *Journal of the History of Ideas*, XXIV, 1: 133–42.
Viczainy, M.	(1979)	The Deindustrialization of India in the Nineteenth Century: A Methodological Critique of Amiya Kumar Bagchi, *Indian Economic and Social History Review*, XVI: 105–46.
Vidal-Naquet, P.	(1964)	Karl Wittfogel et le concept de 'Mode de production asiatique', *Annales*, xix, 3: 531–49.
Vitkin, M.	(1981)	The Asiatic Mode of Production, *Philosophy and Social Criticism*, 1, 8: 45–66.
Vitkin, M. and Ter-Akopian, N.	(1965)	In the Pages of the Journal *La Pensée* (A Discussion of the Problem of the Asian Mode of Production), *Soviet Anthropology and Archeology*, IV, 2: 46–51.
Voltaire, F.M.A. de	(1768)	*L'ABC, dialogues curieux traduits de l'Anglais de Monsieur Huet; in Voltaire, Oeuvres*, vol. XXVII, Garnier, Paris.
Voltaire, F.M.A. de	(1819)	Commentaires sur quelques principales maximes de l'Esprit des Lois, in Appendix to *Oeuvres de Montesquieu*, Laquien, Paris, vol. vii.
Voltaire, F.M.A. de	(1963)	Sur l'Esprit des Lois' in *Politiques de Voltaire*, (ed. R. Pomeau), Armand Colin, Paris.
Walker, R.	(1957)	An Inquiry Into Totalitarianism, *Problems of Communism*, vi, 3: 48–9.
Wallerstein, I.	(1974)	*The Modern World System*, The Academic Press, New York.
Wallerstein, I.	(1981)	*The Capitalist World System*, The Academic Press, New York.
Warren, B.	(1981)	*Imperialism: Pioneer of Capitalism*, Verso, London.
Weber, M.	(1978)	*Economy and Society*, vols 1 and 2, University of California Press, Berkeley, Cal.

Welskopf, E.	(1957)	*Die Producktionsverhältnisse im Alten Orient und in der Griechisch-Römischen Antike*, Akademie-Verlad, Berlin.
Welskopf, E.	(1981)	Problems of Periodisation in Ancient History, in A.M. Bailey, and J.R. Llobera, eds, *The Asiatic Mode of Production: Science and Politics*, Routledge and Kegan Paul, London, 242–8.
Wessman, J.	(1981)	*Anthropology and Marxism*, Schenkman Publishing Co., Cambridge, Mass.
Wheeler, R.E.M.	(1953)	*The Indian Civilization*, Cambridge.
Wickham, C.	(1985)	The Uniqueness of the East, *The Journal of Peasant Studies*, 12, 2/3: 166–96.
Wielenga, B.	(1976)	*Marxist Views on India in Historical Perspective*, Studies on Indian Marxism Series: No. 2, Christian Institute for the Study of Religion and Society, Bangalore.
Wilks, M.	(1810)	*Historical Sketches of the South of India*, vol. 1, Longman, Hurst, Rees and Orme, London.
Wittfogel, K.A.	(1931)	*Wirtschaft und Gesellschaft Chinas*, Hirschfeld, Leipzig.
Wittfogel, K.A.	(1953)	The Ruling Bureaucracy of Oriental Despotism: A Phenomenon That Paralyzed Marx, *Review of Politics*, XV, 3: 350–9.
Wittfogel, K.A.	(1959–60)	The Marxist View of Russian Society and Revolution, *World Politics*, XII, 4: 487–508.
Wittfogel, K.A	(1969)	Results and Problems of the Study of Oriental Despotism, *Journal of Asian Studies*, 28: 257–65.
Wittfogel, K.A.	(1981)	*Oriental Despotism, A Comparative Study of Total Power*, Vintage Books, New York, reprint of 1957 edition published by Yale University Press.
Wolfter, R., ed.	(1978)	*Rudolf Bahro: Critical Responses*, M.E. Sharpe, White Plains, New York.

Wolpe, H., ed. (1980) *The Articulation of Modes of Production*, Routledge and Kegan Paul, London.

Wood, E.M. and Wood, N. (1978) *Class Ideology and Ancient Political Theory. Socrates, Plato and Aristotle in Social Context*, Basil Blackwell, Oxford.

Wright, E. Levine, A. and Sober, E. (1987) Marxism and Methodological Individualism, *New Left Review*, 162: 67–84.

Yadov, B.N.S. (1976) Problems of Interaction Between Socio-Economic Classes in Early Medieval Complex, *Indian Historical Review*, 1, 3: 43–58.

Zel'in, K.K. (1968) The Morphological Classification of Forms of Dependence, *Soviet Sociology*, VI, 4: 3–24.

Zinoviev, A. (1984) *The Reality of Communism*, Victor Gollancz, London.

Name Index

This index does not include any references to Marx or Engels. References to authors and names in footnotes are included.

Subject Index